Bathers Baseball

A History of Minor League Baseball at the Arkansas Spa

Best wishes –
Don Duren

Don Duren

xulon PRESS

Bathers Baseball
A History of Minor League Baseball at the Arkansas Spa
by Don Duren

Printed in the United States of America

ISBN 9781613795422

Cover design: Keith Beasley-Clayton Everett Design-Dallas, TX

For information, please contact:

Don Duren
2508 Banner Elk Circle
Plano, Texas 75025
972-618-2501
E-mail: don.duren@verizon.net

www.xulonpress.com

Dedication

To former players, management and fans of the Hot Springs Bathers baseball teams.

To individuals who furnished me with first hand information concerning the Hot Springs Bathers.

To my lovely wife who assisted me during this publication.

"Similarly, if anyone competes as an athlete, he does not receive the victor's crown unless he competes according to the rules" (II Timothy 2:5).

Contents

Acknowledgements

This book would not have been possible without the generous assistance of many people. Thanks to the Garland County Historical Society, the Garland County Library, Arkansas History Commission, the Society of American Baseball Research (SABR), *The Sentinel-Record* and the National Baseball Hall of Fame. Thanks to all of the former players, Bathers' management, front office personnel and fans. A special thanks to those who donated information concerning the Hot Springs Bathers.

As a youngster growing up in Hot Springs, I had no knowledge of the struggles people experienced to keep the business of professional baseball afloat in the city. Thank you to all individuals who received wages or volunteered their time, effort and resources in order for baseball fans in the area to enjoy many exciting times observing the hometown team, the Bathers. I experienced many lasting memories at Jaycee Park. I recall many of the players who played for the Bathers such as Herb Adams, Jackie Bales, Tony Zini and the late Bob Passarella. Listed are many more within the pages of this book.

In 1950, following a Bathers game with Pine Bluff, my father and I met Ryne Duren, a Pine Bluff pitcher, at Jaycee Park. Since we had the same last name, we wanted to find out more about his ancestry. As a seventh grader at the time, I thought he was one of the biggest men I ever saw. He was actually 6' 2" and weighed around 185 pounds, but he had his Pine Bluff uniform on, standing in cleats. To me, he was huge. Since his family was from Wisconsin, there seemed to be little, if any, correlation between our ancestries.

The history of the Bathers intrigued me. Earl Hudson and I were in the same high school class and he married the daughter of Louis Goltz, once an owner of the Bathers. The family graciously allowed me to visit with them. The Goltz's granddaughter, Madeline Hudson Bull was delighted that I had questions concerning the Bathers and readily shared much information. Then, they brought out two or three old scrapbooks of Mr. Goltz. That was the spark that ignited the flame of interest that led to the research and writing of this book. Thanks so much to the generosity of the Goltz family.

Thanks to those individuals listed in Chapter 17. Additionally, many more have assisted in the research of this book including John Wells and Adam Webb of the Garland County Library. Others include Debbie Lax, granddaughter of the late "Spike" Hunter; Joanne Ensminger Moore, daughter of the late Joe and Evelyn Ensminger; Charles Butler, former coach and school administer of Hot Springs High School. In addition, others who have assisted are John Back, retired Army sergeant; Betty and Susan Elder, wife and daughter of the late Jim Elder; Kelly Zini, son of Tony and A. J. Zini. Others who have assisted include John Watkins, attorney in Fayetteville, AR; Dan Duren, technical support; Mark Blaeuer, former Park Ranger, Hot Springs National Park, Sharon Shugart, former employee, Hot Springs National Park, Tim Conn, son of Billy Conn, Ilitch Holdings, Inc. and Caleb Hardwick of Benton, AR.

Others who have assisted in this project are two former Bathers, Joel Callaway and Ed Herlein; Tim Wiles, Director of Research at the Baseball Hall of Fame and John Zajc of Society of American Baseball Research (SABR). Donny Whitehead who furnished information concerning the Greenwood Dodgers and other material was an excellent resource. Much appreciation is due to Keith Beasley of Clayton Everett Design of Dallas, Texas, who designed the book cover and to Julie James Punjak of Dallas, Texas, who assisted in editing the manuscript.

Introduction

This book is about the history of minor league baseball teams in Hot Springs, Arkansas. The city saw great baseball players before Hot Springs became a member of professional baseball. In fact, baseball engulfed the city each spring when major league teams traveled to the Arkansas Resort for spring training. Mr. A. G. Spalding, president of the Chicago White Stockings (forerunner of the Chicago Cubs) sent his crew down to the Ouachita (Wash'-uh-taw) Mountain-region in the spring of 1886. Spalding's splendid idea was to boil out the "alcoholic microbes" of the young men on his team. Spalding, who disapproved of drinking and gambling, realized that some of his players drank a little too much alcohol during the winter. Therefore, his desire was to have his team physically fit by taking the hot springs baths, climbing the mountains and playing baseball. The White Stockings won the 1886 National League championship.

Through the years, Hot Springs baseball fans gazed on many great players such as Cy Young, Grover Cleveland Alexander, Walter Johnson, Honus Wagner, Tris Speaker, George "Babe" Ruth, Rogers Hornsby, Josh Gibson, "Satchel" Paige, "Dizzy" Dean, George Sisler, Bill Dickey and many more. Major league teams such as the Boston Red Sox, Pittsburgh Pirates, Cincinnati Reds, St. Louis Browns, St. Louis Perfectos (Cardinals), New York Highlanders (Yankees), Brooklyn Dodgers and many more trained at Hot Springs. Several Negro League teams including the Pittsburgh Crawfords also traveled to the Spa. In addition, several minor league teams trained at the resort.

Hot Springs jumped into the professional ranks as early as 1887, perhaps due to the exposure of the White Stockings training in the city. It was a less sophisticated time in sports. In those early years, low salaries, small team budgets, wool uniforms, smaller rosters, unorganized scheduling and poor equipment were all part of minor league baseball in the city. However, the young players loved the game of baseball and most had aspirations of becoming a major league player.

This book reveals both the positive and the negative ideas in American culture. It is a scrapbook of Americana. Listen to what players, front office personnel, league officials, the media and fans say about their minor league team in Hot Springs…usually called the Hot Springs Bathers.

Currently, there are two major leagues in professional baseball, the National and the American, where the most talented baseball players in the world perform. The major leagues are composed of 30 teams, 16 in the National and 14 in the American. About 190 minor league teams in the United States rank below the major leagues. They are under the umbrella of Minor League Baseball, formerly called the National Association of Professional Baseball Leagues. In addition, over 50 minor league teams, under the same organization, are located in the Dominican Republic, Mexico and Venezuela. In the United States, professional baseball league classifications begin with the highest league, the major leagues. The minor leagues rank leagues from the highest to the lowest classifications. The six professional minor league classifications include Triple-A, Double-A, Advanced-A, Single-A, Short Season-A and Rookie. The defunct classifications are Open, A-1, B, C and D leagues. Most of the time, the Hot Springs team was a Class C or Class D team. Beginning in 1938, the Spa entry participated in the Class C, Cotton States League.

Numerous nicknames for professional baseball teams exist across the country. Major league teams include designations such as Tigers and Pirates. Those titles tend to present themselves as powerful, intimidating monikers. However, certain team logos seem less daunting. Examples of less fearsome sounding team labels include the Red Sox (a sock that is red); White Sox (a sock that is white); Cubs (baby bears); Orioles (beautiful black and orange songbirds); Cardinals (beautiful red songbirds); Padres (preachers); Twins (a team representing two cities); Dodgers (originally individuals who dodged streetcars in Brooklyn) and Angels (heavenly beings).

Due to the 47 hot springs flowing from the base of Hot Springs Mountain, located in Hot Springs National Park, one appropriate logo for a baseball team representing Hot Springs could have been Heat. Since the picturesque mountains surround the city, Mountaineers would have been a suitable logo. Native American tribes such as the Caddo, Quapaw or Cherokee once occupied the area near the Spa; therefore, one of these names could have been a fitting title. Popular birds that soared in the area are eagles and hawks, which was a possible consideration. The 100-year-old Arkansas Alligator Farm is part of the "things to see" in the city. Therefore, Gators could have been a possible designation for a team from Hot Springs. However, none of these nicknames caught the fancy of team ownership.

One year in the 1880s, the management named the Hot Springs team the Blues. Later, since the well-known hot springs emit vapor or steam, the Hot Springs Vapors and the Hot Springs Vaporites were tags that grasped the imagination of the owners for two or three seasons. Supposedly, a Vaporite is a person who lives near a vapor. The team, called the Vapors and Vaporites, existed briefly in the early years and made perfect sense for a team's name from the area. However, the name that topped the list was a unique handle called the Hot Springs Bathers. Most people laugh when they hear the name Hot Springs Bathers related to a baseball team. Following their laugh, they smiled and asked, "Hot Springs what?" Again, they would laugh! Okay, so the name does not sound intimidating. The word "bather" signifies a person taking a bath. However, through the years, the name "Bathers" has become the most notable team handle for the Hot Springs professional baseball team. By landing on the name "Bathers," the leadership of the minor league entry believed that specific name publicized the area. Hot Springs National Park, Arkansas, is a world-famous resort where people bathe in sparkling hot mineral waters.

In 1832, President Andrew Jackson signed legislation to set aside "...four sections of land including the hot springs, reserved for future disposal of the United States, shall not be entered, located or appropriated, for any other purpose whatsoever…" Congress didn't label this special land a national park because there was no such entity as a national park or even the National Park Service at that time. The land at the "hot springs" was under government jurisdiction 40 years before Yellowstone National Park became the "first national park." In reality, Hot Springs was the first park established by Congress in 1832; however, on March 4, 1921, congress established Hot Springs National Park as the 18th National Park. Therefore, the Hot Springs Bathers is a perfect name for a team that played baseball near the area of 47 hot springs.

Chapter 1

The Early Years
1886-1909

"The base ball fever has broken out in a new sport. The towns of Little Rock, Hot Springs and Fort Smith have, as the Southerners say, 'all been taken down.'" - The Sporting News

The earliest record of professional baseball in the Spa took place in 1886; however, it was of the major league variety. Major league baseball spring training in Hot Springs, Arkansas, began with an idea developed inside the cranium of A. G. Spalding, president and eventual owner of the Chicago White Stockings. In the maiden issue of *The Sporting News,* March 17, 1886, Spalding's plan revealed to the world his intentions. It was an experiment for his major league team to venture south for spring training. *The Sporting News* stated that the White Stockings, forerunner of the Chicago Cubs, planned to conduct their spring training in Hot Springs, Arkansas. Spalding surmised that some of his players enjoyed drinking the spirits, especially in the off-season, so he planned for his team to be in excellent shape at the beginning of the season by taking daily dips in the hot springs at the Arkansas Spa. Some players were overweight and he intended to introduce them to his idea of weight management.

Manager Spalding, of the Chicago Base-Ball Club, is now completely wrapped up in a plan. March 13 he will start from Chicago for Hot Springs, Ark., with all the members of the Chicago Base-Ball Club. There he will boil them for two weeks.

'It's a great scheme,' said Mr. Spalding yesterday, leaning back in his chair and stroking his forehead. 'I wonder whatever made me think of it. All the boys are enthusiastic about it and all want to go. I have written to a professor down there and he is making arrangements to build a vat in which he can boil the whole nine at once. You see, the beauty of this scheme is that I get a brand-new nine on April 1. I boil out the alcoholic microbes, which may have impregnated the systems of these men during the winter while they have been away from me and Anson. Once (they) get the microbes out, the danger of a relapse is slight. If that don't work I'll send 'em all over to Paris next year and have 'em inoculated by Pasteur. But it will work, and we shall win the championship again this year. The professor writes me that he will boil down the men in over flesh and boil up the fellows who have got there since the season closed.'[1]

The White Stockings were composed of several future Hall of Fame players including "Cap" Anson, Mike "King" Kelly and John Clarkson. In addition to these great players, Chicago sent the following talented players to the Spa in 1886: Fred Pfeffer (2b), Ned Williamson (SS), Tommy Burns (3B), Jim Ryan (RF), George Gore (CF), Al Dalrymple (LF), "Silver" Flint (C), John McCormick (P), Jocko Flynn (P) and Billy Sunday (OF/Utility). Spalding, an excellent pitcher, retired as an active player in 1878. The Hall of Fame committee inducted him into the elite group as an executive in 1939. Spalding prepared his team to train for about two weeks in the Spa. While the team was in the city, players "boiled out" the alcohol in their system, played baseball and climbed the mountains.

While in Hot Springs, the young men enjoyed joking around with each other. There was a story told about "King" Kelly and Al Dalrymple. Within several days of arriving at the Arkansas Resort,

Ed Williamson, shortstop for the White Stockings, wrote a letter to Spalding in Chicago, updating his boss on the team's adventures in the Spa City.

On St. Patrick's Day, we had quite a laugh at Dalrymple's expense, as he fell victim to one of Mike Kelly's jokes. The day previous Kell was out for a run through the woods and becoming very thirsty, he went in search of a spring and succeeded in finding one. Mike thought it was one of the prettiest springs he had ever seen. Every pebble and grain of sand through which the water bubbled up was coated with a beautiful green tint that made the cool water look all the more inviting to Mike's parched lips. He laid flat on the ground and was about to take a gulp of the water when he heard a yell just behind him that caused him to jump to his feet and face a big fellow who, Mike says, was the dead cut of Kit, the Arkansas Traveler.

'You might as well shoot a man as scare him to death,' said Mike, as he prepared to kneel down for his interrupted drink.

'Look here, young feller,' said the stranger, 'if yer hair or moustache was to touch that ar water it would turn as green as grass. That ar is a green sulphur spring; didn't yer know it?'

Kell thanked the big fellow and asked him if he had a bucket. The fellow did not have a bucket, but he had a pint flask, and, after purchasing it from him, Kell emptied its contents (on the ground, of course) and filled it with the spring water. Kell and Dal have been rooming together since we have been here, and when he got home that night Kell emptied the spring water in the wash pitcher. He got up in the morning and sneaked down stairs to the hotel washroom, where he made his toilet. Dal came down to breakfast an hour afterwards with a mug like St. Patrick himself. He had washed hurriedly and had gone out for a half hour's spin before breakfast, so that he did not know of the change, but so help me

Moses, his hair and beard were as green as any badge worn that day in horror of the Irish Saint.

'Look at the mug of his,' laughed Kell, and then he doubled up and howled until he turned red in the face.

'Dal, what in the world have you been doing to yourself?' asked the Secretary John Brown, with fatherly concern. Everybody began to grin and pretty Mrs. John Clarkson's face was red with laughter as she hid it behind her napkin. Other guests in the dining room began to drop to the emerald hue of our left fielder's whiskers, and Dal began to get correspondingly mad.

'What's the matter with you people, anyway?' he asked.

'Look at your whiskers, Dal,' said Mike. 'They're greener than my parrot.'

Dal took hold of a lock of his beard and pulled it out so that he could see it, and his face turned red. 'You all think you're funny, don't you?' he blurted, and with that, he walked out of the dining room. We all look for more fun as Dal swears that he will get even.[2]

The White Stockings won the 1886 National League championship. However, during the post-season there was a hiccup. Most baseball fans considered the National League the real major league. There was no American League at this time. However, another professional baseball league, the American Association, did their best to compete against the National League for money and pride. The American Association existed from 1882-1891. There were eight teams in the American Association, but the St. Louis Browns was, by far, the only team of any significance and they won the 1886 American Association championship. Player-manager Charlie Comiskey of the Browns had some excellent players on his squad including star pitchers Dave Foutz and Bob Caruthers. Other outstanding Browns players were Arlie Latham (3B), Tip O'Neill (OF) and Yank Robinson (2B).

The mighty Chicago White Stockings weren't too concerned about playing St. Louis in the championship series; however, St. Louis had other ideas. Considered by some in the baseball world at this time, the post-season playoffs were merely exhibition games, but the Series did produce revenue through gate receipts and refreshments. Seemingly, Chicago didn't take the "World Series" too seriously as the Browns upset the White Stockings four games to two. The Browns reaped the total gate receipts of $13,920 and each of the 12 St. Louis players garnered about $580. That gave the White Stockings, and Spalding, something to think about all winter.

Spalding enjoyed his spring training concept so much that he returned to the Spa the following spring. Spalding's idea caught on! From 1886 through the 1940s, there was a steady stream of professional baseball teams including major league, minor league and Negro league players training in the Arkansas Spa during the springtime.

Baseball interest caught on in a big way in Hot Springs during 1886. Perhaps interest grew due to the Chicago White Stockings spring training actions in the Spa. In the October 4, 1886, issue of *The Sporting News,* an article about a baseball game between Hot Springs and Little Rock must have been an "event." It may not have been a game played by professional players, but both teams were out to win. During this time, the writers spelled baseball with a space between base and ball like base ball.

The base ball fever has broken out in a new spot. The towns of Little Rock, Hot Springs and Fort Smith, have as the Southerners say, "All been taken down." The people of Little Rock seem to have it the worst, while those of Hot Springs are not far behind. The other day nines representing these two cities came together at Little Rock. So great was the feeling over the game, that no one could be found brave enough in the town of Little Rock to umpire it. In the emergency, St. Louis was called on, and she sent John Hunt to the frontier. He had umpired games in the center of Kerry Patch and had never taken a bluff.

When he called a game, he met a sight that chilled his very heart's blood. Upon all sides were the good and bad men of the rival towns. Some had Arkansas toothpicks, while others were weighted down with big bore rifles or long sixes. It is needless to say, that Mr. Hunt was alarmed, and that he gave those who were in the majority the best of it.

It is scarcely worthy of mention, too, that the Little Rocks shut out the Hot Springs gang by a score of ten to nothing. It is but fair to state, however, that at the close of the game Mr. Hunt was the biggest man in Little Rock and that he was toasted and feted until the sun went down and arose again. So deep was the interest felt in the game by the people of Little Rock, and so confident were some of the citizens in the ability of the home team, that one hackman bet his hack and team against another hack and team on a shut out. It was a wild bet, but a fortunate one for him.

On the day following, Mr. Hunt was requested to go to Hot Springs and umpire the game there. Having had glory enough, however, for the time being, and content to rest on the honors he had already gained, Mr. Hunt folded his tent and returned to his native heath. He says the people of Little Rock are the biggest hearted people in the world, but when it comes to base ball, things must come their way though the heavens fall.[3]

During the 1800s, "base ball" began sweeping the country. The passage in the quote above that states, "…as the Southerners say, all been taken down," meant that the cities were smitten by the baseball fever. Although, it seemed that umpires were difficult to find, especially when contests involved rival teams. The article noted that Hunt umpired games in Kerry Patch, sometimes called "The Patch," a section of St. Louis. The Patch, composed of Irish-Americans, seemed to have been a tough place in which to call balls and strikes. The article intimated that if Hunt could officiate in that section and survive without an incident, his integrity allowed him to umpire anywhere. At the Little Rock-Hot Springs game, some serious fans toted "Arkansas Toothpicks" and "long sixes." An "Arkansas Toothpick" was a long knife, sort of like a Bowie knife, with a blade length of between 12 and 20 inches long. The "long sixes" were "six-shooter" pistols with long barrels. The quote, "When he called a game, he met a sight that chilled his very heart's blood," perhaps meant that he was a little on edge due to the fans "close companions." He may have been an unbiased arbiter, but his tendency to lean a little toward the side of the home team, is understandable due to the circumstances. After the game, he celebrated with the victors, but he wanted to leave well-enough alone, so he decided to by-pass the invitation to umpire in the Resort City.

The first reported venture of a Hot Springs team into the professional baseball ranks occurred in 1887, as a member of the six-team, minor-league, Southwestern League. Team locations and vague rosters are about the only sketchy records that exist. The league included the Fort Smith Indians, the Hot Springs Blues, the Little Rock Giants, the Pine Bluff Infants, the Springfield Indians and the Webb City Stars. The latter two teams were from Missouri, while the other four teams were from Arkansas. Research did not reveal the league standing in this independent league. The vague roster of the 1887 edition of the Hot Springs Blues consisted of 20 players, four of which played major league baseball. One of those players, catcher Emmett Rogers, played professional baseball from 1887-1898. Rogers, born in 1870, hailed from Hot Springs. "J. H. D.," initials of the author that wrote the article, stated, "Emmet Rogers, our favorite ball tosser, is corresponding with St. Joe. We would hate to see Emmet leave us and if the St. Joe people sign him, they will secure a faithful player. We wish him luck." All the teams with whom Rogers played were in the minor leagues, with the exception of one year. In 1890, Rogers played with the Toledo Maumees of the American Association. Toledo is located on the shores of the Maumee River in Ohio. The three major leagues during the 1890 season consisted of the National League, American Association and the Players League. Rogers passed away in Fort Smith in 1941.[4]

Additionally, "J.H.D." penned an article in *The Sporting News,* March 5, 1887, which stated, "At Hot Springs - The Ball Players Gathering There From All Points." He revealed that the major league team, the Chicago White Stockings was on their way to the Spa for spring training. His article indicated that A. G. Spalding, president of the major league team, accepted the terms to use the Spa's baseball facilities offered by W. F. Bassett, manager of the Hot Springs team.[5]

The first meeting of the 1887 Southwestern League game between Hot Springs and the Springfield Indians of Missouri, occurred on Saturday afternoon May 28, 1887, in the Spa City. Hot Springs led all the way, as they trumped the Indians 11-2. More than 1,000 fans saw Frank Hoffman allow the visitors only nine hits as the Hot Springs Blues pounded Homer, the Springfield hurler, for 20 safeties. Both teams committed four errors each. It was Springfield's turn on Monday, May 30, as the Missourians lambasted the Spa Boys 21-7. Hot Springs was on top at the end of two innings 3-2, but unfortunately, they had to play the remainder of the game. The Indians got to the Hot Springs battery of Wiekart and Creely, from St. Louis, for nine runs in the explosive third frame as Hot Springs never recovered. To add to their woes, the Blues committed 15 errors. The aforementioned games were the only two Hot Springs games reported by *The Sporting News* during the 1887 season.[6]

Several years later, in 1894, Hot Springs entered the four-team Arkansas State League. The circuit consisted of the Camden Yellow Hammers-Rainmakers, the Little Rock Rose Buds, the Morrilton Cotton Pickers and the Hot Springs Bathers. This is the first time that the nickname "Bathers" appeared in connection with a Hot Springs professional baseball team. The total games played by each team in the independent league, with vague rosters, ranged from 14-17 games.[7]

Three years later, the final standings of the 1897 Arkansas State League listed the Little Rock Senators as champions. In second place stood the Hot Springs Bathers, followed by the Fort Smith Indians and the Texarkana Nobles. No other records existed for the league.[8]

Hot Springs only won two games and lost 10 in the loosely organized 1898 Southwestern League campaign. The four teams that played over 25 games each were Shreveport, LA, Texarkana, TX, Paris, TX and Denison, TX. Four teams that played about 10 games included Hot Springs, Little Rock, Sherman, TX and Bonham, TX. One player from the Hot Springs 1898 Spa team, center fielder George Bristow, played major league baseball. He hooked up briefly with the Cleveland Spiders of the National League in 1899.[9]

Hot Springs organized a baseball team in 1902, but it probably wasn't a pro team. On Sunday morning, June 15, 1902, *The Sentinel-Record* published a note about the Forest City baseball team visiting Hot Springs to play a baseball team called the "Arlingtons."

Baseball

Forest City Filibusters Coming Next Week for Three Games

The Forest City Filibusters and the Arlingtons will meet on the Whittington Park diamond for a series of three games beginning Monday next. Time will be called by Umpire Murray promptly at 3:30 and the public should not all expect to catch the last car for the ground. The visiting team is reputed to be a strong aggregation of ball tossers, and will give the locals a hard battle for honors.[10]

The Hot Springs Vapors, under the managerial leadership of Jack Love, joined the Class D, Arkansas-Texas League in 1906. The three other teams in the league were Camden (AR) Ouachitas, Pine Bluff (AR) Barristers and the Texarkana (TX) Shine-Oners. Vapors, Barristers, Ouachitas and Shine-Oners were four unusual team nicknames. Perhaps these names can be justified. Hot Springs National Park is a Spa and its hot springs produce vapor. In fact, Vapor City is another label for Hot Springs. Therefore, the team name became an advertisement for the city and the world famous national park.[11]

A barrister is a lawyer and it seemed that Pine Bluff wanted to let the world know that they were the judges of the league. In fact, later, Judges was the name of the Pine Bluff baseball teams in the Cotton States League. In 1930, due to a "name-the-team contest" in Pine Bluff, the nickname

"Judges" won first place. The baseball title was "a tribute to County Judge R. H. Williams, who devoted much time and effort in making baseball possible in the city again."[12]

The Camden Ouachitas, pronounced Wash'-uh-taw, derived its name from the Ouachita River. Additionally, Camden is the county seat of Ouachita County. The word Ouachita, derived from a Native American tribe, is a popular name in the state. Among some of the entities in the state, which include Ouachita in its name, are Ouachita Mountains, Ouachita National Forest, Lake Ouachita, Ouachita River, Ouachita State Park, Ouachita County and Ouachita Baptist University. The Ouachita Mountains are not the same as the Ozark Mountains, which are located mainly in northern Arkansas and southern Missouri.

The explanation of Texarkana Shine-Oners is more difficult. Nobody seems to know the real reason for the Texarkana label. Perhaps the front office wanted the team to continue to shine, no matter the score or the standings.

By 1894, major leaguers established Whittington Park as their main playing field for their spring operations. Historians believe that the team called the Vapors played their games at Whittington Park, where the "big boys" trained. Little information exists regarding the 1906 Vapors because several fires and floods devastated Hot Springs through the years and left little or no historical records. Only bits and pieces of some earlier written material remain.

In 1908, Hot Springs entered the Class D, Arkansas State League and the *Sporting Life* printed the league schedule on April 18. The season opened April 20 and closed Sept. 6, as each team played a 60-game schedule. The league included Argenta (AR) Shamrocks, Helena (AR) Hellions, Hot Springs (AR) Vaporites, Newport (AR) Pearl Diggers, Pine Bluff (AR) Pine Knots and Poplar Bluff (MO)-Brinkley (AR) – no nickname listed. On May 14, the *Sporting Life* printed the league standings and Hot Springs was on top.[13]

On April 24, 1908, *The Citizen Daily Bulletin*, a Hot Springs newspaper, registered the results of a game played on April 23, in which the Spa Boys trounced Helena 10-1. The lineup for the Vaporites included Richard Fay-cf; Roy Liles-3b; Elmer Coyle-1b; Otto Besse-rf; Will Parrott-c;

Steve Crummins-2b; Edgar "Cobbie" Cowan- lf; Albert O'Hern-ss and Wray-p. The offensive standouts for Hot Springs were Fay and Besse with three hits each, followed by Cowan with two safeties, while Cummins and Parrott finished with one hit each.

Notes on the Game

Fay lined a three-bagger to deep center in the seventh and drove in the last two runs. Bruce sent "Cobbie" Cowan scurrying up the mountain and into the woods after another one yesterday.

The locals (HS) negotiated three double plays. The one in the seventh, when Fay in the center garden took a Bigg's skyscraper and doubled (Rudy) Kling at first before the manager could get back to the sack, being the most noteworthy.

Kinman was busy elsewhere yesterday and "Scotty" Moore, an old performer on local diamonds, umpired and did most creditable work.[14]

An interesting sidebar occurred in Hot Springs a few hours after the game and the event had nothing to do with baseball. However, high school boys were high school boys!

The Seniors Triumphant – And still, the senior flag floats from the flagstaff on the new high school despite the attempts of the undergraduates to remove it.

Last night a crowd of juniors braved the threatening weather and crept up to the school with their banner of yellow and light blue, hoping to substitute their banner for the crimson and white of the seniors. But the foresight of two of the senior boys frustrated their plans and the banner of the class of '08 still waves in the April breeze.[15]

By early June, Brinkley (AR) replaced Poplar Bluff in the Arkansas State League. The Vaporites traveled to Helena Tuesday night, July 14, 1908. *The Citizens Daily Bulletin,* a local Hot Springs paper, printed the results. The Vaporites again came out on the long end as they squeezed by Helena 5-4. William Wright tossed a seven hitter against the Hellions, while Hot Springs collected 11 hits off Rogers, the Helena hurler. Both pitchers tossed the complete game.[16]

The second-game lineup for the Spa Boys was different. The batting order was as follows: Elmer Coyle-1b; Richard Fay-lf; Rupert Blakeley-2b; Otto Besse-rf; Arthur Riggs-c; sub-for Riggs – S. Rainey-c; G. Smitheal-ss; Roy Liles-3b; Edgar Cowan-cf and Will "Lucky" Wright-p. Coyle was the leading batter for Hot Springs with a double and a single, while Liles contributed to the cause by blasting a two-bagger. Ejected from the game was Herbert Benham of Helena. What did Benham do that was so ruthless? The player "laughed at one of the decisions" by umpire Gampfer.

The Vaporites copped the Arkansas State League championship on September 7, 1908, with a 78-38 won-loss record, while Newport was runners-up with a 65 - 44 mark. There was no mention of a playoff. However, *The Sporting News* labeled the league the "Arkansaw League" not Arkansas League. The number of total games played by each team differed. None of the teams played the same number of games, but that seemed to have occurred frequently in those early leagues. Hot Springs played seven more games than Newport, 116 to 109. Third place Helena played 115 contests, while fourth place Pine Bluff engaged in 112 games. Fifth place Argenta came in with 117 and last place Brinkley played the least number of matches at 107.[17]

A small town of Argenta was located on the north bank of the Arkansas River across from Little Rock. In the early 1900s, Argenta changed its name to North Little Rock. The historical Argenta Drug Store in downtown North Little Rock remains in operation.

James "Hippo" Vaughn, southpaw Hot Springs pitcher, was a dynamic force for the Spa in 1908, as he posted nine victories against one loss. The 9-1 record enabled him to continue to climb the baseball ladder. The year 1908, was a fast moving year for "Hippo." Before the season was half over, he captivated the eye of the New York Highlanders (later Yankees) and quickly became the property of the Highlanders. "Hippo" played four years with the Highlanders. In 1912, they traded him to the Washington Senators and in 1913, he became a Chicago Cub where he spent nine-exceptional years, winning 20 games, five times.

During his 13-year major league career, he threw 41 shutouts and registered a 178-137 pitching mark. Even though, as a Cub, his 1918 World Series pitching record was 1-2, he wound up with one of the greatest World Series ERA grades in history. The Red Sox scored three runs in three games off Vaughn, as he ended up with an ERA of 1.00. The Series scores were 1-0 loss to Ruth, 2-1 loss to Mays and a 3-0 win against Jones. It was a truly remarkable pitching performance! Perhaps the "Hippo tag" was undeserved since Vaughn was 6' 4" tall and weighed 215 pounds.

In early October, *The Sporting News,* listed the Hot Springs players' contracts that were reserved for the following 1909 season. The list included Joe Herglefort, Otto Besse, R. D. Fay, William "Lucky" Wright, R. D. Liles, Rupert Blakely, Edger Cowan, Elmer Coyle, Rube Walters, T. Naylor, S. W. Rainey, G. W. Smitheal, Joe Bunch, Herbert Benham, A. Naylor and A. H. Jones. Hot Springs acquired a few players who played against them during the regular season.[18]

In December 1908, a meeting in Little Rock of the Arkansas State League delegates voted W. W. Hurst of Argenta, league president for the coming 1909 season. Since he was elected president, immediately following the election as league president, Mr. Hurst "tendered his resignation as president of the Argenta Base Ball Association to take effect at once." At the conference, discussions of other issues took place including league membership. There was a discussion of the legitimacy of the ownership of the Hot Springs club. Arthur S. Riggs produced evidence and signed by T. J. Craighead that stated that Riggs was the owner. Dr. W. O. Forbes, as president of the Hot Springs Athletic and Base Ball Association protested Riggs' action. At the conclusion, harmony was restored to the group and Riggs was the owner of the Hot Springs franchise.

Riggs presented canceled checks and vouchers showing that he had put up the $200 guaranty money, the $15 protection fee, and paid other expenses of the club prior to April 20, amounting in all over $700. [19]

About a month later, R. M. Rider, of Helena, took over the reigns as league president from Mr. Hurst. In 1909, the fragile eight-team Arkansas State League included five Arkansas contingents: Argenta Shamrocks, Ft. Smith Soldiers, Helena Hellions, Hot Springs Vaporites and Jonesboro (no team name found). The Louisiana entries were the Monroe Pearl Diggers and Alexandria Hoo-Hoos, while Texarkana represented the Lone Star State.

The Arkansas State, Class D, League opened the season with Arthur Riggs as owner/manager of the Hot Springs team. It was reported in the May 28, 1909, Hot Springs *Citizens Daily Bulletin*, that the Spa toppled Texarkana by a 6-2 margin at Whittington Park. Ware, second sacker for the Vaporites, led the hitting attack with three singles in four trips to the plate. Shortstop Smitheal, catcher Naylor and pitcher Heigelfort contributed two hits each for the Spa. The base stealers were Bromley, Coyle and Smitheal with one theft each. The lineup for the Vaporites included Bromley-cf; Coyle-1b; Smitheaf-ss; Russell-lf; Ware-2b; Naylor-c; DeHaven-3b; Heigelfort-p and Murphy-rf. Hot Springs scored two runs in the fourth and four runs in the fifth inning, while Texarkana managed only two runs in the sixth frame. The league standings listed in the May 28, issue of *The Citizens Daily Bulletin* were (1) Helena, (2) Jonesboro, (3) Argenta, (4) Monroe, (5) Alexandria, (6) Hot Springs, (7) Texarkana and (8) Fort Smith.[20]

Argenta, Alexandria and Monroe disbanded by early June. The league voted Monroe out of the league for failure to meet its obligations. Newport-Batesville took over Monroe's place and nickname. League officials decided to close the first season on June 13 and restart the second season the next day. Following are the league standings of the first season listed in *The Sporting News* on April 29, 1909: (1) Helena, (2) Jonesboro, (3) Hot Springs, (4) Monroe, (5) Texarkana and (6) Fort Smith.[21]

R, M. Rider, new league president from Helena, drew up a new second season schedule. The league continued until July 7, when the Newport-Batesville team dropped out. Since attendance was low, Rider decided to disband the league. At league's end, *The Sporting News* listed the finals standings as: (1) Texarkana, (2) Jonesboro, (3) Helena, (4) Fort Smith, (5) Hot Springs and (6) Newport-Batesville.[22].

The nickname for Alexandria, the Hoo-Hoos, is unusual, but it seemed to have acquired its origin in January 1892, in the small town of Gurdon, Arkansas. The name referred to a lumberman's organization. Hoo-Hoo International was, and still is, "The Fraternal Order of the Forest Products Industry." The organization was the brainchild of Bolling Arthur Johnson, lumber trade journalist. Mr. Johnson desired to organize a national lumberman's association that would promote high ideals and produce a code of ethics for the business. In addition, he thought fun and fellowship should be a staple of the group. Perhaps the Hoo-Hoo's or a member of the organization sponsored the Alexandria team.

The term "Hoo-Hoo" had been uttered for the first time only a month earlier (Dec. 1891) by Johnson to describe an alarming tuft of hair that grew on top of the otherwise bald head of lumberman and friend, Charles H. McCarer, who later became Hoo-Hoo's member #1 and the group's first Snark.[23]

Chapter 2

Major Leaguers Only
1910-1937

"President Ebbets has taken advantage of his trip to Hot Springs to do a little conditioning himself." - William J. Granger

Hot Springs continued to encounter professional baseball each spring as the major league teams traveled to the Spa for spring training. However, no professional baseball teams representing Hot Springs existed during this time. In 1910, the Pittsburgh Pirates, Boston Red Sox, Cincinnati Reds, Brooklyn Dodgers, including players from other major league teams, trained in the Spa. Minor league teams also dotted the baseball landscape at the Spa.

In 1912, the Philadelphia Phillies trained at the park next to the Alligator Farm. Grover Cleveland Alexander, called "Alexander the Great," was in his sophomore season when he pitched for the Phillies that year. The park was later named Fogel Field in honor of Horace Fogel, owner of the Phillies. The field, also known as Older, McKee or Fordyce Fields, received its names by whoever owned the property. In the 1940s, the property took on the name of Legion Field, since the American Legion baseball team practiced at that location.

The Boston Red Sox spent many spring-training seasons in the Resort. In 1912, the Red Sox won the World Series beating the New York Giants four games to three, as second place Pittsburgh

Pirates finished 10 games behind the Giants in the National League race. During the 1913 training sessions in Hot Springs, the managers of the Red Sox and Pirates thought it would be a clever idea to play a series of games between the two teams and call it, "the Little World Series." Even though the Pirates finished second in 1912, they thought they could win the National League pennant in 1913. It was sort of like a "crystal ball" series. Of course, both teams wanted to be in the World Series in 1913, but who knew what would happen? It seemed that one of the main reasons for the spring series was to increase spring gate receipts, which would be good for both teams. They scheduled nine games between the two powerhouses, but the teams reduced the series as Boston won three of five games with one tie. The "Hot Springs World Series" was not a tremendous success due to several things. Injuries occurred to several key players, the games were grudge matches and the second team players, called "yanigans," played sparingly. There was too much pressure to win each game because the media from many parts of the country flocked to the Springs and reported the games almost like a real World Series. Both managers stated that their starting lineups were in good condition and ready for the season, but the yanigans needed more work. Fred Clarke, manager of the Pirates, stated that games with the yanigans would have been more productive.[1]

Major league owners were always on the lookout for ways to reduce team expenses, even at the expense of player contracts. In fact, as war seemed eminent in 1917, the owners used "war" as an excuse to reduce expenses and Charles Ebbets, owner of the Brooklyn Robins, was no exception. Some owners thought that teams might cut back on expenses by staying closer to home for spring training. However, Ebbets decided to take his team to Hot Springs and stay at the luxurious Eastman Hotel. In fact, Ebbets traveled with the team to the Spa and took part in the baths himself. Ebbets had it all figured out. Following the spring drills in Hot Springs, he worked out an itinerary to play the Red Sox in five or six cities on their return to Brooklyn in order to recover some expenses. In addition, he arranged a three-game exhibition extravaganza with the New York Americans upon the team's arrival at Ebbets Field.

Ebbets was a busy man, but William J. Granger, *Sporting Life* reporter, caught up with the man from Flatbush and discovered his daily routine while visiting Hot Springs.

President Ebbets has taken advantage of his trip to Hot Springs to do a little conditioning himself. The head of the Brooklyn club was in bad physical condition at the close of the World Series. In a letter to the scribes of Brooklyn he says, 'I have been here almost three weeks, spending a most strenuous time daily. My routine has been: Rise at 6 o'clock, take hot shower in these wonderful waters for 25 minutes, then in hot room for 25 minutes; cool off under shower for five minutes, massage and electric treatment for 45 minutes; breakfast at 9 o'clock: 9:30 to 11:00 horseback riding.

Yes, I have learned to ride a nice easy-going horse; luncheon at 12:30; golf, 18 holes - about five and one-half miles chasing a little ball, 1:30 to 4:30; dinner at 6:30; a short walk after dinner; to bed – that is supposed – at 11:00, but I get to bed more frequently after 11 o'clock than before because that is the only time to read the papers to learn what is doing in the outside world and attend to my mail. Some strenuous day? Yes, and believe me, I have never felt better in my life. Have lost ten pounds in weight and would have lost more, but I linger in the dinner room, caused, I presume, by my hard daily work. However, it is doing me a world of good. If my ear would only stop buzzing. Possibly, it is improving, but so slightly, that is not perceptible. Certainly, it is not getting worse. I expect to arrive home February 12th.[2]

Beginning around 1915, Babe Ruth spent several springs at the Spa preparing himself for the long seasons. There is a story that Paul Krichell, a New York Yankees scout, revealed about Ruth while training in Hot Springs in the spring of 1925. The Babe boiled out in the Spa that spring and reported late to the Yankees regular spring training camp in St. Petersburg, Florida. Manager

Huggins and Jake Ruppert, owner and president of the Yankees, didn't take too kindly to the big man's tardiness.

Ruth reported (to Florida) and sat himself in an easy chair in the hotel lobby. Jake asked him when he planned to go to work and Ruth said, 'I should be dead now. In Hot Springs, I had a fever of 105 8/5. The croaker (doctor) said he never saw the like.' Jake assured the Babe that 105 8/5 was quite a fever, and gently pushed him in the direction of Crescent Lake Park, now Huggins Field. [3]

Speculation still exists as to the real reason of Ruth's ailments at the Spa. The 1925 season was one of Babe's worst seasons because he only played in 98 games due to his illness. Even though 1925 was a sub-par season for the Bambino, most major league players would have taken his numbers in a second. Ruth hit .290 with 25 homers. Bob Meusel, Babe's teammate, hit 33 homers to lead the American League, while the Cardinals' Rogers Hornsby smacked 39 to pace the National League. Ruth and Ken Williams of the Browns tied for second in the homer race in the American League.

The Philadelphia Athletics, managed by 66-year-old Connie Mack, crushed the Chicago Cubs four games to one, to take the 1929 World Series. What a surprise and a delight for the students of Hot Springs High School to welcome several of the World Champion Athletics on February 17, 1930. Over 2,000 students and faculty gathered in the high school auditorium on Oak Street, to hear outfielder "Bing" Miller and other players talk about the World Series and the prospects for the 1930 season. Many Athletics traveled to the Spa for pre-spring training conditioning. Some of the players included Al Simmons-outfielder, Joe Boley-shortstop, Max Bishop-second baseman, catchers-"Mickey" Cochrane and "Wally" Schang, pitchers-Jack Quinn, Bill Shores, "Rube" Walberg and Bill "Kid" Gleason-coach.

In 1934, "Babe" Didrikson, voted the greatest female athlete of the first half of the 20th century, visited the Spa to check on her brother, "Bubba" Didrikson, who was a student at the Ray Doan's Baseball School. "Babe" played briefly with the House of David baseball team. During the same spring, other players took the baths and exercised in the Spa including "Dazzy" Vance-pitcher, St. Louis Cardinals; Bob O'Farrell-catcher, Cincinnati Reds; "Shanty" Hogan-catcher, Boston Braves; Riggs Stephenson-outfielder, Chicago Cubs and Clyde Milan-manager of the Birmingham Barons and former major leaguer.

In 1936, instructors at the Doan's Baseball School flooded the area with a wealth of major league baseball expertise. The talented instructors included Earl "Oil" Smith, "Dizzy" Dean, Tris Speaker, George Sisler, Lon Warneke, Rogers Hornsby, Burleigh Grimes, "Schoolboy" Rowe, "Dutch" Zwilling, Hank Severeid, Lew Fonseca, Johnny Mostil and Guy Sturdy.

Carl Hubbell, Leo Durocher, Mel Ott, Bill Terry, "Cookie" Lavagetto, Hal Schumacher and many more players, coaches, managers, umpires, front office personnel visited the Spa in the late 1930s. By then, it was time for Hot Springs to jump back into the professional baseball market.

Chapter 3

Birth of the Modern Bathers
1938

"Hot Springs has been offered an opportunity to have a baseball team in the Cotton States League." - Douglas Hotchkiss

The custom of major and minor league teams training at the Arkansas Resort during the spring continued in 1938. During the same year, the well-established Ray Doan's Baseball School was entering its sixth year of operation at the Spa. Additionally, George Barr, major league umpire, conducted his umpiring school in coordination with the baseball school. Professional baseball scouts rode in from all parts of the country to check out Doan's young talent.

Both institutions were the product of the fertile mind of Doan, nationally known sports pro- moter who won national-wide fame with his bewhiskered House of David baseball teams on barnstorming tours. It was upon a trip through Hot Springs several years ago with the House of David team that he hit upon the idea of the baseball school.[1]

Actually, a small percentage of students from the renowned baseball school ever received more than a "cup of coffee" from the major leagues, but it kept hopes alive for many young men as they learned baseball skills and exploited their talents in front of scouts, managers and former players. The school seemed to have been excellent publicity for the city and, no doubt, aided in strengthening the local economy and increased Doan's bank account. Doan hired exceptional instructors for the school. The 1938 version of the baseball school headlined such major league stars as Lon Warneke, Johnny Mostil, "Kid" Elberfield, Hank Severeid, "Red" Faber, "Dizzy" Dean, Rogers Hornsby and the great "Cy" Young.

During the latter part of 1937, after nearly thirty years, interest in professional minor league baseball became apparent in the Spa. There was a vacancy in the Cotton States League and several cities showed an interest in filling the position. Representatives from Hot Springs and Camden, Arkansas, planned to sit in at a meeting with directors of the Cotton States League on October 31, 1937, in Monroe, Louisiana.

Douglas Hotchkiss, secretary-manager of the Hot Springs Chamber of Commerce, notified J. Walter Morris, league president, that "local baseball enthusiasts and business men have expressed great interest in the movement." In early November 1937, Hotchkiss, sent a letter to several interested parties.

Dear Sir:

Hot Springs has been offered an opportunity to have a baseball team in the Cotton States League. The president of the Cotton States League will be at the Chamber of Commerce Wednesday morning (Nov. 11) at 10:30 to present the details.

I am advised by Mr. Dillon that Whittington Park will be available if we effect an organization. Since there are improved or paved roads connecting the towns and the club travels by motor bus instead of by rail, I do not think a club in this league will be top heavy with expenses.

Bathers Baseball

We would contemplate having night games, which would furnish our visitors some amusement and some place to go for the summer season. Hot Springs might pay its way very easily in such a league and might possibly make some dividends.

I am calling you and several others to meet at the Chamber of Commerce on Wednesday morning, at 10:30 to consider this proposal, which the president of the league will make. Our summer business has been growing steadily each summer and the more we can provide entertainment the more we can build our trade.

Kindly attend this meeting and put forth your views or at least understand the story.

Yours very truly,

Douglas Hotchkiss
Secretary-Manager[2]

Excitement permeated the meeting. President of the Hot Springs Chamber of Commerce S. A. Kemp appointed Roy Gillenwater to chair the baseball meeting. Following the conference, Gillenwater kicked-off the movement immediately to raise 300 subscriptions of $25 each. Before the exhilarating meeting concluded, the group secured 13 subscriptions. The subscription committee, headed up by Mose Holiman included Richard M. Ryan, Dallas Vance, Walter Ebel, Henry Murphy, Roy C. Raef, Cy M. King, Bill Kimball, Jack McJunkin and George Pakis. An executive committee of Roy Gillenwater, Miles "Spike" Hunter, Lloyd Adams, Gil Wootten and S. H. Allman planned to work with the subscription committee. President of the Cotton States League, J. Water Morris discussed the circumstances with the Hot Springs committee.

Morris explained to the group, which met with him yesterday, that $7,500 would be an ample sum to start a club here. He explained that the franchise would cost the city nothing

37

and that the cost of operation would run between $13,000 and $15,000 per year. An annual attendance of 30,000 will enable any club to 'break even,' he said. Between 60 and 65 home games are played by each club.³

On November 18, 1937, Charles Warneke, 11-month-old son of Lon and Charlene Warneke of Hot Springs, became the second youngest stockholder of a professional baseball team. About a month before this meeting, the Cubs traded Lon Warneke, the talented pitcher, to the Cardinals. The Warnekes, who made their winter home in the Spa, were stockholders of the newly formed Bathers baseball team.⁴

Elected president of the newly proposed Hot Springs Bathers Baseball Club was Lloyd Adams, a well-known wholesale merchant in the city. In attendance at the historic, November 23, 1937, meeting was J. Walter Morris who said the meeting, held at city hall, was one of the most enthusiastic conferences of this type. Everyone seemed to recognize the positive spirit. The newly elected directors included Van Lyle, Dr. H. King Wade, I. Moscowitz, Lloyd Adams, H. H. Jeffries, Roy Gillenwater, S. H. Allman and Warren Banks.⁵

During the assembly, Cleveland Indians pitcher Willis Hudlin entered and said, "I heard they were going to try and organize a ball club here tonight, so I had to come along, too." The Hudlins made their winter home on Lake Hamilton.

"Brother, may I ask if you have subscribed for any stock in this new club?" Lon Warneke, Cardinal pitcher asked.

"No one has asked me," replied Hudlin.

"Well consider yourself invited," declared Warneke. "Give me a subscription blank."

Warneke got the necessary blank and handed it to Hudlin, who subscribed for two shares of stock.⁶

"Considerable improvement" concerning old Whittington Park was on the agenda at the meeting. Adding box seats and enlarging the bleachers at the park were also in the plans. The newly elected directors planned to draw up a constitution and by-laws for the club. Within a few days, the group met at the Arlington Hotel, at which time the league planned to vote on the admittance of Hot Springs into the Cotton States League. The ground maintenance staff of the Milwaukee Brewers of the Class AA International League, who used Whittington Park during the spring, planned to work on the grounds and get it in tip-top shape by opening day.[7]

The *New Era,* the evening Hot Springs paper, stated on Dec. 1, 1937, that the Hot Springs Baseball Association, Inc. obtained a charter to operate a franchise in the Cotton States League. The article listed the capital for the club at $10,000 and the incorporators were Van Lyell, H. H. Jeffries, Lloyd Adams, S. H. Allison and I. Moscowitz.[8]

On December 5, 1937, the Chicago Cubs planned to furnish baseball talent to the new community-owned Spa team. Five applicants for the job of manager of the Hot Springs team included Earl Smith, former major league catcher and "Spike" Hunter, former player-manager of the Jonesboro Giants in the Class D, Northeast Arkansas League in 1937. Both men were residents of Hot Springs. Two other applicants included Lena Styles, manager of the 1936-1937 Greenville Bucks (MS) in the Cotton States League and Wally Dashiel, manager of the 1937 Tyler Trojans of the Class C, East Texas League. Additional officers of the new club were Van Lyell - vice president, Warren Banks - secretary-treasurer and Roy Bosson - official scorekeeper. The Chicago Cubs owner reserved the right to approve the team manager.[9]

Even though the Bathers planned to affiliate themselves with the Cubs, the team was community-owned. The Bathers decided to operate its own concessions as club officials continue to organize the new team. "If outside interests can afford to offer us $1,000 or more for the concessions, there must be some profit in it," said Lloyd Adams, club president. He said the club should run the program.[10]

Jack McJunkin became the concessions manager for the season. He drummed up business by printing lucky numbers in the baseball programs. Two numbers were drawn and posted on the new electric scoreboard each night. The two lucky fans each received a free ticket to a Bathers game.

In late December 1937, nearly every public official in Garland County met at the home of Judge Earl Witt to honor Lon Warneke for his work in aiding to establish a professional baseball club in Hot Springs. It was largely through Warneke's effort that the Chicago Cubs planned to have a working agreement with the Bathers. Both Witt and Warneke were natives of Mt. Ida in Montgomery County, Arkansas, about 40 miles from Hot Springs.[11]

Respected local newspaper sports editor, Roy Bosson, interviewed the President of the National Association of Professional Baseball Leagues, Judge W. G. Branham. The minor league kingpin, vacationing in the Resort during January 1938, stated that the minor leagues were on a sound basis.

'Under the present rules no team can enter a league unless it has sufficient funds to start with,' he said. 'As a result the financial instability of the past has been eliminated.'

...'Formerly we had as much trouble keeping teams out of leagues as we had in keeping them in,' he declared. 'Anyone with a little interest in the game could organize a club regardless of how much money he had. Some even tried to start without as much as a home plate. The new rules requiring the clubs to have sufficient money to start with has done away with all that.'[12]

Barnham said attendance in the major and minor leagues was on the rise. During the 1937 season, 26,000,000 fans attended professional baseball games in the United States. Of that number, 13,500,000 fans visited games at minor league sites. The Durham, North Carolina native added that night baseball was on the increase in the south. He praised Hot Springs for jumping into the minor league arena. Barnham, during his several weeks stay in the Spa, brought most of his baseball files, rented a typewriter and "is all but conducting the affairs of the association from his room at the Majestic Hotel." In 1999, the NAPBL changed its name to Minor League Baseball.[13]

Otis Brannan, former major league second baseman for the St. Louis Browns and first to sign a Bathers contract for the 1938 season, was ready to play ball. After a two-year layoff, the 39-year-old infielder was anxious to return to professional baseball.[14]

Lloyd Adams, president of the community-owned Spa team, named Miles A. "Spike" Hunter as player-manager of the new Bathers. The Chicago Cubs, who had a working agreement with the Bathers, approved the nomination. Hunter, beginning his 12th-season as a minor league pitcher, brought experience to the Bathers club. Hunter, from Hot Springs, won 17 games for Jonesboro during the 1937 season. Manager Hunter stated that he was not going to predict a first place finish the first year, but he said he would have a hustling ball club. "'If the players didn't hustle, they wouldn't play, he declared.'"[15]

A letter from the general manager of the public utilities in Hot Springs to the Federal Light and Traction Company in New York, dated February 4, 1938, sought authorization for the immediate installation of baseball lights at Ban Johnson Field. "Seventy foot poles will be installed on the ball grounds and there will be a total of eighty lamps of 1,500 watts each. This gives a load of 120 K. W." By early April 1938, lights became a reality at the old ballpark. The total cost for the lights, including a new power line costing $1,000, was $3,752. The light money made a heavy dent into the stockholders pocketbook, but if attendance stayed above 600 per game, the Bathers would break even. Average attendance during exhibition games was 1,000 per game, so if that trend continued, the Bathers would be in good shape financially.

After many years of professional-less baseball, Hot Springs climbed back into the pro ranks. The Hot Springs Bathers, appropriately named, threw their hat into the CSL baseball ring for the 1938 season. The league had been in existence as a Class D league during 1902-1908, 1910-1913 and 1922-1932. However, in 1936, the league launched into the higher Class C division, two years before Hot Springs jumped into the loop.

The 1938 Cotton States League version included three teams from Mississippi, four teams from Arkansas and one from Louisiana. The Clarksdale Red Sox, the Greenville Bucks and the Greenwood Dodgers represented Mississippi. The El Dorado Lions, the Helena Seaporters, the Hot Springs Bathers and the Pine Bluff Judges were the delegates from Arkansas, while the Monroe White Sox was the ambassador from Louisiana.

On February 13, 1938, at El Dorado, the loop moguls adopted a 140-game schedule for the 1938 season. The schedule, submitted by Harry Faulkner, an official of the Dallas Steers, in the Texas League, drew several complaints. Some discussions concerned the Bathers as they received home games on opening-day game and July 4. However, the directors decided to allow Hot Springs to have both home games since they were the new team on the block. The directors recognized that Greenwood did not have opening day or July 4 home games, so they decided to change the schedule to accommodate a home game for Greenwood on July 4. There would be 10 double-headers and August 28, 1938, was the last day of the regular season. The group voted against a mid-season All-Star game and elected July 21 to be an off day.

El Dorado and Hot Springs representatives voted for an All-Star game, while Pine Bluff and Clarksdale abstained. The other four teams voted against the All-Star game. Lloyd Adams stated that he would like the All-Star game played in Hot Springs so it would generate more league interest. Sentiment seemed to be in favor of having a game in July until Sam Anderson of Greenville disapproved of the game "on the grounds that the clubs would lose money among 'other cross currents of confusion' it would create." The Hot Springs representatives were Lloyd Adams, Warren Banks and "Spike" Hunter. There was no All-Star game played in 1938.

The league voted on keeping a 15-player limit for each team. In addition, it required each team "to have at least six rookies, with less than three years experience and not more than nine players with more than three years experience." The league retained the rule "to keep the $1,500 monthly salary limit for each club."

The schedule for the Shaughnessy playoff between the top four clubs was clarified to provide that teams having the highest percentage at the close of the regular season would have the choice of starting the series in their respective towns. The semi-finals will be five-games and the finals seven.[16]

Manager Bill Terry of the New York Giants brought several players, mainly pitchers and catchers, to the Spa to begin pre-spring training workouts. Activities included thermal water treatments at the bathhouses, hiking on the mountains, playing a little baseball and testing out their golf swings at the Hot Springs Country Club. Among Chief Terry's crew included Carl Hubbell, Hy Vandenberg, Harry Schumacher, Dick Coffman, Don Brennan, Tom Baker, Harry Gumbert and Cliff Melton, all pitchers. The catchers included Gus Mancuso, Harry "The Horse" Danning, Jimmy Sheehan and Ted Duay. Infielders included Freddie Lindstrom and Sam Leslie and one outfielder Henry Leiber.

Originally affiliated with the Chicago Cubs, the Bathers had the carpet pulled out from under them due to a new ruling instigated by Baseball Commissioner Kenesaw Mountain Landis. A major league team could not be affiliated with more than one minor league team in the same league. Since the Cubs had a working agreement with Helena, also of the Cotton States League, the Cubs cancelled the deal with Hot Springs.

Lloyd Adams, president of the Hot Springs baseball club of the Cotton States league, announced last night that the Chicago Cubs have severed affiliations with the Spa team, but added that a 'much better' working arrangement has been arranged with the Detroit Tigers of the American league.

'The agreement with Detroit does not provide quite as much in the way of cash.' Adams pointed out, 'but the other provisions make it all the more acceptable to us.'[17]

The major league team affiliations in the Cotton States League were Clarksdale (Boston Red Sox), El Dorado (Cincinnati Reds), Greenville (Independent), Helena (Chicago Cubs), Hot Springs (Independent - but ties with the Detroit Tigers), Monroe (Chicago White Sox), Greenwood (Brooklyn Dodgers) and Pine Bluff (St. Louis Cardinals). Under the new arrangement, the Bathers received players from the Beaumont Exporters, of the Class A Texas League. As soon as the Cubs contacted Adams about the cancellation, Adams called the Cotton States League president, J. Walter Morris. The league czar quickly called Detroit to get the ball rolling on a new pact.

During his lifetime, J. Walter Morris was a player, manager, owner, and later, president of several minor league teams in Arkansas and Texas. Early in his career, Morris managed the Dallas Steers, Fort Worth Panthers and the Shreveport Sports in the Texas League. His first managerial job was with the Savannah Indians of the South Atlantic League in 1908. He helped organize 13 leagues and was president of six, including the Texas League and the Cotton States League. Inducted into the Texas Sports Hall of Fame in 1966, Morris passed away in 1961 in Dallas.

On February 17, 1935, dedication ceremonies occurred making Ban Johnson Field the formal name of the baseball field at Whittington Park, the official ballpark of the newly formed Hot Springs Bathers. The field, known only as Whittington Park at the time of its establishment around 1894, was the primary spring training grounds for many major league teams. At the time of the dedication in 1935, Ray Doan's school utilized the diamond. Today, the Weyerhaeuser Company offices and parking lot occupy the location. The long-standing Arkansas Alligator Farm, founded in 1902, was, and still is, located across the street.

In the 1930s, Ban Johnson Field continued to be the main baseball diamond in the city. Who was Ban Johnson? In 1894, Ban Johnson, a sportswriter from Cincinnati, became the president of the Western League, the strongest minor league in baseball. Charles Comiskey, owner of the St. Paul franchise in the Western League, was the big man behind the move to promote Johnson to the office. In 1900, the Western League, renamed the American League, appointed Bancroft Johnson its first president. In 1901, the new league went head to head with the National League and claimed major league status. They competed for the same players by offering higher salaries.

Johnson served as the American League president from 1901 through the end of the 1927 season. Will Harridge, who took over the reigns as head of the league following Johnson's retirement stated, "He (Johnson) was the most brilliant baseball man the game has ever known. He was more responsible for making baseball the national game than anyone in the history of the sport."[18] Johnson enjoyed visiting Hot Springs and, in return, the city enjoyed having him as a guest. While visiting the Spa in 1927, he suggested that it would be beneficial for major league pitchers to bathe in the Spa's thermal waters in order for them to get in shape at a faster pace. He was an excellent promoter of baseball spring training in Hot Springs. Ban Johnson passed away in 1931, in St. Louis, at the age of 67.

The first regularly scheduled exhibition game of the newly formed Hot Springs minor league team occurred on Sunday, April 3, 1938, at Ban Johnson Field. The game started at 2:30 p.m. as the hometown team hosted the Milwaukee Brewers of the Class AA, American Association League. The Brewers had been in the city training for more than two weeks, but the Bathers, late starting camp, played "catch up."

Miles A. "Spike" Hunter, Bathers' player-manager and well-known Hot Springs native, released the following batting order for the first exhibition contest with Milwaukee. The hometown lineup consisted of: Eddie Dancisak - center field, Doyle "Pop" Brannan – shortstop, Hal Grant - first base, Otis Brannan - second base, Albert "Lefty" Tolles - right field, Jimmy Hogg - third base and Albert Robinson roamed in the left garden. Paul Rucker, Lawrence Duff and Lowery shared the catching responsibilities. Pete Gains, Benny Trovich, Left-handed Pat White and Dempsey Alexander received turns on the mound. Young Gil Wilson, a Hot Springs boy, sought a tryout at second base with Milwaukee. The students at George Barr's School for Umpires called the game. In 1935, George Barr, National League umpire, opened the first umpire training school in association with Doan's Baseball School in Hot Springs. The Bathers put their best bats forward and eased by Milwaukee 8-7. It was only a practice game, but during their first outing, the Bathers beat a team from the Class AA, American Association. It was a great start.[19]

An extra feature at a subsequent practice game with Milwaukee was a "pepper game," performed by members of the famed House of David Baseball Team. An excellent semi-pro team from Greenbrier, Arkansas, was the Bathers next spring opponent scheduled on Sunday afternoon, April 10. The Bathers scooted past the semi-pro crew 9-5. A few days before the Greenbrier game, the new floodlights passed inspection. "An official stated that the park will be one of the best lighted in the entire Cotton States circuit."[20]

The Bathers strutted out, at home, in their new uniforms as they played the last tune-up tilt on Sunday afternoon, April 17, with the Texarkana Liners of the Class C, East Texas League. However, "Lady Luck chose to put her arms around the Texarkana team" as Texarkana won the practice game 6-4.

There were two balls, both hit into the tree-tops in deep center, that were marked home runs when they left the bat, but which the trees sent back into the park, knocking the Bathers out of two runs. Two close decisions, one at third and one at first, also proved costly as the arbiters decided in both instances against the hometown gang.[21]

A group called the "Whittington Avenue Gang" planned a get-together on opening night to observe the first night baseball game on Wednesday, April 20.

Ernest Gibbs, John Dugan, Brandon Kaufman, Milton Nobles, Mike Reed, and Eddie Cockburn, gang officers, invited all of the old-timers who now live on Whittington or folks who have lived on the fine old street, to attend this special night ball game.[22]

On Wednesday, April 20, 1938, a new era began for the Hot Springs professional baseball. "Hot Springs baseball fans tonight will see a home club in organized baseball for the first time since the old Arkansas State League was disbanded in 1909." The Bathers opened the Cotton States League season by playing host to the Pine Bluff Judges for a brief two-game series.[23]

An editorial on the front page of the April 20, *The Sentinel-Record* written by R. S. Dean, attempted to stir up the baseball interest in the area. Dean named his article, "Baseball Comes Back." He stated that it had been a long time, 1909, since Hot Springs had a professional team.

Now we are staging a comeback with a berth in the expanded Cotton States League, one of the oldest minors in the South. The club has made beneficial connections with Beaumont of the Texas League, and Detroit of the American League…

…If we want baseball on a permanent basis here, we must support the team. The club is a cooperative organization underwritten by 300 businessmen and sportsmen of Hot Springs. It is not primarily for profit, but for supplying clean pastime for our residents and visitors.

…Hot Springs needs baseball, which still is fundamentally the great American sport. It is not only the source of entertainment, but organized baseball is a valuable medium of publicity for any city.

Let us give organized baseball every opportunity to make good in Hot Springs and become a permanent fixture here.[24]

In pregame festivities, Mayor Leo McLaughlin pitched; assigned to the backstop duties was Earl "Oil" Smith, former major league catcher; Dr. H. King Wade, Sr., former semi-pro star, was the batter and the designated arbiter was, of course, Judge Earl Witt. The game commenced at 8:00 p.m. and the admission was 40 cents for adults and one thin dime for children under 15-years-old. The 65-piece Hot Springs High School Trojan Band played as the "Whittington Gang" roared for the local players. Nearly 3,500 noisy fans cheered the Bathers as they reintroduced professional baseball to the Spa. The grandstand and bleachers were packed. "Every seat in Ban Johnson Field was filled, even to the newly constructed bleachers and many of the fans took to the mountainside adjoining the park to find places to view the contest."[25/26]

Manager Hunter toed the rubber for the Spa team, at home, on April 20. The Hot Springs lineup included the batting order and position: (1) Eddie Dancisak-cf; (2) Jimmy Hoagg-3b; (3) Hal Grant-1b; (4) Otis Brannan-2b; (5) Al Tolles-rf; (6) Robby Robinson-lf; (7) Doyle Brannan-ss; (8) Bill Costley-c and (9) Hunter-p. Hunter, the leading pitcher in the Northeast Arkansas League in 1937, began throwing in a light rain. Since Hunter was from the "City of Water," the drops didn't seem to affect him. The Bathers shot out of the gate with a 1-0 lead in the first inning, but the Judges tied the contest in the fourth frame. The Spa turned up the heat in the fifth inning as they crossed the plate four times. Hal Grant, newly acquired Bathers first baseman from Pine Bluff, leaped on Dunkle, the Judges pitcher for three hits, including a fifth inning blast over the short right field fence. Hunter scattered five hits, while the boys from the Spa garnered 10 bingles as the Bathers took a 5-2 debut decision. The big guns for Hot Springs were center fielder Eddie Dancisak and slugging first baseman Hal Grant, as they collected three safeties apiece. Umpires English and Doughty called the speedy game that took only an hour and 33 minutes. At the end of the night, the Bathers sat atop the Cotton States League with a 1-0 record, tied with Greenville and Monroe. After 30 years, Hot Springs was back in the professional baseball saddle.

The following night, limited to only four hits, the Bathers lost to the Judges 2-1 in the opener on the road. The bats didn't come alive for either team as the Spa Boys garnered four hits, while the Judges mustered six. The score was tied 1-1 going into the last of the ninth frame when Pine Bluff shoved over a run for the win.

Hot Springs came out on the short end of another road game on April 24, this time to Helena. The Seaporters energized themselves in the sixth inning, scoring four runs to beat the Bathers 5-1.

Grant was the only Hot Springs player to collect two hits. Three Helena players gathered two hits each off two Bathers' pitchers, Zalsko and Alexander.

The Clarksdale Red Sox trounced the Bathers 6-1 on April 27, in Mississippi. Hot Springs did not have too many pitchers, so many times the pitchers, even though overmatched, threw the complete nine innings. Hunter, rapped for 14 hits, pitched the entire game as Hot Springs only acquired seven hits. Due to several rainouts, the Bathers were in next-to-last place with only a 2-5 record in the young season. On Sunday, May 1, the Bathers suffered their first defeat at home 10-7, as Clarksdale mounted a 13-hit attack.

"The Bull Ring," was the place where Roy Bosson, excellent sports editor of *The Sentinel-Record,* spoke out about the local and national sport scenes. After the Bathers played about a dozen games, the question Bosson asked was, "What's wrong with the Bathers?" The sportswriter stated that they had only two front-line moundsmen, Floyd Speer and "Spike" Hunter. The team was in dire need of three more pitchers, he remarked. "The Bather mound performances have been plenty spotty."[27]

In the same editorial, Bosson wrote about how the league divided team revenue. In 1938, the home team kept what it made from home games without giving revenue to the visiting teams. The Bathers averaged more than 500 paid adult admissions each night. To break even it was essential for the team to average only about 400 per game and smiling "Kingfish" Adams enjoyed the fan support. However, there was one problem. It seemed that the scorekeeper was having a problem with the scorecard. How do scorekeepers keep score if they don't know the players?

Complaint department: Whomever the guy is who prints those scorecards for the baseball games, we resent the barkings of the scorecard vendors to the effect that 'You can't tell a ballplayer from an umpire without a scorecard.'

…You can't tell 'em with a scorecard. In one game the card failed to list any numbers at all by the names of the visiting players, and in another only five of the numbers were correct…Which doesn't help John Fan and ye scorer any.[28]

Hunter made a "save the Bathers" telephone call when he contacted southpaw "Burley" Grimes. Hot Springs quickly purchased Grimes, a strikeout artist from the Jonesboro Giants of the Class D, Northeast Arkansas League. His 1937 record was 17-10 with the Giants. Hunter contacted the Detroit Tigers in hopes they would send pitching relief down his way. After the Bathers lost four straight, Roy Bosson wrote, "Those howling wolves are already howling." He attempted to downplay the losses, but fans will howl from time to time. He also stated that all the ballparks in the Cotton States League are equipped with lights.

Jack Zeller's, chief scout of the Detroit Tigers, joined the Bathers on the road trip to determine the team's needs. Hot Springs needed mound assistance and the fans knew it. A few days previously, Zeller sent the Bathers a couple of promising hurlers. In addition to "Burley" Grimes, "Buster" Bryant, former Kentucky-Illinois-Tennessee League (KITTY) hurler and 19-year-old Johnny Sain, 6' 2", 185-pounder, joined the fold. Hunter picked up Sain who was pitching with the Osceola Indians of the Northeast Arkansas League, but the Bathers still needed more good hurlers.

Douglass Hotchkiss, secretary-manager of the Hot Springs Chamber of Commerce, wrote a letter to the hometown fans and to Bosson. It seemed that Bosson, in his editorial comments concerning the weaknesses of the Bathers, previously stirred up a hornet's nest among certain people in the city and Hotchkiss was one of those hornets. Hotchkiss suggested for fans to cool it. He said that the baseball team is a young organization and it will have its growing pains. In spite of the circumstances, he thought the fans should support the team and have patience with the fledging club. Hotchkiss stated how he felt in the *Hot Springs New Era* on May 10.

…I speak from the viewpoint of a Chamber of Commerce representative, which sponsored this baseball organization and speak from the viewpoint of an individual who has put a fair proposition of money into the movement.

…I am as disappointed as others of our baseball fans that we did not get off to a good start, but I am not discouraged in the least but that our baseball organization will prove amply sufficient and amply competent before even this year in baseball has gone very far.

This is not a word to quiet some of the discontent that seems to exist on the part of friendly baseball fans, who perhaps expected too much in the immediate beginning. Let's all be a little more patient, until our officers and our managers, have a full opportunity to prove their worth, which I am sure will occur…[29]

The negatives continued to roll in. On Tuesday, May 10, 1938, the *Hot Springs New Era*, the evening paper, stated that, "Baseballs traveled to all corners of the lot last night at Ban Johnson Field as manager 'Spike' Hunter's Hot Springs Bathers dropped their seventh straight game as the White Sox of Monroe cut loose with a barrage of 18 base hits." The Sox shelled the hometown boys 17-9, as fans recovered from sore necks as they followed an offensive volley of 28 base hits. The team from Louisiana scored 17 runs on 18 hits, while the Spa team scored nine runs on a 10-hit spree. Shortstop Doyle Brannan, the cousin of second baseman Otis Brannan, was the hitting star for the Bathers as he collected three safeties. Left fielder Harvell, right fielder Bennett and third baseman Hacknep garnered three safeties each for Monroe.[30]

It was just that kind of year for the Bathers. Newcomer and starting Bathers' pitcher Johnny Sain unfortunately saw too many White Sox stroll to the plate. Sain gave up six runs on nine hits in 3 1/3 innings on his first outing with the club. Pullig followed Sain on the hill as the races continued. Hunter slowed it down when he relieved Pullig in the sixth. Hunter attempted to solve some of the problems, but it was too little too late. A week later, Sain and Pullig received their release notices from the Bathers.

Hunter attempted to shake up the team by revamping the lineup. The next game the Bathers lost to Monroe 10-5, making it four straight setbacks. There was not much shake in his shake-up. The Bathers couldn't sink much deeper into the cellar, but sportswriter Bosson had the answer.

Statistician R. L. Taylor has the answer. His figures show that the present Bather pitching staff has hurled 159 innings of baseball. During these 159 innings, they gave up 146 runs, nearly a run per inning, and likewise gave up 189 hits. They struck out 80, but walked 71. They have won four and lost 14 for a .222 average. So, it all comes back to the same spot – pitching.[31]

On May 13, the Bathers, after losing 10 straight, took out their frustration on the Buckshots from Greenville. Left-hander "Burley" Grimes and company overwhelmed the Mississippi group, 18-6.

On May 14, the local media listed the Bathers' batting leaders as Costley (.347), Grant (.330) and Robinson (.306). Grant was leading the team in RBIs at 20. In the pitching department, Grimes had a 1-0 record, Hunter 1-1, Speer 2-3, Zelasko 1-3, Garnish 0-4 and New 0-2. The departed pitchers, Pulling and Sain registered no wins, with one loss charged to Sain.

On May 16, 1938, the *New Era* announced that Ray Doan sold his baseball school to Rogers Hornsby, former major league star. Doan said that the main reason for the sale was the lack of "decent playing fields" in Hot Springs. George Barr, owner of the umpiring school in Hot Springs, stayed with his instructional school.

Bosson related that umpiring in the CSL was a tough career as James E. Wilder and Perry Hunter, CSL umpires affirmed. The arbiters worked on a 30-day schedule, which they received in the mail from the CSL office. They worked in teams and used their own cars to travel to the parks. Of course, they did not eat or stay at the same places as players. They worked no more than four games with a team. Hunter, who had been an umpire for four years, stated, "A man is either out or safe. A pitch is either a ball or a strike. We call 'em like we see'em."[32]

First place Greenville played last place Hot Springs on June 3, and both teams played good baseball. The Bucks shot down the Bathers 6-2 at home, but in doing so, Robby Robinson, Bathers third baseman, exploded for three singles and a triple during his four trips to the dish. Another star of the game was Jimmy Brown, Bathers center fielder. His throw from the outfield was the play that received a huge ovation. From deep right center field, strong-armed Brown threw a perfect strike to Robinson at third, seizing the runner by a dozen feet. The ball from Brown to Robinson "was on a rope," as it never touched the ground.

However, a week later, the last place Bathers pulled the plug on Hunter as the board of directors relieved him of his managerial duties on Thursday night, June 9. At a board meeting, Bathers president Lloyd Adams said that the front office decided to go in another direction; however, Hunter continued to take his rotations on the mound. First baseman, Hal Grant became the Bathers' temporary pilot. When Grant assumed his new duties, he led the CSL in homer runs and doubles. In addition, the well-liked player-manager was hitting over .300.

Grant didn't say much about his additional duties, but he spoke highly of his former boss, "Spike" Hunter. He said that he "enjoyed playing under 'Spike'" and he would hope that Hunter continued to pitch for the Bathers. Grant added that he thought "Spike" was "a good baseball man."[33]

Two days later, Adams announced that Hunter, in addition to his pitching duties, became the traveling secretary of the club. President Morris revealed, "Hunter had operated the local club on the road $25 per day cheaper than any of the other clubs in the circuit and his appointment as secretary followed."[34]

In a talk before members of the team Friday night in the clubhouse, Hunter declared he bore no ill will toward anyone over his release as manager of the team. *"I appreciate the way you boys hustled and played baseball for me," he said, "and I hope you'll continue to do your best for Grant. I intend to be putting out all I have when I'm out there on the mound."[35]*

Within days, the committee chose Bathers hard-swinging outfielder-third baseman, Joe Barnett, the team's manager, to take over the reins from temporary-manager Grant for the remainder of the season. In addition, Hunter continued to pitch for the Bathers.

On Sunday, June 19, 1938, headlines in *The Sentinel-Record* stated that Babe Ruth, "the man that baseball forgot," returned to baseball. The 44-year-old retired player and former Yankee slugger signed with the Brooklyn Dodgers as a coach. His reported salary was a meager $15,000 compared to his gigantic salaries of the past. Some thought that he would be in line to take over the Dodgers managerial duties from Burleigh Grimes (not the Hot Springs "Burley" Grimes). Ruth didn't get the manager's nod, so what did that have to do with the Hot Springs Bathers? Not a thing, except that Ruth's headlines received top billing above the Bathers loss to the El Dorado Lions 8-4 in the hometown paper. The Lions jumped on pitcher Hunter and the Hot Water Boys for 13 hits against only eight hits for the Bathers.[36]

The front office of the Bathers accommodated the hometown crowd on a special Wednesday night in June. Part of the evening included the Bathers hosting the Greenwood Dodgers. The second part of the twin activities was the radio broadcast of the Joe Louis-Max Schmeling heavyweight bout, which had international significance. The political world began to change. In February, Hitler seized control of the German army and put the Nazis in key posts. In March, Germany invaded Austria and Germany annexed Austria in April. The friction between the United States and Germany continued at an extremely high level. The boxing match represented the United States (Louis) against Germany (Schmeling).

Fight Party Tonight

A radio and loudspeaker will be installed at Ban Johnson field tonight to enable local fans to listen in on the Joe Louis-Max Schmeling heavyweight championship bout in New York. The fight starts promptly at 8 o'clock. [37]

It took much longer to hook up the loudspeakers than the amount of time it took Louis to take out Schmeling. Louis knocked out the German in two minutes of the first round. That was the good part. There was another knockout at the hands of the Greenwood Dodgers as Hot Springs went down for a 9-6 count.

El Dorado beat the Spamen in 10 innings on Friday night, June 24, at Ban Johnson Field by the score of 9-5. Hunter started on the mound for the Bathers and was relieved in the 10th inning of a 5-5 game. The bullpen could not hang on to win as the Lions scored four runs in the tenth frame.

The Bathers personnel had an altered appearance as the season progressed. The roster against El Dorado included Eddie Dancisak – cf, Jimmy Brown – lf, Otis Brannan – 2b, Doyle Brannan – ss, Art Robinson - 3b, Albert "Lefty" Tolles – rf, Hal Grant – 1b, Larry Steinberg – c, Jim Hogg – ss, "Spike" Hunter – p, W. Langston – p, Ed Hughes – p and Duke Wells – utility. Duke Wells became the legendary coach of Henderson State University in Arkadelphia, Arkansas. Other Bathers were Joe Barnett - 3b, Doyle Brannan - ss, Bill Costly - c, Paul "Bucket Head" Rucker – c, Walt Schafer – lf, Spinetti, "Big Jim" Mabry – lf, Jabbo New – p, C. Wilson – p, Burnell "Burley" Grimes - p, Albert Williamson - p, Claude Tarrant - p and Floyd Speer – p.

Five-hundred fans showed up on Ladies Night, June 26, as each woman received a free ticket with one paid admission. The crowd saw a "brilliant mound duel" between Grimes of Hot Springs and 6' 9" Gore of El Dorado. Grimes pitched a five-hitter, but lost the squeaker 2-1. Grimes' wife and baby were in the crowd watching the southpaw pitcher.

At the end of June, two Bathers, Robinson and Grant were in the league's top ten in three categories. Arthur "Robby" Robinson, third baseman, was in third place in the CSL's hitting stats with a .346 mark. First-sacker Hal Grant was in seventh spot with a .329 score. Additionally, Grant was leading the league with six home runs. As a team, Hot Springs was clouting the ball at a .278 pace, well enough for third place in the league, only six percentage points behind the team hitting leader, Greenville that produced a .284 mark. Hot Springs was last in fielding and weak in the pitching department.[38]

On Monday evening, July 4, 1938, the Bathers invited fans to help fill the stands at Ban Johnson Field as they played host to the Helena Seaporters. The special occasion was dubbed "George Raft Night." Mr. Raft, famous movie star of the era, known for his starring roles in several gangster movies, was the special guest of the Bathers. Raft, beginning a two-week vacation venture in the Spa, was the guest of his boyhood friend, Owney Madden, a well-known citizen of the Spa. A day earlier, Mr. Madden picked up Raft at the Missouri-Pacific train depot in Hot Springs. Raft's first question to Madden was, "How's the boat?" A few months before, Raft sent Madden a high-powered motor boat. Within a few days, they headed to Lake Hamilton for a spin in the new craft.

Owney Madden was the former owner of the Cotton Club in New York. From time to time in Hot Springs, he entertained friends connected to the gambling industry, such as Frank Costello and "Lucky" Luciano. Mamie Ruth Abernathy remembered that the Bathers "signed Raft to a Bathers contract" and gave him a uniform. Even though it was a rainy night, the ballpark was full of excited fans. Raft, sitting in the press box, didn't get to see much of the game because admirers flocked around him seeking autographs. Raft, who resided at the Arlington Hotel, signed autographs on ties, baseballs, hats and pieces of paper. Guinn Daniel, the Bathers batboy that season, obtained Raft's autograph on a baseball. Nowadays, Daniel is a retired physician living in Hot Springs.

Although he had never seen either the Hot Springs or Helena teams play, Raft proved himself the rabid baseball fan that he is by immediately recognizing two former Major Leaguers in the lineup of the teams.

A Hot Springs infielder fielded a ball and threw to first.

'Isn't that Otis Brannan who played for the St. Louis Browns?' Raft inquired. It was.

'And there is Old Hoss Riggs Stephenson.' he added as the veteran Helena manager walked out on the field.

…Movie topics were shunted aside as he said, 'Let's talk about Hot Springs.' This is the place I should come to take off a few pounds. I'd say he was one of your best boosters.'

The movie star came here to fulfill a promise to Madden to visit Hot Springs and take a course of the world-famous baths.[39]

Mary Sue Adams, daughter of Bathers' president Lloyd Adams, presented red roses to Mr. Raft. Mamie Abernathy made the white dress that Mary Sue wore for the occasion. Little publicity about the eventful evening found its way into the local papers because the umpire "called the game" early, due to rain.

On the last day of July, the league-trailing Bathers continued their losing ways as they dropped both ends of the doubleheader, 8-1 and 6-5 to the Greenville Buckshots. After the second bad call by the umpire, cushions and pop bottles began to fill the air. One poor call was enough, but two bad calls by R. B. Ellis, plate umpire, added to fan frustration. As Ellis scurried off the field at the end of the game, debris flew through the atmosphere. "The sky looked like a rainstorm," as many of the bottles found their mark. Following the game, a fan followed Ellis to the dressing room and conked the ump on the head with a walking cane. The police arrived and escorted Ellis to safety.

On Monday, August 1, the *New Era* posted the following sports headings, "Umpire Bombarded as Spa Club Loses Pair to Bucks." It seemed that fans throughout the Cotton States

League had their fill of poor calls. Roy Bosson wrote an article concerning umpiring, or the lack thereof, in the CSL.

The Bull Ring

The general opinion around this neck of the bushes is that Umpire R. B. Ellis, who "called" that last game at Ban Johnson field yesterday afternoon, is in dire need of a pair of dark glasses, a police dog and a walking cane...(He could also have had walking papers as far as the Hot Springs fans are concerned).

Not that he got up on the wrong side of the downy this morning, but the umpiring in the Cotton States League is about as spotty as a leopard with the measles. One day it is good and the next it is terrible—-but mostly it is terrible.

Sometimes it makes you think that the umps opinion of a strike is a blow to the chin... And boy, how they can deliver it at the most inopportune times. Yesterday's game was merely an example. It has been going on all season and the newspapers all around the circuit have been crying louder than the Wailing Walls of Babylon.

But no one ever pays any attention to the newspaper guys, so the real squawks should come from the presidents of the various clubs. We're just putting in our little cackle to get the rest of the barnyard started.[40]

Under the same editorial, Bosson related a human-interest story concerning a telephone conversation between two baseball coaches who spearheaded amateur teams in the city. On the surface, the story was humorous, but underneath, it was poignant. It illustrated how a coach cared for his team. He wanted something better for his team and he didn't mind asking for assistance. It showed the tenacity and desire of youngsters to play a simple game of baseball. It also demonstrated the generosity of a coach who shared with a team in need.

Comes a rib-tickling yarn concerning the one and only "Meathouse," announcer and ex-quarterback for the Langston High School (Negro) football team.

It seems that "Meathouse" has a baseball team this summer, but they're just a bit shy of equipment. So, "Meathouse" got on the telephone and called Roy Gillenwater, coach of the local American Legion team and official of the Hot Springs baseball nine.

"Mr. Roy," he said, "I got a baseball game scheduled and we (the team) are kinda short on equipment."

"Well, "Meathouse," just what have you got to play with?" Gillenwater questioned.

"To tell the truth," said "Meathouse," "we got a ragged ball and no bat."

"How have you been having batting practice then?" queried Gillenwater.

"O, we been gettin' along all right there," replied "Meathouse," "we been using an old pick handle."

Gillenwater confessed that he fixed "Meathouse" up with the needed equipment.[41]

Bosson uncovered information concerning the local Bathers club for next year. He heard that the Spa team was very interested in hooking up with Detroit for the 1939 season. If the event occurred, "the team would remain in the hands of the local officials and only the actual field management of the team would be under the Detroit-named manager."[42]

By August 3, Hot Springs was still in last place, but Grant, Otis Brannan, Robinson and Tolles were all hitting above .300. In addition, Barnett, Brown, Wells and Costley were hitting in the high .200. Grant topped the Bathers team with 63 RBIs. At the plate, the Bathers' bats were connecting, but fielding and pitching seemed to be lacking. Schafer pitched in 12 games and was the only hurler with a pitching percentage above .500. The pitcher's records were Schafer 5-4, Speer 8-10, Grimes 7-11, Langston 3-5, Hunter 6-10, Barnett 0-0, Williamson 0-2. Sain left the club with a 0-1 record.

Hunter threw a textbook 2-0 shutout at the Greenville Bucks in Mississippi, on August 5, as the Bathers broke a five-game losing streak. The Bucks were in next to last place, but the Bathers would take a win anytime. Barnett and Doyle Brannan each singled twice to lead the Bathers attack. Manager Joe Barnett and Otis Brannan scored the two runs for the Spa team as both teams played errorless ball. The game lasted only one hour and 37 minutes. The next night, Hot Springs came from behind to nip the Judges at Pine Bluff 6-4. Speer went all the way on the mound, winning his ninth game against 10 setbacks. Speer gave up nine scattered hits as the Bathers jumped on the Judges moundsmen for 10 safeties.

The Hot Tub Boys, riding a four-game win streak, pulled themselves up closer to seventh place. In early June, the Bathers were 12 ½ games behind the seventh place Greenwood Dodgers. The team won 9 out of 14 games as they played steady baseball, but they had a long way to go just to overtake the Dodgers.

The *New Era* reported on August 9, "Spike" Hunter, veteran fastball pitcher and former manager became a member of the El Dorado Lions in the same league. The Bathers obtained Spinetti, a rookie hurler, for the veteran pitcher. Hunter, who pitched a brilliant six-hit shutout against Greenville during his last outing, ended his Bathers career with a 7-10 record. El Dorado was in second place and needed a good pitcher for the playoffs, so Hot Springs traded "Spike" to El Dorado to lend mound support for the Lions. In addition, Bathers president Lloyd Adams said Hunter made a larger salary than the rookie pitcher, Spinetti. Hot Springs hoped that the younger player might develop into a real find and eventually "sell for a nice price."[43]

Statewide election results were important to the community. When the Bathers hosted the Helena Seaporters on August 9, a radio, with loudspeakers, installed at Ban Johnson Field, gave the fans the opportunity to hear the results of the various statewide political races. The fans heard the election results and the Bathers heard from the Seaporters as the Spa team used every player on the roster to attempt to halt the visiting team, but it didn't happen. The east Arkansas team ripped the Bathers 18-9 on 17 hits. Pitcher Al Williamson, who had pitched just two nights before, was the only player that the Bathers allowed to sit on the bench the complete game. The Bathers only had 14 players on the roster.

In 1938, Rogers "Rajah" Hornsby, owner of the spring baseball school in Hot Springs, replaced Louis Millies as manager of the Chattanooga Lookouts of the Southern Association Class AA League. In August, a Nashville, Tennessee, reporter interviewed Hornsby in which the former major league great unloaded his opinions concerning the status of the 1938 major league. He said that the big league "is 30 per cent under the standard of a decade ago..." he continued, "The minors have slipped 50 per cent in the same length of time." He listed several factors that he believed were the culprits.

I think the game has slipped so much because the youngsters of today are so much less rugged than those of several years ago. They have fine looking bodies, but they haven't the stamina or love for the game that characterized kids of the generation before.

Soft living and automobiles have had a lot to do with it. Last spring we had 400 boys working out at our baseball school in Hot Springs, Arkansas, but few of them ever will see the big time. They were built well, but they would wilt under competitive battling.

Then, night baseball has contributed to the decline. Say what you please, night baseball can't touch daylight playing even if the club installs the best lightning system that money can buy. It saved many Minor League clubs from bankruptcy, but there is little justification for it in the majors.

Another thing, kids in my time played baseball exclusively. It was the universal game. Now boys play golf, tennis, softball and dozens of other games in addition to baseball. That has made a big difference in their attitude toward the game. That explains to some extent the scarcity of potential Major League stars.

But don't get me wrong. Baseball is the national pastime by a wide margin and always will be. Attendance is growing in the majors despite the brand of baseball played. But baseball men should lose no opportunity to increase boys' interest not only as spectators, but also as players.[44]

While Arkansas Governor Carl and Mrs. Bailey vacationed in Hot Springs for two weeks, the Bathers rolled out the red carpet for the state's chief executive. "Carl Bailey Night" occurred on Friday, August 12, at the Bathers-Clarksdale game. Mayor Leo P. McLaughlin introduced the governor at the pregame ceremonies. In a brief statement at home plate, Governor Bailey mentioned that he enjoyed visiting the Spa. He stated that the city of Hot Springs had been good to him and he valued its friendship. Among his comments he said, "You've got a great place here and one of the most unusual in the entire world."

Mary Sue Adams, daughter of Lloyd Adams, president of the local baseball club, presented the governor, the mayor and Walter Ebel, master of ceremonies, with gifts of appreciation from the club.[45]

The Clarksdale game was a good one through the fourth inning, as Clarksdale was only leading 2-1 when rain delayed the contest. When the game resumed, the Bathers lost their focus, or something, as the visiting Red Sox went on a rampage. Both teams put up goose eggs in the fifth inning, but Clarksdale dried out and Hot Springs was still wet. The Red Sox scored at will for the remainder of the game as they ran over the Bathers 18-1.

The Bathers split the Sunday twin bill with El Dorado as Otis Brannan continued his consecutive-game hitting streak. The Bathers second sacker hit safely in his 24th and 25th consecutive games. An unusual twist occurred during the first game. Joe Barnett, Bathers manager, was the starting pitcher for Hot Springs, while the former Bathers manager and pitcher "Spike" Hunter opened the game on the hill for the Lions. Hunter, who showed the Bathers that he still had it, went all the way for the El Dorado win as he scattered 12 hits and beat his old mates 9-6. Barnett was relieved in the 6th inning and took the loss.

The Bathers ended their last home stand as they dropped a 2-1 decision to the Greenwood Dodgers 4-1. During that home series, August 26, Otis Brannan's long hitting streak of 29-games ended as a crowd of nearly 500 turned out for the final home game.

The 1938 season started with a flare, but the flare soon fizzled for the Bathers! The hometown boys finished in last position in an eight-team league and failed to place a man on the first-team All-Stars. The top four finishers in order were Greenville, Helena, Monroe and El Dorado. The second division included Clarksdale, Pine Bluff, Greenwood and Hot Springs. The bad part was that the Bathers finished last…way last, but the good part was that they completed their rookie season and seemed excited as they looked forward to their sophomore year.

The Greenville Buckshots dominated All-Star honors (no game) as they placed four players on the top-notch squad, picked by the circuit's sportswriters and team mangers. Hot Springs, Pine Bluff and Clarksdale failed to place a player on the first team, however, Hal Grant and Jimmy Brown of the Bathers came close to leaping on the select team. All teams donated at least one representative in the honorable-mention category. The Bathers placed several players on the honorable-mention group: Hal Grant - 1st base (.323), Otis Brannan-2nd base (.325), Duke Wells-of (.292), Arthur Robinson-of (.295), Lefty Tolles-of/p (.295), Jimmy Brown-of (.299), Floyd Speer-pitcher (10-13), Schafer-of/p (.286), Joe Barnett-3rd base (.300) and Bill Costley-catcher (.267).

The Bathers' Board of Directors issued a statement of thanks and appreciation to the baseball fans in the area for supporting the Bathers through a difficult rookie season. Lloyd Adams, president of the Bathers said that the group was working on next year's arrangement with the Detroit Tigers. It wasn't a done deal, but they planned to pursue the interest.[46]

The playoff series confronted first place Greenville with the fourth place finisher El Dorado. Monroe, 3rd place finisher faced Helena who wound up second. The teams played the best of three games in the first round, while the two winners faced each other in a best of seven games that determined the champion.

On August 29, just before the playoffs began, League president, J. Walter Morris, slammed a five-day suspension and a $25.00 fine on the Greenville Bucks manager Powell. The reason for the suspension and fine was simple. During the Greenville-Monroe game of August 11, the Bucks manager argued "over decisions."

In the first-round playoffs, the rejuvenated third-place Monroe White Sox polished off the second-place finisher, Helena Seaporters, three games to one to gain the finals. First-place Greenville did the same to fourth-place El Dorado and won their series 3-1. The championship series pitted the Greenville Bucks against the Monroe White Sox. Monroe continued their winning combination as they upset the Bucks four games to two to take home the Cotton States League championship trophy.

Roy Bosson ended the season with a note about Dave Lockwood and his clothing give-a-ways.

Dave Lockwood, the clothier who offered the $2 in merchandise to each Bather who hit a home run here the past season, almost went broke, paying off during the latter part of the season. The boys were just beginning to find the range. So, now Dave is a strong advocate of that movement to lengthen and raise that short right field fence.

Incidentally, strange as it may seem, the larger number of home runs hit here by visiting players were hit by right-hand hitters and not left-handers.[47]

Chapter 4

Playoff Bound
1939

"Officials of the Spa club hadn't planned to do much improving to Ban Johnson Field this year until…" - Roy Bosson

The Bathers stockholders re-elected Lloyd Adams as president for the 1939 season and increased the number of board members. The committee approved a working agreement with the Beaumont, Texas club. In addition, the group vowed improvements to Ban Johnson Field.

Stockholders of Hot Springs' community-owned Cotton States League club voted to increase their board of directors from five to 11 members and re-elected Lloyd Adams, groceryman, as president, at a meeting last week. Van M. Lyle was renamed vice-president and Warren Banks, secretary-treasurer.

Members of the new 11-man board are Adams, Banks, Owen Poe, Roy Gillenwater, Mose Klyman, J. Gus Borland, L. V. (Rip) Freeman, Jimmie Phillips, Dr. H. King Wade and George Collier.

A working agreement with the Beaumont club of the Texas League was approved, a provision in the agreement being that the Spa club must improve the park. Both the infield and outfield must be made smoother and the short right field fence heightened.[1]

The diminutive right field fence was a real dilemma for the club and league. A deluge of white orbs flew over the short 200-foot fence at Ban Johnson Field in 1938. The number of homers was tops in the league. Roy Bosson typed up the report for *The Sporting News*.

Officials of the Spa club hadn't planned to do much improving to Ban Johnson Field this year until they read the report of Club Secretary Warren Banks. It showed an expenditure of $894.04 for baseballs, 84 dozen of them. Most of them, Banks explained, went over the 200-foot right field fence. So, the club decided to raise the fence by 15 feet, along with the other improvements.

More home runs were hit in the Spa park last year than in any other park in the Cotton States circuit. Club officials also pointed out that the short field had long been a hindrance to pitchers, many fly balls which should have been easy outs going for hits against or over the barrier.[2]

In addition, the renovation of Ban Johnson Field increased the seating capacity to over 2,000 seats. There were 14 new box seats in front of the current grandstand. The do-over included a 50-foot extension of the bleachers on the north side, known as the "wolves den." In addition, the installation of a press box and public address booths enhanced the media area.

Dave Lockwood, owner of Lockwood's Men's Store, stated that he planned to lose his shirt this baseball season. Every Spa player that clouted a homer at home during the 1939 season received a free shirt from generous Dave. The practice continued from the previous season when the Dave lost $120 worth of expensive shirts. The clothes closets of Hal Grant and Otis Brannan were loaded with last season's attire and gifts from the many generous Bathers' supporters.

At the beginning of the season, the Bathers 1939 roster included catchers – Conard Fisher (mgr.) and Lester "Red" Johnson, pitchers – Gene Devine, Dale Jones, Martin Zachar, Ed Albosta, Jim Rickey, Harry Sublett and Rex Mitchell. Infielders included Bob Henney, Pete Haynes, Alan Grisworld, Joe Wessing, Dick Newhouser and Al Gardella. Stationed in the outfield were Steve Carter, Ted Bloch and Ed Rockey.

In addition to popular Lloyd "Kingfish" Adams as the club's president, Mamie Ruth Stranburg (later Mrs. Abernathy) served as secretary to the president. She said that through Mr. Adams, she wrote several letters to the Baseball Commissioner, Judge Kenesaw Mountain Landis. Miss Stranburg served as secretary to Adams in 1939, 1940 and early June 1941. Mamie Ruth stated that during road games, each player received $1.00 per day for their meals. She served faithfully as the organist at Second Baptist Church for 38 years, Central Baptist for 15 years and other churches in Hot Springs for a total of 58 years. She retired as organist at Central Baptist on Oct. 4, 2009, her 90th birthday. In addition, the talented Mrs. Abernathy, affectionately known as Mamie Ruth, taught music at Jones Elementary School in Hot Springs for many years.[3]

With Judge Emmet Harty as CSL president, the 1939 version of the Cotton States Loop included four teams from Arkansas, three teams from Mississippi and one from Louisiana. The Arkansas squads consisted of the Hot Springs Bathers, the Pine Bluff Judges, the Helena Seaporters and the El Dorado Lions. The Mississippi teams included the Clarksdale Red Sox, the Greenville Buckshots and the Greenwood Crackers. The Monroe White Sox represented the Bayou State. The Bathers were an independently owned team, but had a working agreement with the Beaumont club in the Texas League. The league calculated the proposed travel mileage of each team for the coming season. The CSL's road mileage ranged from around 3,700-4,500 miles per team with Hot Springs and Monroe totaling near the high end.[4]

Starting the season on the road, on Wednesday, April 19, manager Conard Fisher's team met the Judges of Pine Bluff at Taylor Field, their new $40,000 recreation complex. The lineup for the Spa team was as follows: Haynes - 3b, Gardella - 1b, Wessing – rf, Carter – lf, Block – ss, Rockey – cf, Griswold - 2b, Fisher - c and Albosta pitcher.

Al Gardella, first baseman, tallied the first run ever at the new Taylor Field in Pine Bluff as he put the Bathers in front by launching a fastball over the right field wall in the first inning. The Judges pushed three runs across the plate in the third stanza as they led the contest most of the game. The Bathers made it a one-run contest in the seventh as Carter walked and Block, Bathers shortstop, slapped a double to drive in Carter. Three hits and two runs in the eighth inning contributed to the Hot Springs 4-3 win. The two Spa pitchers, Albosta and Hickey combined for 12 strikeouts. The climate was more like football weather; however, 600 fans braved the chilly conditions to watch the opening game for both squads.[5]

Hot Springs, Monroe, Greenville and Helena carded wins in their first games of the season. In anticipation of opening night with Pine Bluff in Hot Springs, the article appeared in *The Sentinel-Record* on April 21.

Manager Conard Fisher, especially assigned to Hot Springs by the Detroit Baseball Association in order to develop young players for faster baseball, has a fine aggregation of youngsters here this year. None of them, Fisher expected, has more than four-years experience in the organized game...But all are prospects for the Major Leagues. Otherwise, they would have been cut loose before this.[6]

At the home opener, 1,239 excited Hot Springs fans braved the cold weather on April 22, as they bundled up on Whittington Avenue. Admission prices were set at 40 cents for adults and ten cents for children under 15-years-old. The complete opening-day roster for the Bathers included catchers - Conard Fisher and Lester "Red" Johnson; pitchers Gene Devine, Dale Jones, Martin

Zachar, Ed Albosta, Jim Hickey, Harry Sublett and Rex Mitchell; infielders Bob Henney, Pete Haynes, Alan Griswold, Joe Wessing, Dick Newhouser and Al Gardella; outfielders Steve Carter, Ted Bloch and Ed Rockey. However, the hometown crowd went home disappointed as the Judges drubbed the Bathers 13-5 in the home opener.

Jim Hickey, Bathers pitcher, tossed a dazzling shutout, as the Bathers took care of the Helena Seaporters, 3-0 at Helena on April 28. The young pitcher gave up only five hits and struck out five Seaporters to notch the win. His teammates collected only four hits, but it was enough to do the trick. Gardella, first baseman and Steve Carter, left fielder, picked up two hits each, while infielder Alan Griswold banged out a triple for the winners.

A tragic accident occurred at Ban Johnson Field the night of Tuesday, May 2, 1939, during the Hot Springs-Monroe game. Wallace Montgomery was sitting on top of the right field fence. Due to a Bathers' rally, the excited fan fell 15 feet to his death. The cause of death of the 32-year-old truck driver was a broken neck.[7]

On May 3, pitcher Frank Narbut of Monroe suffered an injured hand in a game with Hot Springs in an unusual matter. In the seventh inning of a tight game, he ran across the plate and scored one of the important Monroe runs. As he crossed home plate, he fell over the batboy! Due to the injury, Narbut left the game in which the Bathers won, 4-3.[8]

About the same time, the Bathers had their troubles. Within a week, two Spa players checked in at the local hospital. Shortstop Alan Griswold was out of action due to a leg injury. Soon, he was back in uniform, but only helped the Bathers by cheering from the bench. Manager Conard Fisher suffered from a severe cold. Outfielder Dick Newhouser took over Fisher's duties behind the plate.[9]

Around the middle of May, a five-game winning streak excited the Bather fans. The Spa team climbed into first division for the first time all season, but it seemed that the hometown fans became a little too energized. During the El Dorado series, umpire Vennari was the target of a thrown bottle, while small rocks tossed by "bleacherites" bombarded manager Frank O'Rourke and pitcher Mike Gore of the Lions. The incident drew a stern warning from league officials.[10]

The Sentinel-Record pictured Lloyd Adams, president of the Bathers, wearing an immensely large 32" head-sized sombrero on Sunday, May 28. The essence of the article was that after the Bathers won five-straight games, Adams had a swollen head and he could actually fit into a size 32" hat. The picture and article of Adams, taken following their three-game skid, noted that his head had shrunk to normal size.

On June 9, Bosson stated that the won-lost figures didn't jive in the Hot Springs papers. Something was amiss. Both papers reported the Bathers in fifth place in the CSL. Stop the presses! After further review, the official standings ruled that Hot Springs was in third place, eight games out of first place. Bosson's "The Bull Ring" continued with a note about Willis Hudlin, Cleveland pitcher.

Tops among the baseball wives who come to Hot Springs is a Hot Springs resident, Mrs. Willis Hudlin. The blonde 'boss' of the Cleveland hurler says she fears her hubby is about to rebel against her play to let him clear 10 acres of land out on Lake Hamilton each year in order to get into condition for the next season. That's just a "subtle" way of getting me to do the work,' Hud declared.[11]

Jeweler Lee Ragsdale had a sure thing. He offered a 15-jewels Elgin wristwatch to the first Spa hurler to toss the first shutout of the season. The kicker was that the feat had to be accomplished at the home "cracker box" ballpark. Two Spa pitchers hurled shutouts on the road, but according to the Ragsdale rule, that didn't count. Bosson concluded, "A pitcher is lucky to get through a game without having a home run hit off him, much less one run scored."

Bosson stated on June 14, that Conard Fisher was one happy fellow when Tom Tighe arrived from Toledo because the new catcher shared behind the plate duties with manager Fisher. Bosson said, "Fisher has been working harder than a preacher at a revival since the season started…"

Just a few days later Martin Zachar, Spa tosser, pulled off a major feat on Sunday, June 18, at Greenville, Mississippi.

Young Martin Zachar, tireless side arm hurler for the Hot Springs Bathers, carved himself a niche in the Cotton States league's Hall of Fame here Sunday afternoon when he enacted the 'iron man' role to perfection by shutting out the Greenville Bucks in both ends of a doubleheader by the scores of 1-0 and 3-0.

To make it all the more impressive, Zachar gave up only five hits in the two games, three in the first and two in the abbreviated nightcap.[12]

Zachar aided his cause by driving in the winning run in the second game. He was Superman, Batman and Captain America all rolled into one. In two games, he pitched 16 innings, which upped his pitching record to 9-7. After Zachar's two stellar performances, he earned the nickname "iron man," and rightly so.

Why did Zachar pitch two games? President Adams said that Zachar "especially requested to pitch the doubleheader because he 'felt right.'" The Hot Springs pitcher, in his second year of professional baseball was from Detroit, Michigan. He reached the Bathers via Beckley of the Mountain States League in West Virginia. His teammates called him "Rube." Zachar, during his short four-year minor league career, won 18 and lost 16 playing for three teams in 1941. The 1941 season was his last season in professional baseball.

By June 19, Monroe was way out in front of the CSL, but it was a close race among Greenwood, Clarksdale and Hot Springs for second position. All three teams had won 34 games each. Hot Springs was sixth in team batting, but Bathers outfielder Steve Carter was the batting ace of the

CSL with a whopping .366 mark in 135 games. Al Gardella, Bathers first baseman, was one of the top home-run swatters with 10.

On June 21, the New York Yankees management announced the retirement of "the Iron Horse," Lou Gehrig and proclaimed July 4, as "Lou Gehrig Day" at Yankee Stadium. The sports page headline in the *Hot Springs New Era* on June 22, stated, "Gehrig Pulled Self Out of Game Just In Time, Report Of Mayo Clinic Reveals."[13]

In a related article, Hot Springs residents extended a double invitation to the Gehrigs to bathe in the thermal waters. Optimistic that the baths may help Gehrig's condition, Mayor McLaughlin of Hot Springs wired Ed Barrow, president of the Yankees, and invited the Gehrigs to the Spa. In addition, Mrs. Willis Hudlin, wife of the Cleveland hurler and an acquaintance of Mrs. Gehrig, sent a message to Mrs. Gehrig urging them to visit Hot Springs. Mrs. Hudlin sent along information concerning the treatment of the paralysis that was available in the city. However, there is no information that the Gehrigs visited the Spa.

On July 3, Hot Springs staged a comeback as they nosed out the El Dorado Lions 6-4 in 13 innings at the Oil City. Gene Devine, starting pitcher for the Bathers, left the mound in the seventh inning in favor of Martin Zachar. In relief, Zachar gave up only four hits during his innings on the hill as the Bathers' "iron man" registered win number 11. Carter continued leading the Bather bats with a .365 average on July 13. Zachar was the club's leading pitcher with 11 wins, while Walt Schafer posted nine skins.

In early August, the Bathers were still in the fourth spot, but they were slugging it out with Greenwood as they closed in on third place. The Bathers remained in fourth position going into the last home stand. At home, in the last series of the season on August 27, the Bathers played Pine Bluff in which the teams split a doubleheader. The Judges walloped Hot Springs 18-9 in the opening game, while the Bathers took the nightcap 7-4. The Bathers ended the season and the game on a high note with a double play. In the seventh frame of the first game, Al Gardella smacked his 32nd home run of the season as the mighty jolt cleared the center field fence. The highlight of the second game was Ted Newhouser, the Bathers all-around player, who played all nine positions for one inning each. When he took the mound, he gave up only one hit and no runs.

The Monroe White Sox ran away with the 1939 regular season CSL race. Under the managerial leadership of Conard Fisher, the Bathers finished in fourth position, which assured them of a berth in the post-season playoffs. The CSL playoffs, called the Shaughnessy Playoffs, matched first place Monroe against the fourth place finisher Hot Springs. Clarksdale and Greenwood, second and third place respectively, completed the playoff tournament.

In 1933, Frank "Shag" Shaughnessy, general manager of the Montreal Royals, devised a post-season playoff system. Named in his honor, the system was set up for the first and fourth place teams to oppose each other, while the second and third place finishers tangled. The winners advanced to the finals to determine the champion. His idea kept more teams in the race, sustained interest and landed more funds in the team's coffers.

1st Round Playoffs

(Best of five)
Game 1 – Tuesday, August 29, 1939 – Monroe, Louisiana
Monroe White Sox – 9 Hot Springs Bathers - 4

Hot Springs traveled to Monroe and powdered John Yelovic, Monroe's hurler, for three hits on three runs in the first stanza of the opening round of the CSL playoffs. Most of the fun for the Spa team stopped right there. Kelton Maxfield and Tom Perry held the Spa to only one run the rest of the way, while the Sports racked up nine runs. Maxfield and Perry struck out six Bathers each. In the seventh inning, Hot Springs attempted a comeback, but with the bases loaded, Perry took over on the hill and the Bathers rally fizzled as a lone run crossed the plate. The Hot Springs battery of Schafer and Fisher had their problems. Schafer marked up one wild pitch and hit a batter, while Fisher ended up with one passed ball. It's difficult to win when a team tallies four runs, on four hits, one passed ball, one hit batsman and one wild pitch. Walt Schafer went all the way for the Bathers, striking out four and giving up nine runs on 11 hits. Series umpires included Rowe, Newman and Gribbon.[14]

Game 2 – Wednesday, August 30, 1939 – Monroe, Louisiana
Monroe White Sox – 15 Hot Springs Bathers – 10

Outs were hard to come by in the 32-hit offensive explosion as nine pitchers went to the mound for the two teams, five hurlers for Hot Springs and four for Monroe. The White Sox popped the sphere around the yard for 17 hits; however, the Bathers were only two hits behind with 15. Monroe's outfielders Taitt, Hargrove and third sacker Pruitt blasted three hits each to lead the Sports at the plate. Hargrove and Taitt added three tallies each. High-powered Hot Springs slugger, left fielder Steve Carter copped the hitting honors for the losers as he slammed four hits, including two doubles, during his five trips to the dish. The Spa went up 10-7 in the top of the sixth inning as they scored eight times in the inning. The lead was short lived, however, due to a six run uprising by the White Sox in the bottom of the inning. Monroe tagged on two more insurance runs, one in the seventh and one in the eighth frame, to complete the scoring. Martin Zachar started for the Bathers, but Ed Albosta, the second pitcher in the merry-go-round affair, took the loss. It looked as if it were going to be a fast series as the White Sox went up two games to none in the best of five games. The defeat seemed to have awakened the Bathers.[15]

Game 3 – Thursday, August 31, 1939 – Hot Springs, Arkansas
Hot Springs Bathers – 15 Monroe White Sox– 3

It was payback time for Conard Fisher's Bathers. The Spa Boys leaped on southpaw Lawrence Hinton in the first inning for six big ones. Bathers' bats began to boom and the Spa pitching began to silence the Sox. It was smooth sailing after that as the Bathers supported the two Bathers hurlers with a 15-hit attack, demolishing the White Sox 15-3. Relief-pitcher Ray Hoffman entered the tussle and he picked up where Hinton left off. Al Gardella, league home-run champion with 32, cranked out two round-trippers, as he registered four RBIs on three hits during his five times up at the plate for the Bathers. Frank Masters limited the White Sox to seven scattered hits and struck out 10, as he went the distance for the Spa team.[16]

Game 4 – Friday, September 1, 1939 – Hot Springs, Arkansas
Hot Springs Bathers – 12 Monroe White Sox - 1

With their backs against the wall, Ed Albosta (10-10) allowed nine hits as Hot Springs detonated the Pale Hose 12-1 in an 18-hit barrage. The win tied the series at two all. The bombardment fired off in the second frame when Gardella lifted a pitch out of the park and Ed Rockey sent a rocket over the fence with two men on. When the fireworks ended in the second inning, the Bathers notched six runs on the scoreboard. The Bathers were only halfway finished. In the sixth inning, the hometown team etched five more points on the scorecard and added another mark in the eighth frame. Dick Newhouser also notched a solo homer. Leadoff batter for the Spa, third baseman Pete Haynes netted four safeties during his five times at bat. Every Bather, including the pitcher, smacked at least one hit during the contest.[17]

Game 5 – Saturday, September 2, 1939 – Hot Springs, Arkansas
Hot Springs Bathers – 10 Monroe White Sox – 5

It was the big-bat era at Ban Johnson Field as each Bather stroked the ball, again, for at least one hit, in the 17-hit attack as the Spa gained a 10-5 victory over Monroe. The White Sox jumped on Walt Schafer for 10 hits, but Schafer remained steady on the hill to notch the win for Hot Springs.

Steve Carter was, again, the game's big gun as he collected a homer, a double and two singles for a 4-5 day at the plate. Monroe's infield gave up five errors to add to their collapse. In the five-game series, the Bathers notched 51 runs to Monroe's 33 tallies. When the smoke cleared, the Bathers advanced to the championship series with Greenwood who beat Clarksdale in their series.[18]

Championship Series
(Best of Seven)

Game 1 – Sunday, September 3, 1939 – Greenwood, Mississippi
Hot Springs Bathers – 3 Greenwood Crackers - 0

The defensive-minded Bathers blanked the Crackers 3-0 in the first game of the championship series played in Mississippi. It was Hot Springs' fourth consecutive playoff win. Martin Zachar flung a six hitter, as the hurler went all the way for the win. The visitors scored twice in the first inning on a Haynes walk and a single by Rockey. Outfielder Steve Carter blasted a double to score Haynes and Rockey. The Spamen added an insurance run in the seventh inning to cap the shutout victory.[19]

Game 2 – Monday, September 4, 1939 – Greenwood, Mississippi
Greenwood Crackers – 3 Hot Springs Bathers – 2

Frank Masters, Hot Springs hurler, yielded only six hits and three runs to the Mississippi team; however, the Bathers jumped on Hardin for eight safeties, but only scored twice. Greenwood took the second game of the series 3-2. Ed Rockey, Steve Carter and Al Gardella posted two hits each for the Bathers. The two teams moved to the Spa for the third game.

The Citizens Cigar Store on Central Avenue carried the radio play-by-play action of the Bathers. The store personnel invited interested fans to come and listen to the game in air-conditioned comfort. "A box score of the proceedings is kept upon a board in view of all."[20]

Game 3 – Tuesday, September 5, 1939 – Hot Springs, Arkansas
Greenwood Crackers – 15 Hot Springs Bathers - 10

"In a free-hitting and loosely pitched contest" the Crackers out-muscled the Spa Boys 15-10 in the Spa City. Hot Springs was moving right along until the seventh and eighth innings when Greenwood ran across 10 runs. "Base hits rained off the fences like buckshot." The game rang up 36 hits as the Bathers out hit the Mississippi team 19-17, but a trio of Spa errors proved costly. The night's offensive activities included six home runs, a triple and five doubles. Hot Springs used four hurlers to Greenwood's three pitchers. The Crackers went up two games to one in the series.[21]

Game 4 – Wednesday, September 6, 1939 – Hot Springs, Arkansas
Greenwood Crackers – 8 Hot Springs Bathers – 7

Ed Rockey and Dick Newhouser collected three hits each, while the Spa's pitcher Walt Schafer acquired two safeties to lead the Arkansas team in hitting. Those stats sound good, but another big inning squashed the Bathers, 8-7. Greenwood scored four runs in the sixth frame to make it an 8-5 game. The Bathers rallied in the ninth but fell one-run short.[22]

Game 5 – Thursday, September 7, 1939 – Hot Springs Arkansas
Greenwood Crackers – 6 Hot Springs Bathers - 5

Crackers shortstop Nig Lipscomb proved too much for the Bathers as he hammered four hits, including a three-run, game-winning homer in the ninth inning to ice the championship for Greenwood, 6-5. Lipscomb ended the night with four RBIs. Carter of the Bathers tried to keep pace as he popped the ball out of the yard twice, including three RBIs. Those big innings again hurt the Spa team. Greenwood took home the 1939 Cotton States League crown by beating Hot Springs 4 games to one.[24]

In one year, Hot Springs went from worst to second. It was a tremendous one-year turnaround for the boys from the Springs. The City of Vapors was proud of the hustle and blue-collar effort on the part of the hometown edition of the 1939 Hot Springs Bathers.

Following the close of the season, manager Fisher stated that the major leagues were interested in looking at several players from the Bathers organization. Bather president Lloyd Adams planned to resign at the end of the season because he said he needed rest. However, the fans circulated a petition urging Adams to remain as president of the club.

Steve Carter, the 22-year-old Bather outfielder topped the Cotton States League batting championship with a hefty .369 average. In addition to his hitting exploits, Carter gained first place honors as he slapped in 132 RBIs, second high with 307 total bases (only three behind the leader) and second with 191 hits. Bronx native, Al Gardella, Bathers young first baseman, strutted home with the long ball trophy with 32 homers. Gardella was eight ahead of the second place finisher Naylor of Greenville. Hot Springs finished last in team batting, but the Bathers held their heads up high when the bean counter added up the team's total bases and home runs. Their 1,327 hits during the season allowed them to accumulate 3,358 bases, including 118 home runs.

The Spa team placed two players on the Cotton States League All-Star squad, as left fielder Steve Carter and second baseman Joe Wessing joined the 1939 honors team. Wessing, regarded by many to be the best defensive second baseman in the league, posted a .237 batting average. The Detroit Tigers planned to take a closer look at the two All-Stars during the following season at their spring training camp in Beaumont, Texas.

The Bathers led the league in "hit by pitch" as 46 Bathers limped down the line to first base. Three Bathers topped the "Gold Glove" categories. Although not called "Gold Glove" awards in 1939, they were still the best fielders at their position. The top fielders included Conard Fisher, catcher, with a .989 average. Shortstop Bob Henny posted the best fielding mark in the CSL at his position with .973 and pitcher Jim Hickey was the leagues' best fielding pitcher with a perfect 1.000 record.

Chapter 5

Landis Cleans House
1940

"Spa Club Stripped by Landis Ruling, Loses Manager, Too." - Roy Bosson.

Judge Kenesaw Mountain Landis took over as Major League Baseball Commissioner in November 1920, and immediately began to clean house. His first act was to deal with the 1919 Black Sox scandal. The court acquitted eight Chicago White Sox players suspected of fixing the 1919 World Series. However, when Landis took over, all bets were off. He banned the eight players from ever playing major league baseball, including "Shoeless" Joe Jackson. Incidentally, Joe hit .375 in the series. That was Landis' beginning and he didn't put on the breaks.

In 1939, Landis discovered irregularities occurring in the Detroit Tigers farm system in which Hot Springs was a part. The Bathers had a working agreement with the Detroit Tigers. So, what was going on? The front page of the January 28, 1940, issue of *The Sporting News* related "Landis Lays Down Law for Farms, Working Agreements; Detroit Loses Title to 91 Players, Must Pay 15 Others." Hot Springs was right in the middle of Landis' ruling. Of the 91 players, there were 22 players from the Bathers' squad involved in Landis' "cover up" ruling. They included William Mueller, Alfred Gardella, Garrett McBryde, James W. Haynes, Ed Rockey, Chandler Duncan, Allen Griswold, Charles E. Moore, Richard Newhouser, Robert J. O'Brien, John Sain, Howard

Sweckard, Walter J. Schaefer, James A. Bleasdale, Edward Bongard, Clifford Carlson, James Pollock, Warren Fehler, John A. Scheifele, Robert Cottrell, James Fuller and Stephen Andrade. Roy Bosson, local sports editor, reported the news.

Spa Club Stripped by Landis Ruling, Loses Manager, Too

Hot Springs, Ark. – When Commissioner Landis finished with his investigation of the Detroit farm system a few weeks ago, the Hot Springs club of the Cotton States League was left with only Manager Conard Fisher on its roster. Twenty-two players were declared free agents.

Now, the Bathers don't even have a manager.

Club President Lloyd Adams received word the other day that Fisher, who piloted the Bathers into the runner-up spot in the league last year, had decided to keep a year-round job with a Michigan manufacturing company instead of returning here. He had already signed a 1940 contract with the club.

The only player on the Bather roster now is 21-year-old Gordon Hurst, southpaw pitcher, signed from the Mississippi semi-pro ranks recently.[1]

Jack Zeller, general manager of the Tigers, maintained a large Detroit farm system. Landis discovered a myriad of improprieties including "cover up" of players and making secret deals with players on different teams in the same league. A major league team could not be affiliated with more than one team in any one league. In some cases, Detroit owned or had a working agreement with two teams in one league. *The Sporting News* summarized Detroit's irregularities in the January 18, 1940 issue.

Among these illegal methods were: (1) the filing of false or fictitious documents, forcing players to sign blank contracts, in which the name of the club or clubs later was inserted; (2) the misleading of players in causing them to think they were signing with Major League clubs; (3) running of try-out camps for the purpose of cornering green talent; (4) faking notices of releases and other methods that practically eliminated all the players' rights and gave the clubs a monopoly on material. [2]

Johnny Sain, who had briefly pitched for the Bathers in 1939, was one of those "covered players." In 1946, Sain, interviewed by a reporter for *The Sporting News*, discussed his minor league days in the Detroit organization.

In 1936, Sain, from Havana, Arkansas, tried out in front of Doc Protho in Little Rock when he was 19 years old.

He warmed up with Skeeter Dickey, brother of Bill Dickey. Prothro saw possibilities, so Johnny was signed to an Osceola contract in the Northeast Arkansas League. The first man he faced hit a home run, but Johnny won the game, 3-2. He won five and lost three on the season. The next year he copped five and lost eight. With Newport (a Detroit farm) of the same loop in 1938, he won 16 and lost four. He thought he'd go up, but he didn't. The next season he won 18 and lost 10 and still didn't move.

'I'd been satisfied if they'd only sent me out of the state,' he said.

When the following spring came around and Jack Zeller, then business manager of the Tigers, sent him another contract for Newport, Sain sent it back and asked to be assigned elsewhere.

'I got the contract back a week later with the notation, "You'll go where we send you,"' said Johnny. [3]

Before spring training of 1940, there was a note in *The Sporting News* concerning Johnny Sain.

John F. Sain, a pitcher on the reserve list of the Hot Springs Bathers and one of the 91 players made free agents due to the decision by Commissioner Landis and the Detroit Tigers, was trying to make the Nashville Vols team in Sanford, Florida.[4]

In 1942, Sain got his shot in the major leagues, hooking up with the Boston Braves of the National League. After that first season, he enlisted in the Naval Air Corps. He returned in 1946 at 28-years-old and won 20 games with the Braves. He was off and running for an 11-year major league stint.

What happens when a team has no players? Lloyd Adams, president of the Bathers announced that Hot Springs received several thousand dollars assistance from loyal fans in order to continue playing in the Cotton States League. New 1940 Hot Springs manager Cecil Combs "indicated the Bathers would receive many of their players on option from higher clubs."[5]

Springtime in Hot Springs meant spring training and Judge Emmet Harty began his second year as president of the Cotton States League. Bathers' spring training began at the historic Ban Johnson Field. It was only three weeks before the first game and Combs anxiously geared up for the workouts.

With a bright spring sun giving off midsummer heat waves, the beads of perspiration rolled today at Ban Johnson field as 34 youngsters greeted Manager Cecil Combs for the opening of spring training by the Hot Springs Bathers.[6]

Activities on the first day of training camp included meeting the new manager, light warm-ups, pepper and hitting practice. Combs said that the team only had three weeks before the first game and they had a lot of work to do. Nearly half of the 34 players paid their own way to spring training in hopes of obtaining a contract with the Bathers. The other half were under contract by the team, as the team planned for a few more players to arrive in the Vapor City the next day.

Among the pitching candidates included a young right-hander from the Eastern Shore League, Louis Briganti. Louis was the son of Frank Briganti, head of the Department of Sanitation of New York City. Other new pitchers included Don Thompson and Jack Holt of Ft. Worth; Webb Salsbury, Detroit; Carroll Wilson, Jacksonville, Texas and Bob Howe, Moline, Illinois. John and Ray Phillips came from the Hollywood Stars in the Pacific Coast League. Roy Bosson, put it plain and simple in his article "Spring Training Stuff."

These old familiar postcard words, "Dear Ma, they started curvin' em today. Be home tomorrow," will be scribbled again here Monday afternoon for Cecil has sent out the word that he is sharpening up his axe for another operation to cut down the size of the Bathers squad...[7]

Manager Cecil Combs and Bathers president Lloyd Adams scrutinized their 1940 edition of the Hot Springs Bathers at Ban Johnson Field on Sunday, April 15, by playing an exhibition game. As expected, Hot Springs shelled the Kroger semi-pro team from Little Rock 12-5. The offensive weapons for the Spa team were Crosby, Scott, Brockelmann, Sowell and McCullom as each collected two safeties. Jullian Sowell, new arrival from Tulsa, started the barrage in the third stanza with a four-bagger over the left field fence. In the sixth inning, second baseman Hudson, lofted one out of the park, while Scott, the 16-year-old, waited until the eighth to rip his round tripper.

Conn started on the mound for the Bathers and pitched perfectly for three innings as he struck out three. He handed the reins over to Wilson who gave up three runs on three hits in three innings. Briganti finished the contest by giving up two runs on one hit and three walks. Umpires for the contest were local residents and baseball buffs Jack McJunkin and Roy Gillenwater. Following the practice match, Combs stated, "We still need a lot of polishing. We have a lot of fine players on the club and I expect them to improve rapidly just as soon as we get into a few tough games."

The manager's "A" team included Jerry Crosby – shortstop, Joe Scott - first base, LaMonte Duncan - center field, Roy Wilson or Ed McCullom - left field, Bernard Broeckelman - right field, Vern Hudson - second base, Sowell - third base, Joe Boynton and Norman Albertson - catchers. The four moundsmen included Lou Briganti, Hampton Conn, Carroll Wilson and John Phillips. Of course, line-ups were always subject to change during the year.

With several more exhibition games under their belts, Hot Springs was ready for the season to begin, but first things first. Predictions are a part of any sporting event and local sportswriter, Roy Bosson prophesied that Hot Springs would finish in the fourth position. However, he said that Hot Springs was "the sleeper that might wake up."

They're off in the Cotton States Derby tomorrow and in case you want a little 'morning line' on how this horse picker sees 'em, here 'tis.[8]

His predictions were as follows: (1) Clarksdale; (2) Monroe; (3) El Dorado; (4) Hot Springs; (5) Greenwood; (6) Pine Bluff; (7) Greenville and (8) Helena. Bosson continued, "Of course, we're the same guy who picked Seabiscuit's first offspring to be a gal, but don't let that bother you when you start to get your bets down…"

On Sunday, April 21, an elaborate parade, recognizing the new Bathers, began at 1:30 at the Grand Avenue – Central Avenue intersection. The Hot Springs High School and Junior High bands led the parade. Others who took part in the parade were the Bathers management, members of the Junior Chamber of Commerce, about 200 Bathers' Boosters, equivalent to the "Knothole Gang," the Bathers and the Pine Bluff Judges, the Bathers opening-day opponent. Jett Brothers Grocery Company provided the "Boosters" baseball caps. The parade ended at the Whittington junction.

In other events, the "Whittington Avenue Gang" offered a prize to the section of town that produced the largest number of fans on opening day. The sections of fans that were in competition included Whittington Avenue, Malvern Avenue, South Hot Springs (Jonestown), Park Avenue, Lower Central Avenue and Oaklawn Avenue. Dave Lockwood, owner of Lockwood's Men's Store, continued his tradition by giving away BVD shirts to the Bathers who hit home runs at the local ballpark.

On-field pregame ceremonies included pitcher, Mayor Leo McLaughlin; batter, Dr. Lawrence Akers, president of the Hot Springs Junior Chamber of Commerce; catcher, Joe McRae, chairman of the Jaycee opening-day committee and 86-year-old Martin Eisele, veteran druggist and baseball enthusiast served as umpire. Mayor McLaughlin lobbed the ceremonial first pitch to Dr. Akers who immediately fouled off the pitch into the bleachers. Akers swung and missed the second toss. It seemed that two strikes were enough baseball for the celebrities. As soon as the school bands completed their rendition of the "Star-Spangled Banner," it was time to "Play Ball!"

Nearly 1,250 paying customers flooded Ban Johnson Field to get their first glimpse of the 1940 model Bathers. In 1938, the first year back in professional baseball, the Bathers drew 1,410 at the first game and in 1939, 1,239 showed up at the first game.

The Spa's first-game starting lineup was Jerry Crosby – ss, Joe Scott - 1b (16 years old), LeMonte Duncan – cf, Ed McCollum, lf; Bernie Broeckelman, rf; Julian Sowell, 3b; Vern Hudson, 2b; Joe Boynton – c and Hamp Conn - p. The game was a little sloppy as the Bathers committed four errors, three by Crosby, while the Judges caused five miscues. At the end of the sixth inning, the Judges were up 6-5. However, in the seventh inning, fireworks echoed all over Whittington Avenue as 10 runs blazed across home plate. Unfortunately, the Judges added six scores, while the Bathers increased their runs by only four. The Spa out-hit the Judges 13-11, but the Judges got the last laugh by crossing the plate 12 times to the Bathers nine tallies, to spoil the opening-day game for Hot Springs. Hitting stars for the Hot Springs were McCollum (lf), with three hits and scored twice; Scott (1B) with two hits and one run to his credit; Hudson (2B) who scratched out two hits and Crosby popped one double and scored twice. Both teams used three pitchers as Hot Springs used Conn, Louis Briganti and Jack McLaughlin, while Conn received the defeat.[9]

In early May, Hot Springs lost eight of 10 games and was in last place in the CSL. They needed more help on the mound as evidenced by the Helena game on May 2. The Bathers jumped on the Helena Seaporters for seven runs on 16 hits. In most circles, 16 hits win games. Helena collected "only" 14 hits, but Helena outscored the Bathers 11-7. Losing usually produces less fan interest and Hot Springs was no different.

Mayor McLaughlin issued a proclamation asking the baseball fans to meet with him at the Auditorium Theater in downtown Hot Springs on the night of May 14, to discuss the future of the hometown team. The team was on financially shaky grounds. The citizens responded and the Bathers continued playing in the league.

Baseball support continued to lag, so the Junior Chamber of Commerce sought to revive interest in professional baseball. They selected a committee to explore ideas on increasing attendance and determine that a wider area of advertising would be beneficial. Marketing the smaller towns and communities around Hot Springs seemed to be an excellent idea. They planned to focus on the entertainment value of the Bathers upon the area and the wholesome family atmosphere it presented to the community. The report stated, "We do not intend to take part in any ticket or money-raising campaign, but will endeavor to talk baseball, see baseball and sell baseball."[10]

Not everyone in the world was thinking baseball. On May 18, 1940, *The Sentinel-Record* reported a story about a more stressful situation. World War II was on the rise in Europe. On May 10, the Nazis invaded France, Netherlands, Belgium and Luxembourg. Louvain is about 12 miles from Brussels, Belgium.

Saved from Nazis

Suzanne Thompson, 11-year old daughter of the American assistant military attaché at Brussels, was in Louvain when Nazis began their invasion. The Father rushed to Louvain, found his daughter and several of her schoolmates huddled in the basement of the school. He brought the children to safety after a harrowing ride over roads bombed and machined-gunned by Nazi fliers.[11]

In Hot Springs, on May 18, baseball was at the forefront. For the first time since the season began, the Bathers climbed out of the cellar. The Spa team outslugged the boys from Greenville by a 17-13 victory at home. Hard-hitting Bathers shortstop, Ed Zydowski, plastered one of the longest home runs ever to fly out of the Spa field. The first inning blast sailed over the center field fence, over Whittington Avenue, beyond another fence located across Whittington Avenue and into the Alligator Farm. Now that was a major league smash!

Squabbling and injuries were a part of the game. In the eighth inning, Greenville's manager Andy Reese disagreed a little too much with a call by Thomason, home plate umpire, as the arbiter quickly ejected Mr. Reese. Before his eviction, Reese hammered a grand slam home run in the sixth to put the Bucks back in the game. Bucks' second baseman Bert Hodge left the game in the first inning due to an injury he received from Ed McCollum who slid into him at second base.

The league standings were very close. Pine Bluff was barely in first place with a 15-9 mark, while eighth place Clarksdale graded out with a 10-16 record. Sixth place Hot Springs supported a 10-15 won-lost count. The first four places in the standings were still up for grabs. The first division, the first four spots in the final league standings, was the goal of all teams, thereby gaining a post-season playoff berth.

An unusual event occurred on May 19, when the Spa team swamped the Greenwood Choctaws in a doubleheader at home. In the first game, Hot Springs scored 16 runs on 17 hits to Greenwood's four runs and 10 hits. At the end of the second inning of the first game, Greenwood was ahead 1-0. At the end of the third inning, it was a tie game, 1-1. Then, the floodgates opened. Following the second frame, Hot Springs scored in every inning. All nine Bathers scored at least one run and every Bather collected at least one hit. Vern Hudson, second baseman, collected three hits during his five plate appearances. Two of Hudson's three hits were four-baggers as he amassed five RBIs and scored three times. Broeckelman, Bathers first basemen, garnered three hits and scored once. Center fielder Duncan contributed six RBIs, two home runs and scored twice. Even the Spa pitcher, Kramer scored three times.

In the seven-inning nightcap, the Bathers added more fuel to the fire. Hot Springs scored 20 runs on 21 hits, while Greenwood ended up with three runs on eight hits. The big guns for the Bathers were outfielder McCollum who topped off the day with a perfect 4 for 4 at the plate, including a home run, double, two RBIs and scored five times. Again, every Bather collected at least one hit and scored at least once during the second encounter. The Bathers may have set some sort of record in the two tilts by scoring 36 runs on 38 hits for 71 total bases as they scored in 12 consecutive innings. It is amazing that in two games, every Bather scored at least once and garnered one or more hits. Kramer was the winning pitcher in the first contest, while Frase was the winning hurler in the second game.

On May 20, the red-hot Bathers did it again. Overcoming Greenwood's eight- run lead, with the aid of seven Greenwood errors, the Spa team rolled past the Choctaws 15-8. The contest gave Hot Springs an eight-game sweep at home. During the winning streak, the Bathers scored 109 runs against the opponents 47. Manager Cecil Combs used three pitchers, Martin, Conn and Wilson during the game "and strangely enough it was Conn who pitched to only two batters who was credited with the victory." Zydowski, Bathers shortstop, produced five RBIs. Hudson knocked in three runs, including a homer. However, following the eight-game explosion, the Spa was no higher than sixth place in the CSL standings. It was early in the season, but it continued to be a horse race from top to bottom.[12]

By the middle of May, the league runner-up in the batting race was Eddie Zydowski with a blazing .407 mark. Tom Gwin, outfielder for Pine Bluff paced the circuit with a blistering .420 average. Vern Hudson topped the base stealers with 12 and Zydowski was on top of the RBI list with 30. On May 19, at El Dorado, shortstop Billy Marshall, second baseman Ray Viers and first baseman Hal Grant of Clarksdale pulled off the league's first triple play of the season. Hot Springs was in second place in team batting and registered fourth in team fielding. However, they were still in the sixth spot in team standings.[13]

What a difference a few days make. The Bathers walloped the Oilers from El Dorado, 12-7 to climb into third position by the slimmest of margins. Hot Springs took advantage of four errors and six free passes by Lund, the Oilers hurler. L. J. Fox made his debut for the Bathers and gave up only three hits in seven innings. However, Fox issued the Oilers nine free passes to first base, as Conn relieved the young Fox. Conn pitched well for a while, but his wildness allowed rangy Carroll Wilson to finish the contest. Conn was the winning pitcher, but by the end of the game, 20 players reached first base by the ball-four method.

In less than three weeks, the Bathers jumped from the cellar to third place. On June 1, one of the largest crowds of the season attended the Hot Springs-Monroe game at the Spa. The Bathers sponsored "Civic Club Night" and all five Hot Springs civic clubs competed for the high-attendance trophy presented to the civic club with the most fans at the game. Monroe edged Hot Springs 10-8, as the Lions Club won the attendance trophy.

In the seventh inning, with the score tied, Vern Hudson, Bathers second basemen, lifted the sphere over the right field fence at Ban Johnson Field to allow Hot Springs to post a 9-7 victory over the Pine Bluff Judges on June 3. The hard-hitting Bathers, managed by Cecil Combs, won their 20th game out of 26 contests. The game didn't lack excitement because it was a slugfest. The two teams collected 28 hits, as the Bathers out hit the Judges 15-13. Carroll Wilson went the route for the Bathers, but he was in trouble during the first four innings.

On June 16, the Bathers were in third position in the league standings, second in team batting and third in team fielding. Zydowski led in home runs with 10 and RBIs with 54. Mr. "Z," hitting a tremendous .399, still held down second spot in the batting race. Pine Bluff's Gwin topped the circuit with a .401 mark. Infielder Vern Hudson led the circuit with 48 runs scored. Bathers' Ed Kramer led the hurlers in pitching percentage with a .857 mark (6-1 record). Judge Harty, league president, toured the Cotton States loop and declared that umpiring and attendance weren't as bad as reported. However, the league released umpire Jack Wallace, due to a number of complaints.[14]

It was batting practice for the Bathers as the Greenwood Choctaws marched into Hot Springs on June 22. Ed Kramer went the distance on the hill for the Bathers as the Spa Boys upended the last place Mississippi guests 20-2. Kramer allowed five scattered hits as Hot Springs collected a rousing 24 hits to win going away. Zydowski blasted the ball all over the yard as he went 4-6 at the plate, including three home runs, eight RBIs and scored four times. Second baseman Hudson may have established a league record by handling 13 assists without a miscue.

The league proposed to play the first league All-Star game on Saturday, July 13. They suggested that the first-place team, at the time of the All-Star break, would play the All-Stars of the league. The team that was league leader on July 4, would be the host city, while all proceeds would go to the host team. Lloyd Adams, president of the Bathers opposed the financial structure because he believed that the proceeds should go to the league, instead of going to any one team. However, Adams said that he would go along with the majority. The sportswriters planned to select the 12 All-Star players.

On June 27, the last place Greenwood Choctaws nipped the Bathers 6-5 in Mississippi, while the Bathers and Helena tied for third spot, 10 games back of the leaders. El Dorado, five games behind Monroe, was solidly in the runners-up position. Since Monroe anchored down first place on July 4, the All-Star game headed to the twin-cities of Monroe-West Monroe, Louisiana.

On July 7, the Bathers were hanging onto third place, but the Oilers rallied to beat the Bathers 15-13. The two teams scored twenty-eight runs in the whack fest, but that was not all the action that occurred at Ban Johnson Field. In the tenth inning, umpire Gray ejected three Bathers, pitcher Leonard Frase, pitcher Ben Melton and outfielder Ed McCollum. The unruly fans began to throw cushions and a couple of pop bottles, but fortunately, they missed their intended mark. In the fifth inning, a line drive hit the Bathers starter Thompson on the foot. Fox relieved him, but not until Thompson gave up six runs in the inning. McCollum was the hitting star as he went 5-5, including a homer.

On July 9, the sportswriters selected only one Bather, Ed Zydowski, to represent Hot Springs in the All-Star contest on July 13. However, he and Thurman Tucker of Clarksdale were the only two unanimous selections. Tucker and Zydowski were one, two respectively in the All-Star voting. At the All-Star break, the Monroe White Sox lead the league, while the Bathers were barely in third place, with an even .500 percentage.

The All-Star selections, picked by the scribes from the CSL cities, competed against league-leading Monroe on Saturday, July 13. The selection committee named L. L. "Cowboy" Jones, Clarksdale Red Sox manager, the All-Star manager. All-Star infielders included Reese - first base, Greenville; Hodge - second base, Greenville; Savage - third base, Helena and Zydowski - short-stop, Hot Springs. Outfielders were Tucker - Clarksdale; Gwin - Pine Bluff and Zarilla - Helena. The two catchers were Van Antwerp - El Dorado and Boden - Helena. Pitchers were Anderson - El Dorado; Adkins - Pine Bluff and Douthat – Greenville.

The 1940 CSL's first All-Star contest, delayed for 20 minutes, began under drizzling conditions. It sprinkled during the first three innings, but the game continued through the seventh inning when the umpires decided to call the abbreviated contest. Ed Zydowski drove in a run and singled during the contest. Helena's right fielder Al Zarilla, who later played a decade in the major leagues, slapped a triple and scored on an infield out. Both teams generated only five hits each as Dewey Adkins, ace pitcher for the Pine Bluff, collected the win. The All-Stars soaked the White Sox 3-1.

The league had financial problems. So what else was new? Pine Bluff and Clarksdale were at a point of folding. "Recent inclement weather reportedly cut heavily into the attendance figures of the league teams…"

The Cotton States League will continue as an eight-team circuit, the directors decided today, after voting to take over and operate the Pine Bluff, Ark. club, which surrendered its franchise.

The Pine Bluff club made its final showing on the home grounds in a doubleheader with Clarksdale and from now on will be operated on the road in the seven other cities of the Arkansas-Louisiana-Mississippi circuit.[15]

CSL president Judge Harty, indicated that he planned to take a fact-finding trip to other cities in hopes to locate interest to replace the Pine Bluff team. Specifically, he planned to visit Vicksburg, Mississippi. In the meantime, there was good news from Clarksdale. President Jimmy McCain of the Clarksdale Red Sox stated, after a meeting with the club directors, that they planned to continue in the league. Clarksdale was playing mediocre baseball because they were in sixth place, but only a few games out of the fourth slot. However, cellar dweller, Pine Bluff seemed as if they dug themselves into a deep, deep hole.

On July 30, the Bathers were hanging on to fourth place. The Spa Boys continued to stay in fourth position in the CSL in early August. However, a few days later, as hard as they tried to remain in fourth spot, they found themselves in fifth place.

Since the team returned to the professional baseball ranks in 1938, the lack of money continued to hinder the Spa teams. However, on August 13, the newspaper reported that an individual who was contemplating purchasing the Bathers was in town to watch the Bathers play host to El Dorado.

For the past three years, the Bathers have been operated as a community-owned team with poor financial success and club officials agreed recently that the best method of its operation would be for someone to take it over to operate as an advertising medium for a business.

During the three years, the club franchise has been in Hot Springs mid-season financial drives have been necessary to keep the team going. A few businessmen have borne the larger load of these drives which bad weather, 'free agent' rulings and Baseball Commissioner Judge Landis and other causes made necessary.

While the club officials declined to give the name of the prospective purchaser, they said he was interested in the game both as a sport and as an enterprise and would seek to build up an interest here.

Inactivity to 'peddle' several of the outstanding players on the Bather team to clubs of higher classes has also hurt the Bather finances at this time.

'Club owners tell us they don't want to buy any soldiers,' Lloyd Adams, Bather president declared after conferring with several. 'They are afraid that as soon as they lay the money down, the conscription will get them.'[16]

That last statement meant that the United States Army, by way of the draft, could obtain the services of any person at any time. Therefore, if the military drafted a player, the team could lose that player's services for several years. Suddenly, there seemed to be no record of the prospective buyer.

On August 25, in Clarksdale, Ray Viers, second baseman for the Mississippi club, faced a Hot Springs pitcher. Viers slapped the ball over the center field fence. Well, sort of. A ball hit a hard-headed fan sitting on top of the wall, square in the noggin and bounded back into the field of play. The man rubbed the bump and continued to watch the game. Viers stopped at third, but umpire Dowdy ruled the ball a home run because the man was not a permanent fixture on the fence.[17]

It was mostly a fair season for the Bathers, but the front office personnel knew how to have a little fun. Near the end of the season, on Tuesday night, August 27, an old-timer's game, preliminary to the Clarksdale – Bathers clash, was on the agenda at Ban Johnson Field, beginning at 7:45 p.m. Many of the local "old heads" decided to get into the act and play one or two quick, non-professional innings.

The pregame battle that everyone awaited occurred between two well-known titans of the city, the Hot Springs Chamber of Commerce and the Hot Springs Junior Chamber of Commerce. "Roy Gillenwater will manage the seniors with Dr. H. King Wade acting as field captain, while almost anybody will be in charge of the juniors." The starting lineup for the senior team included Tommy Bosson- shortstop, Roy Gillenwater – catcher, H. King Wade - third base, Otis Brannan - second base, Cy King - center field, Bill Kimball - left field, Jack McJunkin, first base; Henry Murphy, right field; and "Dumb" Johnson - pitcher. Kelly White, Jack Coats, Louis Kinnard, Earl Spencer, Ben Harrison, Dr. Gaston Hebert (a'-bear), Martin Eisele and all other Chamber members, and anybody else that showed up, were substitutes.

The Jaycees roster, known as the Junior Chamber of Commerce, included pitchers "Red" Swaim, Warren "Statistics" Banks, "Red" Carpenter and Haskel Hardage. Leroy Lyons, Morris Hand and Mike Reed, catchers; Louie Longinotti, Paul Longinotti, "Doggie" Annen, Harold "Taillight" Jackson, "Mickey" Callahan, H. Brenner, Miller Merritt, Lee "Rehbein" Martin, George Callahan and Ralph Morris played the infield and outfield. In the end, the two teams had fun for a couple of innings because that was about all the contestants and the fans could take.

The Bathers last game of the season was unusual, to say the least. It wound up being a practice game between the cellar dweller Pine Bluff Judges and the fifth place Bathers. Okay, the Judges won 20-10, but it was one of those "who cares" games. It was like kids playing sandlot baseball. Frankly, the kid's game would have been more entertaining. The players hit the ball all over the yard and out of the yard. That was the problem. Because both teams ran out of baseballs in the eighth inning, they decided to put the game on hold...until next year! "They played the seventh and eighth heats with only one ball, having to retrieve each foul ball before the game could be resumed. Some three dozen balls were used." The players played at different positions and not only that, they changed positions several times.

The tilt was a farce from start to finish with practically every player on both sides playing practically every position on the diamond before the game was over. Five Bathers worked on the mound and the rest of them shifted about so much the scorekeeper finally gave up the ghost and quit trying to keep up with them. He left on his vacation today to recuperate.[18]

There is more! County Tax Assessor Roy Gillenwater, who played professional baseball in his day, came out of retirement (more like, came out of the stands) and caught the first inning for the Bathers. Club president Lloyd "Kingfish" Adams managed the team.

Red Rollings, the Judge's pilot, pitched the fifth inning dressed in a skirt. His remarks from the mound were classic.

'You're a liar,' he yelled at Umpire Gribbon when the arbiter called his first pitch a ball. And then, a little later, after the ump had called a strike, he yelled: 'Thank God you saw one.'[19]

There wasn't much to crow about at season's end. In addition to finishing fifth, Hot Springs finished in the fifth spot in team fielding and second in team batting. Ed Zydowsky led in the batting race most of the season, but right at the last, Thurman Tucker of Clarksdale nipped him at the wire by one point. Tucker finished with .390 and "Mr. Z" completed the season with a .389 clip. In addition, Zydowsky set an RBI record of 157. The Chicago White Sox called up Tucker for the 1942 season. The outfielder, who played for Chicago and Cleveland, completed a nine-year major league career in 1951. Two Hot Springs players selected to the end-of-the-year (non-playing) All-Star honorable-mention squad were second baseman Vern Hudson and center fielder LaMonte Duncan.

Chapter 6

"The Little Yankees"
1941

"(BATHERS) COP SEVENTH TRIUMPH FOR CLEAN SWEEP OF PLAYOFF SERIES"-The
Sentinel-Record

On December 12, 1940, Lloyd Adams, president of the Bathers, stated that Ellis "Mike" Powers, under an agreement with Nashville of the Southern Association, Class A-1, was the new manager of the 1941 Bathers. Ten players from the Anniston (AL) Rams, Class B, Southeastern loop were part of the deal to play with Hot Springs.

The Bathers, with Powers at the helm, opened their 1941 spring practice at Ban Johnson Field on Friday, April 4. The first two batters, shortstop Lloyd Heitmann, a Little Rock product, and outfielder "Dutch" McCall drove the ball out of the park. It was a good start to a new year! The next evening, Walter Ebel, introduced the team on his "Pleasure Party" radio show on station KTHS. The station initials stood for "Kome (Come) To Hot Springs."

Judge Harty, league president, appointed the following umpires to be the 1941 league arbiters. The CSL umpires were Uley E. (Irish) Welsh, Sr. - Jackson, Mississippi; Frank Dehaney - Elizabeth, New Jersey; Henry Gribbon - Birmingham, Alabama; Bud Newman - Shreveport, Louisiana; Earl Porter - Fort Lauderdale, Florida; Harold Johnson - Milford, Delaware; G.T. Cate

- Commerce, Texas and Cy Pfirman Jr. - New Orleans, Louisiana. Welsh and Gibbon had worked in the league during the 1940 campaign, while Newman and Cate had formerly umpired in the league, while the other men were newcomers.

The eight-team league representatives were Hot Springs (AR), El Dorado (AR), Helena (AR), Clarksdale (MS), Vicksburg (MS), Greenville (MS), Monroe (LA) and Texarkana (TX). The league conducted a 140-game schedule lasting 18 weeks. Two new members to the circuit were Texarkana, "orphaned by the disbanding of the East Texas league," and Vicksburg, Mississippi. Texarkana took over the spot vacated by Greenwood, Mississippi and Vicksburg, Mississippi replaced Pine Bluff, Arkansas.

The Bathers commenced the 1941 season on Sunday afternoon, April 27, at 2:30 p.m. at Ban Johnson Field against the Texarkana Twins. In the pregame ceremonies, a half-inning tilt occurred "to the delight of the spectators." Mayor Leo P. McLaughlin tossed the first pitch to W. Clyde Smith, president of the Bathers. Smith promptly singled through shortstop. Dr. H. King Wade was the backstop. In other pregame action, it was welcome time for the new manager Mike Powers. He received an engraved bat and flowers from Mrs. Lewis Brenner, president of the Jaycee Auxiliary. However, that was nothing to what Virginia Kettlecamp received during the seventh inning. In a lucky-number scorecard drawing, the local beauty-shop owner won a new Ford car!

Manager Powers, who guided Bowling Green of the Kitty League, to a pennant last year, will be making his first appearance in the Cotton States league. A hard-hitting first baseman, Powers will return Hot Springs to the select class of teams having player-manages.[1]

The starting lineup for the Bathers included Coleman Powell - center field, Lloyd Heitman – shortstop, Bob McCall - left field, manager Mike Powers - 1st base, Bob Duncan - 3rd base, Ted Pawelek – catcher, Lisle Davis - right field, Theole - 2nd base and Eldon Lindsey - pitcher. Mike Powers was the sixth Bathers' manager in four years. In 1938, the team's first year in the Cotton

States League, the Bathers used three men in the pilot's seat as "Spike" Hunter, Hal Grant and Joe Barnett stayed in the cellar. In 1939, the team, managed by Conard Fisher, finished in fourth place and played well in post-season play, losing out in the championship series. "Fisher resigned when Commissioner Landis broke up his team during the Detroit farm scandal." In 1940, Cecil Combs guided the team to an "almost first division spot," but fell short late in the campaign, ending in fifth place.

Fans like exciting games, so the lively 1,500 supporters got their wish at the opening game of the Bathers season. Well-known Charlie Mead was the hitting star of the day as he powered three home runs over the short right field fence at Ban Johnson Field. There was a man on base when Mead hit one of his monster homers, but there was one problem! Mead, a former Bather, played for the Texarkana Twins.

The teams were tied 7-7 going into the bottom of the ninth inning when the Bathers came to the plate. With one out in the last of the ninth the bespectacled manager-first sacker Powers slapped a single and went to second on a wild pitch. Duncan struck out. Two out, bottom of the ninth, the scored tied…this is what baseball is all about! The next batter, stocky-catcher Ted Pawelek thumped a single, driving in Powers from second with the winning run.

The Bathers had their share of problems, but so did a former Spa pitcher, optioned by the Hot Springs Bathers to Americus, Georgia, in the Georgia-Florida league. He wrote to family or friends explaining his quandary.

Young Spa Pitcher's Hard Luck Story Is a Classic Tale of Woe

Dear Croachers: Well, it's a hot day in this jerkwater town and a sad day for we boys. Our manager's nine-month-old son died this morning, his daughter is very ill and not expected to live. His wife and mother are sick also. Our third baseman is sick with malaria. One pitcher has a bad appendix, but may not have to have it removed. Our second baseman hit a line drive against the left field wall and fell rounding first and chipped a bone in his elbow. He will be out for two weeks or more. We have been using a sub second, third and catcher and don't have a manager with us...I may have to catch tomorrow as our second string catcher has a badly bruised toe. And, the doctor said if he played he was taking a chance.

I got lucky and won my first game relief pitching. I think we will snap out of it and have a fair ball club by July or August. We have a shortstop that keeps me from looking like the worst ball player on the field. He made 10 errors in the last two games, and got caught off second base two times flat-footed.

G.B. Burchfield.

P.S. Think nothing of this poor writing for I have a sore arm.[2]

In early May, at Ban Johnson Field, the Vicksburg Billies and Hot Springs were tied 7-7 with two outs in the bottom of the ninth. The Bathers' pitcher strolled to the plate. In that position, most managers would substitute a pinch hitter for the pitcher. Since manager Powers knew his players, he allowed southpaw pitcher Jodie Howington to hit. Howington, who pitched the complete game, faced the second Vicksburg hurler, Higgins. Rhodes drove in Bob Duncan with the tying run just a few minutes before Howington ambled to the plate. The situation did not seem to bother Howington because he slugged a single, driving in Duncan for an 8-7 Hot Springs win. Howington pitched nine innings and gave up 14 "scattered" hits. Hot Springs got their share of hits off two Vicksburg pitchers, by stroking 15 safeties...a total of 29 base hits between the two teams during the game.

For the next few days, big scores piled up on the Hot Springs scorecards. The Greenville Buckshots were in town for a three-game series. Hot Springs scored 24 runs in two games, but it wasn't enough.

The official scorer turned in his resignation last night at Ban Johnson field after the Greenville Buckshots had hammered out a 24-12 decision over the Hot Springs Bathers in the final game of their series here.

The one game itself wouldn't have been so bad had the scorer not had to keep account of the happenings of a similar game the preceding night in which the Mississippians walloped the Bathers 20-12.

Last night's three-hour battle saw a total of 44-base hits, including 18 doubles, 3 triples and a home run slammed out by both teams. Greenville used only two pitchers to hold the Bathers to 18 scattered hits, while the Bathers called up three moundsmen to dole out the 26 Greenville safeties.[3]

On May 15, the Bathers lost 15-2 to Monroe as the White Sox bounced the Spa hurlers for 13 hits. The next night, Monroe again ripped the Bathers 12-5. Greenville was in first place, followed by Vicksburg, Helena and Clarksdale to round out the first division. Monroe, in fifth place, headed up the second division, followed by Hot Springs in sixth, El Dorado, seventh and Texarkana in the cellar.

Losing got the attention of the big boys. Larry Gilbert, manager of the Nashville Vols of the Class AA, Southern Association, visited the Bathers when his team played at Memphis, since the Bathers had a working agreement with Nashville. The Bathers were in first division during the first several weeks of the season, but he didn't understand why they slipped so fast in the standings. He was sure it was the lack of good pitching. The last five games, the Bathers and their opponents scored 117 runs. In the last two games of the Greenville series, the two teams scored 68 runs on 80 base hits. Gilbert certainly had a cause for alarm.

A picture of Bob Duncan, Bathers third sacker, appeared in *The Sentinel-Record* receiving a new pair of shoes from Maurice Kallsnick, owner of Maurice's Shoe Store. Kallsnick offered the new shoes to the first person to hit a home run over the center field fence at Ban Johnson Field. The owner paid up. The admission to see Duncan and the Bathers play their home games was 40 cents for adults and 10 cents for children per game. Most of the night games began at 8:15 p.m., while the Sunday games started at 2:30 p.m.

It seemed as though football season arrived early in Hot Springs. Texarkana visited Hot Springs on May 20 and the Twins walked away with a 26-15 drubbing of the Bathers. Twenty-four batters recorded ninety-six at bats during the game that lasted three hours and ten minutes. The next two games with Helena continued to seem like football scores. On May 22, Helena beat Hot Springs 21-10, while two days later the Seaporters hung 27 runs on the Bathers as Hot Springs only mustered six tallies.

By May 24, Bob Duncan, Bathers third baseman, led the CSL in several departments. The rangy infielder led with 7 home runs, 30 RBIs and 67 total bases. The third baseman was only two back of the leader in runs scored with 26. Duncan had an 11-game hitting streak going until Tuesday, May 13. His batting average was a neat .365. The team was fourth in batting and second in team fielding.

"Dutch" McCall went all the way on the mound for the Bathers as he tossed an eight hitter and beat the Clarksdale Ginners 6-5 in 11 innings on May 26, at Hot Springs. It was unusual for a former outfielder to pitch 11 innings and on top of that, win the contest. McCall, during his 11-inning stint, gave up 10 walks and struck out six Ginners. The win gave the Bathers a clean four-game home sweep.

On June 1, Hot Springs was leading the league in batting with a .316 mark, last in team fielding and sixth place in team standings. There were five Bathers hitting over .340, but their opponents scored 284 runs against the Spa's 230 runs in 31 games. Bob Duncan tied for the league's home-run lead at nine. The next evening in Spa Town, the home team took care of Texarkana by a 9-8 score. However, following the game, Spa visitor, Van Camp and his party from Hardey, Illinois, noticed his car didn't look the same. The windshield was shattered from the second inning homer off the bat of Bathers' catcher John Jordin.

On June 18, Hot Springs eased past the Vicksburg Billies 7-6, but the game got out of the blocks late due to the Joe Louis-Billy Conn heavyweight boxing championship. The Hot Springs-Vicksburg game wasn't the only game delayed due to the fight. In the bottom of the fourth inning, the Pittsburgh Pirates and the New York Giants delayed their baseball game at Forbes Field in Steel Town. They resumed the contest 56-minutes later, when Louis decked Conn in the 13th round to remain the Heavyweight Champion of the World. What was the reason for the delay in Pittsburgh? Conn was from Pittsburgh and sports fans in the Pennsylvania city, glued to their radios, listened to their native son take on Louis. Before the Bathers game, Hot Springs baseball fans listened to the championship bout on loud speakers at Whittington Park.

At 27-years-old, heavyweight champion Louis was Conn's senior by four years. The 6' 2" Louis had a reach of 76" and Conn measured 6' 1 ½ "with a 72 ½" reach. Louis weighed 204 pounds, while Conn checked in at 169; however the "announced weight" was five pounds more for each boxer. Conn started out slowly, but progressed as the fight lengthened. By the end of round 12, two officials had Conn ahead, but the third official had the fight even. In the 13th round, Louis jarred Conn a few times, but Conn countered. Then, Conn started slugging it out with the champion. That was a gigantic mistake. Louis knocked the challenger down with two seconds left in the 13th round. Many boxing fans stated that it was one of the greatest fights in history.[4]

Strange things happened in the CSL. Hot Springs was on the road in Northeast Louisiana playing Monroe when an unusual event occurred.

Monroe, La., June 23 (AP) - Manager of the Monroe White Sox made it plain tonight that only necessity made him break a gentleman's agreement among Cotton States league clubs that no infielder or outfielder will be called in to pitch.

After Hot Springs had pounded his starting hurler for 11 runs, Taitt took the mound in the sixth and held the Bathers to one hit the rest of the way.

In the ninth inning, he asked the umpire behind the plate to announce to the 3,500 fans, 'the only reason I went in was that I have no pitchers.'

One Monroe hurler is in a Helena hospital recovering from an appendectomy; another recently had his tonsils removed; a third has a torn ligament in his back, and a fourth has a sore arm.

'But,' Taitt added, 'nothing was mentioned in the agreement about managers pitching.'
Hot Springs won 11 to 4.[5]

Charlie Pescod, one of the Bathers' top pitchers, stuck it to El Dorado on June 25, in the Oilers backyard. The hurler displayed "uncanny control and a sharp-breaking curve," as he tossed an eight hitter, striking out 14, to bamboozle the South Arkansas team 5-2. With the victory, the fifth place Bathers inched closer to the magic first division. A major change transpired in the CSL on July 10. The Clarksdale team folded and Marshall, Texas, took their place. Otis Brannan, former Bathers second baseman, signed with the Marshall Tigers as their new manager. Brannan played for Hot Springs during the 1938 season.

On the same day, July 10, Arkansas Governor Homer M. Adkins made "The Arkansas Hummingbird," Lon Warneke, an official Arkansas Traveler. Warneke, hurler for the St. Louis Cardinals, was a 14-year veteran of the major leagues. Lon, a native of Mt. Ida, Arkansas, lived in Hot Springs during the off-season. Previously, in late June, over 200 of Warneke's friends and supporters from Arkansas traveled by a special train to St. Louis to honor the famous Arkansan at a special "Lon Warneke Day Celebration" at Sportsman's Park. The Arkansas delegation and fans from St. Louis presented the lanky pitcher "with a 1941 Cadillac, hunting dogs, silver service, guns and other items."

Monroe and Greenville played a CSL game at Monroe's Casino Park on July 10, but it wound up being more than just a game. Some of the irate fans and Monroe's radio announcer disagreed with several decisions by the umpires. A frenzy resulted and the state police escorting the umpires from the field. "Some fans got in a few punches and stones were hurled at the arbiter's car as it rolled away from the park." The same two teams played the next evening and Emmet Harty, league president, issued a strict warning that the league would come down hard on the people involved. If any negative action ensued toward the umpires, Harty said that he "would relegate Monroe to the ineligible list and have the territory abandoned." John C. Carlisle, a baseball fan that attended the game, suffered a heart attack and died as he drove home from the game.

Harty fined the Monroe club $50 for failure to provide adequate police protection for Umpires Cy Pfirman and Bud Newman in last night's game. A Monroe radio announcer handling the park loudspeaker system was ordered suspended by the president 'pending investigation of inciting to riot.' Players of both clubs were directed to show cause 'why disciplinary action should not be taken against them for failure to protect umpires.'

Announcing Pfirman and Newman would again work tonight's game. Harty said: 'If a hair of their head is touched, I plan to place everybody connected with baseball in Monroe on the ineligible list and have the territory abandoned.' [6]

Players selected to the mid-season CSL All-Star Classic tangled with the first place team, Helena Seaporters. The Bathers placed second sacker, Roy Marion, brother of Marty of the St. Louis Cardinals and pitcher Charlie Pescod to the elite unit. Both players excelled during the game as Marion collected three singles during four trips to the plate and scored twice. When it was little Pescod's time to toss "his last three innings," the Bathers hurler pitched big as he allowed only two hits and no runs. The All-Stars humbled the eastern Arkansas Seaporters 7-1.

During July, the Bathers climbed up slowly in the standings. On July 29, Hot Springs slid past the Oilers of El Dorado 21-1 as they scored 13 runs in the fifth inning at the Spa. The Bathers collected five homers, seven doubles and nine singles for 21 base hits. Vicksburg led the league, followed by Monroe, Hot Springs and Helena to round out the first division. Second division teams were Greenville, Texarkana, Marshall and El Dorado. The first division was a close race. In one day, teams could move up or down a spot or two in league standings.

In late July and early August, the Bathers got hot! On August 8, overcoming a seven-run deficit in the fifth stanza, the "hit happy" Bathers peppered the White Sox of Monroe, 23-14. The 41-hit assault lasted two hours, 35 minutes. The win put the Water Boys in 3rd place.

There are good problems to have around the clubhouse. "Babe" Ruth entered the major leagues as an excellent pitcher, but he was such a good hitter, they transferred the multi-talented player to the outfield. Hot Springs realized they didn't have a Ruth on their hands, but they did have two 20-year-old players that were good enough to play two positions. Outfielder-pitcher Bob "Dutch" McCall rode into the Spa as an outfielder. The Bathers needed pitching, so manager Powers allowed the six foot, southpaw to pitch often in relief. He looked good throwing his blazing fastball and sharp curve. In fact, manager Powers used the versatile McCall as a starting pitcher, relief pitcher and an outfielder. .

Pete Rhodes traveled to Hot Springs as a pitcher from Alexander City, Alabama. He had a sensational first game, striking out 11 men in six innings, but he caught a line drive on the muscle of his throwing arm. He was put on the injured-reserve list. Later, the Bathers needed outfield help. After recovering, but not 100% ready for mound duty, Powers used Rhodes in right field. After moving to the outer limits, Rhodes hit a cool .350 and had an unimpressive 3-4 record on the mound. Powers said he did not always know the best position to use some of his players, but it was a good problem to have as a manager.

Anything can happen at a sporting event and it did at Ban Johnson Field on Aug. 11. There was a Marshall-Hot Springs game on tap that night at Hot Springs, scheduled to begin at 8:15 p.m. The Marshall team contacted the Bathers and told them that they had bus problems on the way to Hot Springs. What now! Since the league instituted a midnight curfew rule, there was nothing for the players and umpires to do, but wait…at least until midnight. So, in the meantime, what are the players suppose to do? The swift thinking, creative Bathers decided on a rare course of action. Never in the annuals of CSL history, have pregame activities been so ingenious and so lengthy. Since Marshall was a no-show for the time being, the innovative festivities began at the old ball yard. Pitcher Charlie Pescod was the self-appointed event coordinator.

During the summer of 1941, there was much talk about the United States entering the war. During World War I, some baseball teams, usually at pregame ceremonies, recognized the men and women in the military by marching with bats on their shoulders (like rifles). The Bathers reverted to the WW I exercise by entertaining the crowd with that type of marching drill.

Little 'General' Pescod ordered the manual of arms from six Bathers using bats for rifles and staged army drills. 'Privates' McCall, Powell, Heitman, Reggino and Pawelek were put through the 'mill' but the pre-game fun didn't hamper their slugging arms.[7]

The second activity featured a "wrestling match" between "Hammer Head" Heitman and "Bone Crusher" McCall, two Bather players. McCall won the match, because Pescod said he won. The third event was not a smart one. Pitcher Charlie Pescod challenged former Welterweight Boxing Champion of the World and Hot Springs native, Tommy Freeman to a sparring match. Actually, the men were about the same size, around 5' 7", but Freeman had a few more professional bouts than Pescod. Freeman clashed in the ring 219 times, won 176 bouts and lost 20 with 22 draws. The champion went down for the 10 count five times, but he won 81 of his matches by knockouts. On the other hand, Pescod had zero boxing experience. Freeman was 37-years old at the time of the challenge, but he still looked in shape. After sizing up his competition, the 26-year-old Pescod decided to take a rain check on the proposed "fight." That was the best idea Pescod had all evening.

The fourth event was just the opposite of a fight. The great activities director Pescod enlisted manager Powell and catcher Pawelek to dance at home plate! However, there was more. They danced as partners! That was the last time anybody ever saw the duo dance together. The next idea of Pescod's came straight from the Olympic Games. It was just a flat-out foot race. However, the contestants were far from well-trained athletes. The competitors included four famous Hot Springs "boys", Jack "The Great" McJunkin, Van Lyell, Tommy Freeman (the boxer) and manager Mike Powers. Starter Pescod awarded the race to McJunkin.

The fans had a great time watching the pregame happenings, but they paid to witness a baseball game. Following a two-hour wait, the fans, the umps and the Bathers were ready for some baseball! When Marshall arrived at the park, the unlucky Texans were just too exhausted to play baseball. The Bathers drained them, 13-3. The fans went home with loads of hilarious memories and delighted with a hometown win.

Toward the end of the season, the Bathers inched up into second place and then slipped back to third position. They were playing much better than earlier in the season. "Ironman" Pete Rhodes allowed only 10 hits as he and the Bathers beat the Vicksburg Billies 5-4 on Aug. 16. What did the papers mean when they reported "only 10 hits?" That's a bushel of hits! Hot Springs tallied a run in the last inning; however, reaching the last inning took a long time. It is hard to believe, but Rhodes threw the complete 14 innings! So, the words, "only 10 hits" made sense.

There were some strange scores near the end of the campaign. Hot Springs climbed back into second position by demonstrating an array of offensive power as they demolished Helena 28-4 on August 18. The Seaporters were actually up 1-0 in the top of the second inning, but that was the last time they saw the light of day. The Spa team scored six runs in the bottom of the second, two in the third, four in the fourth, 10 in the fifth, four in the sixth and two more in the eighth to end their scoring spree. By the end of August, the Bathers were solidly in second place.

Arkansan Lon Warneke was hot in St. Louis. On Saturday, August 30, in Cincinnati, the St. Louis Cardinals pitcher, Warneke, tossed the first no-hit, shutout of the 1941 major league campaign. The 11-year veteran topped the defending World Champions 2-0, as the lean 31-year-old pitched to only 28 batters. It was Warneke's 15th victory against seven losses for the season. The modest pitcher didn't ride off the field on someone's shoulders. When interviewed in the locker room, the easy going Warneke said, "I gave them a little of everything I had..." He continued, "The main thing is we won, 2-0." That was Warneke!

By the last game on Sept. 4, the Bathers headed to the league playoffs in second position. There was no pressure on their last regular season game. The Bathers ended the season at home with a 14-7 thrashing of the El Dorado Oilers. In order to save his pitchers for the playoffs, manager Powers used three pitchers against the seventh place Oilers. Ed Kramer, Jodie Howington and Pete Rhodes toed the rubber for the Spa Nine, as they tossed three innings each. Starting pitcher, Kramer, the most effective of the three, gave up only one hit and no runs during his time on the hill. El Dorado went up by one run in the top of the fourth inning 4-3, but Hot Springs blasted back with a four-run barrage in the bottom of the inning. In the seventh with another four-run outburst, the Bathers nailed down the win. Due to the shortage of umpires for the match, Hot Springs citizen, "Jack McJunkin, donated his services as base umpire." At the beginning of the eighth inning, the Bathers were introduced to the crowd "and won its applause for the fine spirit shown throughout the season."

At the end of the regular season, an All-Star selection committee elected three Spamen to the 1941 Cotton States League All-Star Team. The top three Bathers were Roy Marion - second baseman, Charlie Pescod - pitcher and Mike Powers - first baseman-manager. Powers barely beat out Doug Taitt of Monroe for the managerial All-Star spot.

Two Roys finished one-two in the CSL batting race. Greenville's Roy Bueschen captured the batting crown with a .370 average; while Roy Marion, Bathers second sacker, ended up five points behind in second place with a .365 mark. Manager Mike Powers wound up with a .356 batting mark, while Bathers center fielder Colman Powell finished with a .348 average. Bob Duncan, Bathers outfielder, finished second in the home run derby with 23 homers, as Connors from Texarkana, won the four-bagger award with 29. Manager Powers led the CSL in the doubles category by popping 47 and won the RBI race by one (137) over Kramer of Greenville. Marion collected the most hits with 207, while Coleman Powell scored the most runs as he crossed the plate 136 times.

The Bathers ended in the top spot in team batting average with an exceptional .315. Second place Monroe had a .297 average. In addition, amazingly, 10 Bathers hit for an average of over .300 and two others were just a few points short of the magic .300 mark. The mighty Bathers amassed 1,007 runs and 1,595 hits to lead the CSL in both categories. Pescod led the pitchers with the best won-lost percentage with a .739 with a record of 17-6. Howington was not far behind with a 16-8 mark and Lindsey maintained a 17-11 record.

The top four-playoff teams were, in order of finish, Monroe White Sox, Hot Springs Bathers, Greenville Bucks and the Vicksburg Billies. Hot Springs opened the Cotton States League's Shaughnessy playoff series, best of five games, at home against the Greenville Bucks.

First Round Playoffs
(Best of Five)
Game 1 – Saturday, Sept. 6, 1941 at Hot Springs, Arkansas
Hot Springs 19 Greenville 4

Before the game, it was "Mike Powers Appreciation Night." The fans presented the manager with a traveling bag and the players gave him a belt and buckle. Each Bather received a watch chain from the fans.

Stanley Todd (19-7) pitched the complete game for the Bucks, but he gave up 19 runs on 19 hits as the Bathers startled the Bucks 19-4 in the first round of the playoffs. Little Charlie Pescod (17-6), after a three-week layoff due to a sore arm, pitched like a giant as he scattered eight hits over nine innings. The Bathers jumped on Todd early and scored in every inning except the second stanza. Catcher Ted Pawelek blasted two homers and added another hit to his three-hit attack for the Bathers. Center fielder Mike Powell and left fielder Ed Rockey collected one round-tripper each. Powell, Rockey and Lou Roggino gathered three hits each. All-Star Roy Marion, not to be outdone, amassed four hits in five trips to the plate as he led the Bathers bombardment in the quick one hour and 50 minute game. Umpires were Gribbon and Porter.[8]

Game 2 – Sunday, Sept. 7, 1941 - at Hot Springs, Arkansas
Hot Springs – 7 Greenville – 5

At the end of five innings, Greenville was up 5-0 as the Bathers' guns shot blanks. Bathers' relief hurler Jodie Howington (16-8) took over from starter Eldon Lindsey (17-11) in the top of the sixth inning. During the first five innings, Greenville blasted four spheres out of the park to the Spa's no-homer night. Greenville's Prather was the hitting standout as he blistered two pitches over the Whittington Park fence. However, in the sixth inning, the Bathers finally discharged their cannons scoring six times. At the end of the sixth frame, Hot Springs was up 6-5. They added one more insurance run in the eighth inning to down Greenville Bucks 7-5. Greenville out hit the Bathers 9-8, but Hot Springs pulled off their second straight win. Howington was the winning pitcher in the two-hour game.[9]

Game 3 – Monday, Sept. 8, 1941 – at Greenville, Mississippi
Hot Springs – 4 Greenville - 2

The Bathers traveled to Mississippi for the third encounter on Sept. 8. The Bathers ran across the white slab four times in the seventh inning, but that was all the Spa team needed to defeat the Bucks 4-2. Greenville tried to make a game of it in the ninth frame as they scored twice, but the Arkansas unit held on to cop the victory and advance to the final round of the CSL playoffs. Ed Kramer (6-11) went the distance for the Spa as he allowed 10 hits in the two hour and three minute game.[10]

While Hot Springs was taking care of business with the Greenville crew, fourth place Vicksburg upset the first place Monroe White Sox to gain the finals against the Spa team. It was September and that meant high school football. The Bathers found out that Friday-night football in Arkansas was important. The CSL moved the championship home opener scheduled at Ban Johnson Field with Vicksburg from Friday night to Saturday night. It was a smart play!

In order to obtain postponement of the opening of the final playoff for the Cotton States League pennant here until tonight so as not to conflict with last night's football game, the Hot Springs baseball club had to agree to permit the Vicksburg Billies to pick a second baseman from the other six clubs in the league to replace Henry, injured Vicksburg second sacker, Bather President W. Clyde Smith revealed last night.

Vicksburg chose Keith, brilliant fielding Monroe second baseman, and that young star will be at the keystone bag at Ban Johnson field tonight when the two clubs clash in the first game of their four-out-of-seven series for the pennant.[11]

The hard-hitting Henry, who hit .333 during the regular season, was out of the lineup due to an injury he received in the Monroe series. Keith, considered the best glove man in the league, was a lighter hitter than Henry, posting a .236 season batting average.

Championship Series
(Best of 7)
Game 1 – Saturday, Sept. 13 at Hot Springs, Arkansas
Hot Springs – 7 Vicksburg - 6

Bathers' southpaw, Charlie Pescod (17-6) and Al Kelley (22-10) of the Vicksburg Billies were the starting pitchers for the opening game of the series at Hot Springs. Pescod had the league's best won-lost twirling percentage, while Kelley, 22-game winner, was the only pitcher in the CSL to win 20 or more games. Hot Springs led the league in team hitting with an excellent .315 average. Vicksburg finished fifth in the team batting with a .282 mark. The two teams were closer in the fielding numbers as Hot Springs finished third at a .951 clip, while Vicksburg was in fifth in fielding with .948. Ban Johnson Field was full of excited Bather fans as 1,334 paid their way through the turnstiles.

The Bathers rallied in the ninth inning to pull past the Vicksburg Billies to take the opening game of the CSL playoff series 7-6. Both pitchers went the distance as Vicksburg collected 15 safeties to the Bathers 9 hits. Hot Springs' Charlie Pescod, diminutive left-handed pitcher, was on top of his game as most of the Billies were on strike, as 15 struck out. Pescod made it tough for the Mississippi team by not walking a single batter. The only home runs of the night came off the bats of Roy Marion, Bathers second sacker and Harold Lee, Vicksburg's first baseman, with one each. Marion, Lee and Zimmerman all had three safeties each. Marion clouted two doubles in his hitting spree. The Billies committed three errors. It took two hours and 30 minutes to complete the contest.[12]

Game 2 – Sunday, Sept. 14 at Hot Springs, Arkansas
Hot Springs – 11 Vicksburg - 3

The second game at Hot Springs totaled 14 runs, 27 hits and 5 errors. Fortunately, Hot Springs collected most of the runs and hits, as they downed the Billies 11-3. Ed Kramer (6-11) went all the way for the Spa Boys as they blasted three Vicksburg pitchers, Joust, Baker and Lee. After one out in the fourth inning, Baker relieved the starter, Joust. Colman Powell, Bob Duncan and John Jordin garnered three hits each for the Bathers. Over 1,200 fans witnessed the Bathers second straight win of the championship series. The Billies gathered three of the five errors. Time for the contest was a quick two hours.[13]

Game 3 – Monday, Sept. 15, 1941 at Vicksburg, MS
Hot Springs – 9 Vicksburg - 4

The playoffs moved to Vicksburg for the third game where Bathers Eldon Lindsey (17-11) and the Vicksburg pitcher Ed Clement (1-3) were the starting hurlers. It was a 3-3 game in the sixth inning. Hot Springs scored once in the top of the seventh inning, while Vicksburg zeroed out in the bottom of the seventh inning. The eighth frame was the big inning for Hot Springs as they scored four times, while the Billies went blank in the bottom of the eighth. The Arkansas team added an insurance run in the top of the ninth. Vicksburg could only match their run in the bottom of the inning as the Bathers took their third straight playoff game from the Billies by the tune of 9-4. Al Welland of Vicksburg hit the only round-tripper of the contest, but six Bathers including Powell, Powers, Duncan, Raggino, Pawelek and Lindsey, the pitcher, attacked the Billies pitchers for two hits each. Vicksburg committed four errors to only one for the Bathers. Time of the game was 2:28.[14]

Game 4 – Tuesday, Sept. 16, 1941 at Vicksburg, Mississippi
Hot Springs – 16 Vicksburg - 7

The Bathers felt confident with a 3-0 lead in the best of seven-game series. One more win and they could wrap up the championship, but they knew they couldn't look ahead as they remembered that old cliché, "Take one game at a time." However, facts are facts. The Bathers had won six straight playoff games while losing none. That's good in anybody's league!

Jodie Howington (16-8) started for the Bathers and Al Baker (12-8) began the mound duties for Vicksburg. The Bathers started the ball rolling all over the park in the first stanza as they scored three tallies, while the Billies scored once in the bottom of the first inning. In the fourth inning, the Billies came back strong as they scored three times. Hot Springs scored one in the top of the fourth. At the end of four innings, the score was tied, 4-4. This was not what the Bathers wanted, but they played out their hand. The Bathers brought out the artillery as they pounded Vicksburg's pitching in the last five innings to crush the Billies 16-7 on 19 hits! Bathers' manager-first baseman Mike Powers was the heavy hitter with four hits, six RBIs and a home run. Powell, Heitman and Pawelek collected three hits each, while Pawelek added a homer to his resume'. With two outs in the fourth inning, "Dutch" McCall relieved Howington to pick up the win for the Bathers. Time of the championship contest was 2:30. Umpires for the final game were St. Charles, Gribbon, Porter and Newman.[15]

On September 17, the headlines on the sport page of *The Sentinel-Record* stated it best! **BATHERS TAKE CHAMPIONSHIP WITH 16-7 FINAL VICTORY. SPAMEN MAKE IT FOUR IN A ROW OVER VICKSBURG. COP SEVENTH TRIUMPH FOR CLEAN SWEEP OF PLAYOFF SERIES.** Yes, the Bathers went undefeated in the playoffs with seven straight wins! The Bathers were the 1941 champions of the Cotton States League!

Following their record-breaking seven-game playoff sweep, *The Sentinel-Record* called the Bathers "The Little Yankees." The 1941 Bathers may have been one of the best teams in Cotton States League history. In fact, some said that the team was "the greatest single season effort on the part of any club in 50 years." Some of the regular-season facts of the 1941 team included Roy Marion's second place finish in the batting race with .365; manager Powers averaged .356 in batting and Coleman Powell hit a .348. The Bathers set five team records during the 1941 season. They finished first in team batting average with a .315 mark; finished first with 5,079 times at bat; collected the most base hits with 596; popped 312 doubles and collected 2,379 total bases. Individual records included Powell's 137 runs scored, Marion's 207 hits and Charlie Pescod's highest pitching percentage .739 with 17-6 record.[16]

A few days later, sportswriter Roy Bosson noted that Bathers president Clyde Smith did not receive remuneration for the services of some of his players. The situation involved Smith and Larry Gilbert, Nashville Volunteers manager. Gilbert did send most of the Bathers to Hot Springs, but Nashville took away several of the promising players and Hot Springs was left holding an empty purse.

Nashville sent five players here on option and as expected, they recalled all of them. However, under the terms of the working agreement with the Bathers, the Vol. pilot also retained the privilege of calling up any other Bathers he desired...Among those he desired were little Charlie Pescod, whom the Bathers purchased with their own good dough, and who, incidentally, led the Cotton States League in pitching, and another youngster named Coleman Powell, who developed into a brilliant prospect here...Prexy Smith admitted he had had visions of fattening the Bather exchequer no little from the profits of the sales of Coleman and Pescod to faster company...When they sign that playing agreement for next year, Prexy Smith will read all clauses.[17]

Following the season, Charlie Pescod, named director of the Hot Springs Boys' Club, took charge of the 300-member organization on September 27, 1941. Pescod formerly served as director of physical education in the Cristobal High School, Canal Zone, and as assistant coach at the Dumas High School in Arkansas. Nashville, of the Southern Association, sent word to Pescod that they wanted him to pitch for the Vols during the 1942 season.

Pescod, born in Salinas, Ecuador, South America and raised in the Canal Zone, was one of 12 children. He had six brothers and five sisters who, in 1941, lived in the Canal Zone. Pescod entered professional baseball in 1937. He weighed 145 pounds and stood 5' 7" when the 26-year-old southpaw hurled for the Bathers. In 1943, he was the most talked about player at spring training before entering military service. His overall minor league won-lost record was 73-52 for a pitching percentage of .584, while his ERA was a very good 2.89.[18]

In 1943, Pescod enlisted in the Army and in 1944, Private Pescod left his wife and daughter in their family home in Dumas, Arkansas. Soon, he was on his way to Europe, where on December 2, 1944, Charlie Pescod was "killed in action" in France.[19]

Chapter 7

The War Years
1942-1946

"The Cotton States League would cease operations until further notice."

- Judge Emmet Harty

Due to the war, disbandment of the Cotton States League was a real possibility. In the December 18, 1941, issue of *The Sporting News*, president of the Hot Springs Bathers, W. Clyde Smith stated, "The directors agreed operations during the 1942 season would be too much to undertake." Soon after this statement, league president, Judge Emmet Harty announced that the Cotton States League would cease operations until further notice.[1]

Professional baseball was quiet in Hot Springs during the war years, but there was activity related to baseball. *The Sporting News* was a popular sports paper during WW II. Under the heading, "In Camp It's Like a Postcard in a Country Post Office," military personnel around the country praised the publication. Lieutenant James M. Keating stationed at the Army-Navy Hospital in Hot Springs, stated, "The enlisted personnel at this post apparently enjoy the issues very much, as evidenced by the inquiries received relative to it."[2]

In early January of 1943, Blake Harper, concessions manager at Sportsman's Park in St. Louis, contributed to the War Bond drive in Hot Springs. He donated 1942 World Series autographed baseballs and pennants which were auctioned for a total of $55,250. The baseballs, autographed by members of the St. Louis Cardinals and the New York Yankees, brought high dollar to the event sponsored by the Hot Springs Business and Professional Women's Club. The 1942 World Champion Cardinals beat the Yankees four games to one. John Sturgis of Arkadelphia, Arkansas, purchased one ball for $20,000. Another baseball sold for $10,000 and none sold for less than $1,000.[3]

Lon Warneke, veteran pitcher of the Chicago Cubs and formerly of the St. Louis Cardinals, took his preliminary draft board examination at Hot Springs on January 4, 1944. "The Arkansas Hummingbird" notified the Cubs not to count on him for spring training. He was right. The 34-year-old father of two, served in the Army in 1944 and part of 1945.

President Clark Griffith of the Washington Senators (sometimes called the Nationals), sent five Nats to "boil out" at Hot Springs around February 1, 1945. Griffith was "a believer in Hot Springs conditioning, particularly for the more ancient of his players," like pitchers "Dutch" Leonard and Roger Wolff. Joining the duo were pitcher Sid Hudson, catcher "Jake" Early and shortstop Cecil Travis. The latter three players were former servicemen who, Griffith thought, needed to get back on track before regular spring training commenced. The pre-conditioning contingent boiled out for about three weeks before reporting to spring training camp in Orlando, Florida.

Professional baseball protected former professional baseball players who served in the military. "Returning servicemen, who were on the rolls of clubs before joining the armed forces, are entitled to certain general privileges of re-employment..." Within certain guidelines and a pre-scribed time, baseball urged the reinstatement of players to their old teams.[4]

Due to WW II, there was no minor league baseball played in Hot Springs from 1942 through 1946. However, the Army-Navy Hospital baseball team, located in Hot Springs, needed a place to play league games. The Junior Chamber of Commerce owned several acres around Belding and Carson Streets. The large tract of land, called Dean Field, seemed to be a good area to con-struct a suitable field. The older Jaycees, over 40 years-old, called Exhausted Roosters, took the lead in helping to generate funds for the construction of a new field in the area. Appropriately called "Roosters Field," construction began in 1945. The field, located across the road from the future Jaycee Park (Bathers Field), was the answer to the dilemma. The military team, made-up of personnel from the hospital staff in Hot Springs, played other military installations in and around Arkansas. Orval Allbritton recalled the construction of the field took place in the spring and summer of 1945.

Much of the work force to build Roosters Field was furnished by the German prisoners of war (POW) camped at Lake Catherine State Park, near Hot Springs. Named Camp Hot Springs, it was one of several POW branch camps of Camp Joe T. Robinson in North Little Rock. Camp Hot Springs opened in March 1945 as a German POW camp. Mr. Allbritton stated that the Germans were excellent workers. When the POWs completed their daily tasks at Roosters Field, the Army guards would load them into 6x6 Army trucks and head back to camp. Allbritton said that he noticed the American driver, from time to time, stopped at the Purity Ice Cream Company on Malvern Avenue and treated the POWs to ice cream cones. Allbritton lived near the ice cream company.

Allbritton stated that the first contest at Roosters Field was a practice game between the Army-Navy Hospital and an African-American team from Hot Springs. The military team had first-rate uniforms and good players, while the Hot Springs African-American team had no uniforms and wore regular clothes and shoes. They rolled up their pants legs and played ball. The small group of spectators knew that the game was just for fun, but both teams wanted to win. The hospital team had talent and included at least one professional player. Mr. Allbritton recalls a professional player who played for the Army-Navy team named Tucker, who he believed was Thurman Tucker, a Chicago White Sox outfielder. If this was the same Tucker, he was the leadoff man and starting center fielder in the 1944 Major League All-Star Game representing the White Sox. His nickname was "Joe E." because he resembled Joe E. Brown, the movie actor.

The military team was surprised when they ran into a buzz saw. The African-American team played well, in fact, well enough to beat the Army-Navy team in the first game ever played at Roosters Field. Allbritton said that the American Legion baseball team, on which he played, practiced at Roosters Field. The upgrading of the field became a special project for the "Exhausted Roosters."[5]

On November 17, 1946, forty representatives of six cities met in Greenville, Mississippi, to discuss the revival of the Cotton States League. The league considered an eight-team league. Monroe, Helena, El Dorado, Pine Bluff, Clarksdale and Greenville signed applications for membership. Three teams, Greenwood, Mississippi, and two Arkansas teams, Camden and Hot Springs, waited in the wings.

Joe DiMaggio and Hank Greenberg, two major league All-Stars, "boiled out" in the Spa by taking a series of 21 baths, which they completed on Dec. 13, 1946. Following the war, the two former GIs had trouble resuming their baseball careers as they got off to a slow start in 1946. Following his course of baths, DiMaggio said that a seven-year-old twinge in his shoulder disappeared. In addition to the baths, Greenberg played golf with Al Simmons, coach of the Athletics, and Toots Shor, New York restaurant owner.[6]

Chapter 8

Jaycee Park - The New Home
1947

"Sod is being laid on the infield and box seats are being constructed at the base of the big 2,000-seat grandstand." - The Sentinel-Record

A fan base in the city wanted to explore the idea of Hot Springs returning to professional baseball, because many baseball enthusiasts missed the Bathers. They remembered the successful baseball year of 1941, when "The Little Yankees," won the Cotton States League title. In early 1946, the Hot Springs Junior Chamber of Commerce approached Blake Harper about becoming the president and owner of the new Hot Springs Bathers, if Hot Springs received the franchise.

Blake Harper had several interests with banks, including two in Hot Springs. In addition, he served in the front office on several baseball franchises. He was the concessionaire at Sportsman's Park in St. Louis, home of the National League St. Louis Cardinals and the American League St. Louis Browns.

As an optimistic person, Harper, in 1944, defied logic. During the 1944 season, it seemed there would be an all-St. Louis World Series between the Cardinals and Browns. The Red Birds won 105 games and soared past the Pirates to take the NL crown by 14.5 games. From the concessions standpoint, Harper and the world knew it was the Cardinals year, again! The Birds were on their way to their third consecutive wartime pennant.

However, the American League Browns was a different story. The Brownies, as some called them, were pennant poor in the 43-year-history of the franchise, so why should 1944 be different? The Browns began the season winning their first nine games! That was unheard of for the Browns. With only a few weeks remaining in the season, they were in first place. However, everyone knew the history of the Browns and the Brownies didn't disappoint their fans. They began to slide! The pennant came down to the last week of the season.

But there was at least one St. Louis citizen who still believed in the Browns. Blake Harper, concessionaire at Sportsman's Park, was busy preparing a Browns' World Series program…[1]

Harper stocked Sportsman's Park high with concessions for the coming World Series between the Cardinals and Browns. Some knew he would have to stuff down thousands of hot dogs, hundreds of bags of popcorn and drink tons of soda pop until he turned green, because they were sure the Browns would slither into next year, as always. At the tail end of the 1944 season, the surprising Browns shackled the Yanks five times, as they won the American League pennant by one game over the Detroit Tigers. Due to Blake Harper's confident prognostication, he sold many refreshments during the 1944 World Series in St. Louis.

In December 1946, the Cotton States League granted Hot Springs a baseball franchise and, soon after, Harper decided to take the offer extended to him by the Hot Springs Jaycees. He knew the ends and outs of baseball, but one major problem that usually existed in the minor leagues faced Harper and that was the lack of money. Harper had his work cut out for him. He had to "sell" the minor league Bathers to the city and surrounding area. An encouraging sign was that the Jaycees moved from old Whittington Park and planned to build a new field. The Jaycee Park recreation area looked promising, but there were major problems to be ironed out before any baseball occurred at the possible future home of the Bathers at Jaycee Park.

In January 1947, the Jaycees sent two committee members to St. Louis to discuss with the management of the Missouri-Pacific Railroad about the removal of a spur line from the middle of the large recreation area called Jaycee Park. A railroad track through the middle of the ballpark had to go, if the possibility existed for a baseball park in the area. Soon, the green light to eliminate the railroad tracks became a reality. From that moment on, it was full-speed ahead. Leveling and drainage by Jack Smith and his crew were the next items on the agenda. Subsequently, the strategy was to begin erecting a 2,000-seat stadium within 30 days. Mr. Smith was in charge of the field prior to turning it over to the general contractors.

Lusk and Grubbs, Texarkana contractors, won the contract to build the grandstand for the estimated 2,000-seat structure. "The construction of the baseball field and grandstand is the first step planned by the Jaycees toward development of the big tract into a city-wide public recreational area." The cost of the baseball field and grandstands, built by the Jaycees, exceeded $55,000.[2]

In the meantime, the drive for funds for the structure continued with the Initial Gifts committee headed by Jimmy Phillips reported making excellent headway. After the conclusion of the Initial Gifts drive sometime this week, the general campaign for funds will be launched with County Collector Ray Owen in charge.[3]

In January 1947, Jim Griffith, a division superintendent of the Arkansas-Louisiana Gas, Co., in El Dorado, became the president of the new Cotton States loop. Griffith, former president of the El Dorado baseball franchise from 1937-1939, served on that team's board of directors beginning in 1932. Former CSL Boss, Judge Emmet Harty declined to serve as president, but he did assist Griffith as vice president of the circuit.

The new post-war, six-team, professional Class C, Cotton States League was nearing opening day. Teams from Mississippi and Arkansas equally divided the league. The Mississippi teams included Greenwood, Greenville and Clarksdale, while Hot Springs, El Dorado and Helena made up the Arkansas group.

The circuit voted to begin playing a 120-game schedule on April 20, and finish on Sept. 1. The loop adopted the Rawlings ball as the official baseball. Hosting opening-day games were Hot Springs at El Dorado, Clarksdale at Helena and Greenville was on the road at Greenwood. The top four teams at the end of the season would participate in the Shaughnessy playoffs. The league also voted to play Sunday doubleheaders, while Saturdays would be a day of rest.

The loop set a club salary limit of $2,600 a month for 15 players including the manager, with the roster to consist of seven class players and eight non-class men…

…Minimum admission prices were set as follows: General admission, 60 cents plus tax; bleachers, 40 cents plus tax; children under 12, 10 cents.[4]

By the start of the season, a spacious new $40,000 home for the Bathers was nearing completion at Jaycee Park. The Bathers used Legion Field, formerly Fogel Field, for spring training. Legion Field was located across the street from Ban Johnson Field on Whittington Avenue, next to the Alligator Farm.

The Sentinel-Record printed Blake Harper's letter to the area baseball fans on March 16, 1947. He wrote about how he wanted to answer some questions concerning the Bathers and the new ownership. Excerpts from the letter appear below.

About fourteen months ago, the Junior Chamber of Commerce contacted me and advised that they would like to have me take over the Hot Springs Franchise in the Cotton States League.

At that time, they also advised me that they would build a suitable park and the park is now under rapid construction.[5]

He dangled a carrot in front of the fans by saying that he encouraged the National Association of Professional Baseball League to hold their meeting in Hot Springs in December 1947. The convention would draw around 1,500 delegates and emphasized that the city would receive "untold publicity" and revenue.

Harper continued to let the fans know that he wanted good ball players and if they were good enough to advance to a higher team, he would sell them so that the Bathers received adequate compensation. He realized baseball was a business and he wanted to be a good executive.

I made an agreement with the Junior Chamber of Commerce that no time would the club solicit donations to finance the Club, which is usually the practice in other towns of this size in order to have organized baseball.

Sometime in April, we expect to mail to all automobile and truck owners two windshield stickers which reads as follows: 'We Bathe the World' 'Support the Bathers.'

Our training camp will be in charge of our Manager, Joe Santomauro, a graduate of the University of Alabama and Earl Smith, a local boy, who was one of the great catchers of Pittsburgh, N. Y. Giants and the Cardinals for 12 years. We also expect to have the services of Carey Selph for a few days. Mr. Selph is formerly of Arkadelphia, and played his first year for me at Fort Smith. Later, he was with the Cardinals and the White Sox and managed Houston for many years.

...The club has purchased two sets of uniforms, one used at home and one on the road. The material in these uniforms is the same used in all Major League clubs. The wording on these will be Hot Springs Bathers.

The Ball Club has all the concessions and what money is made from this source will be used to finance the Club.[6]

Harper acknowledged that the cost of running a franchise in this league was around $32,000 to $35,000 a season. He added another incentive when he said that he contacted the Commissioner of Baseball, A. B. "Happy" Chandler, and asked him to attend a game sometime during the summer. In addition, he said that the park would seat between 3,500 and 4,000.

Workers transformed Ban Johnson Field, former home of the Bathers, into a midget auto race-track. In addition, renovation of the new Whittington Park amusement area took place. The grand opening of the modernized amusement park, owned by Playground, Inc., occurred on Saturday, April 19. The new area featured a dance pavilion, roller skating, rides, miniature golf, wading pool for children, swings, seesaws, picnic grounds and other forms of family entertainment. Hot Springs' own George Maki, "the King of the Trumpet" and his orchestra was a magnificent drawing card for dancing. There was always free admission to the grounds.

Harper selected Chancellor Sam Garratt as team president, while the field general was Joe Santomauro. Mrs. Evelyn Ensminger was the club secretary-treasurer. Additionally, Harper continued to serve as the veteran concessions manager at Sportsman's Park in St. Louis. Harper, who was a continual Spa visitor, hired 51-year-old former major leaguer Earl Smith to help assemble and coach the Bathers. Harper planned to use Smith as a pinch hitter.

In 1919, as a 23-year-old rookie, Earl "Oil" Smith, began his major league employment with the New York Giants. His manager was the "no-nonsense" pilot, John McGraw. Once, McGraw fined Smith when he hit a homerun. McGraw told the Sheridan, Arkansas, native to lay down a bunt, but Smith politely swung at a pitch of his liking and slammed the ball out of the yard. That was how McGraw managed the team! However, McGraw praised Smith by saying he was "the greatest judge of batters of all time." During his playing days in New York, Earl acquired the nickname of "Oil." The New York fans pronounced Earl, like "Oil." So, he became "Oil" Smith.

During his 12-year major league career, Smith played with the Giants, Pittsburgh Pirates, Boston Braves and the St. Louis Cardinals. Smith finished his career with a hefty .303 batting average and caught in five World Series.[7]

During spring training, the Bathers opened their exhibition schedule against the Army-Navy Hospital Red Sox. The men who were on the staff at the large local military hospital, formed the team and they played other military teams in the area. Since Jaycee Park was not ready for play, the Bathers used Fogel (Legion) Field for workouts and practice games. The Bathers were up 6-4 at the end of the sixth inning, but then the fireworks exploded for the Bathers. Hot Springs scored 10 runs in the next two frames to wrap up the 16-4 win over the GIs. First baseman Bill Haschak, a newcomer to the league, led the Bathers at the plate with five hits. Walt Schublon and Joel Callaway were the tossers for the Bathers.

The last exhibition game for the Hot Springs team was a blow out. The Bathers' opponent was "Mutt" Carrigan's American Legion Baseball team, made up of local high school players. Of course, the score was a lopsided 16-1 victory for the Bathers, but the pro team needed the practice. It was just that, a scrimmage, as the Legion team proved little resistance against the older and more experienced Bathers. However, the practice aided the Legion boys, a team made up of very good players. Two members of the Legion team, Jack Bales and Rex Wehunt, signed professional contracts within a year. In fact, both players played for the Bathers in the 1950s. Rex, a left-handed pitcher, hurled for the Bathers in 1951 and Bales, a popular catcher-manager, participated for Hot Springs during the 1952-1955 seasons.

In late April, the YMCA, in cooperation with the Bathers organization, began registering boys for the "Knot Hole Gang." All boys, ages 8-16 who signed up, obtained a membership card. The "Gang" received free admission each Thursday night to the Bathers home games.

On April 20, *The Sentinel-Record* reported that the momentum on the baseball diamond and stands rapidly increased.

Sod is being laid on the infield and box seats are being constructed at the base of the big 2,000-seat grandstand. Fence posts had been set. All light poles have been erected and fixtures are due to arrive at the Arkansas Power and Light (AP&L) office here April 21.[8]

The steel and concrete grandstand at Jaycee Park awaited the crowd, but the light fixtures did not arrive in time for the opening game. Instead, the Bathers traveled to El Dorado to begin the season with a four-game road trip.

World War II left a baseball void in many cities in the United States. However, the war was over and the Spa was ready for some professional baseball. The home team did not have an affiliation with a major league club, but the Chicago White Sox was looming in the background.

The 1947 edition of the Hot Springs Bathers started the season with infielders Walt Lenczyk-third baseman, Bill Haschak-first baseman, Harley Briggs-second baseman, Earl Drenning-shortstop, Paul Green-shortstop and J. W. Crain-third baseman. Catchers included Tony Zini and Doyle "Red" Morris. Outfielders were Mike D'Antonio-center fielder, Walt Lakics-center fielder, Tom Mabry-left fielder and Jim Wilson-right fielder. The four hurlers were Walt Shublom, Joel Callaway, Art Hamilton and Ralph Sheldon. Ben Smith was on the roster as batting practice pitcher. Coach Earl Smith and manager/pitcher Joe Santomauro completed the opening-day roster.

Baseball returned to the Spa! However, it was not a good start for the Spamen as the El Dorado spanked the Bathers 17-8 in the 1947 opener on the Oilers muddy field on April 29. The Bathers returned the favor the following evening by trouncing the Oilers 20-7. The winners collected 18 hits to the losers 10. The big guns at the plate for Hot Springs were first baseman Bill Haschak who went 5-5, outfielder Tom Mabry collected four hits, second baseman Harley Biggs garnered three raps and Tony Zini smacked two safeties. Bathers' pitcher, 24-year-old Art Hamilton, in his first professional start, helped his cause by stroking two singles. Hamilton, who went the distance on the mound, struck out four and only walked two during his first outing of the season. In the first game, the Bathers botched the ball all over the yard, but it was a different story on night two. While El Dorado collected five errors in the field, the Bathers were errorless.

The Bathers returned home from El Dorado with a 1-3 record. However, Hot Springs was ready to play host to the Clarksdale Planters in a twin-bill home opener at their new home, Jaycee Park, on Sunday, May 4, at 2:00 p.m. Season tickets were on sale at the Medical Arts Drug Store, Central Cigar Store, Stell and Adams Hardware, Sporting Goods Store, Oaklawn Supply Company and C. J. Spencer Cigar Store. Season box seats sold for $55.00. Interested fans purchased box seats from Mrs. Ensminger at the Bathers office located at the Southern Grill on Central Avenue.

The Bathers prepared to launch the home campaign, but Blake Harper, the team's owner, was missing. Mr. Harper had two jobs. As earlier stated, he was head of the concessions at Sportsman's Park in St. Louis. Even though he enjoyed owning the Bathers, it seemed difficult for him to split his interests equally. Eventually, that seemed to be a big problem for the Harper ownership.

The local newspapers seldom printed a front-page editorial concerning baseball; however, on May 4, a baseball editorial appeared in the *New Era,* the evening paper. The editor, in his lengthy article, urged all baseball fans in the area to support the Bathers and minor league baseball in Hot Springs.

Hot Springs will welcome the return of organized baseball this afternoon. The Cotton States League has been revived after a five-year wartime lapse and this occasion will mark the opening of the home season of the Hot Springs Bathers. Truly, this is a real indication that the city is in the last stages of its return to peacetime normalcy.

...The Bathers return to action under new management and in a new setting. Hot Springs is indeed fortunate that such an experienced baseball man as Blake Harper evidenced his faith in the city by obtaining the city's franchise in the Cotton States loop. Mr. Harper is a longtime friend of Hot Springs and knows its people. He will do everything in his power to give Hot Springs a winner.[9]

An overflow crowd of over 2,500 excited fans jammed Jaycee Park, on Sunday afternoon, May 4, as they welcomed the Bathers' new team, new season, new park and a new era. The park was much larger and better designed than the old Ban Johnson Field. The newly organized Hot Springs Municipal Band, under the direction of Loyce Biles, played. During the preliminaries, Judge Clyde Brown, president of the Junior Chamber of Commerce, "gave a brief history of Jaycee Park." Following the history lesson, Earl Ricks, mayor of Hot Springs, tossed out the ceremonial first pitch and the game was on.[10]

The league leading Clarksdale Planters spoiled the Bathers' opener by drubbing the home team, 19-1 and 16-6. In the fourth inning, of the first game, Planters' center fielder Paul Mauldin made history when he swatted the first home run at Jaycee Park. The historic blast sent Bathers starter Walt Shublom to the showers. The Bathers mustered only two hits in the first game. The bright spot for Hot Springs came in the seventh inning when third baseman Wally Lenczyk lifted a four-bagger over the fence. He was the first Bather to hit a home run at Jaycee Park. The event occurred in the first game ever played at the park, Sunday, May 4, during a doubleheader on opening day of 1947. Due to the length of the contests, the games were snoozers because the twin bill lasted five hours. Due to the scores and length of the games, many of the fans departed, long before the last out.

Bathers entertained the Greenville Bucks on Wednesday night, May 14. The headlines in *The Sentinel-Record* stated that it was the first professional night baseball game held at the Spa since the war.

Not since the pre-war Bathers performed at Ban Johnson field has professional night-baseball been played here. The present edition was scheduled to open the season under the lights May 1, but reflectors did not arrive until the club was ready to go on the road again last week. [11]

The Bathers made history! On May 14, the Bathers won the first "under the lights game" played at Jaycee Park by the tune of 6-1 over the Greenville Bucks.

On May 15, Blake Harper, owner of the Bathers, and Leslie O'Conner, vice president and general manager of the Chicago White Sox met for a high-level conference that centered on the possibility of the White Sox taking over the ownership of the Bathers from Blake Harper. Harper was a good man, but it seemed that he bit off more than he could chew.

The contemplated purchase by the White Sox has been in the talking stage for some time, but came to light last week when 'Red' Ormsby, former Major League umpire and now Chisox front office man, investigated interests here, and the possibilities of support if the Major League club did add the Bathers to its comparatively small farm system.[12]

Emmett "Red" Ormsby was born in Chicago in 1895. From 1923-1941, he was a well-respected American League umpire. During those years, Emmett umpired five World Series and the 1935 All-Star game. He umpired his first World Series in 1927, which pitted the mighty Yankees and Pirates.[13] As any major league umpire, Ormsby experienced problems. On one occasion, he umpired an Athletics game that ended in a riot.

In 1927, he was involved in an argument in Philadelphia with Ty Cobb and Al Simmons of the old Athletics, over a ball that Cobb hit out of the park, which Ormsby called a foul. He ordered both players from the field, but the fans rioted and the umpire had to be escorted from the field by the police.[14]

On the other side of town, midget auto racing was set to begin its first season in Hot Springs on Friday night, May 23. The new Whittington Park Midget Speedway, former Ban Johnson Baseball Field, was the first professional auto racetrack in the history of the area. L. S. Hamilton, manager of the speedway, said that around 30 drivers planned to participate in the opening stanza. Time trials began at 7:00 p.m. and main events started at 8:00 p.m. at the oval track. Hamilton scheduled midget races every Friday night.

A C-47 plane, affectionately nicknamed "Gooney Bird" during WW II, transported several of the midget cars to the Hot Springs Memorial Airport. A parade of cars rolled down Central Avenue at 2:30 p.m. in anticipation of the evening's event. Mr. Hamilton said, "Drivers will be coming here each week from Kansas, Oklahoma, Mississippi, Texas and Louisiana." In addition, the track manager stated, "The driver who builds his own racers invests from $5,000 to $10,000."[15]

A serious baseball conference took place at the Majestic Hotel on May 27, as Chicago officials and leaders of the Hot Springs Junior Chamber of Commerce closed the deal on the sale of the team. The front-page headlines in the Wednesday morning, May 28 edition of *The Sentinel-Record* stated, "Chicago White Sox Take Over Bather Baseball Franchise." Joe Kuhel, former major league player, became the new manager of the Bathers. Released outright were manager-pitcher Joe Santomauro and Earl "Oil" Smith, coach/pinch-hitter.

Hot Springs joined the growing Chisox farm system. The Hollywood Stars of the Pacific Coast League was the only Triple-A team listed in the White Sox organization in 1947. Fall River Indians (MA) of the New England League and the Waterloo White Hawks in the Illinois-Indiana-Iowa League, called the Three-I League, joined the White Sox farm program in the Class B division.

The three Class C White Sox affiliates were the Superior Blues (WI) of the Northern League, the Oil City Refiners (PA) of the Middle Atlantic League and the Hot Springs Bathers in of the Cotton States League. The Class D teams in the Chicago's farm system were Lima Terriers of the Ohio St. League, Wisconsin Rapids White Sox of the Wisconsin State League and Madisonville Minors (KY) played in the Kentucky, Illinois and Tennessee League.

Leslie O'Conner was a seasoned veteran in the business of baseball. He had served as assistant to the late Judge Kenesaw Mountain Landis, former czar of major league baseball. The first order of business for O'Conner was to inspect and determine needs of the slumping Bathers. "Patsy" O'Rourke, chief scout and scout "Red" Ormsby scrutinized the team on road trips.

However, one of the more important topics left on the table was the concern about park leasing. The Junior Chamber of Commerce owned the Jaycee playground development area, including the minor league baseball park.

Under tentative provisions of the new lease, semi-pro clubs will be able to use the park only for special games, but the plant will be open to American Legion or Army nines on off days.

'The point of difference is the use of the park by semi-pro clubs,' O'Conner told the small group of Jaycee baseball leaders in his hotel room. 'It is not a satisfactory situation when two or more clubs occupy the same premises. We intend to help improve the grounds, for the diamond is now in bad condition.'[16]

O'Connor stated that he planned to send Gene Bassett, head groundskeeper at Chicago, to Hot Springs and instruct local workers as they refurbished the playing field at Jaycee Park.

The White Sox agreed to advance the necessary money to the Junior Chamber to construct dressing rooms and showers underneath the grandstands. According to the agreement, the money must be paid back within a year.[17]

Harper decided to step down, as not only owner, but also president of the club. He said that his decision was due to pressing business and health issues. O'Conner asked Nathan Schoenfeld, president of the Jaycees and other members of the organization to select a local person as president. Bill Purnage, business manager of the Waterloo, Iowa team, stayed in Hot Springs to assist Mrs. Ensminger with the day-to-day business dealings.

Next day, *The Sentinel-Record* reported that Chancellor Sam Garratt was the new president of the Bathers. O'Conner remained as executive-vice president and Dr. Stough continued as vice president. Mrs. Evelyn Ensminger, the wife of Joe Ensminger, high school coach, remained as the business manager and secretary-treasurer. The business office of the Bathers was located on the second floor of the Southern Grill Club on Central Avenue.

The Sentinel-Record, on Sunday, June 1, revealed the personalities involved in the closed meeting at the Majestic Hotel. Bathers' former owner Blake Harper and Leslie O'Conner, vice president and general manager of the White Sox met with other leaders concerning the sale of the team. Those in attendance with Harper and O'Conner were scout Emmett "Red" Ormsby, Herbert Brenner, chairman of the Jaycee development project; Nathan Schoenfield, Jaycee president; Leland Leatherman, chairman of the baseball committee and Joe Kuhel, new team manager. In addition, others attending the meeting were Mrs. Ensminger, "Patsy" O'Rourke, chief scout and Dr. D. B. Stough, vice-president and club advisor.[18]

Competition for the entertainment buck was a big problem for the Bathers. On Friday, May 30, the same night the Bathers hosted Helena at Jaycee Park, midget auto racing fans began to flood the oval on Whittington Avenue. An estimated crowd of 3,000 excited racing fans showed up to watch the spills and thrills. Admissions to the auto races were general admission - $1.25, reserved seating - $1.50, Box Seating - $1.75 and children under 12 (general admission) - 60 cents. A $14,000 "Offy" driven by Leland Music of Dallas plowed into hay bales and overturned on the first lap as flames leaped from the car. Numerous spectators ran to assist the driver, but he was unscathed; however, there was expensive damage to the car. Fred Offenhauser, inventor of the "Offy" engine, dominated Indianapolis Motor Speedway for decades.[19]

As of May 11, Joe Kuhel, new Bathers manager, concluded his 18-year major league career with the Washington Senators and the Chicago White Sox. The left-handed first baseman maintained a .277 major league career batting average. Joe Kuhel, pronounced "Cool," was an ideal name for the new, handsome manager. The players knew they had a talented, well-known former major leaguer at the helm. The players were excited for him to be the field general. Joel Callaway, the 19-year-old right-handed hurler for Hot Springs in 1947, recently related, "When Kuhel arrived in town that was a big deal." All the players knew that Kuhel was a good major league player and it was a good morale booster for the Bathers. Callaway pitched for the Bathers a few months and the team traded him to Amarillo where he met his wife, Ann.[20]

Kuhel began his long professional career in 1924, as he played first base for the Flint Vehicles in the Class B, Michigan-Ontario League. He also played with the Kansas City Blues of the American Association, Springfield Senators in the Illinois-Indiana-Iowa League (Three-I League) and Lincoln Links in the Western League. When returning to the Kansas City Blues, the Washington Senators bought the 6' 180 pound first baseman for $65,000 in 1930.

In 1940, Kuhel blasted 27 round-trippers to tie Zeke Bonura for the most home runs in one season in a White Sox uniform up to that time. In a memorable game in 1937, Joe smacked the ball all over the field as he hit three triples. The new Spa manager played with the Washington Senators in the 1933 World Series against New York Giants. The Giants took the Series in five games and "Red" Ormsby was part of the umpiring crew during that Series.

Two ads, printed side by side, appeared in *The Sentinel-Record* on Friday, June 5. The baseball admission prices: adults – general admission: 75 cents, children: 25 cents and box seats: $1.00 (tax included). There was free admission (except tax) to all females attending a Bathers game on "Ladies Night," as the first pitch began at 8:00 p.m. The auto races advertisement listed $1.25 for adult general admission, children (under 12) general admission 60 cents, $1.50 reserved seat (tax included) and $1.75 for box seats (tax included). Time trials began at 7:30 p.m. and the main events started at 8:00 p.m. Paid attendance for the baseball game was 875 that evening, while the attendance for the auto races was over 2,000. Of course, the races ran once a week and the Bathers played more frequently.[21]

At this time, the Greenwood Dodgers shared the lead with the Greenville Bucks in the CSL. However, Greenwood was all alone at the top in paid attendance, while the total figure for the

Bathers was dismal. The office of Jim Griffith, president of the Cotton States League, released the paid attendance numbers on Sunday, June 8. Greenwood topped the circuit with 16,577. Clarksdale's figures were 12,570, while El Dorado tallied 11,256. The bottom half of the league included Greenville - 10,750, Hot Springs - 6,379 and Helena -5,062.

On Monday, June 9, manager Kuhel conducted a baseball clinic for the younger generation at Jaycee Park. Kuhel, assisted by other Bathers, demonstrated the fundamentals of baseball to about a 100 youngsters. The high school athletic department, the Boys Club and the YMCA requested the clinic and the Bathers were delighted to take part in the event.

The fans of Hot Springs were getting to know the new manager and they liked what they saw. On June 26, Kuhel's 41st birthday, the fans gave the manager a party before the Greenwood game at Jaycee Park. Kuhel received a birthday cake, traveling kit and a kiss from attractive Miss Dorothy Gullett, runner-up in the recent Miss Hot Springs beauty contest. Bill Bailey, local radio personality, was the host for the party. The Greenwood Dodgers celebrated in another way as they thrashed the Bathers 11-6.

"Civitan and Lion Clubs Set Baseball Back 50 Years, But Bring In Dough For Junior Chamber Baseball Fund" was the title of an article on the local sports page. About 800 fans turned out at Jaycee Park on Tuesday evening, July 1, for an enjoyable time as the crowd donated nearly $300 to the Jaycee Baseball Fund. After nearly three-hours, fatigue was rampant on both teams, so they just called it quits after 6 2/3 innings.

Dr. Henry Van Patter, Dr. L. E. Reed, J. R. Smith and football coach Joe Ensminger tossed for the Lions. Dr. Van Patter returned to the mound to extinguish the red-hot Civitans as the Lions roared to victory. Many regular baseball rules were heaved over the fence or some place. The trio of Civitan pitchers included Al "Lefty" Lasky, Lee Martin and Leonard Ellis.

The hitting star of the night was Leonard Ellis who collected a triple and a double for the second place Civitan team, while teammate George Eckel spanked a double. Roy Bosson and George Callahan were the umpires. In the third inning, the Civitans complained to Callahan of a bad call. Due to the call, the Civitans presented Callahan with a seeing-eye dog, dark glasses and a tin cup. "Emcee Bill Bailey's caustic quips from the public address booth were well received."[22]

When the smoke had cleared, the Lions were leading 19-13, but because the game had been declared over midway in an inning, the score reverted to the previous inning. The final count gave the 'Roaring' Lions a 15-13 victory and the right to clash with the Optimists in a similar exchange of antics.[23]

Dorsey "Rod" Roddenberry, a local Hot Springs commercial photographer, "traded his darkroom for a diamond." Roddenberry, former semi-pro baseball player and professional umpire, signed a contract in July to umpire in the CSL. Jim Griffith, president of the CSL, assigned Roddenberry to the four-game Hot Springs-Helena series beginning Tuesday night, July 22, at Jaycee Park. Roddenberry worked with Jim Elder of Philadelphia, PA, in a two-man officiating crew.

Elder told Jack Bales about an amusing incident that occurred in 1947 when Elder was umpiring in the Cotton States League. Bales remembered, "Elder was scared of Harry Chozen," then player-manager of the Greenville Bucks. One night, Elder made a call at home plate and Chozen came tearing out of the dugout toward Elder. The umpire was thinking, "This could be it." Chozen ran up to Elder and said, "Have you ever eaten at Coy's Steak House?" Chozen told Elder, "You don't have to be afraid of me; I'm just out here having fun." Jack said that Jim Elder was a "good guy."[24]

The facilities at Jaycee Park were still in the process of being completed. "All but a small portion of the aluminum roof has been placed on the Jaycee grandstand. Club and shower rooms are now available for both home and visiting teams."[25]

The Chicago White Sox considered Hot Springs to be a prime target as a baseball-training center. "The purpose," Leslie O'Connor said, "is to get as many boys who want to play baseball and give them a chance to show their wares before competent men who are experts at the game."

He also remarked that he was focusing on high school graduates who enjoy playing the game of baseball. There was no mention of a starting date. [26]

Hot Springs was a hotbed of baseball and softball. On Aug. 3, four articles appeared in *The Sentinel-Record*, that pertained to baseball teams in the area and the other article was about softball. The baseball contests involved a twin bill with the Bathers and Greenville. The Bucks topped the Spa team twice by the scores of 7-0 and 7-4. In semi-pro baseball action, the Julius Greyhounds from Memphis ran into a hornets nest at Sam Guinn Stadium as the Purity Negro All-Stars of Hot Springs whopped the visitors 13-5. Purity won 36 of their 38 scheduled games. The white semi-pro team of Hot Springs traveled to Glenwood and lost in their Sunday afternoon affair, 10-3. The local American Legion team, known as the Hot Springs Junior Bathers, managed by "Mutt" Carrigan, lost in the state Legion tournament at Little Rock. Hot Springs hosted the district fast-pitch softball tournament at Legion Field, located next to the Alligator Farm on Whittington Avenue. One of the greatest fast-pitch softball pitchers in Arkansas history, Charlie Mowery, threw for the Spa squad. The southpaw fastball specialist hurled his team, the Colony Center, to the championship by overpowering the Army-Navy team from Hot Springs, 8-3. [27]

The fans honored manager Kuhel with "Joe Kuhel Night." The event occurred before the Bathers-Oilers game at Jaycee Park on Thursday, August 28. The popular manager received gifts for his first-class managerial efforts. Joe McRae, Johnny Robbins and James Dowds headed the "Kuhel Night" committee, sponsored by the Optimist Club. Kuhel also received a life membership to the Hot Springs Optimist Club.

We are honoring Joe Kuhel for his untiring efforts to re-establish organized baseball in Hot Springs, declared McRae. Also, we appreciate his efforts in the summer baseball program in which the Optimists participated. On the field and off, Joe has endeared himself to all the people of Hot Springs for his clean sportsmanship and other traits of character. [28]

Kuhel stated in reserved fashion, "It's baseball and I love it." He said that the fans and media were tremendous to work with and he had an excellent experience in Hot Springs.

I was sent here primarily to teach kids the fundamentals of baseball and get them ready for the big leagues. I like this job of manager, and hope to be skipper of a Major League club sometime in the future.[29]

As soon as the season ended, Joe planned to fly to Chicago to be with his vacationing wife and son. After a brief rest at his home in Kansas City, Missouri, he would return to Hot Springs in late September to prepare for the Chicago White Sox tryout camp at Jaycee Park on Oct. 1.

On Sunday, August 31, "Mrs. Baseball," Mrs. Marie E. "Mom" Peters, a 20-year resident of Hot Springs celebrated her 70th birthday by attending a Bathers doubleheader. Later, the Bathers planned to escort "Mom" to the DeSoto Hotel's Mural Dining Room for an exquisite dinner. Manager Kuhel, pitchers Bill Matte, Pete Wojie, Paul Wright and Tom Hamill prepared to be her dinner escorts. The amazing Mrs. Peters had perfect attendance at Bathers' home games since Hot Springs joined the Cotton States League in 1938. A native of Missouri, her favorite major league team was the St. Louis Cardinals.

The same day, the Bathers played host to the El Dorado Oilers. Hot Springs was attempting to stay out of the cellar. The weather crept into the triple digits as El Dorado made it even hotter for the Bathers. The Oilers drubbed the Bathers in the two-game, 37-hit attack, 16-4 and 15-3. Losing a doubleheader was not all that went wrong.

To make matters worse, irate fans, who couldn't hold their cushions or pop bottles, took after Umpire Jim Elder. A police escort had to be called for the young Philadelphian, who had ejected Manager Joe Kuhel from the second game following an argument in the third inning. Elder was showered with cushions and bottles at the close of the dismal double-header. Kuhel had questioned a decision Elder had made at third base.[30]

Following the game, about 150 fans hung around the clubhouse, but the police said there were no other incidents "other than a little profane language." Chancellor Sam Garratt, president of the Hot Springs Bathers Baseball Club stated that the cushion-throwing incident was "disgraceful."

Quarter-horse racing at Whittington Park Speedway, a golf tournament at the Hot Springs Country Club, recreational fishing and boating on Lakes Catherine and Hamilton challenged the baseball dollar on Labor Day, Monday, Sept. 1. Seven quarter-horse races took place at the Whittington Park Speedway. Thirty-seven horses entered the contests that began at 8:00 p.m. The last race was a "run-off race" or challenge race in which the winners of the first six races ran in order to determine the overall winner.

The same day, the Bathers closed out their season with a doubleheader against El Dorado. Excellent crowds were at all events. Around 1,300 fans sat through the sizzling heat of 106 degrees to watch the Bathers drill the Oilers 6-5 and 7-6 in the final battles of the season. The National Park Service recorded a light rainfall of .01 inches in mid-afternoon.

At intermission an awards presentation took place. Bathers' right fielder Jim Wilson collected two watches. Lewis Jewelers donated a watch to Wilson for hitting the most home runs, while Edwards Art Gallery gave the slugger a watch for being the team RBI leader. A watch from Lewis Jewelers went to first baseman, Bill Haschak, for copping the team batting title. Haschak finished third in the Cotton States League batting race with a .334 mark. In addition, each player received $29.00 from the Bathers appreciation fund headed by Clarence Miller and Mrs. Marie "Mom" Peters.

The final CSL season standings were, in order of finish, (1) Greenwood, Greenville, (3) El Dorado, (4) Clarksdale, (5) Hot Springs and (6) Helena. The Bathers missed the post-season playoffs.

The Nick R. Overstreet Award went to Dr. H. King Wade as he captured the Labor Day Handicap Golf Tournament by posting 134 in the 36-hole match. Tommy Dodson shot a 137, followed by a tie among R. L. Jacobs, Billie Joe Wilkins and Dr. Bobby Lee with 139. Approximately 50 golfers participated in the Hot Springs Country Club's annual amateur event.

On Sept. 7, the Bathers announced that the White Sox filed articles of incorporation in Little Rock. "This is a mere technicality made for tax purposes." The Spa team stated that the majority stockholder is Leslie O'Connor, business manager of the White Sox.

At a meeting in Hot Springs, September 21, the Cotton States League tentatively accepted teams from Pine Bluff, Arkansas and Natchez, Mississippi, as members of the loop for 1948. Eligibility of the new franchises included posting $1,500 by each team no later than November 1, 1947. Jim Griffith, president of the circuit, stated that the acceptance vote was unanimous.[31]

The White Sox planned to promote Joe Kuhel to take over the managerial reins of the 1948 Muskegon Clippers of the Class A, Central League in Michigan. However, on October 4, Clark Griffith, owner of the Washington Senators, phoned him from New York and asked if he wanted to manage his old team, the Senators. "Kuhel all but shattered the phone's mouthpiece with his eager acceptance." That was a big step from Class C to the major leagues. The Senators finished in seventh place in 1948, but they lacked top-notch players for them to make a run for the pennant.[32]

A successful 15-day Chicago White Sox tryout school ended on October 15, in Hot Springs as the Pale Hose signed 14 of the 143 players. According to "Patsy" O'Rourke, Chisox scout in charge of the project, the average age of the participants was 19-years old. Perk Purnhage, tryout school secretary, stated that among the 14 signed players included a catcher, nine pitchers and four infielders. Among the Arkansas signees were Bennie Smith, Hot Springs; Tilford Owens, Hot Springs; Mahlon Winston, Sheridan and J. C. Peckham, Little Rock.

Instructors at the school included Johnny Rigney, Joe O'Rourke, "King" Lear, Jack Onslow, Johnny Mostil, "Red" Ormsby, Tony Chernetsky and Joe Kuhel. Following the World Series, Rogers Hornsby flew in from New York and held an hour and a half instructional batting clinic daily, for the last ten days of the school.

Whittington Park – Dedicated Ban Johnson Field in 1935 –
first home of the Bathers from 1938-1941 [GCHS]

"Spike" Hunter – Pitched for HS in 1938 - picture taken c.1927 –
spring training when he played for the Dallas Steers - Whittington Park [Debbie Lax]

"Spike" Hunter – (p) taken spring 1927 – Whittington Park –
with Cleveland Indians hurler Willis Hudlin [Debbie Lax]

Philadelphia A's and Dallas Steers – Spring Training 1927 – Thomas Edison's home in
Florida – Thomas Edison (center front) - "Spike" Hunter (Dallas Steers) is top left – 3
over (next to "Lefty" Grove). Many baseball notables in this picture: Connie Mack,
"Lefty" Grove, Eddie Collins, Al Simmons, Jimmie Foxx, Rube Walberg, Ed Rommel
and Earle Mack (son of Connie) [Debbie Lax]

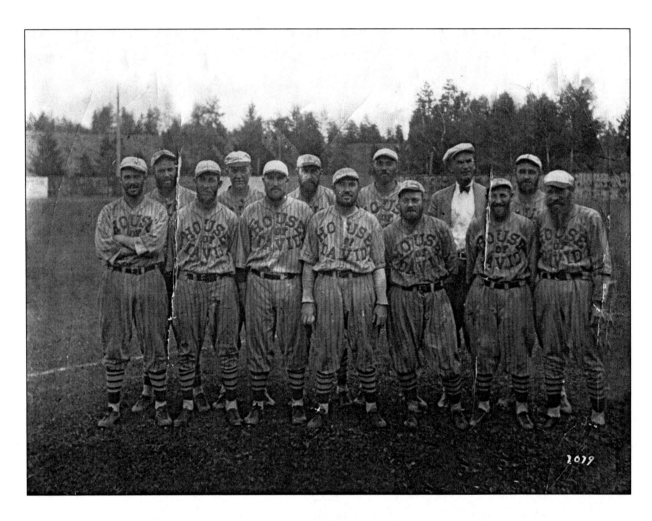

House of David - c. 1934 – "Spike" Hunter – Top row left -

next to Grover Cleveland Alexander [Debbie Lax]

Erb Wheatley, owner of one share of 1938 Bathers stock worth $25.00 [GCHS]

1941 Hot Springs Bathers – "The Little Yankees" [The Sentinel-Record]

Mamie Ruth (Stranburg) Abernathy - late 1930s & early 1940s –
Bathers secretary [M.R. Abernathy]

Evelyn Ensminger - 1947-48 Bathers secretary - [Joanne Ensminger Moore]

1947 Bathers – Front row: (L-R) Walt Lenczyk (3b), Pete Green (ss), Pete Wojey (p), Joe Kuhel (Mgr/1b), Joe Callaway (p), Tony Zini (c), Mike D'Antonio (of). Back Row: Art Hamilton (p), Joe Santomaturo (p), Tom Mabry (lf), Jim Wilson (rf), Harley Biggs (2b), Doyle "Red" Morris (c), Bill Haschak (1b) and Bill Lakics (cf) [Joel Callaway]

1947 (3 Catchers) – L-R-Catchers Doyle "Red" Morris and Tony Zini receive instructions from former major league catcher Earl "Oil" Smith (center) [Tony Zini]

1947 - Ed Herlein – ss/3b [Ed Herlein]

1948 Team – Front row: (L-R) George Kuchurek (of), Jim Kamis (p), Tony Zini (c), Ed McGhee (rf), Herb Adams (cf), Dick Strahs (p), Joe Holden (Mgr.), Harry Salvatore (Inf), Bill Haschak (1b), Ray Rapacki (p), Russell Kurowski (p) and Bill Jackson (c). Back row: Dominic Coughlin (p), Andy Baud (lf), Martin Kaelin (inf), Ed Herlein (p), Charlie Schmidt (ss), Dick Fuller (3b), Bob George (c), Bob Newbecker (p), Art Hamilton (p) and Jeff Peckham (p). [Tony Zini]

1948 Team (in circle) - Dick Strahs p-(with ball), (continue right) Herb Adams (cf), Ed McGhee (rf), Andy Baud (lf), George Kuchurek (rf), Harry Salvatore (ut), Bill Haschak (1b), Charlie Schmidt (ss), Ed Herlein (inf), Martin Kaelin (2b), Dick Fuller (3b), Tony Zini (c), Bill Jackson (c), Bob George (c), Jim Kamis (p), Bob Newbecker (p), Jeff Peckham (p), Art Hamilton (p), Dominic Coughlin (p), Ray Rapachi (p) and Russ Kurowski (p). Joe Holden (Mgr) in middle. [GCHS]

1948 Team – Front row: (L-R) Johnny Rigney, White Sox farm director, George Sobek (Mgr./2b), Herb Adams (cf), Paul Wright (p), Andy Baud (lf), Ed McGhee (rf) and Harry Salvatore (inf). Top row: Fred Shaffer (scout), Charlie Comiskey II (White Sox front office), __?___, Ray Rapacki (p), Charlie Schmidt (ss), Art Hamilton (p), Bill Haschak (1b), Tony Zini (c), Warren Kjellenberg (c), Nick Coughlin (p), Jim Kamis (p), Pete Heinen (p) and Carl Fuller (3b) [Tony Zini]

1948 Spring training with Rogers Hornsby (middle)

& Herb Adams (far right) [Tony Zini]

Herb Adams – 1948 – centerfielder[Herb Adams]

Baseball History of Herb Adams

Year	Team/State/League	Class
1947	Madisonville Miners (KY) -- KY-Ill-Tenn	D
1948	Hot Springs Bathers (AR) Cotton States	C
1948	Chicago White Sox - Majors	ML
1949	Chicago White Sox - Majors	ML
1949	Memphis Chicks (TN) – Southern Assoc.	AA
1950	Chicago White Sox - Majors	ML
1950	Buffalo Bisons (NY) – International	AAA
1950-52	United States Army	----
1953	Springfield Cubs (MA) - International	AAA
1953	Indianapolis Indians (IN) – Am. Assoc.	AAA
1954	Los Angeles Angels (CA) - Pacific Coast	AAA
1954	Columbus Red Birds (OH) - Am. Assoc.	AAA
1955	Houston Buffaloes (TX) - Texas	AA
1955	Omaha Cardinals (NE) – Am. Assoc.	AAA
1956-58	Houston Buffaloes (TX) - Texas	AA
1959	Mobile Bears (AL) – Southern Assoc.	AA

Herb Adams – data [Herb Adams]

Tony Zini-1947-1948- Catcher [Tony Zini]

Baseball Career of "Tony" Zini

Year	Team	Class
1944	Knoxville Smokies/Mobile Bears – Southern Assoc.	AA
1944	Kingsport Cherokees (TN) - Appalachian	D
1944-46	United States Army	----
1946	Zanesville Dodgers (OH) - Ohio State	D
1947	Hot Springs Bathers (AR) - CSL	C
1948	Hot Springs Bathers (AR) - CSL	C
1949	Helena Seaporters (AR) - CSL	C
1949	Natchez Indians (MS) - CSL	C
1950	Natchez Indians (MS) - CSL	C

Tony Zini data [Tony Zini]

Joe Kuhel- (Mgr./1b) -1947 - Fans celebrate Kuhel's birthday with birthday cake - Bill Bailey (MC) & Dorothy Gullett (contestant in the Miss Hot Springs Pageant) [GCHS]

Bill Bailey kisses Mgr. Kuhel at BD party – 1947 [GCHS]

Dorothy Gullett kisses Mgr. Kuhel at BD party – 1947 [GCHS]

Dick Strahs – (p) 1948 [M. R. Abernathy]

Ed McGhee – (of) 1948 [M. R. Abernathy]

Charlie Schmidt – (ss) 1948 [M. R. Abernathy]

Andy Baud – (of) 1948 [M. R. Abernathy]

Art Hamilton – (p) 1948 [M. R. Abernathy]

Bill Haschak – (1b) 1948 [M. R. Abernathy]

Art Hamilton (p) & Tony Zini (c) – 1947-1948 [Tony Zini]

Herb Adams – Receives 1948 MVP trophy [Tony Zini]

George Sobek – 1948 (Mgr./2b) [GCHS]

Dick Strahs – 1948 hurls perfect game – carried off field [Tony Zini]

Dick Fuller – (3b) 1948

"Mom" Peters – Recognition Night – 1948 – She had perfect attendance
at Bathers home games since the 1938 season [Tony Zini]

"Mom" Peters – Recognition Night – 1948 [Tony Zini]

Herb Adams – Chicago White Sox bought outfielder following
1948 season. [Herb Adams]

Billy Conn - pro boxer- Bathers delayed game in 1941 to listen to the Louis-Conn fight -
Conn in buggy with Hot Springs Mayor Leo McLaughlin – late 40s [Tim Conn]

1949 Team – Front row: (L-R) Ray Wallace batboy, Pel Austin (inf/of)(4th from left)
and Claude "Swifty" Dick-batboy (far right front row). Back row:
far left – Jack Drobena (team trainer). [GCHS]

1950 Team – Front row: (L-R) Claude "Swifty" Dick (batboy), Bill Gingerich (p), Ray Baer (p), Tony Gubicza (p), Bill Maley (c), Marty Lee (c), Erv Rabka (2b), Jerry Brazen (3b), Alex Cosmidis (ss) and Bob Hoeft (of). Back row: Johnny Antonelli (Mgr.), Don Tierney (p), Danny Caccavo (p), Steve Solis (of), Fred Wasiluk (c), Ed Schafer (p), Dan Phalen (1b), Joe Jaworski (of), Joe DeGrazia (2b), Jack Colburn (p) and Harry Montgomery (p). [GCHS]

1951 - Rex Carr – Mgr. [GCHS]

1952 – Team – Front row: (L-R) Wally Rasmussen (rf), Don Hilbert (of), Ben Day (p), Bill Gingrich (p), Bob Benish, (mgr./p), Kirby Dickens (ss), Olen "Tuffy" Owens (of/p), Richard Collins (p), Jerry Durnin (2b) and Clarence "Babe" Tuckey (3b). Back row: Bob Passarella (1b/util), ?McCalman, Ed Jacobson (lf), Ken Fentem (p), Vernon "Moose" Shetler (1b), Joe Stern (lf), Fred Wasiluk (c), Bob Zolliecoffer (p) and Wayne Parks (p) [GHSC-identified by Bob Passarella] – Many players rotated in and out during season [GCHS]

1952-1953 - Bob Passarella (inf/of) – [Bob Passarella]

Baseball History of Bob Passarella

Year	Team	Class
1945-47	United States Army	----
1947	Hornell Maples (NY) - PONY	D
1948	Semi-Pro	
1949	Sioux Falls Canaries (SD) - Northern	C
1949	Carthage Cubs (MO) - KOM	D
1950	Semi-Pro	
1951	Cordele A's (GA) - GA/FI	D
1951	Americus Rebels (GA) – GA/FL	D
1952	Hot Springs Bathers (AR) - CSL	C
1953	Hot Springs Bathers (AR) - CSL	C

1952-1953 – Passarella Data [Bob Passarella]

1952 – Jim "Shanty" Hogan – (p) [GCHS]

1952 – Clarence "Babe" Tuckey – (3b) [GCHS]

Bert Shepard (p) – played for Bathers in 1952 - Shepard slips on his
artificial leg as a Washington Senator - 1945 [National Baseball Hall of Fame].

1952 – Fred Wasiluk (c) [GCHS]

1952-1955 – Jack Bales (c) In 1949 Thomasville, GA uniform [Jack Bales]

Baseball History of Jack Bales

Year	Team/State/League	Class
1948	Montgomery Rebels (GA) - Southeastern	B
1949	Durham Bulls (NC) - Carolina	B
1949	Thomasville Tigers (GA) – GA/FL	D
1950	Rome Colonels (NY) – Canadian/American	C
1951	Davenport Tigers (IA) – Three-I	B
1952	Durham Bulls (NC) - Carolina	B
1952	Greenville Spinners (SC) Tri State	B
1952	Hot Springs Bathers (AR) - CSL	C
1953	Hot Springs Bathers (AR) - CSL	C
1954	Hot Springs Bathers (AR) - CSL	C
1955	Port Arthur Sea Hawks – Big State	B
1955	Lake Charles Lakers – Evangeline	C
1955	Hot Springs Bathers - CSL	C

1952-1955- Jack Bales Data [Jack Bales]

Umpires – Cotton States League c. 1948 – (L-R) Harold Willson,
Dorsey "Rod" Roddenberry and Jim Elder [Betty Elder]

Jim Elder – Umpire – Cotton States League 1947-1948 [Betty Elder]

Professional Career
James Albert Elder

Year	Location	Occupation
1947-48	Cotton States League	Umpire
1949-50	Southeastern League	Umpire
1951	Hot Springs Bathers	Gen. Mgr.
1952-53	Florida International League	Umpire
1953-64	Youth/School Leagues	Umpire/Ref
1960-93	Arkansas Travelers (LR)	Play-by-Play
1965-98	KARN Radio Network (LR)	Sportscaster
1970-97	Arkansas Razorbacks Football	Statistician

Jim received "Arkansas Sportscaster of the Year" honors 11 times. The Arkansas Sports Hall of Fame inducted Jim to the high honor in 2007.
Jim Elder (1924-1998)
Family notes Aug. 2009

Jim Elder Data [Betty Elder]

c. 1950s – Jaycee Park – winter scene [Caleb Hardwick]

1953 – Major league players visit Hot Springs during pre-spring training (L-R) Jack McMahan (p) in Yankees farm system, (child-Roy Campenella II), Roy Campanella (c) Brooklyn Dodgers, Joe Black (p) Brooklyn Dodgers, Jack Bales (c) Bathers and Guy Cook (p) Bathers [The Sentinel-Record]

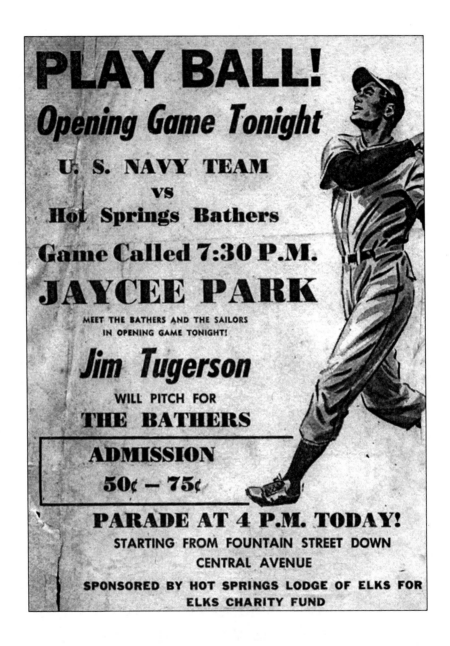

Jim Tugerson advertisement in local paper – 1953 - He pitched against the Navy team during a pre-season exhibition game [The Sentinel-Record]

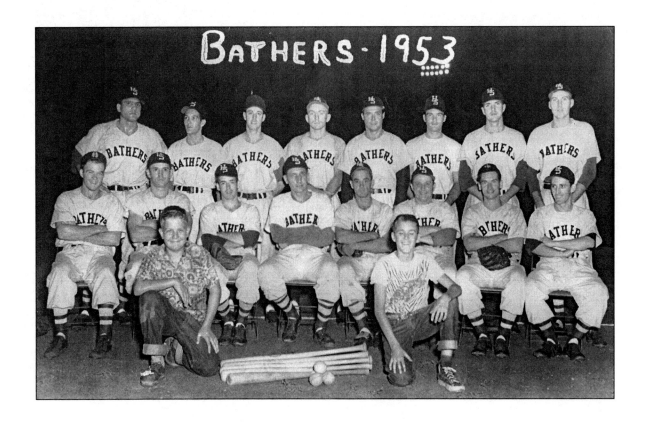

1953 Team – Front row: (L-R) Billy Bales and M. D. Graham (batboys) 2nd row: Claude "Swifty" Dick (p), Bob Adcock (lf), Bob Gibbons (p) Vernon "Moose" Shetler (mgr/1b), Hal Martin (cf), "Babe" Tuckey (3b), Steve Korfonta (rf) and Nellie Campver (p). Back row: Nick Demus (c/p), Manny Fernandez (p), Bob Passarella (ss), Jack Bales (c), Al Ronay (p), Bill Giddings (2b), Tommy Ward (p) and Kenny Siefert (p) [GCHS]

1953 – April 23 - Opening Night – Jaycee Park – Hot Springs dignitaries ready for pre-game activities - Front row: (L-R) – Judge Clyde Brown, Milton Nobles and Judge Sam Garratt. Standing - "Blind" Bill Durant, Tony Zale (pro boxer), ___?__, H. King Wade, Sr., Louis Goltz, ___?___, Earl Ricks (coat on arm), Jack McJunkin (behind Ricks), Will Lake (fishing hat), Q. Bryum Hurst, Dr. Lawrence Akers (behind Hurst), Warren Angel and Van Lyell, Sr. [Goltz family]

1953 - Lewis Goltz swinging – Pre-game activities -
opening night – 1953 [Goltz family]

1953 – Jim Tugerson (p) with the Knoxville Smokies –
[Minor League Baseball]

Jim and Leander Tugerson planned to pitch for the Bathers – 1953 [The Sentinel-Record]

1953 – Jim Tugerson (p) and other Bathers listening to a report from the league commissioner that was read over the loud speaker at Jaycee Park denying Tugerson to pitch in the league. The game against Jackson declared a forfeit. [The Sentinel-Record]

1953- Hal Martin (cf) – Set home run record in the CSL
smashing 41 round trippers. [Don Duren]

Bob Passarella – (inf./OF) 1952-1953 [Don Duren]

Tommy Ward (p) – 1953 [Don Duren]

SEASON
1954

The COUPONS IN THIS BOOK

00247

Est. Price 11.48
Fed. Tax 2.30
State Tax .22

Total $14.00

ARE EACH GOOD FOR ONE ADMISSION TO
HOT SPRINGS BATHERS
20 Grand Stand Tickets for $14.00
AVOID CONGESTION AT GATE

Issued to

TICKETS ARE NOT GOOD IF DETACHED FROM THIS BOOK

WELDON, WILLIAMS & LICK, FT. SMITH, ARK.

1954 - Bathers season coupons booklet [Donny Whitehead]

1954 – Paul "Daffy" Dean (Bathers owner/mgr) [Don Duren]

Uvoyd Reynolds

1954 – 18-year-old Uvoyd Reynolds (of) broke the color line in the Cotton States League on July 20. The recent Langston High School (Hot Springs) graduate and three-sport letterman played right field for the Bathers. He turned down several college football scholarships to play professional baseball. [The Sentinel-Record]

1955 - Rudy Mayling (of) [Goltz family]

1955 – Rod Tangeman (p) [Goltz family]

1955 – Kirby Dickens (ss) [Goltz family]

1954-1955 – Ed White (p) [White family]

Lon Warneke
"The Arkansas Hummingbird"

Lon "The Arkansas Hummingbird" Warneke – Major League Pitcher -
Instrumental in obtaining Bathers franchise in 1938 [Don Duren]

Mike Ilitch – Played 2nd base for Bathers in 1952 – currently owner of Little Caesar's Pizza, the Detroit Red Wings (NHL) and the Detroit Tigers (MLB). Ilitch hoisting American League trophy won by Detroit in 2006 [Ilitch Holdings, Inc.]

Argenta Drug Store today – A team from Argenta, AR (now North Little Rock)
participated in the early 1900s against Hot Springs teams. The historic
drug store is located on Main St. in NLR [Don Duren]

Jaycee Park today – used by youth & high school teams [Don Duren]

Jaycee Park today – [Don Duren]

Chapter 9

Herbie and the Red Hot Bathers
1948

"Bathers Stop Greenwood 5-2, to Cop Playoff Title." The Sentinel-Record

In the second post-war season, the Cotton States League re-elected Jim Griffith, from El Dorado, as league president. Griffith stated that the financial status of the league was in good shape, but the ballparks needed upgrading. The expanded league greeted Pine Bluff, Arkansas and Natchez, Mississippi to the loop. The new eight-team Cotton States League represented four teams from Arkansas that included Hot Springs, El Dorado, Pine Bluff and Helena. Greenville, Greenwood and Clarksdale represented Mississippi. The league drew up a 140-game schedule, 70 at home and 70 on the road for each team.

Joe Holden, 34-year-old manager-catcher of the 1948 Bathers, piloted the Fall River Indians of the Class B, New England League, in 1947. Holden's brief major league stint consisted of catching a few games for the Phillies from 1934-1936. Leslie O'Connor, vice-president of general manager of the Chicago White Sox guided the management of the Bathers. The White Sox purchased the Bathers on May 28, 1947, from then owner, Blake Harper. Chancellor Sam Garratt served his second term as president of the Bathers, while Mrs. Evelyn Ensminger, starting her second year in the Bathers front office, was the club's secretary-treasurer.

Communication among the league newspapers and radio stations needed improvement over the 1947 season. Charles Kerg of the *Greenville Delta Times Record* served as the head of the

Cotton States League sportswriters and that distinguished group planned to improve the league's media program.

There was a boost in player salary and squad limits rose from 15 to 17 players per club. Griffith said that he believed the increase would bring better talent to the league and would allow the teams to carry one or two additional pitchers in their lineups.

Beginning April 1, Johnny Rigney, farm director, supervised spring training for four White Sox farm teams that trained at Hot Springs for several weeks. The highest classification team to train in the Spa was the Class A, Muskegon (Michigan) Clippers of the Central League managed by Bennie Huffman. Pete Fox managed the Waterloo (Iowa) White Hawks in the Class B, Illinois, Indiana & Iowa (Three-I) League. Hot Springs was the Class C representative, while Wisconsin Rapids White Sox came out of the Class D, Wisconsin State League, managed by Frank Demaree.

The 1948 Hot Springs Bathers, led by Joe Holden and affiliated with the Chicago White Sox, received a rousing ovation from the 3,700 excited fans, as the team played their home opener against the Pine Bluff Cardinals on Tuesday night, April 20. Celebrities on hand at the pregame ceremonies included Johnny Rigney, J. P Heil, former Wisconsin Governor and a surprise visit by Tony Zale, then former middleweight boxing champion of the world. Zale, training in Hot Springs for his third fight with Rocky Graziano, geared up for his bout on June 10, in New Jersey. Other celebrities included Hot Springs Mayor Earl Ricks and Lewis Goltz, former president of the Junior Chamber of Commerce, who assisted in the pregame activities. The crowd roared with laughter as many dignitaries participated in a "mock baseball game."

Night games started at 8:00 p.m. at Jaycee Park with the grandstand admission price ranged from 35 cents to 75 cents each. Box seats sold for $1.00 each, while the bleacher seats costs 25 cents to 50 cents per person. The official scorecard, which sold for a nickel, included advertisement, a lucky number and the Bathers season schedule.

The opening home-game hype wasn't enough to help the Watertown Boys win, as the Cardinals squeezed past the Bathers 7-6. By May 6, the Bathers trailed league-leading Greenwood by only a half a game, but Helena was hanging a game behind the Bathers in third spot. A few games later, Pine Bluff bit the dust when shortstop Charlie Schmidt slammed the ball out of the yard in a dramatic 6-3 Bathers triumph.

On May 10, outfielder Andy Baud pulled off one of the most astonishing base stealing feats in CSL history. He singled in the seventh inning to score Ed McGhee. Later, Baud, caught off first, was in a rundown. "Through sly back and forth maneuvering, he dodged four Greenville players." Catcher Martin had him nailed, but slippery and speedy Baud succeeded to outrun all of them to second base. He scored later on Tony Zini's single.[1]

The Bathers and Greenville were deadlocked 13-13 going into the seventh frame on Wednesday, May 13 at Jaycee Park. Tony Zini laced one down the left field line and watched it clear the fence, scoring Martin Kaelin ahead of Zini. The ball bounced back into the field of play, but the umpire ruled it a home run. Lindsay Deal, Greenville manager, rushed out from the visitor's dugout, headed straight to the umpire and vehemently disagreed with the call. The Bucks pilot said it was foul because it hit the light pole; however, the light pole, located close to the foul line, was outside the park. No doubt, it was a close call, but the ump declined to change his original call. The Bucks manager decided to protest the call and the remainder of the game was under protest. Following the protest, "the Bucks took their leisure." Hot Springs won the three hours and 18 minutes game 22-13. Nine pitchers took the hill during the contest as the two teams swung for 31 hits; the Bathers totaled 18 to the Bucks 13 hits. The winning pitcher was Dickie Strahs as 1,600 fans attended the lengthy tilt.[2]

Days later, *Friend News Service* compiled the CSL stats and Herb Adams, diminutive center fielder for Hot Springs, was in third position in the CSL batting race with a strong .391 mark. Three Bathers, Jackson, Zini and Schmidt followed Adams in the race with above .300 averages. Pitchers Kamis and Strahs registered a 3-0 and 2-0 records respectively. The Bathers were off to a good start.

Ed McGhee dazzled the crowd with his hitting display as the Bathers rapped the Seaporters from Helena 7-4. McGhee put on a batting clinic on May 16, as he amassed a pair of doubles and three singles for an incredible five-hit day! Due to McGhee leading the way, the Bathers regained second place in the CSL on May 17.

Ray Rapacki twirled a sparkling 8-0, eight-hit shutout against the Clarksdale Planters at home on May 19. It was a shaky night in the field for the Planters as they racked up nine errors. Steady Herb Adams, the speedy center fielder, made two sensational catches in the center garden for Hot Springs.[3]

The next night, Clarksdale turned the tables on Hot Springs. It was the same score as the night before, but the eight runs were on Clarksdale side of the ledger, while Hot Springs gawked at the zero in their column. The Bathers committed four errors to go along with their seven hits. Strahs (5-1) was the loser for the first time during the 1948 season. Catcher Zini took a spill at home plate and Bill Jackson replaced him behind the plate as over 1,000 fans witnessed the shutout at Jaycee Park.

Hot Springs had some good nights including the 13-3 win over Helena at home on May 21. The next evening the Bathers rallied for two runs in the eighth frame to tie the Seaporters 5-5. In the 14th inning, the Bathers loaded the bases and an error by the Helena shortstop allowed the Bathers to edge the Seaporters 6-5. In an earlier inning, the visiting manager, Wood Johnson lodged a protest. He argued that a ball pitched by reliever Dick Strahs, hit the batter before it hit the bat. Umpire Sam Cirpriani ruled it hit the bat first. With the win, the Hot Water Team remained in second place. On May 20, the Bathers swept the Helena series with a 9-4 win as over 1,000 fans turned out for the third game.

By May 27, Greenwood began to pull away from the pack as second place Hot Springs was five games behind the leader. The Bathers flirted with second and third place for most of the season. Bad times hit the Resort Boys. On June 2, Dick Strahs hurls a two hitter and lost a heartbreaker, 2-1 to El Dorado. On June 4, the Bathers tangled with Natchez and lost a doubleheader 5-4 and 11-3.

Due to the serious illness of manager Joe Holden's wife in Easton, Pennsylvania, Holden took a leave of absence. Between the doubleheader on June 4, the fans gave 35-year-old Holden a combination farewell-birthday celebration at Jaycee Park. Holden received a traveling bag, as well as a pen and pencil set. George Sobek of Hammond, Indiana, took over as acting manager of the Bathers. Holden's return to the pilot's position was uncertain at the time, but Joe never returned as manager of the Bathers. Before arriving in Hot Springs, Sobek played for Waterloo, Iowa, in the Class B, Three-I League. He planned to play second base and outfield for Hot Springs.[4]

Genora "Tony" Zini, the mainstay catcher for the Bathers noted that even though manager Holden's stay was short, Zini learned much from Holden about catching. In 1947, Earl "Oil" Smith, former major league catcher helped coach the Bathers. Zini said that he learned a lot from him, too. In 1947 and 1948, Zini's salary of $400 a month was an excellent salary for a Class C catcher at that time. He said that he received the same salary when he played for Knoxville, before the war, so the Bathers agreed to continue to pay him the $400 a month.

Tony's grandparents and family arrived in New Orleans from Italy in the early 1900s. At that time, Felix, Tony's father, was 9-years old. The Zini family traveled to a small town in Mississippi where his grandparents began working on a farm. When Felix was 16, he was working as a Red Cap at the local train station. On a wet night, Felix slipped on the rails, rendering him unconscious. The engineer of an on-coming train didn't see the teenager lying on the tracks and the train severed Felix's right arm. Tony said, "It was a tragic accident, but it could have been much worse." The medical community and others in the area nurtured young Zini back to health. He became proficient with his left arm and hand.

Later, Felix and his wife, Stella, moved to North Little Rock, Arkansas, where Tony was born. The family lived in North Little Rock, but when Tony became school-age he attended school in Little Rock because his father owned property in both cities. Felix bought a grocery store in Little Rock and the family assisted in managing the store located in the downtown area of the capital city. The police and firemen frequented the grocery store and from time to time, the police brought prisoners into Felix's store. The prisoners noticed little Zini running around the store, but the prisoners couldn't pronounced his first name, Genora. So, the prisoners nicknamed him "Tony," a good Italian name.

Tony played baseball beginning at a young age in Little Rock. In high school, he was a standout player on the American Legion baseball team. During the 1944 baseball season, Tony's senior year at Little Rock High School, 17-year-old Zini signed a professional baseball contract with the Knoxville Smokies/Mobile Bears of the Southern Association. Even though the Little Rock American Legion Doughboys baseball team, known statewide for their talent, the move from the Legion ranks to the professional scene was huge. Mobile moved their franchise to Knoxville several years earlier and played out of Knoxville until July 1944, at which time the Class A-1 team moved to Mobile. Little Rock High School transferred his high school credits to Knoxville where Tony continued his education. A month before graduation, Tony broke his finger playing for Knoxville. However, upon graduation, he returned to Arkansas and graduated with his class at Little Rock. At his high school commencement ceremonies, he walked across the stage with a broken finger in a cast. Following graduation, the team sent him to the Kingsport (TN) Cherokees in the Class D, Appalachian League.

World War II raged all over the globe. At the end of the season, 18-year-old Zini joined another team, called the United States Navy. After boot camp, the Navy sent Tony to Camp Elliott in San Diego, California, where he made the baseball team. Sports continued to be an important aspect of the military. Base Commanders usually wanted the best athletes on their base, so their military installation would finish high in the athletic standings. Winning was good for morale and it gave the base commanders bragging rights among their peers. For six months, Tony played on the same team with Bob Lemon. Two years later, Lemon signed a Cleveland Indians contract and became one of the elite pitchers in baseball. In 1976, Lemon became a member of the National Baseball Hall of Fame.

After about six months of playing baseball for the Navy, Tony sustained an injury, which ended his military baseball career. He said when injured players were out of action for any length of time, the Navy transferred them to their regular job. Therefore, Zini headed to the ocean and worked on the USS Shipley Bay (CVE-85), an escort carrier. He visited many places in the world including five of the seven seas.

In 1946, at 19-years of age, Zini came marching home. On June 30, 1946, he signed a baseball contract for $315.00 a month with Knoxville, a Brooklyn Dodgers farm team. Since he had been on a ship, he was out of baseball shape, so Mobile released him to the Zanesville Dodgers of the Class D, Ohio State League. He played briefly with them until the end of the 1946 season and then entered Little Rock Junior College (now University of Arkansas at Little Rock). He continued to play professional baseball in the summer and attend LRJC in the offseason.

In 1947, at 20 years old, Tony traveled to Hot Springs to become the popular catcher for the Bathers. The workhorse catcher caught 110 games for the Spa team and batted .266. Zini returned to the Bathers the following season and he stated that the 1948 season was one of his most memorable of his career. He said the people in Hot Springs were great fans and he enjoyed playing in the Spa with a great group of young men. "The 1948 Hot Springs Bathers was the best team I ever played on," declared Zini. He enjoyed reading Maurice Moore's sports columns in *The Sentinel-Record*. Moore followed the team all over the place as he wrote about the Bathers. "He was a tremendous sports editor and supporter of the Bathers," Zini noted. Tony thought Jack Drobena, the Bathers' trainer, did an excellent job keeping the players healthy.

In the spring of 1949, Zini decided to be a holdout by demanding a higher salary, with the Waterloo White Hawks of the Class B, 3-I League. He said that was a bad idea because management didn't like that move. His next stop was Natchez of the Cotton States League.

Tony recalled an incident that occurred when he played with the Natchez Indians in 1950. Zini faced the hard-throwing bespeckled pitcher Ryne Duren of the Pine Bluff Judges. Due to Duren's notorious wildness, many players in the batter's box stayed loose when they faced the big man with thick glasses. Tony recalled once when he faced Duren, the 21-year-old pitcher buzzed a fastball at Tony's noggin and Zini hit the deck! Once was enough. Bat in hand, Zini charged the mound. Zini said he was ready to wrap the club around Duren's head, but the big pitcher quickly apologized to Zini for the incident and there was no negative aftermath. Boys will be boys! A few years later, in 1958, Duren was the number one relief pitcher for the New York Yankees, saving 20 games, a league high. He played 10 years in the majors saving 57 games and ended up with a respectable .3.83 ERA mark.

Following the 1950 season, the 23-year-old Zini decided to hang up his uniform and finish his college degree. He had about two years of college under his belt, so he decided to head to Razorback Land. He earned his business degree from the University of Arkansas in 1952, the same year he married a University of Arkansas graduate, Alyce Jane (A.J.). He and A. J. met at LRJC a few years earlier. Tony was the first in his family to graduate from college and he is proud to say that the younger generation in his family, are all University of Arkansas graduates. Within hours following graduation, EXXON hired him where he worked for 35 years before retiring. He enjoys playing golf "a lot." He enjoyed hunting pheasants and quails, but golf is now his number one hobby. He and his wife are active members at their church in North Little Rock, Arkansas. Since his mother lived to the age of 105, Tony may have many more years to visit the links.[5]

On June 5, 28-year-old George Sobek officially took over the reins as manager of the Bathers. Sobek played baseball and basketball for Notre Dame. The multi-talented athlete won All-America honors in basketball with the Fighting Irish in 1941. While serving with the Navy, Sobek continued his baseball exploits. Following his military duties, the veteran played briefly in the baseball minor leagues and managed several teams. He played professional basketball with the Toledo Jeeps in the National Basketball League (forerunner of the NBA). During the 1946-1947 basketball season, he was the league's sixth leading scorer.

Billy Hornsby's debut with the Bathers occurred on June 13. Billy, son of the Hall of Fame player, Rogers Hornsby, "smashed out two doubles and a triple and made two sensational catches in right field." He arrived in Hot Springs on an option from another White Sox farm team, the Class B, Waterloo (Iowa) White Hawks of the Three-I League. He replaced Ed McGhee, who went on the disabled list due to a leg injury. Hornsby's stay in the Spa was brief, as he was a well-traveled minor league player, returning to Waterloo on June 19. Rogers Hornsby discussed his son Billy. "I'm glad Billy learned early that he wasn't a player." Hornsby continued, "This no longer is a game for guys that are destined to stay in the minors. And imagine how I would have felt, seeing the Hornsby name down in the batting averages with the pitchers." [6-7]

On June 14, Herb Adams led the loop in hitting with an astounding .401 batting average. He was the only Bather in the top dozen in the hitting department. In 53 games, Adams appeared at the plate 237 times, scoring 53 runs. He led the league with 95 hits as he punched in 33 RBIs. Dick Strahs chalked up an 8-3 pitching record, which tied him for fourth in the CSL. Strahs pitched in 12 games, allowing 75 runs, as he boasted a .727 won-loss pitching percentage. The team remained in second place, still trailing Greenwood.[8]

The Chicago White Sox, the parent club of the Bathers, organized a baseball tryout camp at Jaycee Park. The three-day camp directed toward boys 16-26-years-old, who were "out of high school." Another exciting event occurred in June as Mr. and Mrs. Dick Fuller became the proud parents of Terry Fuller born at St. Joseph Hospital in Hot Springs. Dick, Bathers third baseman, hailed from Rockford, Illinois.

There was a rare event in El Dorado when the Bathers traveled to the Oil Town on June 25. The Oilers infielder Julius Pressley had all the heckling he could take and rushed into the stands attacking the stunned fan. Police escorted the player from the park as Hot Springs crushed the Oilers 15-1 on 17 hits. Pressley received an indefinite suspension by Jim Griffith, league president. Harry Brandt, Oilers president, "issued an apology to the fans."[9]

During the first 33 home games, the Bathers drew 36,000 fans by June 27. The total attendance for the 1947 season was 42,000. The Bathers were way ahead of that mark for 1948.

Manager Sobek inherited a quality team because on July 2, the newspaper reported that the Bathers led the CSL for 10 straight weeks in team batting and fielding, but they were third place in the loop standings, only a game and a half behind second place Clarksdale. The Spamen led with a batting average of .272, eleven points better than second place Natchez. In addition, Herb Adams, "center field flash," continued to lead the league in hitting with a .401 mark. Bill Haschak, first sacker, sprayed the ball around the yard for an even .300 clip, while catcher Tony Zini was at a .298 average. Right fielder Ed McGhee had a .285 batting average, while Charlie Schmidt, shortstop, averaged .279.

At home on July 3, the Bathers slid past the Natchez Indians, 6-2. Jim Kamis went the distance on the mound as he scattered six hits and came up with one of the six hits for Hot Springs, to aid his winning cause.

The Sporting News noted in an article "Open Season on Pilots in Cotton States League," that four CSL skippers got the ax within 10 days. George Sobek took over from Joe Holden at Hot Springs; catcher Johnny George replaced pitcher Art Nelson at Pine Bluff; Cal Chapman, veteran infielder, succeeded Howard Roberts at El Dorado and pitcher Tince Leonard replaced another hurler, "Woody" Johnson at Helena.[10]

The Bathers brought the July 4 fireworks in their bats to Pine Bluff as they exploded for seven runs, detonating the Cardinals 7-0. Pitcher Art Hamilton threw a six hitter as he won his second victory within five days. Hot Springs did a bunch of damage in the first inning as they crossed the plate five times. McGhee and Baud were the Bathers firecrackers as both players went 3-5 at the plate. The longest knock for the night was a triple by McGhee. Adams, Sobek, Fuller and Zini added two safeties each. The solid lineup during the Pine Bluff game was as follows: Adams – cf, Haschak - 1b, Schmidt – ss, Zini – c, McGhee – rf, Sobek - 2b, Baud – lf, Fuller - 3b and Hamilton - p. Greenwood was league leaders on July 4, while Clarksdale was five and a half games behind Greenwood. Hot Springs was only six games behind Greenwood in third spot.

Pine Bluff produced nothing but the sound of silence as Dick Strahs tossed a perfect 2-0 game! The rarity materialized on July 8, against the sixth place Pine Bluff Cardinals at Jaycee Park. Hot Springs took the first game of the twin bill 5-2 and Strahs took care of business during the seven-inning nightcap. The 23-year-old Navy veteran dazzled the Cardinals with no hits, no runs and no walks. No Red Bird reached base. His teammates scored a run in the fourth inning and one in the fifth frame. A crowd of 1,408 sat on the edge of their seats as the game rolled into the home stretch. There was "more hush than cheering." In the critical seventh inning, Strahs faced the top of the batting order. The first batter, Stan Hancock, who had launched a homer in the first game, grounded out to second baseman Harry Salvatore. Jerry Giaratano belted a roller to shortstop where Sobek fired to Haschak for the second out. The third batter was Pine Bluff's big belter, Ray Smereck. It was like *Casey at the Bat*. The results were the same. Big Ray went down swinging, just like Casey. Following the last swing, the team and hundreds of fans streamed on the field to congratulate Strahs. It was the first no-hitter and, of course, the first perfect game, ever pitched in Hot Springs since the Bathers joined the CSL in 1938. The two wins placed the Bathers in second place just ahead of Clarksdale and put Strahs in the Cotton States League record books.

A fun game was played at Jaycee Park between the city firefighters and policemen. Over 1,000 astonished on-lookers couldn't believe their eyes as they watched in amazement as the "Fire Balls" took on the "Flat Feet." Little resembled a baseball game except the equipment and the field on which the two teams played. "The Flat Feet won't talk about baseball today. They can't, too many sore muscles, but the smoke-eaters have plenty to say." The Fire Balls blazed past the Flat Feet 25-8 and the crowd went home happy.[11]

At the All-Star break on July 10, Hot Springs edged into second position behind Greenwood and barely ahead of third place Clarksdale. Five Hot Springs players dominated the first post-war All-Star tilt held in Greenwood, Mississippi. The game confronted the Arkansans against their neighboring counterparts from Mississippi. Hot Springs players selected to the elite squad were manager George Sobek; outfielder Herb Adams, leading the CSL in hitting with a sizzling .393;

first baseman Bill Haschak (.322); shortstop Charlie Schmidt (.322) and catcher Tony Zini (.299). Mississippi scored first in the fourth frame, but in the sixth, it was Arkansas' turn. Herb Adams smashed a triple and scampered home on teammate Bill Haschak's long sacrifice fly. Dick Strahs, Hot Springs pitcher, relieved Bill Phillips in the eighth inning. Infielder John Le Gros' wild throw on Herb Adams' roller and walks to Schmidt and Talbert in the tenth inning, set the stage for Helena's third baseman Bob Klien. He smashed a scorcher to the outfield driving in two runs and the victory. Strahs was the winning pitcher as the Arkansas All-Stars defeated the Mississippi All-Stars 3-1.[12-13]

On July 13, Herb Adams headed up the CSL's hitting race with a blistering .397 average. The Bathers speedy outfielder led his nearest competitor by an amazing 41 percentage points. Hot Springs also led in team batting and team fielding, but was in third place in team standings.[14]

On July 14, Hot Springs lost an 11-inning heartbreaker, 12-10, to the Greenwood Dodgers at Jaycee Park. It was 9-9 at the end of regulation. Both teams put up goose eggs in the 10th frame, but the Dodgers scored three times in the 11th inning. The Bathers attempted a comeback, but tallied only a solo run in the bottom of the 11th inning. Greenwood set a Jaycee Park record with five double plays; however, Hot Springs out hit the Dodgers15-14, as both teams demonstrated their offensive power.

In pregame ceremonies, on July 15, Mrs. Marie "Mom" Peters, longtime Bathers fan, presented an engraved watch to Dick Strahs for his recent perfect game. On behalf of the fans, other members of the team received tie clasps. Among the special guests at the game were Marjorie Lawrence, famed Metropolitan Opera star, and her husband, Dr. Frank King. The family lived in Harmony Hills just outside of Hot Springs.

The next night, the Bathers jumped back to their winning ways with a 4-3 triumph over the Greenwood Dodgers before 1,357 fans at Jaycee Park. The Bathers were drawing excellent crowds. Nearly 2,000 (1,943) paying customers showed up at "Ladies Night," July 16.

Charley "Chuck" Comiskey II, heir to the Chicago White Sox dynasty; Johnny Rigney, farm director of the Chicago White Sox and Fred Shaffer, White Sox scout, were in town inspecting one of their 13 Chisox farm teams, the Hot Springs Bathers. The Sox were in charge of about 240 youngsters who were members of White Sox farm system. The Chicago men were looking for young talent and Comiskey said, "If any can show they have the get up and go and the ability to play major league baseball, they will be given ample opportunity to display their wares." Comiskey declared, "There will be many personnel changes in 1949, but we figure that by 1950, we will see that our farm clubs are starting to pay dividends."[15]

Comiskey stated that most of the prospects for the 1949 season would come from the Memphis Chicks of the Southern Association (AA), Hollywood Stars in the Pacific Coast League (AAA) and Muskegon Clippers (A) of the Central Michigan League. However, he noted that Adams, Baud and McGhee were among the best outfielders he had seen in A, B or C leagues during the season. In 1948, "Chuck" Comiskey was gaining valuable baseball experience by serving as president of the White Hawks of Waterloo, of the Class B League. From Hot Springs, he traveled to Nashville, Tennessee, to watch the Southern Association's All-Star game.

Herb Adams' fan club drove all the way from Oak Park, Illinois, to watch the sparkplug play. Herb's father, mother, two sisters and a brother spent their vacation in Hot Springs. The visitors said that they were "having a whale of a time."

Speaking of visitors, a Hot Springs delegation composed of Joe McRae, J. R. Smith, Norwood Phillips and Coy Theobolt traveled to St. Louis and took in a Cardinals-Braves game at Sportsman's Park.

Someone in the crowd watched Arkansas' Johnny Sain and wondered if this is the same lad a certain president of the Bathers told to go back to the cotton patch because he wasn't good enough to pitch in the Cotton States.[16]

Sain became a pretty-fair country pitcher. In 1948, the lanky native of Havana, Arkansas, led the Boston Braves and the National League in "most wins" with a 24-15 record, including four shutouts. *The Sporting News* selected Sain as "Pitcher of the Year" in 1948. He earned a 1-1 record in the 1948 World Series in which the Braves lost to the Cleveland Indians. [17]

Clarksdale Planters visited the Bathers at 2:30 p.m. on July 18. It was a special day because that was the day they gave out free team pictures which many people still have in their collection.

On July 19, Art Hamilton needed help from relief twirler Jim Kamis to cop his 14th victory against six setbacks. Clarksdale got six runs in the last three innings, but the Bathers survived to win 8-7. The hometown swatters came through one more time as Adams, Haschak, Sobek, Fuller and Baud all slammed the ball for extra base knocks.

Herb Adams remained at the top of the individual batting scramble on July 27, as he posted a flaming average of .395. In his bag of talents, the young star from Oak Park, Illinois, scored 88 runs, blasted 164 hits and collected 52 RBIs. Adams remained number one in runs, hits and total bases. The Spamen continued to lead the circuit in team fielding with a .957 grade and team hitting with a .277 mark. The Bathers jumped around from second or third place in team standings.

Before the month was over, Hamilton notched his 11th straight victory, 16 overall wins against six defeats, by downing Helena 3-1 on four hits. The ace right-hander from Austin, Texas, struck out 10 and helped his cause at the plate by rapping out three singles in as many times at the plate.

Tony Zale, world middleweight boxing champion, received a rousing ovation as a special guest of the Bathers. He approved the Bathers 3-1 victory over Helena. Zale, fresh from a third-round knockout of Rocky Graziano, was in the Spa training for the Marcel Cerdan fight in September. Zale was a terrific baseball fan and a frequent visitor to the Spa. Before the game, he posed for photographs with the Bathers. [18]

On August 1, Hot Springs swamped the Oilers in El Dorado 10-4 on 22 hits. Strahs threw an eight hitter against the south Arkansas team. The Spa team scored seven times in the first frame as they worked on three El Dorado pitchers during the contest. Manager George Sobek led the

Bathers' batters by cracking five hits during his six times at bat. Bill Haschak went four for five and Ed McGhee had a four for six day at the plate.[19]

In El Dorado on August 2, Art Hamilton tossed his 12th straight victory and his 17th win of the season, overwhelming the seventh place Oilers, 8-3. The tall Texan limited El Dorado to only eight hits. The third place Bathers connected on 12 hits by only four players. Schmidt (4-6), Haschak (3-5), Sobek (3-6) and Adams (2-5) led the sharp-hitting Bathers to the win. The game was a quick one, lasting only two hours and five-minutes.[20]

Hot Springs was first in team fielding, team batting and third in overall standings in the CSL, as of August 3. In the pitching category, the top five pitchers for the Spa had records of Hamilton 17-6, Strahs 15-6, Kamis 8-4, Rapacki 10-10 and Coughlin 8-8. Adams topped the league in batting statistics with an incredible .370 average. Consistent hitting by Sobek upped his average to .334, tied for second in the league.

In seven games, the former All-America basketball player at Notre Dame pounded out 17 hits in 35 trips to the plate, sending his batting stock soaring 27 points to a neat .334. From July 29 to August 2, Sobek gathered 16 of his total safeties, but sparked his drive last Sunday when he made five hits in six tries.[21]

Thursday night, August 5, was a good night for the home team. Manager Sobek slid across home plate in the 13th inning to give the Bathers a thrilling 8-7 victory over the El Dorado Oilers at Jaycee Park. In pregame ceremonies, a crowd of 1,600 honored Carey Selph from Mount Ida, his "adopted town." Selph, born in Donaldson, Arkansas, stayed close to home to attend college. He starred in football, basketball, baseball and track during his four years at Ouachita Baptist College (now University) in Arkadelphia in the 1920s. Selph played a few years with the St. Louis Cardinals and the Chicago White Sox. He performed five years in the minors with the Houston Buffaloes, a minor league franchise of the St. Louis Cardinals. Managing the Buffs in 1933 and

1934, he led the team to a first place finish in the Texas League, but lost in the first round of the playoffs. Houston finished sixth in 1934, Selph's last year in organized baseball. In 1949, Selph constructed a camp near Mt. Ida and named it Ozark Baseball Camp. The camp, now called Camp Ozark, is a Christian sports camp owned by Sam Torn, an attorney from Houston.

Dignitaries at the pregame activities included the Mayors of Hot Springs and Mt. Ida. Other VIPs included Tony Zale, Mort Cox, Sam Garratt and C. Hamilton Moses.

Mayor Earl Ricks presided as master of ceremonies and introduced Tony Zale, world middleweight boxing champion. Mayor John Froehlich, of Mount Ida, Phillip Kelley, president of the Mount Ida Chamber of Commerce, Mort Cox, president of the Spa Junior Chamber of Commerce and Art Winch, co-manager of Zale.

Chancellor Sam Garratt, president of the Hot Springs Baseball Club, presented Selph with a new model rod and reel on the behalf of the club.

...The tribute to Selph was paid by C. Hamilton Moses, president of the Arkansas Power and Light Company, who called his childhood chum 'one of the finest citizens in Arkansas.' [22]

Attorney C. Hamilton Moses became president of the Arkansas Power and Light Company following Harvey Couch's death in 1941. Moses, the childhood friend of Selph, was an enthusiastic businessman who drew industry worth millions of dollars into the state of Arkansas. Couch named Lake Hamilton in honor of "Ham" Moses.

"Bathers Blast El Dorado, 12-5 to Chalk Up Sixth Straight Victory," was the headline in *The Sentinel-Record* on August 7. Pitcher Dick Strahs struck out 12 Oilers and yielded only six safeties to go all the way on the hill for the Bathers. Ed McGee was the big cannon for the Bathers as he smashed a home run over the left field fence in the second inning. He added a triple and a single during his five trips to the plate, ending with a fantastic five-RBI night. The team remained in third place just a shade behind Clarksdale and seven games behind the league leading Greenwood Dodgers.[23]

After all the praise heaped on Art Hamilton, Natchez tapped the big man for his first loss in 13 outings, nipping the Bathers 4-2 at Jaycee Park on August 7. The loss also snapped the Bathers winning streak at six. Hamilton gave up six safeties in front of 1,800 home fans, but the Spa Boys couldn't pull out the win. On August 18, the Bathers ripped the Greenville Bucks 14-2 as they collected a whopping 19 hits. The Bathers continued to hang around in second or third place in the league standings.

Hot Springs observed "Leslie O'Connor-Old-Timers Night" sponsored by the Bathers and the Optimist Club on August 23. O'Connor served as general manager of the Chicago White Sox and was a frequent visitor to Hot Springs. The group met at the Arlington Hotel in the early evening and later, traveled to Jaycee Park for a brief pregame ceremony. In addition to O'Connor, honored guests included former baseball players from Arkansas. The old-timers lineup included Pulaski County Sheriff Tom Gulley, formerly of the Chicago White Sox; Earl Smith, Hot Springs, formerly with the Pirates and Giants, Carey Selph, Mt. Ida, formerly with the Cardinals and White Sox and manager of the Houston Buffs. The two Boston Red Sox representatives were Leo Nonnenkamp and Lee Rogers, both of Little Rock. Little Rock's Bill Dickey, the great Yankee catcher, was unable to attend. Harry "Steamboat" Johnson, umpire-in-chief of the Southern Association and a colorful baseball figure attended. Other baseball honorees, former minor league stars from Hot Springs, included "Spike" Hunter, Roy Gillenwater and Al Williamson.[24] In addition to the players; other guests were Judge Sam Garratt and Mrs. Evelyn Ensminger, Bathers business manager. O'Connor served for several years as assistant to the late Judge Landis. In charge of arrangements was Calvin Craig, president of the Optimist Club.[25]

Unofficially, it became Strahs-Baud Night! Dick Strahs chalked up his 19th win and Andy Baud went wild at the plate. Thanks to Baud's homer, triple and double, the Bathers slipped past Clarksdale 4-2. Baud went 3-3 at bat and Bathers' catcher Tony Zini contributed three consecutive singles. It was a 2-2 game until the ninth inning when Hot Springs scored twice to take the win before 1,446 excited hometown fans. Strahs struck out seven Planters as the Mississippi team collected eight hits in the one hour and 55 minute game.[26]

There were different circumstances on Wednesday, August 25, when the Planters drilled the Bathers twice 22-13 and 10-5. The midnight curfew helped the Bathers in the second game because the match halted in the sixth inning due to the late hour. It was the first time in two seasons that the league utilized the curfew rule.

On August 27, Dick Strahs went for his 20th win of the season as he took the hill in the late game of the doubleheader at Helena. The first game of a doubleheader went nine innings, while the second contest was a seven-inning affair. In the nightcap, Strahs was pitching a shutout until the seventh frame, but the Bathers were putting up goose eggs, too. In the top of the seventh, with the score 0-0, Helena's Bob Klein singled. Paul Richardville pulled off a perfect sacrifice bunt as Klein moved to second base. Dom Italiano smacked a single driving in Klein. The Bathers came up empty in their half of the seventh, allowing Helena the 1-0 win and denied Strahs his 20th win.[27]

Pregame ceremonies during the last regular season game, on August 31, were special. The Cotton States League's Most Valuable Player trophy went to the Bathers' center fielder, Herb Adams. Adams received the trophy from Mort Cox, president of the Hot Springs Chamber of Commerce. The 20-year-old "overwhelmingly" won the award over 20 rivals. Adams stated. "I don't deserve it, but it is swell." Cox also presented Maurice Moore, sportswriter for *The Sentinel-Record* and *New Era*, a gift for his excellent sports reporting of the Bathers.[28]

Adams, the MVP League winner, ran off with five additional individual league titles. The 5' 5-1/2" speedy center fielder scored the most runs with 122; blasted the most hits, 223 and collected the most total bases with 280. He took home the fourth piece of iron by winning the Cotton States League's batting championship with a whopping .375 average. He added another award for his trophy shelf as he claimed the MVP of the All-Star tilt.

The Bath-Tub Boys ended the season on August 31, with an 11-5 trouncing of the Helena Seaporters in front of 1,622 animated fans at home. Both managers cleared the benches as the Bathers' players changed positions. Andy Baud ended the regular season "in a blaze of glory" as he went four for five at the plate. Baud, the Bathers only player to play in every game, switched from his left field position to third base. In the last inning, Sobek decided to put Baud on the hill, as the multitalented Baud responded by polishing off the last three Helena batters. The first two Seaporters he faced flew out, and in a perfect ending, Baud struck out the last batter to wrap up the 1948 regular season.[29]

Hot Springs finished in third position, gaining a berth in the CSL playoffs. The Bathers began their "second season" of 1948! In 1936, the league inaugurated the two-round Shaughnessy playoff system to determine an overall league champion. The order of finish of the final standings determined the playoff setup. The first round matched first place Greenwood and fourth place Natchez, while second place Clarksdale played third place Hot Springs.

The Bathers playoff hopes rested with a cluster of first-class pitchers including Dick Strahs, Ray Rapacki, Art Hamilton, Nick Coughlin, Jim Kamis and Charlie Stiglich. The hitting arsenal included catcher-Tony Zini, utility – Harry Salvatore, first baseman-Bill Haschak, second baseman/manager-George Sobek, shortstop-Charlie Schmidt and third baseman-Dick Fuller. Outfielders were Ed McGhee, Andy Baud and Herb Adams.

First Round Playoffs
(Best of five)
Game 1 – Thursday, September 2, 1948 at Community Park, Clarksdale, Mississippi
Hot Springs – 3 Clarksdale - 0

Hot Springs opened at Community Park in Clarksdale as Dick Strahs (19-7) hurled a masterful 3-0, three-hit shutout victory over the Planters as nearly 3,000 fans looked on. The Bathers pushed across lone runs in the third, fourth and seventh innings by Schmidt, Adams and McGhee to seal the victory. Clarksdale's 21-game winner Bob Upton weakened and after 6 2/3 innings handed the ball to McLeod. Upton gave up three runs on eight hits and struck out four. McLeod pitched perfect ball for 2 1/3 innings, but Upton took the loss. Adams, Sobek and Baud each contributed two hits in the win. Umpires for the series were McGraw, Grillo and Valencourt.[30]

Game 2 – Friday, September 3, 1948 at Community Park, Clarksdale, Mississippi
Hot Springs – 3 Clarksdale - 2

In another low scoring contest, the Planters bowed to Art Hamilton (18-9) and the Bathers in a close one, 3-2 as Hot Springs took a two-game lead in the first round of the playoffs. Hamilton, who went all the way on the mound, tossed a three hitter to cop the win. "Handy Andy Baud provided the winning run when he cracked out a double into left field and Sobek slid into home safely by a few inches" in the sixth frame. Adams smacked three hits during his five chances at the plate, while Schmidt thumped two doubles. Haschak and Baud banged out one double each. Hot Springs scored first in the third, but the Planters followed with two runs in the bottom of the third. In the fifth, Adams scored on Schmidt's second double of the night. Haschak would have scored on the same play, but umpire Tony Grillo ruled that big Haschak missed third base. Ed "Cotton" Hill, the 14-game winner for Clarksdale, hurled the nine innings and gave up three runs on nine hits. Both pitchers struck out seven.[31]

Game 3 – Saturday, September 4, 1948 at Hot Springs, Arkansas
Hot Springs – 17 Clarksdale - 1

An overflow crowd of 2,700 ardent baseball fans awaited the Bathers return home for the third game of the series. The bats blazed red hot as the Bathers exploded with a 17-1 shellacking of Clarksdale as they captured a berth in the championship finals. Jim Kamis (9-5), from Berwyn, Illinois, limited the Planters to only six hits, while the Bathers jumped on three Clarksdale pitchers for 13 safeties. Haschak, Fuller and McGhee had a field day at the plate as they launched one missile each that landed on the other side of the fence. McGhee's shot went over the 390-feet center field fence, one of the longest balls hit at Jaycee Park during the 1948 season. Haschak, Baud, Adams, Kamis, Fuller and Sobek contributed to the RBI column. Attendance: 2,700.[32]

Championship Series
(Best of Seven)

Game 1 – Tuesday, September 7, 1948 at Greenwood, Mississippi
Hot Springs - 3 Greenwood - 2

The championship series was the best of seven games with a 2-3-2 format. In this system, if the series went seven games, Greenwood hosted the first two games, Hot Springs hosted the middle three and the teams returned to Greenwood for the last two contests.

Hot Springs opened up on the road at Legion Field with their right-handed 19-game winner, Dick Strahs on the hill. The Dodgers countered with their 13-game winner Stan Polonczyk, a curveballer from Michigan. Umpires for the series were Richard Valencourt, Harold Willson (spelled Willson), Jim Elder and Joe Iacovetti. The umpires were from various parts of the country and out of the country. Richard Valencourt lived in Newark, NJ, while Harold Willson came from Ontario, Canada. Jim Elder, born in Pennsylvania, lived in Little Rock, while Joseph "Cooper" Iacovetti hailed from Pittsburgh, Pennsylvania.

Greenwood, aided by a Hot Springs error and two singles by the Dodgers, jumped out to a 2-0 lead in the bottom of the second inning. With the help of four Dodger errors, the Bathers returned the favor in the top of the third by adding three tallies. The game rocked along until the last of the ninth when the Dodgers' sabers rattled. Hollis DeArmond led off the inning with a drive over the first baseman's glove for a double, the only extra base hit of the game. The next batter, pitcher Poloncyzk struck out attempting to bunt. Lukasiuk pushed a single between short and third as DeArmond took off from second headed for home. Charlie Schmidt went far to his right, grabbed the ball and noticed DeArmond halted briefly rounding third. Schmidt threw a perfect strike to Zini as the Bathers' catcher slapped the tag on DeArmond for the second out of the inning. With Lukasiuk on first, Cliff Stewart hit a scorcher down in the direction of Harry Salavtore at the "hot corner." The sure-handed third baseman quickly scooped up the ball and threw to second for the force out on Lukasiuk to end the contest. The Bathers pulled off the first win in the best of seven-game series as Strahs hurled the complete contest giving up only two runs on seven hits, while striking out seven, for a Bathers 3-2 win.[33]

Game 2 – Wednesday, September 8, 1948 at Greenwood, Mississippi
Hot Springs – 8 Greenwood - 7

The next night at 8:00 p.m. in game two at Legion Field, the Bathers started their 18-game winner, Art Hamilton. Greenwood Skipper Jim Bivin chose Lade Dean (11-3) to start on the mound for the Dodgers.

It was a ragged game from the start. Herb Adams starting the game with a grounder to short, Lukasiuk bobbled the ball and that was all the speedster needed to reach first safely. Later in the inning, Adams scored on a sacrifice fly by Schmidt and Haschak scored on a dropped ball at home by Landini, the Dodgers catcher. Three errors and one hit in the opening stanza gave the Bathers a 2-0 lead. The Dodgers Lukasiuk made up for his two boots by lacing four singles during his five times at the plate.

Greenwood led 6-5 at the end of the eighth frame. Hot Springs rallied in the ninth frame as Tony Zini lashed his first hit of the playoffs, a triple, driving in three runs to take an 8-6 lead. The

Dodgers managed one score in the bottom half of the ninth, but Hot Springs held on for the second win of the series, 8-7. The Greenwood paper stated, "The Dodgers mauled veteran Art Hamilton for 16 hits, but wasted a good many of them." However, Hamilton and the Bathers got outs when it counted. Hot Springs gathered 10 hits to aid their cause. Hamilton was the winning pitcher, while Dean was on the losing end. Errors were the real culprit of the contest as Greenwood committed six errors to Hot Springs' four miscues.[34]

Game 3 – Thursday, September 9, 1948 at Hot Springs, Arkansas
Greenwood - 13 Hot Springs - 12

The Dodgers came out smokin', but so did the Bathers. The Greenwood paper called it a "Slam-Bang Thriller." Greenwood got the sparks flying in the third inning by scoring two runs. Then, it was the Bathers turn to hit the ball between the white lines and out of the yard. Adams beat out an infield hit and Haschak politely hit a round tripper over the right field wall to tie the score. Center fielder Cliff Stewart couldn't hang on to Schmidt's smash. McGhee tripled to right and scored Schmidt Sobek singled scoring McGhee. Andy Baud singled and it was time for Greenwood's manager Bivin to make changes and changes he made. Ed Privette took over from Hazle on the mound, Hazle, a good hitter, went to right field, Boston moved over to left and DeArmond trotted out to replace Stewart in center field.

Privette walked Zini and Salvatore, allowing Sobek to score from third. After two balls to Kamis, Bivin had enough. Without any warm-ups, Bivin installed himself on the mound, but that move didn't seem to help. Two more runs crossed the plate before the inning concluded as the Bathers went up 7-2. It was looking bright for the hometown boys. Don't go away, anything can happen in sports and it usually does. By the end of the fourth stanza, Hot Springs led 8-4. Greenwood watched Hot Springs at the plate and imitated their swinging ability.

So, here come the Dodgers roaring back. The visitors tallied three times in the seventh to tie, while the Bathers produced a goose egg in the bottom of the seventh. The Dodgers, focusing on scoring, went ahead in the eighth by one run. By this time, Bivin weakened and he gave the ball to Stan Poloneyzk with two men on base and no outs. Adams greeted the new pitcher with a single scoring Salvatore as Strahs went to second. Haschak forced Strahs at third and Schmidt fanned. The wildness of Polonczyk added three more scores for the Bathers and things were looking good again for the home team.

With Hot Springs up 12-9 in the top of the ninth, the hometown fans, believing the boys could handle the Dodgers for one inning, began to trickle out to the parking lot. Never leave a game until the last batter is out. Everything went south for the Bathers in the ninth. Errors, wild pitch, a couple of hits, a walk and suddenly the Dodgers went ahead 13-12. Perhaps the Bathers could rally, but Poloncyzk said, "No," to that and Hot Springs went down 1-2-3 in the ninth, as the Dodgers pulled off a wild and wooly affair to win, 13-12. Attendance: 2,476. [35]

Game 4 – Friday, September 10, 1948 at Hot Springs, Arkansas
Hot Springs – 7 Greenwood – 5

Sobek, scratching his head as he decided on a starter, settled on 19-year-old, 6' 2" 205 pound, southpaw Chuck Stiglich who finished with a 4-3 regular season record. Greenwood's Bivin started reliable Murray Richardson on the mound. Richardson had a 13-6 regular season record.

The Bathers jumped out to a lead as they notched three tallies in the opening frame. They continued to add one run in the fourth and one more in the fifth for a 5-0 lead heading to the top of the sixth. Well, here we go again! Pearl broke the ice with a round tripper, followed by four-baggers by Hazle and Lukasiuk. The Dodgers were in a groove, but with two outs, Hamilton came in to relieve shaky Stiglich in the seventh and extinguished the Dodger blaze.

With the game tied at five-all in the eighth, Andy Baud's two-run triple in the eighth inning solidified the Bathers cause as he drove in two runs to take a 7-5 lead. The Dodgers threatened in the ninth, but with two men on base and one out, Hamilton took care of Joe DeArmond as he went down swinging. Dodgers' runners occupied first and second with two outs. With a flick of the wrist, wily catcher Zini picked off the unsuspecting Hazel at first to end the threat and the game.

Outfielder Andy Baud, big gun for the Bathers, collected three hits, including a triple, a double and four RBIs. McGhee had a two-hit night including a homer and Haschak added his flair as he popped a double and a single. In addition, Adams affixed his two singles to the hit list The Bathers led in the series 3-1.[36]

Game 5 – Saturday, September 11, 1948 at Hot Springs, Arkansas
Greenwood – 3 Hot Springs – 2

The outlook was bright for the Bathers as the hometown boys returned home. One more game was all the Bathers needed to win the championship. Both pitchers pitched shutout baseball until the seventh inning. Joe Hazle, Dodgers outfielder-pitcher, posted a solo round-tripper in the seventh inning to put Greenwood up 1-0.

A near riot broke out in the seventh inning when Andy Baud slid into catcher Lou Landini as he scored the Bathers first run. Jim Elder, home-plate umpire, quickly stifled the incident. The Bathers garnered three singles to take the lead 2-1 at the end of seven innings. In the top of the ninth, Greenwood's Hazle cranked a double as Polonczyk came to the plate. The pitcher parked a long ball on the other side of the fence to score Hazle ahead of him. The Dodgers blanked the Bathers in the bottom of the ninth to take the 3-2 victory. However, Hot Springs held a 3-2 edge in the series as they shifted to Mississippi for game six. Attendance 2,700.[37]

Game 6 – Sunday, September 12, 1948 at Greenwood, Mississippi
Greenwood - 8 Hot Springs - 2

When the Spa Boys took the field at the middle of the fourth inning, they were in front of the Dodgers 2-0. To be fair, Greenwood needed to have a turn at bat during the fourth inning. In fact, the Bathers were still in front after one out in the Dodgers half of the fourth inning. However, the dam broke. Bathers' southpaw Nick Coughlin hit Ed Nidds. The next batter, George Boston rattled the boards for a triple, scoring Nidds. Joe Hazle grounded out to short, but Bob Kremens followed with a loud double to deep center to allow Boston to lope home. Lou Landini singled home Kremens to put the Dodgers in the lead for good.

The Dodgers capped the victory with a four-run explosion in the sixth frame as they triumphed over the Bathers 8-2. It was a lackluster offense as Dean held the Spamen to only five scattered hits, including one extra base hit, a triple by Baud. The overflow crowd of 3,263 partisan fans at Legion Field got their money's worth as the Dodgers sent the series to the seventh and final game. There were so many fans that they created extra space in foul territory in right field to observe the contest. The final game of the series, scheduled for September 13, was rained out. Suspense mounted as fans in two states waited one more day for the championship game.[38]

Game 7 – Tuesday, September 14, 1948 at Greenwood, Mississippi
Hot Springs - 5 Greenwood - 2

Texan Art Hamilton (18-9) started the final game of the series for the Bathers on Tuesday, September 14, at Legion Field. The *Greenwood Commonwealth* anticipated that Joe Hazel, the "all-around hitter, fielder and pitcher" would get the nod on the mound for Greenwood. It was a minor surprise when Greenwood manager Jim Bivin picked Stan Polonczyk as the starting pitcher for the Dodgers, since it was Polonczyk's fourth appearance in the series. A capacity crowd of

2,000 fans again packed Legion Field. However, attendance was down from the previous game due to the charred rubble of most of the burnt grandstand. The fire seemed to have occurred several months before and the old-wooden stands became a fire hazard, so the fire marshal closed a section of the grandstands. Greenwood fans were fired up and they weren't going to let a little inconvenience douse their enthusiasm of witnessing their Dodgers play host to the Bathers in the finals of the CSL playoffs. This was it! The seventh game was for all the marbles!

In the second inning, the Bathers got the shindig rolling as Hamilton singled, driving home a sliding Andy Baud to put the Bathers on top 1-0. Zini came marching home a few minutes later on Adams' fielder's choice in which Hamilton was forced out at second base. Hot Springs was up 2-0 going into the bottom of the second frame. The Dodgers came back in the bottom of the second inning to score one run. It remained 2-1 until the sixth inning, when the Bathers jumped on the Greenwood starter Polonczyk for two more tallies.

Haschak singled and Schmidt walked, with no outs when Dean relieved Polinczyk in the seventh. However, the Bathers were unable to capitalize in the seventh, as the score remained 4-1 in favor of the Bathers. The bottom of the eighth inning, Greenwood attempted a comeback, but the Dodgers mustered only one run. Bathers were on top 4-2. The Spa Boys countered with a score in the top of the ninth inning. Going into the bottom of the ninth, Hot Springs was ahead 5-2 as Greenwood faced their last gasp.

Hamilton bore down in the final half of the game. In two previous games, the Bathers have lost in the crucial ninth. McGhee made a running catch of Joe Hazel's fly for the first out. Kremens grounded to Sobek at second base. Landini worked Hamilton hard, and finally drew a base on balls. The Texan tossed him nine balls (pitches).

Russ Pearl, pinch hitting for relief hurler Lade Dean also proved a tough batter, but after receiving six pitches he hit a pop fly to Schmidt at shortstop for the final out of the 1948 season. [39]

Sobek and McGhee collected three hits each for the Bathers in the final game as Hamilton won his third series game by tossing a six hitter. In addition to Hamilton's outstanding pitching, Sobek said that the turning point in the championship game was a "sensational catch" by rookie outfielder McGhee off the bat of Kremens. The *Greenwood Commonwealth* put it this way:

McGhee and Sobek led the Bather assault on Polonczyk and Dean with three hits each. McGhee not only had two singles and a double, but made two sensational catches in right field that really hurt the Dodgers…One of them, on a liner by Bob Kremens with two men on and two away in the fourth, cost Greenwood at least two runs. It was one of the best plays of the year at the local field by an outfielder.[40]

Umpires for the contest were Valencourt, Willson, Elder and Lacovetti. The title tilt lasted two hours and 20 minutes. The win gave Hot Springs the second playoff flag since entering the CSL in 1938. In 1941, the Bathers finished second in league play, but swept the championship by winning seven straight playoff games without a loss.

The baseball season of 1948 was an unforgettable season. Not only did the Bathers win the CSL championship, but also led the league in highest attendance with 87,462. It was a tremendous year for individual statistics as well. In addition to the many individual honors that Herb Adams received, Dick Strahs pitched a perfect game. Five Bathers dominated the first All-Star game. The Bathers selected to the mid-season Classic were George Sobek-manager of the Arkansas squad, Herb Adams – center fielder, Bill Haschak – first baseman, Charlie Schmidt – shortstop and Tony Zini – catcher.

In the pitching category, Hot Springs faired well. Dick Strahs ended the regular season with a 19-7 record for a .731 percentage mark, seventh best in the league. Art Hamilton's 18-9 record allowed him to have a .667 percentage; Ray Rapacki finished with a 14-12 record, while James Kamis had a 9-5 mark.

At the plate, Adams topped the league batters with .375, Bill Haschak hit .314 and wound up in fifth place in the CSL's batting race; Charlie Schmidt hit .302; Sobek had a healthy .297 average; McGhee was next with a .273 mark, followed closely by Baud with a .271 batting average. Zini produced a .266 average. Hot Springs finished first in team batting with .279 and ended in second place in fielding with a .956 mark to Clarksdale's .957 first-place finish. Adams, McGhee and Strahs eventually played in the major leagues.[41]

The 1948 Cotton States League attendance figures revealed the following rank: (1) Hot Springs – 83,425, (2) Clarksdale – 63,883, (3) Pine Bluff – 58,342, (4) Greenville - 53,499, (5) Greenwood – 48, 847, (6) Natchez – 38,069, (7) El Dorado – 36,273, (8) Helena – 31,292. League Total – 413,613; Playoffs – 27,701 and the All-Star game – 1,603.[42]

The following night back in the Spa, the players had things to do and place to go. But wait! First things first! A team celebration took place at Barbar's Lodge on Lake Hamilton. It was an Auld Lang Syne-type party as most of the players prepared to travel to their respective homes. Adams received a call from the White Sox and left for the Windy City shortly after the feast. The White Sox purchased his contract for $7,500. He saw action in several of the 1948 season-ending games in a White Sox uniform. In a 4-3, Chicago victory against the Browns at Sportsman's Park in St. Louis, the 20-year-old, belted a double and a single and hauled in three fly balls in the outfield. A few days following his two-hit game, Adams burned his hand cooking at home and was out of action for four days. From a business standpoint, the White Sox were a little unhappy about the accident, but Herb returned to the Chisox less than a week later in a pinch-hitting role.[43]

After a brief rest, manager Sobek planned to play basketball with his hometown team, Hammond, Indiana. However, Hammond wasn't just any hometown team. During the 1948-1949 basketball campaign, Hammond Calumet Buccaneers were members of the professional National Basketball League (NBL). In 1949, the NBL merged with the Basketball Association of America (BAA) to form the new National Basketball Association (NBA). In 1949-1950, twenty-nine year old "Chips" Sobek played with the Sheboygan (WI) Redskins in the new National Basketball

Association. The 6' 0" – 180-pounder scored 346 points in 60 games averaged 5.8 points per game. Sobek, wearing jersey number 6, added 95 assists during the season. Sheboygan ended the season in fourth place in the Western Division. The 17-member league realigned itself into the Western, the Central and the Eastern divisions. Sobek played against George Mikan, the Hall of Famer, who led the Minneapolis Lakers to the 1949-1950 NBA championship. Sobek officiated basketball in the Big Ten conference for several years and the Indiana Basketball Hall of Fame selected him as a member of the class of 1980.[44]

Art Hamilton, winning pitcher of three playoff games against Greenwood, planned to head back home to Austin, Texas, and work at his former post office job. Pitcher Ray Rapacki traveled with Adams, since Chicago was Rapacki's home. Strahs headed to vacationland in Wisconsin. Pitcher Nick Coughlin and his new wife from Hot Springs traveled to Dayton Ohio, to work at his old job at the National Cash Register Company. Outfielder Andy Baud headed home to Midlothian, Illinois, to work on his father's farm. Catcher Tony Zini planned to return home to North Little Rock, Arkansas, and go to college. He later graduated from the University of Arkansas with an engineering degree.[45]

Pitcher Pete Heinen planned to assist his father in distributing brewery supplies in Barrington, Illinois. Working in Chicago was Bill Haschak's plan. Third baseman Dick Fuller, his wife and child traveled to the Fuller's home in Rockford, Illinois. The remainder of the team took vacations and returned to their respective home.[46]

The White Sox finished the 1948 season in the American League cellar, but the 30-minute film, called "Down on the Farm," was a big hit with the Chisox organization. The color movie previewed promising young players of the White Sox organization. "The 'baby star' of the "Down on the Farm" is Herb Adams. This Class C player, a Sox farmhand at Hot Springs, is vaulting all the way to the majors."[47]

In 1984, long after retirement, Herb and Donna Adams were visiting their son in Tulsa, OK. Suddenly, Herb became ill and immediately, the former fleet-footed baseball player's family drove him to the hospital. The hospital staff put him on life support where he remained in a coma for 3 ½ weeks. He regained his health because, as the doctors said, "He had a slow pulse rate." Other than the surprise illness, he was in good physical condition and that seemed to have saved his life. He walked out of the hospital a cured man, except for his hearing. The illness left Herb deaf. By phone, his wife writes questions for him to answer and he answers verbally on the phone. However, Donna stated that Herb is susceptible to pneumonia. For some reason, he has had the sickness five times since his Army days in Korea. His latest bout with the illness occurred in February 2011. In addition, Donna related that in 1947, Herb signed his first professional baseball contract at Madisonville, KY, for $100 a month. One year later, in Hot Springs, he more than doubled his 1947 salary by signing his 1948 Bathers contract for $225.00 a month.[48]

George M. Trautman, president of the National Association, stated the minor leagues employed about 13,000 players during the 1948 season. There were 438 baseball clubs in 46 states, Wyoming and Vermont the only states without teams. Trautman was a guest on Red Barber's "Club House" radio show. In answer to a question, Trautman replied that average Class D players salary was $150 a month, plus board and transportation during road games.

Chapter 10

Eight Men Out
1949

"(Umpire) Willson's action was unprecedented." The Sentinel-Record

L eslie O'Connor, general manager of the Chicago White Sox from 1945-1948, was vacationing in Hot Springs. O'Connor, who was out of baseball for the first time in 28 years, told Maurice Moore, sports editor of *The Sentinel-Record*, that he was "enjoying his first vacation in five years." Asked how he got into the business of baseball, the attorney smiled and told Moore how it all started.

Following the Black Sox scandal in 1920, Judge Kennesaw Mountain Landis became the commissioner of baseball. He was in that position to clean up and regulate the game. Landis was looking for a secretary-treasurer to assist him in his new and important position. Two months later, he heard from Landis.

My law partner and I used to kid each other quite a bit, so when he told me Judge Landis (U. S. district judge in Chicago) wanted to see me, I shot back something like, 'So does the president.' He gave me the private baseball telephone number the judge left, but I still hesitated before I went to see him.

'I went to his chambers, and he proceeded to ask me to name some young attorney who might serve as his assistant in baseball. I gave him the name of one of my acquaintances, and told him of his qualifications. When I had finished, I walked about 50 feet to the doors of the chamber. I had my hands on the handle when he called to me, "What about yourself?"

'I went back and told him I knew nothing about baseball administration, but that I loved the game. He said, "In that respect we can start out together." I told him I would rather talk it over with my partner and wife first. My partner wanted to go into the real estate business, and my wife agreed, so I went into baseball.[1]

The White Sox purchased the Bathers and O'Connor was one of the men responsible for the action. The Chicago attorney enjoyed visiting Hot Springs; in fact, he liked the city so much he bought property on the Arkadelphia highway called Coronado Tourist Court. He also planned to "seek admittance to the Arkansas bar" and write books pertaining to law.

Several teams in the Chicago White Sox farm system reported to Hot Springs during the spring of 1949. Over 130 professional baseball players took over Jaycee Park in late March. About 40 pitchers and catchers started working out the kinks on March 28, while the rest of the players began flexing their muscles two days later. The three-week training camp was under the tutelage of Johnny Rigney, farm director of the White Sox.

Among the instructors who arrived with the "farm boss" were Charles "Red" Ruffing, Benny Huffmann, Glen "Gabby" Stewart, Frank Parenti, Otto Denning, Joe DeMasi, Pete Fox, Paul Schoendienst and George "Specs" Toporcer. Most of the instructors had major league experience. The following teams and managers that trained in Hot Springs were Ruffing (Muskegon, Michigan Clippers, Class A, Central Michigan League), Huffman (Waterloo, Iowa White Hawks, Class B, 3-I League) and Fox of (Hot Springs, Arkansas, Bathers, Class C, Cotton States League). The Seminole team of the Class D, Sooner State League began training on April 6.

Morning training sessions at Jaycee Park began with Waterloo and Muskegon on the field at 9:30, while the Bathers met in the afternoon at 1:30. Jaycee Park, which underwent a face-lift costing several hundred dollars, was under the supervision of Ed Walsh, groundskeeper. The workers raised the field about five inches from the previous season.

The Chicago White Sox farm system presented six exhibition games played at Jaycee Park during the spring of 1949. The schedule was as follows: April 7, Tulsa vs. Muskegon; April 8, Tulsa vs. Waterloo; April 9, Indianapolis vs. Muskegon; April 10, Indianapolis vs. Waterloo; April 11, Milwaukee vs. Muskegon and April 14, Hot Springs vs. Waterloo. All the games began at 8:00 p.m., except afternoon games on April 9 and 10. George "Specs" Toporcer, director of field operation for the Chicago White Sox, was in Hot Springs to check on the training camp and commented on the attitude of some of the players.

Somehow, today's youngsters don't have the earnest desire to play the game as it should be. The publicity, which heralds many of them into the show, gives them the wrong idea.[2]

Toporcer graduated from the sandlots of New York straight to the major leagues in 1921. During his major league career from 1921-1928, "Specs" played the infield for the St. Louis Cardinals and always wore glasses. He said it just seemed natural for him to wear glasses.

The Waterloo Hawks scored a 9-4 exhibition victory over the Bathers on Easter Sunday afternoon, April 17. It was the Hawks second spring win against the Bathers. There were several connections between Waterloo and Hot Springs. Three former 1948 Bathers Bill Haschak, Ed McGhee and Andy Baud played for the Waterloo team. Pete Fox, the 1948 Waterloo manager, became the 1949 field general of the Hot Springs Bathers.

Pete Fox ended a distinguished major league career of 13 seasons in 1945. The 5' 11" outfielder, who tipped the scales at 165 pounds, broke into the big leagues in 1933 with the Detroit Tigers. Fox, traded to the Bosox in 1941, remained with the American League team until his retirement in 1945. Selected to the 1944 All-Star game, Fox did not play in which the American League lost 7-1. His career batting average was a healthy .298 with a hefty .327 World Series batting average.

The young 1949 Bathers launched the season with the following players: (ages in parenthesis) Pitchers – Dan Caccavo (19), Bill Fischer (18), Don Wescott (20), Tony Hoenick (22), Charles (Chips) Veddar (23), George Silliman (19), Ken Skidmore (20), Bill Muldowney (19) and Al Brown (20). Catchers included Fred Wasiluk (18) and George Sojka (20). Infielders were 1st base Ken Landenberger (20), 2nd base Pel Austin (22), 3rd base Bill Mead (18) and 3rd base Tony Donofrio (21). Outfielders consisted of Dick Anderson (21), Coleman "Ding Dong" Bell (23), Gene Creekmore (21) and Steve Solis (25). Seven players were veterans of World War II.

The Class C, Cotton States League, consisted of four teams from Mississippi and four from Arkansas. Clarksdale, Greenwood, Greenville and Natchez were the Mississippi teams, while Arkansas teams were from El Dorado, Helena, Hot Springs and Pine Bluff.

The Bathers opened the season at Pine Bluff in front of 2,800 fans. The Spa Boys garnered ten hits against the Cardinals pitcher, but starter Caccavo, relief hurler Silliman and the Bathers went down to an 8-5 defeat. Caccavo gave up only five hits and Silliman allowed only two bingles, but that was all the Cardinals needed to win. Solis, Austin and Creekmore led the Spa attack with two hits each. Eddie Albrecht, strikeout king of the 1948 CSL season, continued his over-powering ways as he struck out 14 Bathers, but he was touched for 10 hits. The Bathers completed the two-day road trip with a whopping loss to the Cardinals 18-2. The team was ready to get home and play in front of the home crowd.

Manager Fox and general manager Milt Woodard were ready to show off their 1949 team to the hometowners on April 21. A crowning highlighted the colorful inaugural pregame festivities. For several weeks, fans voted for the "king or queen of Bathers." For several weeks, fans voted on the two nominees, Tony Magle and Mrs. Marie "Mom" Peters. "Two of the most ardent rooters were nominated by friends and have waged a dogged campaign to see which one could outsell the other in Bathers ducats." Tony Magle, a native of Greece, and a follower of Hot Springs athletics for many years, won the popularity contest over Mrs. Marie "Mom" Peters. He won a season pass to the Bathers games and to all the Chicago White Sox battles. Mr. Magle's crown was in a form of a baseball cap. Chancellor Sam Garratt, president of the Bathers, also placed a crown on the head of runner-up, Mrs. Peters. Following the crowning, Mayor Floyd Housley strolled to the hill and pitched to Fowler Martin, president of the Junior Chamber of Commerce. Umpiring behind the plate was Dan Watkins, Hot Springs police chief. The Hot Springs Trojan Band and the Langston Drum and Bugle Corps provided the music. They postponed the fireworks display due to the misty weather.[3]

Now, they were ready to begin the home opener. Bill Fischer, 18-year-old right-hander from Marathon, Wisconsin, took the mound for the Bathers. The young Fischer sat down the first three Pine Bluff batters in order. In the bottom of the first inning, Tony Donofrio led off for the Bathers with a pop-up to second base. Gene Creekmore followed with a single to center field. Outfielder Steve Solis, the third batter, was at bat when the rains came.

An estimated crowd of 2,500 was in the stands when Umpires Buck Willson and Bill Fallers called the contest at 8:37 p.m., 30 minutes after players retired to their dugouts because of the downpour.[4]

Everyone was eager to roll the following evening. On April 22, the field, the players, the fans and the weather were ready to raise the home curtain on the 1949 season. Ticket prices ranged from 25 cents to a dollar. After losing two games at Pine Bluff, Hot Springs wanted a win, especially at the home opener. Since Fischer only pitched to three hitters the night before, he started, again for the Bathers. Fischer scattered nine hits, struck out seven, and went all the way as the hometown Bathers triumphed over Pine Bluff 5-3, before a large crowd of 2,331. Bathers' center fielder Gene Creekmore was the hitting star as he went 3-4 at the plate. He slapped a double, two singles, scored twice and contributed an RBI. Newly acquired, Harry Salvatore, a member of the 1948 championship team, helped the Bathers as he collected a single and scored twice.

The next night, Hot Springs hosted the Clarksdale Planters from Mississippi. A crowd of 1,161 saw the Planters take it to the Bathers 9-6. It seemed that the season was going to be much different from the championship team of 1948. New players started to drift in to the club. They needed them. Bill Close- shortstop, Leon Firestone- 3rd base and John Gabos - outfielder were three new players that arrived to lend a hand.

A few days later, Hot Springs had one of their best outings of the season by blasting Clarksdale 11-4 on five home runs, a Jaycee Park record. Clarksdale's Ed "Cotton" Hill, one of the leading pitchers in 1948, had the distinction of tossing up all five homers to the Bathers. Hot Springs went wild in the seventh inning by scoring eight runs. The headlines above the box score stated it all—-"Hill Dynamited."

Early in the season, the Bathers struggled to stay out of the cellar, but a big man from Michigan headed their way. On May 7, the management called up Dan Phalen to furnish firepower at the plate. He was six feet, six inches tall and played first base. Dan, one of the tallest players in the White Sox organization, reported from the Muskegon Clippers (Mich.) of the Class A, Central League. It took Phalen a few games to settle in to the new league and new pitching. Perhaps he bathed in the hot springs, consumed several cups of Mountain Valley Spring Water and received a massage at one of the bathhouses on "Million Dollar Bathhouse Row." Whatever he did, he snapped out of the mediocre hitting slump. Against the Greenville Dodgers at Jaycee Park on May 11, "Big Dan" reminded the fans why he was playing for the Bathers. He exploded with three smacks in four trips to the plate. He blasted a homer, spanked two doubles and knocked in four runs in four trips to the plate. Pel Austin, Bathers leading hitter, cracked three singles in five trips to the plate and scored a run. The Bathers scored nine runs on 11 hits. Does this sound impressive? Greenville nearly doubled the Bathers run output as they rapped out 17 runs on 16 hits. At least it was a good day for two Bathers.

There was a note in the local paper in mid-May concerning a former star player of the Bathers. Herb Adams, 21-year-old outfielder for the Chicago White Sox joined the Memphis Chicks of the Southern Association. In 13 games, he was hitting .302 for the Chisox before a finger injury side-lined the fleet-footed outfielder. Adams, the Cotton States League's leading hitter and MVP, played center field for the Bathers in 1948. Adams joined the Chicks in the middle of May.[5]

Pitcher Jeff Peckham pulled into the city around the middle of May to help bolster the Spa's mound staff. Peckham arrived from the Waterloo White Hawks. The next day he was on the hill at home against the Natchez Indians. Hot Springs exploded for four runs in the first inning as Peckham threw a seven hitter at the Indians, struck out five and won a 6-4 decision. Bathers' shortstop Bill Close was the standout hitter for the Spa team as he connected for three hits. He also scored once and added an RBI. Peckham, a returning Bather, pitched for the Spa team early in the 1948 campaign.

Since the Bathers stayed in second division for most of the season, usually sixth or seventh place, the crowds remained sparse. There were 872 fans at the game between Natchez and Hot Springs in May. However, the Bathers front office thought of ways to entice the crowds to the park. In pregame events of the Natchez game, two opposing left fielders entered the fungo-hitting contest as Natchez left fielder Chandler outdistanced Dick Anderson of the Bathers. Joe Rullo, Indian manager, won a novelty test with Bathers' manager Pete Fox. The Bathers came out on top in the running and throwing challenge. Bathers' catcher Fred Wasiluk won the accuracy throwing competition, while shortstop Bill Close sped around the bases in 14.9 seconds as he outran the Indians right fielder, Bob Sprentall. Lewis Goltz, owner of Lewis Jewelers, presented the winners with fountain pens.

By the end of May, the Bathers, planted firmly in second division, had four players in the top 20 in the league's batting race. Dan Phalen was the CSL's batting leader with an average of .362. Pel Austin, swatting the ball at a .336 clip, held down ninth place. Tied for 16th in the batting race were Bill Close and Charlie Schmidt at .316. Hot Springs was hanging on to third place in team hitting, but they were in fifth place in team fielding.

A surprise move occurred in early June. John Rigney, farm director of the Chicago White Sox, through Bathers general manager Milt Woodard, appointed 36-year-old, Glen (Gabby) Stewart, former New York Giants and Philadelphia Blue Jays (Phillies) infielder as player-manager of the Hot Springs Bathers. Stewart donned a Bathers uniform immediately as he took over the third base spot. Pete Fox, former manager, remained in the White Sox organization as a scout in another league.

A manager knows he is in trouble when greeted by a clown. Jackie (Johnny) Price, famed baseball clown from Bill Veeck's arsenal of tricks in Cleveland, performed the first night Stewart took control of the Bathers. Price, who gave up baseball to become an entertainer, caught fly balls from a jeep, batted and threw baseballs while he stood on his head. He also threw two baseballs at the same time in opposite directions to the crowd's delight. Price performed in front of millions of baseball fans across the country logging around 40,000 miles a year, mostly by driving his car. At a minor league, Class C game, he charged around $125 for each performance.[6]

Clarksdale greeted the new manager on his first outing and slammed Bathers pitcher, Bill Fischer for 7 runs on 17 hits. Welcome to Bathers world! However, the game was not that bad. Hot Springs overcame the 17 hit-barrage, by winning the game 8-7. A crowd of 1,573 welcomed the clown, the Bathers and the new manager.

Even though Stewart's chargers were hot and cold, home attendance on June 16, registered 1,216 paid fans. On June 19, league statistics showed that the Bathers were in 6th place in the team standings, but they had five players batting .300 or better. Steve Solis was the team leader with .310, Dan Phalen .307, Bill Close .301, Pel Austin and Dick Anderson each were hitting at an even .300 average.

In Hot Springs, it doesn't rain many times on July 4, but it did in 1949. It was a washout and the rescheduled game occurred a few days later. The fans returned to Jaycee Park on July 8, to watch the pregame festivities, post-game fireworks and a baseball game between Clarksdale and the Bathers. It was close, but the Planters wound up on top, 9-8. The fireworks display assisted in drawing nearly 3,000 fans to Jaycee Park, the largest baseball crowd in the history of Jaycee Park. "All available seating was filled and fans stood several deep along the third base line." Milt Woodard, general manager, was delighted and sad. Due to the huge crowd, he turned away close to 300 fans. Following the game, the belated July 4th Independence Day celebration began as nearly 50 pieces of spectacular fireworks dazzled the fans. An elaborate American flag display climaxed the 20-minute extravaganza.

The Cotton States League All-Star game, played in Helena, Arkansas, took place on Monday night, July 11. The Bathers representatives were second baseman Pel Austin and pitcher Danny Caccavo. A large crowd of 2,193 saw the All-Stars of Mississippi thump the Arkansas All-Stars 5-3. The Bathers' two players showed up well as Caccavo singled in the fifth inning and Austin rattled the fence by slamming a triple and driving in Caccavo to score.

In late July, southpaw Edward Kuta, a former semi-pro pitcher, signed with the Bathers. In addition, catcher John Gugala, restored to playing status, allowed Stewart to return to pilot the Bathers from the bench. Austin switched from second base to third base in the transition. Martin Kaelin became the regular second baseman as the Bathers currently had 17 players on their active roster.

Hot Springs hosted a national college coach's clinic and several coaches attended the Bathers game on August 4. The honored guests of the Bathers were Frank Leahy, football coach at Notre Dame; Clair Bee, basketball coach at Long Island University; Forrest England, football coach at Arkansas State; John Barnhill, University of Arkansas football coach; George Cole, assistant football coach at Arkansas and Gene Lambert, basketball coach at the University of Arkansas.

Well, it was just one of those seasons. Hot Springs outhit Helena 14-3 on August 16. It was difficult to believe, but Helena posted the win by going 10 innings to squeeze by the Bathers 3-2. Unearned runs due to errors solidified the win for Helena.

251

Eight Men Out is a movie and a book about eight Chicago White Sox players allegedly conspired with gamblers to throw the 1919 World Series. The incident known as the Black Sox Scandal damaged the name of baseball; however, on August 2, 1921, a grand jury acquitted the group. The next day, the first Baseball Commissioner K. M. Landis took office and immediately banned the eight players from playing professional baseball for life.

So, what did the 1919 incident have to do with the Bathers in 1949? The number eight and the White Sox were the two commonalities. Umpire Harold Willson tossed out eight Bathers during a game on August 21, at Helena, but it didn't seem to matter to the Bathers. Hot Springs ran past the Seaporters 9-4 with only the nine starters remaining on the field. Caccavo pitched the entire nine innings for the Spa win. The eight ejected Bathers were part of the White Sox farm system.

Willson's action was unprecedented. It was the first time in the post-war history of the league that eight men had been ejected from a single game. After loud and persistent heckling from the bench, Willson ordered a Helena policeman to escort Manager Gabby Stewart and the following out of the park: Roy Grant, Bill Fischer, Charlie Stiglich, Ed Kuta, Don Schmudlach, and Jeff Peckham, all pitchers: and Pete Grammas, injured outfielder-shortstop.

It was the first time in his 13-year career as a Major and Minor League player and manager that Stewart had been thrown out of a game.

The big rhubarb occurred as the teams changed fields after the Bathers' half of the eighth.

Stewart said he asked Willson to eject those who were doing the heckling, but the umpire told him he couldn't pick out the specific players, so he cleared the bench, leaving the nine starters to complete the game.[7]

In late August, the Bathers were out of the running for a play-off berth, but they tried to make it tough for the playoff bound El Dorado Oilers on Sunday, August 24. The Oilers scored six runs in the ninth inning, but fell one run short of the big comeback as the Bathers took a 12-11 victory. Schmudlach pitched well until the ninth frame when Stewart gave the ball to Jeff Peckham. He was a little wobbly, but settled down to preserve the win for Schmudlach. The big man of the night was Bathers' Dick Anderson who clouted a grand slam home run in the fifth inning. Grand slam home runs were not new to the Bathers' outfielder. It was the third time during the 1949 season that he blasted a grand-slammer. An exceptionally large crowd of over 1,000 attended the game.

The next night, was "Pete Grammas Night" at Jaycee Park. Grammas, steady infielder-outfielder, recently returned from the Bathers' injured roster. The Hot Springs' Ahepa Greek fraternal chapter honored him by presenting Pete with a gift. "The former Mississippi State College star joined the Bathers in July, and has been a sparkplug both in hitting and fielding. He is a member of the Ahepa chapter in his home town of Birmingham, Alabama."[8]

The Hot Water Boys ended the season at Clarksdale by pouncing on the Planters 9-3, in a 15-hit attack. Roy Grant, in one of his best twirling performances of the season, tossed a four hitter and won his seventh straight decision, ending the season with a 10-5 record. Kaelin, Phalen and Austin leaped on the Planters pitchers for three hits each. Following the game, many of the Bathers headed for home via Memphis; however, several players returned on the team bus to Hot Springs before going their separate ways.

Dan Phalen and Dick Anderson posted batting averages good enough to be in the top five in the Cotton States League hitting race. Phalen finished with a .318 mark, nine points behind the leader. Anderson wound up with a .312 batting average. Phalen, the long, tall first baseman copped the CSL's home run trophy by exploding with 22 round-trippers. The Bathers finished in sixth place in the team standings and first in team batting with a figure of .278, four points ahead of second place El Dorado. Hot Springs finished fifth in fielding and sixth in team standings, well off the pace for a playoff berth.

Chapter 11

Antonelli Leads Bathers
1950

"Tierney Hurls One-Hitter as Bathers Cop Playoffs." The Sentinel-Record,

In 1950, the Bathers had a working agreement with the Chicago White Sox. During the middle of February, the White Sox sent out 22 Bather contracts. The list included several players from the 1949 roster, but by opening day, there was a roster revision.

John Antonelli, playing manager; Herbert Anderton, Bathers owner (from Memphis); Chancellor Sam Garratt, club president and Wilson Murrah, general manager, guided the Bathers front office. Garratt was re-elected to his fourth term as president. Members of the Bathers board, appointed by Anderton, were Mayor Floyd Housley, Leland Leatherman, attorney; Prince Cook, auto dealer; Herbert Brenner, mortician; Lloyd Adams, hardware store owner; W. Clyde Smith, theater chain manager; Raymond Clinton, auto dealer; Van Lyell, bottling company owner and Lewis Goltz, jewelry story owner. Manager Antonelli should not be confused with Johnny Antonelli who pitched in the majors during the 1950s and 1960s. Other officers included Anderton as vice president-treasurer and Murrah as secretary-general manager. Anderton, owner of the Bathers, appointed Gus Dickson, local restaurateur, as concession manager for Jaycee Park.[1]

In December 1949, the White Sox sold their club holdings to Herbert Anderton, prominent Memphis restaurateur; however, the Chisox supplied the club players through a working agreement. "Anderton, 36-year-old native of Memphis, spent six years as an amateur and professional boxer before going into the restaurant business." Anderton enjoyed sports; however, this was his rookie year to be involved in a sports franchise.[2]

Anderton's choice to serve as general manager was Wilson Murrah, a former sportswriter for the *Memphis Commercial Appeal*. In 1948, Murrah was the general manager of the Vicksburg Billies of the Class B, Southeastern League and in 1949; he worked at a Memphis sporting goods store.

Park renovations were at the top of the front office's list. Construction of 200 box seats increased the seating capacity of Jaycee Park to around 3,000. Centralized entrances and an additional passageway to the grandstand became realities. In addition to new concession stands, a general manager's office was constructed. Two projects continued to be on the board as they wanted to pave the "dust bowl" around the park and provide better parking for the fans.

Eight teams representing three states made up the 1950 Cotton States League. The three Arkansas teams were El Dorado, Pine Bluff and Hot Springs. Greenville, Greenwood, Clarksdale and Natchez were the Mississippi contingents, while Monroe was the Louisiana representative in the loop. Monroe replaced Helena, which had been a member of the circuit for two years.

John Antonelli, the new player-manager for Hot Springs, born in Memphis in 1915, was an outstanding managerial prospect in the White Sox organization.

He broke into baseball in 1935 as manager and player for the Lexington, Tenn. Club of the Class D Kitty League. He shifted to Union City, Tenn. of the same circuit in 1937, and moved up to Houston, Texas of the Class A Texas league in 1938. As a farm hand of the St. Louis Cardinals, he moved to Columbus, Ohio in 1942 and joined the Cards in the latter part of the 1944 season. Later he was traded to the Philadelphia Phils, and in 1946 played for Buffalo. The next season found him at Baltimore. But it was in 1948 that he reached his peak with the Memphis Chicks. He batted over .300, and kept the Chicks scrapping in the pennant race.

Illness forced him from playing most of the 1949 season. A versatile infielder, he holds distinction of playing under four Major League managers – Eddie Dyer of the St. Louis Cards; Billy Southworth of the Boston Braves; Jack Onslow of the Chicago White Sox, and Bucky Harris of the Washington Senators.[3]

Three White Sox farm teams began a three-week training camp at Jaycee Park on March 26. Farm director Johnny Rigney was in charge of the spring practice sessions. Colorado Springs Sky Sox of the Class A, Western League and Waterloo, Iowa, White Hawks of the Class B, Three-I League joined the Hot Springs Bathers in spring drills. "Buddy" Hassett headed up the Sky Sox, while Otto Denning was the skipper of the White Hawks. Teams that traveled to the Spa to play one of the three teams in camp included Tulsa, Memphis, Little Rock, Hope (Arkansas) and the University of Arkansas.

The men who were in charge of the training camp included scout Freddie Shaffer, John Rigney, farm director, scout Joe Holden, manager "Buddy" Hassett of the Sky Sox, manager John Antonelli, manager Otto Denning of Waterloo, Bill McPhail, general manager of Colorado Springs, Tom Rigney, general manager of Waterloo, scout Frankie Parenti and manager Bennie Huffman of Superior, WI.

The three White Sox farm teams entertained members of the press and radio on the evening of April 8. The buffet dinner, held at the Majestic Hotel, was the third annual press-club party sponsored by the White Sox. Sam Garratt, president of the Hot Springs club, served as host and George Toporcer, field supervisor for the farm system, was guest speaker.

The University of Arkansas Razorbacks' baseball team visited Jaycee Park for a quick exhibition tilt with the Bathers. It was the first time the Hogs played a professional team, as the pros won the abbreviated seven-inning contest, 14-3. Bathers' second-sacker, Leo Grady was the hitting star with a three for three outing at the plate, including a double. Joe Thomasson, Hogs shortstop and Hot Springs product, collected two safeties in four trips to lead the Razorbacks. "Little Joe" Thomasson, star athlete at Hot Springs High School, was a three-year letterman on the baseball and football teams for the Razorbacks.

With the end of spring training and the beginning of league play, the Bathers paraded through downtown Hot Springs on Tuesday afternoon, April 18. Leading the parade were the Hot Springs High School Trojans Band and Langston High School Bulldogs Drum and Bugle Corps. Anderton, Murrah, Garratt and Antonelli headed up the car brigade, followed by 20 cars representing the many civic organizations in the city.

As the Cotton States League opened its new campaign, Al Haraway, president of the CSL, stated that the league drew an all-time high attendance of 437,383 in 1949. All the teams were advertising strongly in order to win the prestigious president's attendance trophy.

Pregame festivities began at 7:45 p.m., with the first pitch scheduled at 8:00 p.m. at Jaycee Park. W. Clyde Smith, member of the Bathers' board of directors presided over the pregame program. Smith introduced Chancellor Sam Garratt, president of the Hot Springs Baseball Club; Herbert Anderton, new club owner from Memphis and Wilson Murrah, general manager. Local radio personality, Bill Bailey, introduced the players of both teams. John Y. Harding, band director at the high school, directed the Trojan band in a brief concert. Dora Jane Ledgerwood, music teacher at Hot Springs High School, led the fans in singing the "Star Spangled Banner." Mayor Floyd Housley got the season cranked up by throwing out the "ceremonial first pitch." More than 1,500 orchids awaited the female fans as they passed through the turnstiles.

Steve Solis - center fielder, Don Tierney - left fielder and catcher Fred Wasiluk were three returning holdovers from the 1949 squad. Manager Antonelli was the seventh skipper to handle the Bathers during their past three seasons following World War II. The Bathers batting order for opening night included Alex Cosmidis – shortstop, Leo Grady - second base, Steve Solis – center field, Don Tierney - left field, Joe Jaworski - right field, Eugene Holder - first base, Fred Wasiluk – catcher, Jerry Brezen - third base and Harry Montgomery - pitcher.

Called into action for the Pine Bluff-Hot Springs series was Dorsey Roddenberry, "umpire-at-large." The well-known Spa photographer and former Cotton States League umpire officiated with regular umpire Bill Maslowski. Due to a death in the family, regular arbiter, Al Troychak took a leave of absence.

Pine Bluff was ready to spoil the Bathers opener as they jumped out to a 2-0 lead in the top of the first inning. Cosmidis belted a homer over the left field wall as he cut the lead in half in the bottom of the first inning. The Judges ran another player across the plate in the third inning, but the lead didn't last long. Hot Springs scored one run in the fourth and another one in the fifth inning to tie the contest. Bathers' bats came alive in the sixth, as they ripped across four runs to take the lead by four. Neither team scored the rest of the game as the Spa Boys won the opener 7-3 on 13 hits. Montgomery went the distance for the hometown crew as he tossed a six hitter, striking out six and walking five. Cosmidis and Tierney collected three hits each for the Bathers; however, Hot Springs was sloppy in the field as they committed five errors.

During the second inning of the 7-3 Hot Springs win, the first rhubarb of the season took place. Center fielder Jack Ramm of the Judges drew a walk. Catcher-manager Harry Chozen, the only CSL "holdover" manager from the 1949 season, hit a grounder to Cosmidis at short who tossed to Leo Grady at second for the force out on Ramm. Base runner Ramm slid in hard at second, upending Grady and spoiled the double play opportunity. Umpire Roddenberry, applying the new interference rule, thumbed Chozen out at first. Chozen rushed over to Roddenberry and began to argue the ump's call. After several minutes, Roddenberry had enough of Chozen's lip and tossed the pilot out of the game. Rookie catcher, Paul Burrows finished the game behind the plate for the Judges. The contest moved along quickly, taking only two hours and 10 minutes.

The Bathers lost the second home game and when Hot Springs arrived to play on Pine Bluff's diamond, the Judges drenched the Hot Water Boys with cold water, 17-0. After three games, the Bathers were in a three-way tie for next to last with a 1-2 record. However, the season was young.

Near the end of April, the Bathers gained a clean sweep in a three-game series with the El Dorado. The last game of the series took two hours and forty minutes, but the first inning lasted a marathon time of 49 minutes.

The league released the opening night fan figures, as the league declared Hot Springs the winner of the opening-game attendance trophy with a crowd of 2,567 fans. Monroe came in a close second as they pulled in 2,307 fans. Hot Springs won the trophy in 1948 with 3,000, but in 1949, the Bathers could only muster up 2,035 on opening night. President of the Cotton States League, Al Haraway reported the totals.

Haraway reported that a total of 17,806 – probably the largest in the 49-year history of the circuit – witnessed openers in eight league towns this year as compared with 15,715 in 1949.[4]

On Friday, May 5, Danny Caccavo took the Jaycee Park mound against the Monroe Sports in the opener of a three-game home stand. The usually wild, lefty from The Bronx, tossed a brilliant two-hitter, blanking the Sports, 3-0. He whiffed 15 and walked only one to win his third game in four starts as the win put the skids to the Bathers four-game losing streak. After an hour and 50 minutes, it was time for the 1,160 fans to head home.

About a week later, Hot Springs chugged into Monroe on a two-game win streak. The results didn't take up much room in the newspaper. In a brilliant pitching duel with Harry Tremel, Caccavo threw another shutout at the Sports, as the Bathers took a 1-0 win. His dazzling performance allowed only seven hits. Tierney of Hot Springs slapped a two-bagger, the only extra-base hit of the game. The Bathers lone run came in the second inning as rookie catcher Marty Lee singled to center to start the action. Don Tierney rattled the right field fence for a double, sending Lee to third. Joe Jaworski loaded the bases as he reached first base on an error. A single by Frank Gabry sent Lee scampering home from third for the winning lone run. Caccavo and Tremel both whiffed nine batters each as Caccavo walked three and Tremel walked one. Hot Springs had eight left on base and Monroe had five stranded. The game only took an hour and forty minutes. The following night, the Bathers posted their 4th win in a row, as they toppled Natchez 7-6 in 11 innings.[5]

On May 14, the Friend News Service of Blytheville, Arkansas, compiled the CSL statistics for the period ending May 9. In the league standings, Hot Springs was in third place closely followed by Clarksdale. The Bathers were in third position in team batting with a .265 mark. Pine Bluff was leading the loop with a whopping .307 team average. Clarksdale, supporting a .960 average in team fielding, was the league's leader, while the Bathers were next to last with a .937 figure. Charles Rugg of Greenwood and Cliff Coggins of Monroe were tops in pitching as each posted a 4-0 record. Hurling leaders for Hot Springs were Danny Caccavo and Harry Montgomery each with a 3-1 record.

Alex Cosmidis posted a .350 batting average, as he was only two percentage points behind first place leader Bob Kurtz of Pine Bluff. The diminutive Hot Springs shortstop also led the circuit in "most hits" with 28 and "total bases" with 46. Joe Jaworski, Bathers outfielder ranked sixth in the batting race with a .333 mark, while Frank Gabry, first baseman, upped his average to .325.

For the second straight night, Hot Springs won in the 11th inning as they ran their win streak to five. This time it was a 2-1 decision against the Planters at Clarksdale, Mississippi. Marty Lee, sensational rookie catcher, provided the fireworks as he cracked a double, driving in the winning run for the Spa team. Ed Schafer scattered five hits as he went all the way on the mound to cop the victory. The Spa pitcher struck out seven and walked four.

The next night, the Bathers won their sixth straight as Clarksdale went down by a 7-6 score. This time the winning run came in the ninth inning as 1,320 fans looked on at Jaycee Park. However, all good things must end and the next evening, Clarksdale won 4-1. On May 17, the Hot Town Boys and Greenwood were even in second position with 15-11 records. Pine Bluff was first with 17-10 mark.

On May 17, the Bathers beat Greenwood 11-6, as Caccavo whiffed 10 Dodgers to win his fifth victory in front of 1,184 home fans. It was the Spa's seventh triumph out of their last eight outings. In the last three games that Caccavo pitched, he whiffed 35 batters.

Bathers' Wilson Murrah, general manager, acquired first baseman Dan Phalen, who played the 1949 season in Hot Springs. The popular 6' 6" tall Phalen, who hit 22 home runs in 1949, returned to the Bathers, by option, from the Waterloo White Hawks. His first game back in the Bathers uniform was on May 18, against the Greenwood Dodgers at Jaycee Park. Hot Springs turned back Greenwood, 5-1 for their second straight victory, as Phalen went 1-4 at the plate. The Iowa native received a round of applause by the 1,267 fans, when he approached the plate in the second stanza. At this time of the season, the Bathers were in second place.

On June 23, a game and a half separated the top three teams in the loop. Pine Bluff was on top, while Hot Springs and Monroe tied for second. The Judges were still pouncing on the ball with a team batting average of .296. The Bathers managed to stay in the second slot with a team average of .263. Fielding was still a weak point with the Bathers sliding in next to last with a .943 score. Clarksdale's .957 was leading in that department. Cosmidis ranked number five in the batting race with a .328 average, while the "new kid on the block," Dan Phalen was not far behind at .320. Roy Jaworski batted a .290 clip.

The weather was hot in Greenwood on June 25, so were the Bathers as they crushed the Dodgers 18-2. The Dodgers were no match for the Bathers on this night as "Danny Boy" and the Bathers had it cooking! This was a night to remember for the Bathers as Caccavo whiffed 13 Dodgers, walked one and gained his seventh victory. The win put the Bathers only ½ game behind the league-leading Judges. It took Caccavo nearly three weeks to reach that lucky number seven win. Not only did Caccavo pitch lights out, he had a monstrous night at the plate, cracking out a homer, double, two singles and scored twice during his five times at the plate.

The Bathers took two from the Judges on July 6, at Jaycee Park 6-5 and 10-6. Ray Baer's relief pitching won in both games as 1,437 excited fans saw the doubleheader. In the nightcap, Bathers first baseman, Dan Phalen cleared the bases with a grand slammer in the 9th inning to assure the Bathers victory. Two days before the All-Star game, Hot Springs hammered the Greenville Bucks 22-1 at home.

The Community Park at Clarksdale, Mississippi, was the setting for the third annual Cotton States League All-Star contest. Harry Chozen, Pine Bluff's manager was in charge of the Arkansas-Louisiana team, while the Mississippi delegation was under the direction of Natchez pilot, Doug Adkins. The four Bathers that made the elite team were Fred Wasiluk – catcher, Dan Phalen - first baseman, Alex Cosmidis - shortstop and Dan Caccavo - pitcher.

Over 2,000 fans watched Hot Springs' All-Star, Dan Phalen slug two out of the park, slash a double and drive in four runs as the Arkansas-Louisiana team whipped the Mississippi All-Stars, 8-3. Pine Bluff's Ryne Duren gave up three runs to the Mississippi contingent in the eighth stanza, but the Arkansas-Louisiana boys hung on for the win.

By the middle of July, the active Hot Springs Junior Chamber of Commerce became the proud owner of Jaycee Park.

The last $500 of the $23,000 note was presented to the Arkansas National Bank. The payment ended a 3 ½ years fund raising campaign. More than 100 benefits were sponsored by organizations, after two campaigns failed to produce the $60,000 needed to construct the field in 1947.

Ten Hot Springs businessmen signed the $23,000 note, which provided the funds to complete the park.

The Chicago White Sox took over and made over $13,000 worth of improvement. The next project is paying for the paving around the park of 1,500 feet, paid over a ten-year period. [6]

Hot Springs was still in second place on July 16, as Cosmidis was batting .326, while Phalen was not far behind with a .312 mark. Caccavo had a 9-5 pitching record. A little over a week later, Hot Springs went into the dumpster as Natchez handed the Bathers their sixth straight loss. A few days later, Natchez gave the Spa team their eighth loss in nine games. On July 28, the Bathers humbled Clarksdale 15-2, as Hot Springs remained in first division. Phalan was the big gun going 4-5 including three round-trippers. Hot Springs, on a won-loss roller coaster, continued to fight back as they beat Clarksdale 10-1 for their seventh straight win.

On August 4, the third place Spa team shutout Clarksdale 1-0, for their eighth straight win. On August 5, Pine Bluff surged out of the gate in the opening frame by running across five runs and that would be all the Judges needed to humble the Bathers 12-4. Fred Wasiluk, Bathers catcher, was the best hitter on the Spa team as he went 2-4, but that didn't make a dent in the score. The next night the first place Judges turned back the Bathers 11-7, for the third consecutive time. On the same day, Hot Springs saw Natchez take a doubleheader from Monroe as Natchez tied Hot Springs for third place in the loop.

By the middle of August, the Bathers were on the move. On August 10, a "Ladies-Night" home crowd of 937 watched Hot Springs ease past El Dorado with an 8-7 victory as they chalked up their third straight win. Phalen's three-hit night, including his 17th homer and 2 RBIs, enabled Hot Springs to win. Left fielder Bob Hoeft, catcher Marty Lee and pitcher Bud Warfel added two hits each to the Hot Springs victory. Alex Cosmidis' provided the winning blow, a double, driving in Ray Baer in the eighth inning.

It was another one-run game for the Bathers winning their fifth straight, as Hot Springs eked out an 8-7 triumph over Greenville on August 11. A three-run splurge in the seventh inning did the trick for the Bathers. Outfielders Don Tierney and Bob Hoeft contributed three hits each and Brezen and Phalen added two hits each. Shortstop Cosmidis drove in two runs during the contest. Caccavo needed help in the seventh inning as "Fireman" Ray Baer lugged his water hose to the mound to help Caccavo gain his 15th victory.

Bathers' pitcher Bud Warfel, 26-year-old right-handed hurler, suffered a broken wrist by a pitched ball at Greenville on August 13. The 5' 9", 195-pound pitcher, ended his career with an 8-4 record and an ERA of 5.22. In 1949, his only other year in professional baseball, Warfel pitched for the Oil City Refiners (PA) Class C, in the Middle Atlantic League where he posted an 11-8 mark with the Pennsylvania team.[7]

A "no mercy rule" existed at Jaycee Park on August 16, as the Bathers handed Greenville a double loss, 12-4 and 4-0. The Bathers pounded out 33 hits in the twin bill as they blasted 20 hits in the first game and 13 safeties in the second contest; however, no player hit a home run in either game. Don Tierney, regular outfielder and part-time relief pitcher, threw his first nine-inning victory of the season. "Big Dan" Phalen connected for six hits during the two games, five in the first game and one in the second contest. Jerry Brezen, back in the line up after an Oiler pitcher beaned him in the noggin two nights earlier at El Dorado, connected for two safeties. The following day, the Spa team chalked up their fourth win in a row and 10 out of the last 11 games as they jumped on Greenville by a more modest count of 4-2.

On August 20, Ray Baer made his 43rd relief appearance for Hot Springs when he took over on the hill for Ed Schafer in the ninth inning, with no outs and two Clarksdale runners on base. The Bathers stopped the Mississippi club as the Bathers walked away with a 4-2 victory.[8]

Hot Springs demolished Natchez 16-1 on August 28, at Jaycee Park. The next evening, Natchez remained in town. The Bathers didn't fare as well on August 29, because two-run homers by Jones and Ruzuta help pace Natchez to a win over Hot Springs, 7-3. However, interesting pregame action took place at home plate. The purpose of the activity was to dedicate Jaycee Park by burning the $23,000 promissory note, which signified the removal of the mortgage on the baseball facility. The honor of burning the note went to Judge Clyde H. Brown, president of the Jaycees during the construction of the park in 1947. Among the special guests were the original signers of the 1947 note. The group included General Earl T. Ricks, Van Lyell, Dr. Louis Martin, Herbert Brenner, W. C. Brown, Judge Clyde Brown, Mose Klyman, Dr. H. King Wade, Sr., Jimmy Phillips and Will Lake.

Dr. H. King Wade, Jr. presided over the ceremonies and reviewed "the work of the organization in establishing Jaycee recreational park."[9]

Shortstop Alex Cosmidis ended the season with a batting average of .301 and shared the 1950 Cotton States League's Most Valuable Player honors with outfielder Jack Ramm of Pine Bluff. The two outstanding players won the trophy over 13 other nominees. The Hot Springs Jaycees first presented the award in 1948, when Bathers' excellent outfielder, Herb Adams overwhelmingly won the honor. Cotton States League sportswriters, managers and club presidents voted for the MVP.[10]

Cosmidis, whose home was Norfolk, Virginia, was a 21-year-old Navy veteran. Rated as one of the outstanding rookies in the Chicago White Sox chain, Cosmidis was the property of the Colorado Springs Sky Sox and played his college baseball at Illinois Weslyan. Ramm, 19, finished second in the CSL's batting race with a .348 average. The St. Louis Browns owned the rights to Ramm, a Detroit native. However, Ramm was a member of the Army Reserves and unfortunately was not around to collect his hardware since he left for active duty a few days before the presentation.

Maurice Moore stated that he appreciated Bathers trainer Jack Drobena. The trainer began his work with the Bathers about mid-season and it paid off. The players thanked Drobena by presenting him with an engraved watch.

Bathers split a doubleheader with Greenwood to end up in third place in the loop standings. They won the first game 12-5 and then, it seemed that it might have been one of those "who cares" games for Hot Springs as the Judges demolished the Bathers 15-0. The playoff format pitted first place Pine Bluff against the fourth place finisher Natchez. Second place Monroe took on Hot Springs.

1st Round Playoffs
(Best of 7)

Game 1 – Thursday, September 7, 1950 at Monroe, Louisiana
Monroe - 7 Hot Springs - 2

Hot Springs traveled to Monroe to begin the best of a seven game, post-season series without 16-game winner, Danny Caccavo. The big pitcher was out of action due to an ailing arm. Monroe hosted the first two games and Hot Springs was the host city for the next three contests. If needed, Monroe had the last two games of the series. The Bathers seemed to have been wobbly from that last regular season 15-0 encounter with Pine Bluff. The Bathers took the first playoff encounter on the chin by a score of 7-2. Bill Gingerich started on the hill for the Spa and lasted six innings giving up three runs on four hits. Monroe greeted relief pitcher Schafer with four runs on four hits during his brief stint. Umpires for the series were Lerch, Maslowski and Vanderhoof.[11]

Game 2 – Friday, September 8, 1950 at Monroe, Louisiana
Hot Springs – 11 Monroe - 10

The second playoff game was a comedy of errors and hits. The Bathers tied the series by out-lasting the Sports 11-10. There were 11 errors committed during the competition, eight by Monroe. In addition, "there were 21 bases on balls issued by seven pitches, 14 of them by four Hot Springs hurlers." The two teams pounded the ball all over the yard as the Bathers whacked 14 hits to the Sports 8. Rabka paced the Bathers with a three-hit night and Phalen's two hits, accounted for five RBIs. Baer, the third Hot Springs hurler, got the win.[12]

Game 3 – Saturday, September 9, 1950 at Hot Springs, Arkansas
Hot Springs – 9 Monroe - 3

The first night at home, the Bathers picked up a 9-3 triumph on seven hits and no errors as 1,290 fans looked on. Monroe came close to comedy game #2 as they erred five times. Converted pitcher Don Tierney struck out nine Sports and threw a no-hitter until the top of the sixth stanza. At the end of the sixth, Hot Springs was up 3-1. In the splendid seventh inning, Hot Springs romped for five runs. Monroe attempted a comeback in the ninth, scoring twice, but it was too late. Paid attendance was 1,290.[13]

Game 4 – Tuesday, September Sept. 12, 1950 at Hot Springs, Arkansas
Hot Springs – 6 Monroe – 2

Following a couple of rainouts, a crowd of over 1,400 fans jammed Jaycee Park on September 12, to witness the Bathers triumph over the Sports 6-2. Jack Colburn was shaky in spots as he walked nine Monroe batters, but three timely double plays got him out of several jams. Colburn tossed a seven hitter to reap the win. Lee, right fielder, was the Bathers hitting star as he went 3-4. The Bathers went up 3-1 in games. All they needed was one more win to be in the championship series with Natchez, who beat Pine Bluff in their playoff series.[14]

Game 5 - Wednesday, September 13, 1950 at Hot Springs, Arkansas
Monroe - 4 Hot Springs - 0

Jim Burns blanked the Bathers 4-0 as he hurled a masterful two hitter on September 13, at Hot Springs. A paid attendance of 1,334 saw a well-played game on both sides. Center fielder Allen Cross slammed the only home run of the game in the eighth frame. Gingerich, who was the losing pitcher against Burns during the first game, registered another loss. However, Gingerich pitched well giving up four runs on five hits in the eight innings that he worked. Umpires were Vanderhoof, Lerch and Maslowski.[15]

League president, Al Haraway of Helena, announced the loop's regular-season All-Star team. The team, chosen by managers and sportswriters, included three Bathers to the roster. The team consisted of 1B - Dan Phalen, Hot Springs; 2B - Harry Schwegman, Pine Bluff (unanimous choice); 3B – George Rezina, Natchez; SS – Alex Cosmidis, Hot Springs; LF – Ben Cantrall, Pine Bluff; CF - Jack Ramm, Pine Bluff; RF – Jim Gilbert, Natchez and C – Lou Landini, Greenwood. Pitchers included right-handers Cliff Coggin, Monroe and Adam Stepkowski, Pine Bluff. Dan Caccavo, Hot Springs and John Miskulin, Natchez were the two southpaw hurlers.

Game 6 – Friday, September 15, 1950 at Monroe, Louisiana
Hot Springs – 5 Monroe - 3

The sixth game of the series switched back to Louisiana as Don Tierney started on the mound for the Bathers. Suddenly, the Bathers were up 5-0 by the end of the third inning. The Monroe Sports started clawing their way back as they posted a tally in the fourth inning and two more in the sixth. At that time, the Bathers were still in charge 5-3. Manager Johnny Antonelli took out Bathers' starter, Tierney and traded him in for reliever Ed Schafer. Tierney pitched 5 2/3 innings and gave up three runs and only two hits. Schafer blanked the Indians the rest of the way. Bivens, the Monroe catcher was the only Sport that hit safely with two singles. The Hot Springs Bathers won the first round of the post-season playoffs by besting Monroe 5-3. Their next step was facing Natchez in the league championship series! Umpires were Maslowski, McGraw and Vanderhoof. Paid attendance was 2010.[16]

Championship Playoffs

(Best of seven)

Game 1 – Saturday September 16, 1950 at Natchez, Mississippi

Natchez – 4 Hot Springs - 2

Natchez took the first step toward the playoff championship as 1,126 fans watched the Indians glide by the Bathers 4-2 at the Mississippi ballpark. Both teams connected for nine safeties, while Solis, center fielder for Hot Springs slammed a homer with the bases empty. Antonelli used 14 players, including himself, to attempt to curb Natchez. Antonelli garnered a single in the eighth as he batted for Hoeft. Natchez scattered five errors, but it didn't hamper the outcome. Montgomery started for the Bathers and gave up two runs on seven hits in seven innings. Usually reliable Ray Baer pitched the eighth inning, but the Indians scored two runs on three hits, while Hot Springs put up a goose egg in the ninth. The Bathers left 13 on base, while Natchez left eight runners stranded. The winning pitcher was John Miskulin who went all the way for the Indians. Baer suffered the loss for the Bathers.[17]

Game 2 – Sunday, September 17, 1950 at Natchez, Mississippi

Hot Springs – 13 Natchez - 4

It was 9-1 at the end of the fourth inning before the Indians knew what hit them. Hot Springs went on to even the championship series by walloping Natchez 13-4 before a crowd of 1,045 in Natchez. Twelve Bathers went to bat in the fabulous fourth as Hot Springs cracked out six hits and dashed across home plate seven times. The Spa team racked up 13 safeties, including a two-run homer by catcher Fred Wasiluk in the second inning. Jack Colborn started for Hot Springs and pitched to one batter, hurt his arm and Tony Gubicza took over on the mound. Colborn gave up one run on one hit. Gubicza went the rest of the way as he gave up eight scattered hits and three runs to take the victory. Gubicza aided his cause by thumping out two doubles in five times at the bat, while Steve Solis ripped three hits off the opposing hurlers.[18]

Game 3 – Wednesday, September 20, 1950 at Natchez, Mississippi
Hot Springs – 7 Natchez - 6

After two days of rain, the series resumed in Natchez as Hot Springs went up a game on the Indians rallying past the Mississippi team 7-6. Three big scores on only one bingle in the seventh frame enabled the Bathers to win their second straight contest.

Starter Bill Gingerich went to the showers early after giving up four runs on four hits in the first inning. Antonelli replaced Gingerich with Ed Schafer who went the rest of the way. Schafer allowed only four hits and struck out six during his innings on the mound. Phalen and Cosmidis led the way with three hits each as Phalen scored the winning run on a walk. Manager Antonelli got the "old heave- ho" in the ninth when he protested a call when a Bather was called out for interfering on a bunt. Hot Springs led the series 2-1.[19]

Game 4 – Thursday, September 21, 1950 at Hot Springs, Arkansas
Natchez – 10 Hot Springs - 3

The fourth contest, on September 21, would have been a close game if Natchez hadn't scored in the sixth inning, but they scampered across the plate six times. Over 1,540 fans saw the Indians gallop away with a 10-3 victory. The series was now deadlocked at two apiece. "The Indians only garnered seven hits off starter Don Tierney and relief pitcher Baer, but they took advantages of walks and costly miscues to chalk up all of their runs in three innings." Both teams earned seven hits each. Second baseman Buddy Coleman, well-known Arkansan of Coleman Dairy fame, scored two runs for Natchez.[20]

Game 5 – Friday, September 22, 1950 at Hot Springs
Hot Springs – 3 Natchez - 2

In the fifth match up, the Bathers won an 11-inning defensive battle by the score of 3-2. An error by the Indians' third baseman George Ruzina enabled the Bathers to come out on top. Both teams managed seven hits as John Miskulin, Natchez pitcher, tossed the complete game. Bill Gingerich gave up only two runs in nine complete innings, but Tony Gubicza, who relieved Gingerich, did his duty in the 10th and 11th innings by holding the Indians scoreless and hitless. A Natchez error in the last of the 11th enabled the Bathers to pull off the victory as Gubicza received the win. Marty Lee, Bathers right fielder mustered two singles to lead the Spa hitting. Over 1,100 fans attended the game at Jaycee Park. [21]

Game 6 – Saturday, September 23, 1950 at Hot Springs
Natchez – 7 Hot Springs – 5

Natchez bounced back in the sixth game with a 7-5 win over the Bathers at Jaycee Park before a crowd of 1,446 paid patrons. The bottom half of the first inning looked promising as the Bathers scored three times. The lead didn't last long as the Indians dashed home with four runs. They added another score in the third inning and that was it for Harry Montgomery, Spa starter. The Indians added one run in the fourth and one more insurance run in the fifth. Hot Springs was unable to catch up. Marty Lee led the Spa Boys with three RBIs and three hits, including a double. Cosmidis added two more hits, including an extra base whack. Ed Schafer, Bathers relief pitcher, hurled 6 1/3 innings giving up only two runs on three hits. Montgomery took the loss. The series was even at 3-3.[22]

Game 7 – Sunday, September 24, 1950 at Hot Springs
Hot Springs – 7 Natchez – 2

Over 1,000 fans turned out to watch the finals of the Cotton States League Championship Series at Jaycee Park. The series had been nip and tuck. In the finals, Hot Springs jumped out to a 6-1 lead by the end of the third inning as Don Tierney hurled a one-hitter for the Bathers. Phalen homered twice as he led Hot Springs to the Cotton States League's Playoff Title. *The Sentinel-Record* printed the results in large letters.

Tierney Hurls One-Hitter As Bathers Cop Playoffs
Phalen Homers Twice As Hot Springs Tops Natchez Indians, 7-2

Thanks to Don Tierney's brilliant one-hit pitching performance, the Hot Springs Bathers are the Cotton States league's 1950 Shaughnessy playoff champions.

Tierney, who didn't start chucking from the mound until nearly mid-season, was touched for only one scratch single as the Bathers trounced the Natchez Indians, 7-2, in the final game Sunday at Jaycee Park. [23]

Not only did Tierney hurl a one-hitter, he struck out 12 Indians and blasted a triple to add to his resume. Utility Dick Moncrief, pinch-hitting for the pitcher Jayne, spoiled Teirney's bid for a no-hitter in the ninth inning when he popped a blooper into right field. Hot Springs jumped on Roy Jayne for 11 hits as he went all the way for Natchez. Brezen, Phalen, Cosmidis and Wasiluk vaulted on Jayne as each player picked up two hits. In the seventh inning, Cosmidis had the honor of rapping in the last Hot Springs run of the season.

The 1950 champion Hot Springs Bathers included Bill Gingerich, Ray Baer, Tony Gubica, Bill Maley, Marty Lee, Erv Rabka, Jerry Brezen, Alex Cosmidis, Bob Hoeft, Don Tierney, Danny Caccavo, Steve Solis, Fred Wasiluk, Ed Schaefer, Dan Phalen, Joe Jarworski, Joe DeGrazia, Jack Colburn, Harry Montgomery, Claude "Swifty" Dick (batboy) and Manager Johnny Antonelli.

The Sporting News, October 15, 1950, issue, listed the Cotton States League regular season paid attendance, including the All-Star tilt, as 437,254. The playoffs drew another 23,686 paying customers totaling 460,940 paying fans. Add 4,337 non-paying patrons to the numbers and the CSL drew 465,277 fans for the 1950 season.[24]

Chapter 12

Ownership: Fruit Basket Turnover
1951

"…we wish to highly commend the efforts and achievements of the Hot Springs Junior Chamber of Commerce in retaining and saving professional baseball in Hot Springs…" A. G. Crawford and W. D. Roddenberry

Three Chicago White Sox farm teams began spring training in Hot Springs. Colorado Springs Sky Sox began spring workouts at Jaycee Park on March 23, while the Waterloo, Iowa White Hawks and the Hot Springs Bathers started on April 1. The Sky Sox represented the Class A, Western League, while the White Hawks were from the Class B, Three-I League. Hot Springs represented the Class C, Cotton States League.

Many minor league teams had financial problems. During the 1950 season, the Bathers went in debt by more that $13,000. The Korean War (1950-1953) was about a year old and it was tough economic times, but the people of Hot Springs wanted to be a part of professional baseball. Owner Anderton and Sam Garratt, Bathers' president, issued a joint statement on April 7, that the team was financially able to participate in the 1951 Cotton States League.

The club has an able playing manager and has been assured sufficient players by the Chicago White Sox organization to field a baseball club.

All attention of the management is now being given to our opening night of April 19, so that we may again capture the opening day attendance trophy.

The cooperation and support of loyal baseball fans is sought with the promise of the management for another hustling baseball club.[1]

Rex Carr, the well-traveled, 35-year-old from Lexington, KY, served as the new Bathers' pilot. In 1950, he guided the Harlan (KY) Smokies to a first place finish and playoff championship in the Class D, Mountain States League. Carr planned to be a catcher-manager at Hot Springs.

The Cotton States League, composed of eight teams, included three Arkansas teams, the Pine Bluff Judges, the El Dorado Oilers and the Hot Springs Bathers. The four Mississippi teams were Clarksdale Planters, Greenville Bucks, Greenwood Dodgers and Natchez Indians. The representative from Louisiana was the Monroe Sports.

The Bathers traveled to Pine Bluff to open the 1951 season. It was not a good opening night for the Bathers as the Judges dunked the Bathers 12-6. Vince Giammario, 22-year-old left fielder from Chicago, was the Bathers hitting standout as he went 3-5. The next night, the Bathers eked out an extra inning 11-9 victory at Pine Bluff. Knotted up at 9-9 at the end of the regular contest, the Bathers took advantage of an error and a wild pitch in the extra frame to cop the victory. Relief pitcher, Don Ehlers who had just arrived on game day, threw hitless ball against the Judges in the 10th inning. Jim Rentschler, right fielder from Spring City, Pennsylvania, blasted a homer and a single for the Bathers. In addition, Pel Austin, strong hitting first baseman, from Peach Orchard, Arkansas, slapped two doubles for the winners.

Officially designated as "Mr. Bather," Corporal Johnny Back, of Paragould, Arkansas, received his new title in a hospital room at the large Army and Navy Hospital in Hot Springs. Chancellor Sam Garratt, club president and Herbert Anderton, Bathers owner, presented the special award to

Back. The Korean War veteran was the special guest of the Bathers on opening night at Jaycee Park. He also served as honorary marshal of the "Meet Your Bathers" parade through downtown Hot Springs. During the pregame ceremonies, Back tossed the first ball from his wheelchair. The ceremonial throw officially launched the baseball season in Hot Springs.

During his high school days at the Greene County Consolidated School in Arkansas, Back was a "pretty fair" shortstop and like many youngsters, had the aspirations of playing big league baseball someday, but he said he "loved the Army better." In 1950, he joined the Army at 17-years old. Soon, he was on a troop ship headed for a place called Korea. In August, thirty days after he landed in Korea, he was in a hot war.

He was wounded near Sobuksah by the same hand grenade that killed his buddy in a fox-hole, but he (Johnny) recovered enough to single-handedly hold off the enemy (Communist troops) until reinforcements arrived.[2]

Blown from the foxhole, Back quickly located his machine gun in the dark and began firing at the enemy. At first light, American reinforcements saw that there were about 30-40 enemy bodies lying within several yards of John's foxhole.

He said he wanted to make the Army a career if they would let him. Following the injury, he landed in Hawaii and entered Tripler Army Medical Hospital. The surgeons fused Corporal Back's wounded ankle so that he would eventually walk, but his ankle would not have full range of motion. For a year and a half, he remained in Army hospitals. When he left Hot Springs in the latter part of June 1951, he walked under his own power.

On opening night, Corporal Back represented 300 Korean War veterans who were convalescing at the Army-Navy Hospital. The previous week, the Army awarded young Corporal Johnny Back the Silver Star for his heroism. Some of his military buddies, including his platoon leader, thought that he should have received the Medal of Honor. Capt. Edna Lynn, a nurse at the military hospital and a native Arkansan, assisted Sgt. Back in his wheelchair at the opening night festivities. John related that Capt. Lynn was a Lieutenant stationed at Tripler Hospital in Hawaii during the surprise attack on Pearl Harbor in 1941.

Mr. Back continues to live in Arkansas. In a telephone interview on August 2009, Johnny stated that he has cancer, and is convalescing at his granddaughter's home in Jonesboro, near Paragould. Retired Supply Sergeant Back, yes, retired sergeant, served 20 years in the Army. A few years after he left the Army and Navy Hospital in Hot Springs, he decided to retire from the Army... and he did. However, within six months, he re-enlisted. Sixteen years following the Korean War, the Army sent him to Viet Nam. In addition to Viet Nam, he served in the United States, Europe, Japan, and long after the Korean War, he served a second tour in Korea. He married Louise on Dec. 24, 1953. During his tour in Europe, Debra, his youngest child, was born in Germany. His two older sons are deceased and after nearly 46-years of marriage, his wife passed away in 1999. In 1970, he resigned from military duty, with 20 years service and returned to his Arkansas roots.[3]

Among other special guests at opening night on April 19, were Mayor Floyd Housley and Col. H. S. Villars, commanding officer of the Army and Navy Hospital. W. Clyde Smith, master of ceremonies, introduced the Bathers and the Pine Bluff Judges to the 1,784 fans. The Hot Springs High School band played a brief concert and Dora Jane Ledgerwood, music teacher at the high school, sang the National Anthem as the Stars and Stripes flew in center field.

The Judges spoiled the opener for the Bathers 13-8. Pine Bluff smacked the ball all over the yard as they popped 16 hits off starter Tony Gubicza. Before the fans had time to purchase their peanuts and popcorn, the Judges piled up five runs on three hits in the first inning. Pine Bluff kept heaping it on. By the fourth inning, it was 9-2. The Judges tallied four more runs in the eighth stanza. The Bathers attempted a rally in the eighth as they garnered five runs, but the uproar fell short. Hot Springs managed eight hits during the struggle. The outstanding play for the Bathers occurred in the eighth frame as Erv Rabka, speedy second sacker, hit the ball to deep center field. The speedy Rabka turned on his afterburner and flew around the bases for an inside-the-park home run. His parents traveled all the way from Rhode Island to see Erv hit one of a very few inside-the-park homers at Jaycee Park.

A few days later, Joe Mattis hurled an exceptional five-hit, 4-0 shutout against El Dorado. It was the first start of the season for the 25-year-old. Following the blanking of El Dorado, the Bathers went on a rampage and won four straight. About a week earlier, Mattis suffered from the flu. What a difference a few days make! The Oilers stuck it to the Bathers at Jaycee Park 18-2, snapping their four-game win-streak. El Dorado ran up 11 runs in four innings and Hot Springs didn't help its cause as they committed 10 errors!

Jim Elder, general manager of the Bathers, stated that ticket sales were going slowly and urged the fans to purchase their tickets soon. Soon, problems began to surface. The main problem continued to be the lack of money. Maurice Moore, the reliable sports editor for *The Sentinel-Record*, spoke very candidly and honestly in his "Sports Shifting" column. True, the team was not clicking on all cylinders, but fan support was down to less than 500 a game for the first 10 home games. Owners of sports franchises are sports fans, but they are in the business to make a buck. Herbert Anderton of Memphis bought the Bathers from the Chicago White Sox and thought the club was salvageable. The team was in a tailspin and so was the club's stock. Increased fan attendance equals profits. In fact, many additional fans needed to walk through the turnstiles in order to keep the team in Hot Springs.

...The franchise could go elsewhere, and if conditions don't change soon, it will...The only financial assistance sought from the citizens at large is through stronger attendance...[4]

Pel Austin was one of the bright spots in the Bathers lineup. He was a popular player for the Bathers in 1949, and he was just as popular in 1951. They called him "Pelting Pel." Following the season, Austin would become the new Athletic Director of Elaine (AR) High School. Minor league players in the 1950s worked at other professions during the offseason and Austin was no exception. However, Pel could swing the timber, but his batting average began to drop. Austin was shifting from first base to third base to second base, but he liked left field the best. He talked to manager Carr and asked him if he could switch from the infield to the outfield, his regular position. He thought his batting average would increase if the change occurred. Carr was accommodating, especially to his star player. The manager pulled off a fruit basket turn over. Carr went to first base, Leo Grady moved to second, Erv Rabka jumped over to shortstop and Tom Galli hopped over to third base. It was sort of like the Bud Abbott and Lou Costello skit, "Who's on First." By May 1, Hot Springs was in a sixth place tie, but Austin raised his batting average 38 points in one week. Pel scattered the ball around the park at a .393 clip and ranked third in the league hitting.

On May 6, Moore reiterated that Hot Springs could be on the verge of losing a professional baseball team. He said that in 1947, the Junior Chamber of Commerce started with nothing and through fund-raising, public subscriptions and any legal means possible, raised money to build Jaycee Park. "The diamond was rebuilt by one of the best groundskeepers in the country – Gene Brossard." He stated that the park was worth more than $100,000. Moore asked the fans to contact Judge Garratt, Elder and/or players, if anyone knew the reason or reasons for the decline in attendance.[5]

On May 10, Hot Springs dropped their fourth straight game, this time a no-hitter to the second place Monroe Sports. Chris Crisco, threw a 5-0, no-hitter at the Bathers in a game that lasted a brief one hour and 45 minutes. By the middle of May, the Spa team was in fifth place in team batting with a .253 mark. The Bathers were last in fielding and sixth in team standings. Austin and Carr led the Bathers batters with a .340 and .325 respectively.

By May 26, the Bathers were in seventh place. Owner Anderton was ready to pull the plug. He lost too much money and was disappointed of the wilting fan support. To financially operate a sound, Class C baseball team, he said it took $9,000 a month and for that to happen, around 900 fans needed to walk through the gates each game. The opening night crowd was a good number, registering 1,700, but soon dropped to 600 per game. Actual attendance per game during the last several weeks in May registered between 250-500 die-hard fans. That wouldn't keep a franchise afloat. Therefore, Anderton decided to cut his losses and get out before he lost more money.[6]

On Saturday, May 26, the management and other interested parties met in the chancery courtroom of the Garland County Courthouse to decide the fate of the club. There seemed to be several options for the Spa club. The options were (1) increase attendance; (2) individual or individuals purchase the club; (3) subscribe to area fund-raising activities; (4) a combination of any of the above ideas or (5) the club throws in the towel and abandons the Cotton States League. Clarksdale was considering the same thing, so the league stared at a possible six-team league. It was not a good situation for Clarksdale, Hot Springs or the league.

Anderton purchased the Class C franchise from the Chicago White Sox in December 1949, and last season operated the club at a loss. After deliberation and consultation with Hot Springs sports enthusiasts, he decided to carry on here again this season.

A general drop in attendance and the fact that the Bathers have won only three out of their last 21 games have chopped the attendance from previous highs of 600 to 700 to crowds averaging from 250 to 500.

Anderton recently paid off $4,100 in back federal taxes, and expended more than $2,000 more on debts left over from last season.

It was pointed out that the Bathers need funds to fulfill their out-of-town schedule at Pine Bluff and El Dorado during the next five days.

Several Hot Springs sports enthusiasts have expressed interest in the club, but no offers have been made.[7]

The Saturday meeting produced another meeting. The second meeting planned for the citizens of Hot Springs to take over the franchise. Anderton's indebtedness amounted to $15,137.75. A stock-selling campaign, conducted by a steering committee headed by Chancellor Sam Garratt, emerged. In addition to Garratt, committee members included W. D. Roddenberry, Van Lyell, Herbert Brenner, Lewis Goltz, Leland Leatherman, Lloyd Adams, Nathan Schoenfeld, W. Clyde Smith and Mayor Floyd Housley. Other members were Dr. H. King Wade, Jr., Ray Smith, Jr., Richard Ryan, Harrison Shepard, Henry Britt, Tommy Ellsworth, Bob McVey, Mrs. Lena Buchannan, Circuit Judge C. Floyd Huff, Jr., Prosecuting Attorney Julian Glover, Pete Flippin, Ish Beam, Norton Meek, Jack Smith, Tommy Dodson and J. R. Smith.

Chancellor Garratt stated that the group planned to sell stocks for $100 per share and $50 per half share. He said that the citizens group must pay $10,637 to the owner and pay an additional $4,500 to the Chicago White Sox. The committee wanted Chicago to pick up the $4,500 tab, but the Chisox were non-committal concerning the debt.

Jack Smith, president of the Junior Chamber of Commerce, got the ball rolling by stating that the Jaycees pledged to pay the $750 rental owed on the park. Garratt mentioned that the overall general debt amounted to $6,164.73 and the current state and federal taxes amounted to $1,472.70. Anderton paid his back taxes of $4,100 to "square away" with the government. Also outstanding were the $2,100 player's payroll and $900 for park personnel. Garratt flatly told people that if they bought shares, they could easily lose money. He suggested that there were four reasons for lower attendance: "(1) bad weather; (2) lack of money; (3) considerable illness in the city; and (4) opposition to outside ownership." Perhaps another huge reason was a losing team.

Before WW II, the citizens owned the Bathers; however, the team had working agreements with the Detroit Tigers and the Nashville Vols of the Southern Association. In 1947, Blake Harper bought the team and soon sold out to the Chicago White Sox in May of that year. Chicago operated the team through 1949 when Anderton bought the team in December 1949. Garratt said that Anderton invested more than $10,000 into the Bathers.

Meetings continued. The committee labored on the project in the attempt to sell stock. Soon, the paper announced that the "sum of $5,000 stands between Hot Springs and retention of its franchise in the Cotton States league." At the meeting, Al Haraway of Helena and president of the Cotton States League told the group that, "there's no reason why Hot Springs can't raise this money and continue in organized baseball."

> *'You are the only judges as to whether you can assume the obligations,' he declared. 'Hot Springs has always been a good baseball town, and the city itself has too much civic pride to lose the franchise.'*
>
> *'It would be a black eye for Hot Springs if the citizens gave up,' he declared. 'Being a member of the Cotton States league is a great advertising medium over the South, and it's the finest a small town can have.'* [8]

One day before the deadline, headlines in the city newspaper declared, "Junior Chamber of Commerce Takes Responsibility of Reorganizing Bathers."

> *Nathan Schoenfeld, member of the board, and president of the Junior Chamber at the time of the construction of the park declared:*
>
> *'When the Jaycees constructed the park, they pledged to the people of Hot Springs they would bring (back) organized baseball. I am asking that we don't go back on that pledge.'* [9]

Therefore, the Jaycees came to the rescue of Organized Baseball in Hot Springs. How long would a minor league team survive in the Spa was anybody's guess. However, for the present, the Bathers continued to be the Cotton States League's representative in Hot Springs.

On Thursday, June 7, the Bathers became a part of history. The Bathers fell to the Greenville Bucks at Greenville 7-6, but the contest lasted 19 innings! It was the longest game in CSL post-war play and probably the longest game in the history of the CSL! The Bucks' marathon victory lasted four hours and fifty minutes. Tony Gubicza, Hot Springs pitcher, walked manager "Arky" Briggs with the bases loaded in the bottom of the 19th frame and Al Yanen trotted across the plate with the winning run. The 1,100 fans saw Gubicza take over on the hill in the second inning. He threw an unheard of 17 innings! It was his best pitching performance since he came to the pros two years previously. However, the hard-luck pitcher had nothing to show for his toil. He lost eight straight decisions. The game, originally scheduled for seven-innings, since it was the front-end of a doubleheader, lasted too long for the second game to be played. They postponed the second game until a later date.

Early Saturday morning on June 9, strong winds blew through the city and damaged the score-board and a large section of the right field fence at the baseball field. Reports estimated the damage at approximately $750. A few weeks before, the Jaycees financially rescued the Bathers. Now, local unions took their turn at throwing out the lifeline to the Bathers. Carpenters Local #891 and Electricians Local (IEBC) #619 volunteered to repair the damage without charge. Heading up the repair work were J. C. Mason of the carpenters union and Jim Mosley and Walter Hardison of the electricians union. The kind act enabled Natchez and the Bathers to play their regularly scheduled game on Monday night.

Financially, the Bathers nearly went down for the count, but thanks to the Jaycees, the revived Bathers continued to slug it out in the Cotton States League. The Jaycees and the management put their heads together and came up with a unique plan. Their plan was simple…go forward and not look back. They hit the restart button and had a "second opening night." It's unheard of, but that's the ingenuity of the people of Hot Springs. "Second Opening Night" was an excellent idea…if it worked.

Sports Columnists, Maurice Moore recorded his thoughts in *The Sentinel- Record* of June 10.

What could be more fitting than a second 'opening night' for the Bathers? Basically, the Bathers is the same (team), which started the season in April, but there have been several roster changes. The ownership is brand new. The Junior Chamber of Commerce *now owns the club, lock, stock, and barrel. And from the amount of the debts left behind by former owner Herbert Anderton, the Jaycees might need those barrels later. Anyway, they're sweeping aside everything that's happened before, and will try to give the young players a new lease on life with a gala celebration Monday night (June 11). More than 1,700 fans turned out on April 19 for the first game. The Jaycees want to top that mark. They've taken on a hard task, one that needs unlimited support if professional baseball is to remain in our midst.*

The new board of directors has outlined a full program, starting with an extensive stock-selling campaign in which it seeks to raise $5,000 to pay off funds borrowed to close out transfer of the franchise from Anderton to the Jaycees. The Jaycees didn't pay the former owner a cent. They merely assumed obligation of paying off debts accumulated last season and so far in this one. Most baseball fans are glad to see Chancellor Sam Garratt back as president of the club. He has wanted to quit several times because of his heavy judicial schedule, but each time he's been persuaded to remain. The judge said the other day, 'I'm going to work even harder than before to help keep baseball here.'[10]

Moore applauded Tony Gubicza, the losing pitcher in the "marathon game" a few games ago. Moore wanted to light a fire under the fans so they would come out to the games and support the Bathers.

Tony Gubicza is in a rut with eight straight losses, but the Philadelphia lad may have snapped out of his slump at Greenville the other night. He relieved Pat Waters in the second inning, and pitched the remaining 17 in that 19-inning thriller. He made Cotton States history with that stint, even though he lost when he walked the winning run across in the 19th with two out. Nevertheless, the Philadelphia kid deserves a heap of credit for his courage and stick ability. The club may not win often, but when they play games as they did against the Bucks in that marathon, how can you help but support them?[11]

The second opening night was a success! Over 1,500 fans came out to watch the newly organized Bathers. During the pregame ceremonies, Henry Britt, new Jaycees president and Hot Springs attorney, awarded Chancellor Sam Garratt an honorary membership in the Jaycees. Other activities included the drawing for a $169.00 electric dishwashing machine. Hot Spring resident, Roy Gentry became the proud owner of the appliance presented by Elliott Butane Gas Company. During the game, Mayor Floyd Housley and the city council operated the concession stands. The outcome of the game was not as enjoyable. The third place Natchez Indians put the pressure on the sixth place Bathers as they soaked the Spa, 13-9 win.

Maurice Moore, in his sports editorial, interviewed an unidentified veteran Cotton States League manager who thought the players of 1951 were spoiled. The unnamed manager said that he couldn't get on their case anymore, because they may get angry and go home, as one player did recently. Some players think they are prima donnas; therefore pampering exists. The manager said that players put themselves ahead of the team. "He blames bonuses as one of the contributing factors." Recently, a seasoned player in the Cotton States League "finished a game the other night, jumped in his car and headed for his home in the East without saying 'hello', goodbye, or I'm gonna leave you now." Even some semi-pro baseball teams were paying decent salaries, which attracted players to leave professional baseball. In addition, "Bonus Babies" rubbed Hornsby the wrong way.

It wasn't too long ago that Rogers Hornsby told friends here what he thought about bonuses to players, and it would have made some of the high-priced 'boys' turn a bright red. Hornsby came from the old school, where a player had to slug or be slugged to stay in the lineup and be assured of a meal ticket.[12]

The league All-Star game at El Dorado pitted the Mississippi teams against the Arkansas-Louisiana group on July 9. Over 2,500 fans watched the Mississippi crew score one run in each of the first two innings, add two more runs in the fifth inning and win the mid-season classic by a 4-1 margin. Starter and league's leading pitcher, Billy Muffett of Monroe took the defeat. Pel Austin and Leo Grady were the only two Hot Springs players to see action in the game, in which Mississippi evened the series two games each.

Henry M. Britt, local attorney and president of the Jaycees, declared that the home team needed more fan support. The team was heading south financially and in league standings. It seemed as though the Bathers would never win enough games to jump up to the first division in time for the playoffs. The front office was doing their best to pay the bills.

One bright spot in the Bathers organization was the family of Pel Austin. The Hot Springs outfielder was swatting the ball at an amazing .350 clip. In fact, he was the top hitter in the league, but Jim Gilbert of Natchez was right on his heels at .348. Amidst his hitting streak, the Austins became proud parents of Randy Austin who was born on July 19. A few days following his birth, the Bathers designated a "Randy Austin Night" in which the youngster received many gifts. Pel and family planned to leave the team in August in order for the star player to assume his coaching duties at Elaine High School near Helena, Arkansas.

Near the end of July, in addition to Austin, Rex Carr continued to hit well as he remained in the top-ten hitting race with a .327 mark. Leo Grady was staying right up there with the big boys at .295. As a team, the Spa Boys were hanging around sixth place in the league standing, fourth in league batting and last in league fielding. Pitching and fielding continued to be suspect as no reinforcements were heading to the Spa.

On Monday night, July 30, the Bathers observed "Blood Recruitment Night" at Jaycee Park. Since the war in Korea continued and there was a tremendous need for blood for the soldiers. Through the Garland County Red Cross chapter, the Bathers gave away two free Bathers tickets to each person who registered to be a donor. The Army-Navy General Hospital blood bank was near depletion and the recipients of the drive were the patients at the military hospital in the city. The Army and Navy's excellent band played before and during the game for the enjoyment of the crowd. Uniformed Red Cross workers, seated at desks under the grandstand, signed up over 60 individuals. Special guests included Major General William G. Livesay (Retired), Mrs. Livesay and 10 Korean War casualties "whose lives were saved by blood administered on the battlefield." Chairperson of the blood drive, Joe Zahalka, presided as master of ceremonies.

The Sentinel-Record reported on August 4, that A. G. "Gabe" Crawford and Tom Stough planned to purchase the Bathers.

The club has been beset by financial troubles ever since the Chicago White Sox sold the franchise to Anderton, who finished the 1950 campaign more than $13,000 in the red.[13]

A few days later on August 8, information of the sale of the club made it official. The Jaycees decided to sell the club to Crawford and Stough. The two new owners paid the Jaycees $7,275 for the franchise. From this amount, the Jaycees planned to pay off as much debt as possible. Perhaps the third time was the charm. Hot Springs seemed determined to continue organized baseball in the Spa city. "Gabe" Crawford, drug store owner and Tom Stough, operator of a deep-freeze storeroom, purchased the 200 shares of stock held by the Jaycees, as they looked to the future. There were 64 other minor stockholders. At this time, Crawford and Stough planned to attend the meeting of minor league owners in Columbus, Ohio, in December.

Herbert W. Anderton of Memphis, who bought the club from the Chicago White Sox in 1950, declared last May that he was unable to continue, and the Jaycees assumed the ownership to continue professional baseball in the resort.

When debts began accumulating at an alarming rate, and attendance began slumping after a brief rise, the Jaycees offered the club for sale.

…Under the provisions of the new contract, signed yesterday afternoon, the Jaycees will be given proceeds of one night's game a year. This practice had been an annual affair until Anderton dropped it in 1950.

Out of the sales money received from the new owners, the Jaycees paid off a $4,000 bank note that they had assumed last June to continue baseball.[14]

On August 9, the Bathers mustered only one run in a double header as the team lost 1-0 and 5-1 to El Dorado. Hot Springs only managed two hits in the first game and five safeties in the nightcap. By August 13, the Bathers lost five games in a row and they spiraled downward to sixth place in the standings. It didn't get better! By August 19, the Bathers were in another tailspin. When the Monroe Sports walloped the descending Bathers 9-0, it was their 11th loss out of 12 starts. It couldn't get worse, but it did. *The Sentinel-Record* reported on August 22, the "off course" Bathers could not find the winning column as they lost their 14th game out of the last 15 contests.

Right-handed Pel Austin, the six foot, 195-pound stalwart outfielder and former Arkansas State footballer, scooted eastward to assume his high school coaching duties in Elaine, Arkansas. Even though there were a few weeks remaining in the season, his .337 average was strong enough for him to wind up in third place in the CSL batting scramble. Austin was among six who received votes for the league's MVP.

On August 25, *The Sentinel-Record* noted that A. G. Crawford became the new president of the Hot Springs Bathers, following a meeting at Phillips Willow Room on Park Avenue. Chancellor Sam Garratt, five-year president of the club, became the chairman of the board. Other new board members included Tom Stough, vice president-treasurer and W. D. Roddenberry, secretary. The meeting was the first meeting of the new board and their first order of business was looking to the future…making plans for the 1952 season.

Near the end of the 1951 season, fans selected John Gabos, center fielder, as the Bathers "Most Valuable Player." Gabos, the defensive sparkplug, hit 20 home runs, batted .248 and established a

Cotton States League record for total walks with 144. For his efforts and honors, Vance Brothers Pawnbrokers presented the diminutive outfielder a shotgun. Gabos was out of action during most of the previous season due to an illness. The Bathers "Most Popular Player" award went to Leo Grady, Bathers left fielder. Grady rocked along with a .284 batting mark.

This was not the Bathers year. Even home-pregame activities went awry. Before a Sunday game on August 26, a faulty parachute kept stuntman Glen Albright from jumping from a height of 3,000 feet. Regulations required parachutist to jump with two parachutes. "Albright was in the plane ready to leap when he discovered the faulty second chute." [15]

On August 31, the last game of the season, Hot Springs topped Pine Bluff 5-2 at Jaycee Park. It was "fan appreciation night" at the park, as Mrs. J. B. Dahl won the $100 cash prize given by the Bathers organization.

An article appeared in *The Sentinel-Record* praising the work of the Jaycees. A. G. "Gabe" Crawford, one of the new owners and president of the club and W. D. Roddenberry, secretary, signed the letter.

'On behalf of the stockholders and the board of directors of the Hot Springs Baseball Club, Inc., we wish to highly commend the efforts and achievements of the Hot Springs Junior Chamber of Commerce in retaining and saving professional baseball in Hot Springs and for the community. The people of Hot Springs should feel gratified to have an organization composed of young men, such as yours, having the ability and the determination to succeed in community service. Even though public support of the organization and its goals may vary from time to time, we feel confident that the general public of Hot Springs recognizes your achievements with pride.

'It is our wishes that you convey this message to members of the Junior Chamber of Commerce at your earliest convenience.' [16]

The Bathers wound up in sixth place in the eight-team circuit, next to last in club batting and last in fielding. Hot Springs finished 25.5 games behind the first place leader, the Monroe Sports. Hot Springs drew 40,564 fans, which put them in sixth place in team attendance in the league. Over 70,200 walked through the turnstiles in Monroe, Louisiana, as the Sports took the top spot in attendance.

Manager Rex Carr ended the season with a respectable .302 batting average and Leo Grady finished up with a .281 batting mark which was the third highest batting average on the Bathers. Even though Hot Springs needed help on the mound, each of the three hurlers had a fair season. John Brumm, 23-year-old right-hander, finished with a 13-12 pitching record and a 3.25 ERA. Don Ehlers, one of the younger pitchers at 20-years-old, had a good ERA at 2.77 and survived with a winning 9-6 mark. Southpaw Joe Mattis won 12 games, but lost 13 with an ERA of 3.57.[17]

Chapter 13

A War Hero and a Future Owner
1952

"Too late to Classify – WANTED: One desperately needed Cotton States League victory. Apply Hot Springs Bathers, Jaycee Park." – Maurice Moore

Bob Benish took over as the Bathers manager in 1952. Previously, Benish managed from 1947-1951 on several minor league teams. In 1948, he led the Troy (Alabama) Trojans to the playoffs in the Alabama State League, but lost in the first round. On August 29, 1948, the Alabama State League suspended him and catcher Bob Odenheimer for attacking an umpire. The suspension took place during the first 60 days of the 1949 season. Following the two-month deferral, Benish took over as the skipper of the Helena (Arkansas) Seaporters in the Cotton States League. Helena finished last that year.[1]

Tom Stough and A. G. "Gabe" Crawford were co-owners of the Bathers and, in addition, Stough served as general manager. Stough was the owner of Freezit Cold Storage Plant in Hot Springs, while Crawford was a druggist. Stough was once a college baseball player and remained a fan of the game. Previously, he served as co-owner of the Okmulgee, Oklahoma, baseball team in the Western League. Formerly connected with the petroleum and construction industry in

Oklahoma, Tom moved to Hot Springs in 1945. He replaced the 1951 general manager, Jim Elder who returned to umpiring in the Class B, Florida International League.

The eight-team Cotton States League was composed of three Arkansas teams representing Pine Bluff, El Dorado and Hot Springs. Mississippi entered four teams from Greenwood, Greenville, Meridian and Natchez. Monroe represented the state of Louisiana. Each team in the CSL played a 126-game schedule, 63 on the road and 63 at home. Teams played each other 18 times. Hot Springs open the season on April 22, at Pine Bluff and ended the season at Greenville on August 25.

Introduction of the 1952 Hot Springs Bathers edition began as the Bathers rode in cars in a parade down Central Avenue on the afternoon of April 22. Players' names were on the side of the parade cars and the Hot Springs Trojan band led the procession, which started at 4:15 p.m. from the junction of Whittington, Park and Central Avenues. Other VIPs, such as the Bathers front office personnel, city officials, county officials and representatives of civic clubs journeyed through the city.

The opener went down the drain...too much rain washed out the opener! However, the game was on tap for the next night, April 23. Several activities occurred during the pregame ceremonies at Jaycee Park. The fans honored three former Bathers presidents, Lloyd Adams, W. Clyde Smith and Chancellor Sam Garratt. Only these men served as president of the Bathers since the team joined the Cotton States League in late 1937. The trio put on an improvised game for the delight of the fans and media. Mayor Floyd Housley and Tom Stough, general manager of the Bathers, spoke briefly, followed by the introduction of both teams. The Army-Navy Hospital's color guard raised the flag as the Trojan band played the Star-Spangled Banner. Young Vernon Bales, cousin of Jack, threw out the first ball. Vernon, a physically challenged young man, knew many sports statistics. Jack said that Vernon was brilliant at remembering statistics. Harvey Stegman, sports director for Radio Station KWFC (Come to Wilson's Furniture Company), was the master of ceremonies for the pregame activities. A crowd of 1,400 fans showed up for the opener.

The Bathers were only one run behind, 6-5, as the contest rocked along in the sixth inning. It remained that score until the fateful ninth frame. The Judges scored three times, while the Bathers put up a big zero. The Judges spoiled the Bathers' opener, 9-5. Don Hilbert - CF, Babe Tuckey – 3B and Jerry Durnin -2B collected two hits each for the Bathers.

By May 1, Hot Springs, tied with Pine Bluff with a 4-4 record, hovered in fourth position. Loop leader, Meridian Millers posted a 6-1 mark. For the first eight games, things seemed to be in good shape even though the team was in the middle of the pack. It was still early in the season.

Big first baseman, Vernon "Moose" Shetler and Don Hilbert center fielder received their unconditional releases from Bathers general manager Tom Stough on May 3. Manager Benish planned to take over the first-base bag and a new recruit, Emery Petty, from the Big State League in Temple, Texas, would be the new center fielder. Benish played first base several years and following the war, played first base for the Atlanta Crackers. However, since the Cracker days, he added pitching to his resume'.

Stough stated that the reason he released Shetler is because the first baseman was not rounding into shape and Hilbert had a sore arm. The real reason that Stough released the two players may have been financial, so he could purchase pitchers.

'It is with regret that we release Hilbert and Shetler because we have grown to like both. But we know we must have pitching to be among the first four in this tough league.[2]

Maurice Moore, sports editor of *The Sentinel-Record* and president of the CSL's sportswriters, asked the question in his column, "What's going on?" Everybody seemed stumped at the release of the two popular players. Bench managers in the CSL were becoming extinct due to the 16-player roster. The managers needed to be playing managers in order to save money. If Hot Springs were drawing a large number of fans, it might be different, but there were too many empty stadium seats to have the luxury of a non-playing manager.[3]

Usually a home crowd drew about 500-600 fans per game. However, the night after a great comeback rally in El Dorado in which the Bathers won, 1,300 fans greeted the Bathers at Jaycee Park. Fans like winners. "Tuffy" Owens, an outfielder turned pitcher, scampered home with the winning run at El Dorado during the comeback victory. A Hot Springs fan stated, "Tuffy looked just like he was toting the ball for Milan Creighton back in 1942 again." Olen "Tuffy" Owens played high school football for Hot Springs a decade previously and Creighton, former Chicago Cardinals football coach in the 1930s, was his coach. [4]

Moore stated that Stough and Crawford were thinking about moving the remainder of the Bathers' Sunday home games to Saturday doubleheaders. The main reason the co-owners wanted to switch to Saturdays is that too few fans showed up on Sundays. They weren't sure what to do, but they were willing to try just about anything to gain more fan support.

In his same editorial, Moore talked with former Philadelphia Athletics pitcher, George Earnshaw concerning pitch count. Big George said that in some games, he counts the number of pitches and a pitcher who throws 120 times in a nine-inning game is "doing a topnotch job." He counted Monroe's Jack Fuller's pitches a few nights earlier and the Monroe Sports pitcher threw 123 times in nine innings, while the four Hot Springs pitchers total tosses added up to 152. In 2011, most managers won't allow pitchers to throw too many pitches past a pitch-count of 100, because of the possibility of injuring their arms or losing their effectiveness.

Moore also mentioned the length of games in the CSL. He stated that the league seemed to be improving because the time of games were shorter. In 1951, home games averaged from 2 hours and 15 minutes to 2 hours and 24 minutes. In 1952, the average game length was 2 hours flat. He recalled that a nine-inning game a few days previously, lasted only 1 hour and 37 minutes. In comparison, the average length of a major league baseball game in 2009 was two hours and 51 minutes.

Bob Passarella played the infield and outfield for the Bathers in 1952 and 1953. Most of the players called him Bob, but he had a couple of nicknames, one was "Passie" and the other was "Grouse." Due to Bob's speed, his childhood friends tagged him "Grouse," just like the fast foul. During the 1950s, many ballplayers were veterans of either World War II or the Korean War. Passarella was one of those vets. During World War II, in 1945, at 18, following his high school graduation in Pennsylvania, "Passie" joined the Army. Stationed in the United States for several weeks, the Army sent him to Italy where he served as an MP (military policeman). The Germans surrendered in May 1945, and the Japanese surrendered in August 1945. Following Sgt. Passarella's military service, he played three years in Class D baseball leagues before arriving at Hot Springs. Bob lived in the same house in which he was born in Scranton, Pennsylvania, until he passed away in 2010.

Passarella, 6'0" 175 pounds, who batted and threw right, was a standout performer in several games during the 1952 season. He hit around .230, but he could field with the best of them. His favorite position was second base, but in 1952, a crisis occurred. Manager Bob Benish, the 37-year-old first sacker enjoyed playing, but due to knee problems, he was unable to move around the bag as he did in previous years. The left-handed Benish asked Passarella if he had ever played first base. "Passie" told him, "No, but I'll give it a shot." The manager began tutoring him. As an infielder, Bob was an excellent glove man and demonstrated good footwork, so he transferred those assists to the first base position. He gave it more than just "the good old college try" because he played around 80 games at first base in 1952. On Memorial Day, the local paper reported the previous night's results in which Bob went one for four at the plate and played a top-notch defensive game in a 3-1 win over Pine Bluff.[5]

Probably the turning point of the game was First Baseman Bob Passarella's expert fielding in the fifth inning.

The utility player who has shown much improvement afield and at the plate in the past few weeks, turned in the defensive gem of the night when he made an unassisted double play with the bases loaded, and then registered the third out, also unassisted.[6]

Up to this point, Passarella was playing first base with his regular infielder's glove, so someone decided to upgrade him to a real first-sacker's glove.

Don't look now, but Bob Passarella is going to be sporting a brand new first baseman's glove tonight.

The much-improved utility-player who has been handling the initial sack off and on this season, has earned his new glove, especially after a brilliant showing there last night. During his previous appearances in this position, he has used a regular fielder's glove.

However, last night Passarella put on a sterling fielding exhibition, making a key double play that helped turn the tide of the game.

A hurry-up call was put out early today for the new prize, and it was soon secured.[7]

Wally Rasmussen, star right fielder for Hot Springs, led the league at the plate with a solid .348 average. The next best hitter for the Bathers was left fielder, Joe Stern with a mark of .291. The team remained in second division in league standings, batting and fielding. Newly acquired Jim Hogan had a 2-0 pitching record, but not much to crow about this early in the season.

On June 2, El Dorado stuck it to the Bathers 13-0. However, on June 6, with the help of relief pitcher Benny Day and a homer by big Joe Stern, Hogan won his fifth straight as the Bathers topped the Monroe Sports 4-3. The quick game took an hour and 50 minutes to complete, but only 641 fans showed up at Jaycee Park.

Stough and Crawford tried to get Detroit, Pittsburgh or Cleveland to assist with the Bathers, but the major league teams couldn't see a financial upside in becoming a major league affiliate for the Bathers. Therefore, the Spa co-owners went the independent route. The backdoor policy went into effect by hooking up with the Texas City Texans of the Class B, Gulf Coast League. Texas City had a working pact with the Washington Senators. Hot Springs received several players through the Texas chain such as Jim Hogan and Joe Grasso – pitchers, Jerry Durnin - second baseman, Chico Escudero - shortstop and Felix Gomez - center fielder.

The question arose concerning the whereabouts of former Bathers' star Herb Adams. Maurice Moore said that the 1948 sparkplug went straight to the White Sox following the 1948 season. In 1949, he played baseball with Uncle Sam at Fort Leonard Wood, Missouri, but the Army had other plans for the young soldier. The Army wanted him to play baseball with the Eighth Army club in Korea. Rev. and Mrs. Clyde Hart of the Spa received a letter from their eldest son, Sgt. Tom Hart stationed in Korea. Sgt. Hart stated that he saw Private First-Class Adams thump two hits, one of them a bases loaded triple. Rev. and Mrs. Hart were the parents of the well-known former Baylor track coach, Clyde Hart.

Over 1,200 fans jammed Jaycee Park on Saturday night, June 13, as the fans saw Passarella pop a double, a single and score a run. However, his exploits were not enough as Meridian eased past Hot Springs 3-2. The crowd was the third largest of the season up to that time, but on all three occasions, the Bathers lost.

The Meridian Millers took two from the Bathers at Jaycee Park on June 16, 3-1 and 5-3. Bathers' newcomer Mike Ilitch ran for "Babe" Tuckey in the seventh frame in the opening game. In the second game, Ilitch started at second base, but went 0-4 at the plate in the 5-3 lose to Meridian. On June 17, in a 13-7 lose against Natchez Indians, Ilitch contributed two hits, an RBI and a stolen base for the Bathers, as they lost their third straight game. Mike played the remainder of the year for Hot Springs. There will be more about Ilitch later.

It was a three-hit night on June 18, for hitting star "Babe" Tuckey. Hot Springs kept it close until the eighth frame as they exploded for six big runs. The score was 8-0 before the Indians scored their three runs in the ninth. Passarella, with a man aboard in the second inning, blistered a fastball over the right field fence near the scoreboard to make it a 2-0 game. "Passie" and Gomez followed Tuckey with two hits each as Hot Springs stopped a three game losing skid.[8]

On June 19, southpaw, Jim Hogan collected his ninth straight victory by dropping the Natchez Indians 1-0 in the second half of a doubleheader at Jaycee Park. Hogan blasted a double in the bottom of the fifth frame and strolled over to third on a balk. Second sacker, Mike Ilitch sent a hot grounder to second base and the second baseman relayed the ball to the catcher as Hogan headed home. The Indians catcher dropped the ball as Hogan scooted across the plate for the only score of the contest. In the first game, the Bathers took it on the chin as they fell 4-1. Hogan was undefeated, since arriving from Texas City.

In 1952, Hogan was a 32-year-old "old pro" of the Bathers. He was born in Fort Worth and lived in nearby Arlington, Texas. During the off-season, he worked for his father-in-law in Gainesville, Texas. Mellowed with age, the lefty was an excellent curve-ball artist. "Pop," as he was called by his teammates, was married and had a year-old son, Raymond Lee "June Bug" Hogan. At this time in his life, Jim was an eleven-year veteran of professional baseball. He served in the Army from 1941-1946. Master/Sergeant Hogan's military stint included a hitch on Okinawa in the South Pacific. Earlier in the 1952 season, Hogan posted a 1-4 record with Texas City Texans of the Class B, Gulf Coast League. A few weeks into the 1952 season, the Texans shuffled him off to Hot Springs and the Bathers were elated to get the talented hurler.

However, the "iron-man" trophy of the day went to Natchez's pitcher Dick Thompson who hurled both ends of the 14-inning doubleheader. The right-hander allowed only 10 Bathers' hits in two games. Moore noted that Thompson "was an effective moundsmen all the way" and showed little signs of weakening. From time to time, the Bathers played well, but the team was still next to last in league standings.[9]

Bob "Zollie" Zolliecoffer tossed a brilliant two hitter as the Bathers stung the Greenwood Dodgers 7-1 at Jaycee Park on June 26. "Zollie" won his seventh game against six losses as Ilitch and Gomez accounted for four of the Bathers' nine hits.

On June 28, the big event of the day included a marathon twin bill between the Bathers and Greenville that lasted 22 innings! In the first seven-inning tilt, the Bathers blasted the Mississippi boys for 12 hits, but only mustered two runs. The Bucks popped the ball around Jaycee Park for only eight hits, but scored eight tallies to slug the Bathers 8-2.

Last year, the Bathers played in a 19-inning event in Mississippi, but the longest game at home up to this point, was the second game of the double header that lasted 15-innings. It was that Hogan person again! Hogan battled "Red" Kenney for 15 innings! Two pitchers pitched 15 innings each! What an exciting match up. Records weren't kept on the number of pitchers thrown by both pitchers. From the fourth inning on, the game was knotted 2-2. It wasn't July 4, but there were fireworks!

(Bucks) Manager (Harry) Chozen, one of the Cotton States Leagues most colorful skippers, heckled Umpires Behrens and Woudstra throughout, but the crowning blow came in the 12th.

A rhubarb over a called strike lasted nearly 10 minutes before officers were called in to 'escort' Chozen from the park. With him went Pitcher Sam Peck.[10]

Right fielder Wally Rasmusseun and two newcomers, Mike Ilitch, second sacker and Pat Saviano, left fielder were the Bathers' heroes of the extended game. In the 15th inning, the players combined their talents to make it an exciting finish.

Ilitch, first batter to face Kenney in the bottom of the 15th, slapped out a single. Wally Rasmussen's well placed sacrifice enabled Ilitch to move to second and the speedy infielder stole third. Saviano then lifted one of Kenney's slants into short centerfield, and Ilitch romped home.[11]

Ilitch scored the third run for Hot Springs to cop the victory as Hogan won his 10th game of the season. Bob Passarella was busy at first base, as he may have established a fielding record of 22 putouts and one assist without an error.

One negative during the week occurred when Texas City recalled Bathers star center fielder Felix Gomez. The Bathers did not want to lose their star outfielder. Gomez hailed from Cuba and among the duties of "Chico" Escudero, Bathers shortstop, was to serve as an interpreter for Felix. Chico, from Puerto Rico, had excellent command of the English language and Felix needed help. However, whatever Texas City wanted, Texas City got and they got Felix.

Ed Jacobson, Bathers outfielder, posted a .353 batting average at the end of June. In the young season, Jacobson, the hard-hitting outfielder, wound up in Hot Springs via Hutchinson, Kansas and the Pittsburgh Pirates farm system. Felix Gomez was hitting .308 when he departed the team for Texas City and Wally Rasmussen was batting .288. The Bathers were last in team batting, sixth in fielding and remained way back in second division in league standings. The Bathers welcomed another good hitter like Jacobson.

Five new Bathers arrived to bolster the line up. Hometown product, Jackie Bales led the quintet. Catcher Bales, former Spa American Legion star, came from Davenport, Iowa of the Three-I League. The four other players were Jim Miller, second baseman from the Durham Bulls, North Carolina; Bob Caberella an infielder, catcher Dick Anderson from Harlingen (Texas) Capitals and Guy Brill a right-handed pitcher rode north from the Texas City Texans.

'We are trying to bolster the club, and the only way to do it is to plug the gaps,' Stough declared. 'We are doing everything within our power to give Hot Springs a winning ball club, and we will continue to make changes with that aim in mind.'[12]

Over 1,800 fans showed up on July 4, at the Bathers home park to watch the Monroe Sports celebrate the Independence Day festivities by detonating the visiting Bathers twice, 11-4 and 4-3.

During the game, catcher Freddie Wasiluk chased a pop fly behind home plate, fought with the backstop screen and the screen won. Wasiluk, injured twice earlier in the season, received a gash on his face when attempting to catch a pop fly from the bat of Monroe's shortstop, George Andrews in the second game. The two games lasted nearly a total of five hours and the fans watched star Bathers' pitcher Jim Hogan lose his second game of the season against ten victories.

Bathers' outfielder, Ed Jacobson remained in the top 10 CSL's batting race in early July, as he batted .337, tops on the Hot Springs roster. Hogan, one of the top hurlers in the league, recorded a 10-2 mark. However, at the beginning of July, the Bathers were near the bottom of the team standing and rested in the cellar in club batting and club fielding.

The Bathers organization celebrated "Jaycee Night" on July 5, as Hot Springs hosted the El Dorado Oilers. Since the Jaycees helped fund the baseball park in 1947, the Bathers donated the proceeds from one game during the season to the Jaycees. A special feature at the game was the appearance of newly crowned "Miss Arkansas," Bonnie Nicksic of Hot Springs. The Jaycees sponsored the "Miss Hot Springs" contest in which Miss Nicksic later won the title of "Miss Arkansas." She received a Nash Rambler car from Rowell Nash Motors of Hot Springs, which she used for a year in her travels around the state.

At Pine Bluff, a few days later, scrappy second baseman Mike Ilitch was the Bathers hitting personality with three singles for four trips to the plate. However, the Judges handed the visiting Bathers their ninth straight setback, 5-2. Over 1,000 fans witnessed Vern Schneider, Pine Bluff's ace hurler, as he won his 13th game against five losses. The quick game, played in less than two hours, may have been the game that broke the Bathers' back.

The Bathers collected too many losses! That was it! Time was up! The Bathers front office decided to make a managerial change on July 9, in favor of pitcher Jim Hogan. The Bathers had a losing record and manager Benish, due to a bad knee, could play only sparingly. Many minor league teams needed to get the biggest bang for its buck. Therefore, teams attempted to get a two-for-one deal by hiring a player and tossing the managerial responsibility on him. The club released

Benish, as Hogan became the new manager. Hogan, 32-year-old lefty hurler, joined the team in mid-May and by the end of May, maintained a 2-0 pitching record. The team knew Hogan the player, so there were no surprises as he added the title of "manager" to his resume'. However, the team continued to lose.

Hogan, quiet-spoken native of Texas, has been in organized baseball since 1937. His first club was Lake Charles, Louisiana, then in the Evangeline League.

In 1939, he played with Helena of the Cotton States League, and was with the old Monroe White Sox of the same circuit in 1941.

Hogan, who is married and the father of a young son, served in the Army Air Force from 1941-46. He was discharged with the rank of master sergeant.

During the summer of 1945, he managed the Westover, MA Air Base club.

Hogan pitched for Gainesville, Texas, of the Big State (Class B) League, from 1947 through 1949.

But, 1950, was his best year in baseball. He won 23 and lost seven with Jacksonville, Texas, of the Gulf Coast League.

He played part of last season with Texas City and served as acting manager for a time. Texas City first optioned and then sold him to the Bathers.

With Texas City he had a 1-4 pitching record. But, after joining the Bathers, he won nine straight without a loss. [13]

Hot Springs had some talented players, but there was not enough of that talent to go around. The fans, as well as the media, were becoming more frustrated. So, an ad appeared in the local paper on July 11, following the Bathers 11th straight loss.

Too late to Classify – WANTED: One desperately needed Cotton States League victory. Apply Hot Springs Bathers, Jaycee Park.[14]

The CSL sportswriters and team managers selected three Spa players to the fifth annual All-Star game. The list, released by Al Haraway, league commissioner, included Jim Hogan - pitcher, Wally Rasmussen - outfield and Fred Wasiluk - catcher. Greenville, Mississippi, was the scheduled site for the mid-season classic on Monday, July 14. The contest pitted the Arkansas-Louisiana All-Stars against the best in Mississippi.

On July 11, against Pine Bluff, Passarella drove in three runs and slapped a double and a single in four tries at the plate as the Bathers broke another losing streak. The number 11 seemed to be the "charmed number." Strange things were happening! The Bathers snapped an 11-game losing streak by the score of 11-10. Hot Springs manager-pitcher Jim Hogan won his 11th game on the 11th day of the month and both starting pitchers wore uniform number 11. Two more numbers seemed important to the team too, as they scored four runs in the last of the ninth inning to win the contest.[15]

Moore said that it would be tough for the new skipper Hogan to move the team into first division. It was going to be difficult to "mold a stabilized organization," Moore remarked. Since the season began, more than 60 players came through the revolving clubhouse doors and about 50 were out the door.

Just before the All-Star tilt, the league released the league standings. Hot Springs was last in club batting with .232, next to last in club fielding with a .947 mark and next to last in team standings. Leading the Bathers hitting attack was Wally Rasmussen with a .279 average and Ed Jacobson with a .272 mark.

The league selected 16 players per team to participate in the All-Star game. The Arkansas-Louisiana Stars zapped the Mississippi squad 10-2. A crowd of over 2,100 saw the Ark-La crew win its third game of the five-year classic on July 14, at Greenville, Mississippi. Wasiluk, Bathers' catcher picked up a single in five trips to the plate. The other two Hot Springs All-Stars did not see action. Hogan was not called on to pitch and Rasmussen, due to a leg injury, was out of action for 10 days. The league reported an amazing statistic. During the five years of the All-Star contest, the Arkansas-Louisiana boys won the big game when played in Mississippi and when the tilt switched to Arkansas, the Mississippi All-Stars won. The classic drew over 2,000 fans every year, while El Dorado drew the largest crowd, 2,400 in 1951.[16]

Hogan, the ace of the Bathers pitching staff, went for his 12th win of the season on July 15. A sparse crowd of over 500 fans saw one of the best pitching duels of the season as the Monroe Sports invaded Jaycee Park. Again, Passarella came to the rescue. "Passarella's Hit Enables Hogan to Win 12th Victory," stated *The Sentinel-Record*. With two outs in the last of the 12th inning, "Passie," waited for a full count. He punched the next pitch into short left field. Former Bather, Pat Saviano attempted to make a sensational shoestring catch, but the ball fell in for a base hit. "Izzy" Carballeria, scampered home from third to give the Bathers a 1-0 hard fought win. "Passarella was the batting sparkplug for the Bathers with three hits in four trips." Those Hogan special numbers popped up again! This time the magic number was 12. Hogan won his 12th game of the season in the 12th inning. It was also the pitcher's 12th season in professional baseball.[17]

Even though Ilitch, Passarella, Jacobson, Tuckey and Brill all singled and Jack Bales hit a line-shot triple, no Bather crossed home plate on July 22, against Natchez as the Indians blanked the Bathers 4-0 in Natchez. Hot Springs remained in seventh place in the league standings.

Since it was blazing hot during August in Hot Springs, general manager Tom Stough announced the rescheduling of the Sunday's afternoon game to 7:00 p.m.

'We are establishing this precedent here because of the oppressive afternoon heat which affects fans and players alike,' Stough declared. 'We feel it will be cooler in the evenings and more inviting to fans.'[18]

An estimated 7,500 fans, the largest crowd ever to see a baseball game in the Resort, streamed to Jaycee Park on July 27, 1952. The Natchez Indians were in town to play the Bathers, but that was not the major reason that people jammed the park, hillside and railroad track around the park. The real reason for the gigantic crowd was politics! The throng attended the game primarily to see and listen to Democratic Gubernatorial candidate Boyd Tackett. Francis Cherry and Tackett were in a hotly contested race for Governor of Arkansas. In addition, the fans saw a close game until the eighth inning when Natchez pulled away and beat the Bathers 6-2 for the Spa's fifth straight loss. Babe Tuckey went four for five at the plate and Mike Ilitch singled twice for the Bathers.

Greenville blew in town on August 5, planning to extend the Bathers losing streak. It looked like it was all over when the Bathers came to bat in the third inning. By that time, Greenville was up 6-0. Passarella's two-run home run got the Bathers on the scoreboard. Bales' grounder forced Tuckey at second, but scored Ilitch from third to cut the score in half. It was eight to five when the Bathers came to bat in the bottom of the eighth frame. Hot Springs cut loose for five runs and held Greenville in the ninth to take the contest 10-8. Right fielder Jack Bales pulled off an oddity that credited him with four RBIs without a hit! "Two of the runs were made on outfield flies, another one on an infielder's choice, and another on a sacrifice hit."

An unusual situation occurred in early August when Bert Shepard took the field at first base. Shepard rode in from Corpus Christi as a free agent and signed a Bathers contract to play first base and bolster the pitching staff. In his first game with the Bathers, he played two innings at first base and made five putouts against the Bucks. He hit a double and flied to left field in two trips to the plate. So, why is this event so rare? Bert Shepard, a WW II veteran, wore an artificial leg.[19]

When he received his release from Corpus Christi, he heard that Hot Springs was looking for pitching. Since the Bathers were in seventh place, he thought he would ask the Bathers front office for a tryout.

'Baseball is my life,' he emphasized. "I'm just hoping my arm comes back so I can do some good.'

Shep is a friend of an old friend of Hot Springs, Joe Kuhel, former Major Leaguer who managed the Bathers in 1947.

'Joe helped me quite a bit and I certainly think he is one great fellow.' He declared. 'Joe always spoke very highly of Hot Springs.'

Kuhel left here in 1948 to man age the Senators.[20]

There were veterans of WW II and the Korean War playing in leagues all over the United States and Shepard was one of those men. Passarella remembered that Bert came to the park with his artificial leg slung over his shoulder. That was his "playing leg." He wore his "everyday prosthetic leg" and in the clubhouse changed to his "playing leg." Bob said that Shepard was a pretty good pitcher and first baseman. Bert was "a nice guy with a good attitude," Bob stated. Passarella remembered Shepard as being knowledgeable about baseball and "Shep" wanted everyone around him to play his best.

The sports headlines on August 7, of *The Sentinel-Record* stated "One-legged Pitcher Impressive Although Bathers Lose to Bucks." Shepard threw a fantastic game against Greenville as he hurled the complete contest. The Bucks scored one run in the fifth stanza. After the fifth inning, only one Greenville player advanced to third base. Hot Springs had their chances as they left the bases loaded and no outs in the fourth and ninth stanzas. The Hot Springs pitcher walked five, struck out four and allowed only eight scattered hits in nine innings, but Shepard lost a heartbreaker 1-0. Passarella recalled an oddity occurred in the ninth inning when Greenville's Kenney hit a wicked line drive back to Shepard. The ball bounded off Shepard's leg toward home plate. It caught Bales, the catcher, by surprise and the ball shot through his legs for an error. The batter ended up on second base. The infielders ran over to Shepard to see how bad he was hurt. Shepard was laughing because the ball hit his artificial metal leg.[21]

In addition, he showed the enthusiastic crowd at Jaycee Park that he was an excellent fielding pitcher. Moore, Greenville's third basemen, laid down a sacrifice bunt. Shepard scooped it up, slipped on the wet grass and hurled to first base in time to beat the runner. The 560 excited fans, including over 50 patients from the Army and Navy Hospital, roared their approval. The patients were guests of the Bathers. "Shepard visited the hospital wards yesterday and talked with many Korean casualties." [22]

During one of the games, Passarella relates that Shepard was on the mound and the batter smacked a scorcher up the middle just past Bob at second base. The hustling second-sacker dove for the ball, but it was barely out of reach. In the dugout at the end of the inning, Bert said, "Bob you should have had that." Bob said, "Bert, I dove for the ball, what else could I have done?" Nevertheless, that was Bert! [23]

The 31-year-old Shepard was born in Dana, Indiana, on June 28, 1920. A star athlete in high school, he spent two years in the minor leagues. In 1941, the 5' 11" 185-pound, left-handed pitcher played with the Bisbee Bees (AZ) in the Class C, Arizona-Texas League. Bert had a 3-5 pitching record, but also played first base and the outfield. In December 1941, the world was at war and Bert joined the Army Air Corps in May 1942. After extensive pilot training, Lieutenant Shepard received his wings and in early 1944, the Army Air Corps sent him to England. Bert served with the 55th Fighter Group stationed at Wormingford, England. He flew the Lockheed P-38J Lightning fighter plane. Due to its design of two tails, the Germans called the plane "forked tail devil."

Shepard, although an active pilot, found time to play baseball. The men were ready to play their first game of the 1944 season on May 21. Bert had flown 33 previous missions and on that day, volunteered for his 34th mission. He thought he would have plenty of time to return to his base in England to play the baseball game because, in his opinion, it was going to be a "milk run" which meant an easy mission.

His orders were to attack an enemy airfield near Ludwigslust, several miles east of Hamburg, Germany. He headed for his mission in Germany. Following the assault on his target, he turned and headed toward his base. He was surprised to hear radio reports of enemy anti-aircraft batteries in the area. As he was flying at a low altitude over a clump of trees, suddenly he "felt something 'like a sledgehammer' pounding on his right foot." He used the radio to contact his base. He recalls saying, "There goes the ballgame." The shell ripped through the plane and tore into his right foot and leg. That instant he also took a slug in the chin from the enemy on the ground.

Immediately he passed out and crashed in a field near Hamburg. Irate German farmers, who worked in the field at the crash site, planned to finish off the American flyer. However, Lt. Loidl, a young Austrian doctor who was serving in the German Air Force, rushed to the scene in time to pull the American pilot from the burning wreckage.

Loidl, with the aid of two armed soldiers, drove the farmers away and checked to see if the pilot was still alive. 'He was unconscious, his right leg being smashed, and he bled from a deep wound on his head,' recalled Loidl in 1993. 'I recognized that the man could be saved only with an urgent operation. My emergency hospital was not equipped for that. So, I drove the wounded man to the local hospital that was headed by a colonel. When he refused to admit the "terror flyer," as he called him, I telephoned the general on duty at the Reich's Air Ministry in Berlin and reported the case. Whereupon the general called the colonel and settled the matter. Lieutenant Shepard was admitted and operated on. A few days later, I inquired about his condition and was told that he was doing fine.[24]

The doctors amputated Shepard's right leg several inches below the knee. Shepard woke up two weeks later and realized he lost part of his right leg. He was a prisoner of war (POW), but the German doctors saved his life. He thanked the doctors for his rescue and successful surgery. Following a lengthy recovery period, the Germans transferred the American pilot to a regular German prison camp. Dr. Doug Errey, a Canadian medic and fellow prisoner, assisted in constructing a temporary artificial leg out of discarded scrap metal, wood and felt. Soon, the American prisoner was throwing a ball within the prison camp yard. A POW for eight months, he returned to the United States aboard the neutral Swedish ocean liner, MS Gripsholm, in a prisoner of war exchange. He arrived stateside Feb. 21, 1945, and the Army transported him to the Walter Reed Hospital in Washington, D. C., where he met Under Secretary of War, Robert Patterson.

When Patterson asked about his plans for the future, Shepard explained that he wanted to play baseball. Skeptical, but impressed with the young flier's attitude, Patterson contacted Senators' owner, Clark Griffith, and asked him to take a look at the young pitcher.[25]

Shepard retired from the military in April 1945, but a few days previously, signed with the Washington Senators as a pitching coach on March 21, 1945. "Shep" did pitch in some exhibition games.

On August 4, 1945, six months after seeing the last of the German POW camp, Shepard stepped on the mound as a relief pitcher for the Washington Senators in a regular-season major league game. In the fourth inning, with two men on base, two outs and Washington well behind in the score, Shepard finished the game by pitching 5.1 innings, as he struck out two, walked one and gave up one run on three hits. The visiting Red Sox beat the Senators that day by a 15-4 count, but the Shepard won a great victory. Amputee Bert Shepard had pitched in the major leagues.[26]

Shepard signed a 1946 Senators contract as a pitching coach and at the end of the season he went barnstorming with major league players. His highpoint during the baseball tour was that he batted two for four at the plate against the great Cleveland Indians pitcher, Bob Feller.[27]

Following the tour, he returned to Walter Reed Hospital for more surgery. "He was in the hospital for two and half years and during that time underwent five operations." However, baseball was still in his veins, so, in 1949, even on crutches, for a brief period, he managed the Waterbury, Connecticut club in the Colonial League.[28]

After two seasons, he had a hankering to get back in the game. He signed as player-manager for St. Augustine in the Florida State League. He posted a 1-1 record, but he had differences with the front office and within two weeks, he moved on. He went to Chattanooga in hopes that the trainer for the Lookouts could help him get his arm loosened.[29]

Shep has some advice for fellow amputees: 'You can do more than you think you can if you give it a good try.' Courage-Bert Shepard has plenty of it.[30]

He continued playing and managing minor league baseball until 1954, including part of the 1952 season at Hot Springs. Following his baseball days, he worked at IBM and Hughes Aircraft in California. He was married and had three children, but later divorced. He married his second wife a few years later. Shepard became a champion golfer winning the National Amputee Golf Championship in 1968 and 1971.[31]

In 1992, Shepard's dream partially came true. During a hunting trip in Hungary, Jamie Brundell, an English businessman, met an Austrian physician named Loidl. The doctor told Brundell about the story of him helping save an American pilot during WW II. Loidl remembered the name "Bert Shepard" on the flyer's dog tags. Brundell wondered what had happened to Shepard. Brundell could have left the story rest there, but suddenly, he became intrigued with the tale. He searched through military records and after several months, located Shepard in Hesperia, California. The businessman contacted Loidl in Austria. In December 1992, Loidl called Shepard from Austria. The next year, Shepard flew to Europe.

In May 1993, Shepard had an emotional reunion with Doctor Loidl, the man who had rescued him from the plane wreckage after he was shot down. [32]

During the conversation, Loidl told Shepard that he gave his parachute to his wife who made a dress from the material. Loidl also related to Shepard that the Gestapo asked him why he helped the American. Dr. Loidl said, "Because he is a human." Bert Shepard, 87, passed away June 16, 2008, in his sleep at a retirement home in Highland, California.

Passarella had a tremendous doubleheader at the plate against Monroe at Jaycee Park on Saturday, Aug. 9. In the first game, Bob, who played left field and split first base duties with Shepard, went 2-3, including a double. In the nightcap, second baseman Passarella hit 1.000 by collecting three singles in three trips to the plate. The Bathers clipped the Sports 6-2 and 6-5. A five for six-night at the plate is good in anybody's league.

The next night, the Sports blanked the Bathers 13-0, but it could have been worse. The umpire called the game at the end of the seventh inning due to a baseball shortage. Simply put, they ran out of baseballs! The Bathers management was waiting on a shipment of baseballs, but they did not arrive in time for the game. They used most of the baseballs during Saturday's doubleheader, in which the Bathers won both contests. The Spa team started the game with only six new baseballs and 13 used playable baseballs. During the blowout, first baseman John Paul Jones of Monroe may have established a single game record at Jaycee Park. Jones blasted the sphere around the yard for eight RBIs on three hits. He hit a homer, double, single and received a free pass to first with the bases loaded to gain his eight RBIs. Bert Shepard started on the mound for the Bathers, but gave way in the third stanza to Ed Baski. [33]

On Saturday, August 16, an "iron man" performance occurred against El Dorado at Jaycee Park. Joe Grasso nearly emulated the 1939's mound performance of Martin Zachar. Grasso was the starting pitcher in the first game of a doubleheader. Joe only gave up five runs on six raps, but the Oilers eased by the Bathers 5-2.

Manager Joe Hogan scheduled himself to start on the hill in the second, seven-inning game. However, before the game, Grasso asked Hogan if he "could pitch until I win." The manager granted Grasso's wish. In the second inning, "Tuffy" Owens laid down a perfect squeeze bunt toward third base that allowed Ed Jacobson to score from third with the first Hot Springs run. It was slow going for the Bathers, but they clawed and scratched for each run. Passarella lifted one over the right field fence in the fifth to help the Bathers cause. Hot Springs played better the second game to skid by El Dorado 5-4. Grasso went the distance in both tilts as he compiled a one-day, won-lost record of 1-1. In the two games, Grasso threw 14 innings, gave up nine runs, scattered 14 hits and struck out four.[34]

On August 20, the Bathers were at home against the Judges. It seemed that "Passie" liked to hit against Pine Bluff because, again, "Passarella was the hitting star as he garnered three for four, including his homer, double and single," but the Judges rolled over the Bathers 8-4.[35]

The next night, Shepard toed the rubber for the Spa Boys against Pine Bluff. Hot Springs was leading 2-1 going into the fifth frame. Three runs came across the plate in the fifth due to hits by Ilitch, Tuckey and Bridges. In the eighth inning, Ilitch singled, stole second and third and "scampered home" on an error. Tuckey scored from third on Passarella's sacrifice fly. Shepard went the distance as he hurled a six-hitter and garnered his first win in Hot Springs, 7-2.

Ilitch had a three-hit game on Aug. 22, at Greenwood, but the Dodgers walloped the Bathers 12-5. Greenwood's attendance was one of the best in the league as 1,008 fans showed up for the contest. The Dodgers needed only 504 fans to walk through the gates during their last home stand to exceed 50,000, the largest since the 1947 season.

Before the season's end, there was a rumor floating around that Tom Stough planned to retire as co-owner of the Bathers following the 1952 season. A. G. Crawford planned to carry on next season, if he could find a partner. Crawford estimated the total losses were about $14,000. For three months, from 300-600 faithful fans per game, traveled to Jaycee Park and watched a losing team perform the best they could. The management appreciated the die-hard fans, but that's not enough interest to support a professional baseball team. Maurice Moore ended his column concerning the Bathers 1953 options by writing, "Cross your fingers sports fans, and hope for the best." [36]

With two games left on the road, the last place Bathers ended their gloomy season by losing their last home game to the Greenville Bucks 6-2, in front of 650 baseball-starved fans on Aug. 25. Ilitch was the big gun at the plate as the Bathers' second sacker collected three hits for five times at the plate. In addition, he made seven putouts and four assists in the field.

Chico Escudero, infielder-outfielder, selected as the team's MVP in a season-long poll, received a suit of clothes from the Dino's Men Store. Chico, who hailed from Puerto Rico via New York, averaged in the low .200s at bat. Babe Tuckey, voted the teams' "outstanding player," received a watch from Edward's Art Gallery. "Iron Man" Tuckey, a veteran third sacker, played in every game during the 1952 season. Each member of the club received a "going away" gift.

The Bathers journeyed to Pine Bluff to end the season with a two-game loss, 12-5 and 10-9. The boys played hard, but they just didn't have enough talent to keep up with the fast Cotton States League. Ed Jacobson led the Bathers with a .293 season batting average and Tuckey hit well with a .271 mark. Hogan was the pitching ace on the Spa's staff with a 12-7 record and Bob Zolliecoffer ended with a 10-14 pitching record. Bert Shepard won one game and lost three. As a team, Hot Springs finished last in team standings and team batting.

Mike Ilitch joined the Bathers on June 13, and was a good player. Who was Mike Ilitch? Teammate Passarella said that Mike was a good scooper at second base and was fast. Mike, blessed with good speed and a good arm, posted a .266 batting average with 10 RBIs during his short career in Hot Springs. Mike's desire, just like many aspiring youngsters, was to become a major league player. In 1952, as a 22-year-old, Detroit signed Ilitch to a minor league contract to play for Jamestown, New York, in the Class D, Pony League (PA, Ontario, NY). Shortly after the 1952 season began, Detroit transferred him to Hot Springs. In 1953 and 1954, he rose to the Class B, Florida International League with the Tampa Smokers and Miami Beach Flamingos. In 1955, he jumped around among three teams, St. Petersburg, Norfolk and the 25-year-old ended his playing career with the Charlotte Hornets of the Class A, South Atlantic League. His career batting average was a respectable .280. However, along the way in his pursuit to the big leagues, an injury halted his progress in mid-stream. The desire to succeed remained with the young man, but he directed his aspirations toward the world of business.

The Director of Archives and Historical Documents at the Ilitch Holdings, Inc. stated that Mike's stats as a Bather, in addition to the above numbers, included: Games Played -72, At Bat – 278, Runs Scored – 44, Total Hits – 74, 2B Hits – 9, 3B Hits– 1, HR – 0, Stolen Bases – 26. "Passie" said that Mike's nickname was "Itch," because it rhymed with his last name.

If you don't know "Itch" personally, you do know something about him. He was born Michael Ilievski, a first generation American of Macedonian decent who became a foremost American entrepreneur. He is the founder and owner of Little Caesars Pizza, owner of the Detroit Red Wings of the National Hockey League (NHL) and owner of the American League baseball team, the Detroit Tigers. In addition, Ilitch is a member of the United States Hockey Hall of Fame. He may not have slugged many baseballs out of the yard at Jaycee Park; however, since then, he has hit numerous "tape-measure" homers in the business world.[37]

Chapter 14

The Tugerson Brothers
1953

"I knew we weren't going to play." - Jack Bales

"Goltz Replaces Crawford as Co-owner of Bathers," was the sports headline that appeared in *The Sentinel-Record* on Sunday morning, March 22, 1953. Lewis Goltz, a jeweler, replaced A. G. (Gabe) Crawford, a druggist, as co-owner of the Hot Springs Bathers Baseball Club. H. M. Britt and Garrett Britt, Hot Springs attorneys, remained co-owners with Goltz. However, it was around mid-season before the league approved the transfer, but Goltz continued as one of the officials of the Bathers' front office.

Hot Springs finished dead last in 1952, 35 games out of first place, as well as last in attendance with 37,796 in the eight-team CSL. The 1953 eight-team Cotton States League consisted of four Mississippi teams, three teams from Arkansas and one from Louisiana. Meridian, Jackson, Greenville and Natchez represented the Mississippi contingent, while Monroe was the lone Louisiana team. The three teams from Arkansas were El Dorado, Pine Bluff and Hot Springs.

In late 1952, the Bathers leadership came up with a unique idea. The inspiration was to sign a talented black player, or players, to the Bathers roster. The Bathers front office personnel, at that time, of Crawford and Britt presented the proposal to Haraway, league president, as early as

315

January 1953. "According to a letter written by Haraway to the Hot Springs Jaycees, Crawford and Henry Britt met with him on January 25 to discuss 'the matter of signing colored ballplayers for Hot Springs.'" Haraway suggested to the group that the matter should not be pursued because it would stir up a "hornet's nets." [1]

Now that Goltz was co-owner, in waiting, and acting president of the club, he yearned for greater interest and enthusiasm by placing a better product on the field, resulting in elevated attendance and higher gate receipts. Goltz seemed to have been a "Bill Veeck-type owner." Veeck, owner of the Cleveland Indians and, later, the St. Louis Browns, was a promotional genius. The innovative and energetic Veeck wanted the fans to have fun at the ballpark, increase attendance and make a buck. Veeck's most historic accomplishment was the signing of Larry Doby, who broke the color barrier in the American League, eleven weeks after Jackie Robinson signed with the Brooklyn Dodgers in the National League. Now, both leagues had a black player. Veeck introduced fireworks following games and hired Max Patkin, "Clown Prince of Baseball" as a Cleveland Indians coach in order to boost attendance. In another promotional venture, Veeck signed 42-year-old, Satchel Paige, the oldest rookie to have ever played in the majors. Attendance soared at the huge 78,000-seat Municipal Stadium in Cleveland. In 1951, Veeck signed 3'7" Eddie Gaedel to pinch-hit in a St. Louis Browns uniform. Gaedel, who wore number 1/8, batted once in the major leagues against the Detroit Tigers and received a walk on four straight pitches. Goltz wanted to build a strong nucleus because he wasn't in the business to lose money. Who is? He had some good players, but his desire was to contend for first place. In addition, he wanted all areas of the city, including the African-American community, to be supportive of the Bathers by their attendance.

The Goltz family members were immigrants from Poland and Russia. His father arrived at Ellis Island in New York, during the early 1900s and the remainder of the family moved to the United States a short time later. Due to overcrowding at Ellis Island, the rest of his family landed at the port in Galveston, Texas. Mr. Goltz, Lewis' father, decided to keep the family in Texas. The family's name was originally Holtz, but the official at the port of entry misread the handwriting and thought the "H" was a "G." The new emigrates didn't argue because they were delighted to be in the United States.

Born in Texas, Lewis, a Jewish-American attended public schools in Dallas and graduated from Forest Avenue High School. The high school, sometimes called, Forest High School, went through a name change in 1956 to James Madison High School, which exists today. The National Register of Historic Places added the school to its list in 1995. Several well-known individuals attended Forest Avenue. One of its celebrated students was the late Stanley Marcus, former president and CEO of Neiman Marcus Department Stores of Dallas. Additionally, the late Henry S. Miller, Jr., renowned Dallas realtor and the late Aaron Spelling, film and television producer were students at Forest. In the sports world, the late Dwight White, four-time Super Bowl Champion with the Pittsburgh Steelers and two-time pro bowl selection was a standout athlete from Forest Avenue High School.

Following high school, Goltz attended SMU in Dallas and the University of Texas at Austin, but dropped out of the college scene because he ran out of money. He became interested in a Hot Springs girl and later moved to Hot Springs and married her. Hot Springs became his new home, a city that he truly loved. His granddaughter, Madeline Goltz Hudson Bull said, "Grandfather, who was a member of the NAACP, respected all people regardless of race, color, creed, or religion."[2]

Goltz was a promoter extraordinaire. He had taken chances before and came out on the long end. He seemed to have enjoyed living on the promoter's edge.

Goltz had already proved himself a capable promoter of weekly 'rassling' events at the old Boys Club building, one of which featured Gorgeous George and drew 4,000 people. His showman's instincts told him that the black hurlers would be a good draw. This would save the franchise, and they might even win a few games.[3]

By 1953, Jackie Robinson established himself as a tremendous player with the Brooklyn Dodgers. However, not all professional baseball leagues followed suit by signing black players, especially in the south. The Cotton States League, a Class C, minor league, had been in existence for over 50 years and no black player had shown up on any of the team's rosters.

The Bathers' officials decided to take the leap and sign two black players, but they did not realize what a dilemma awaited the Spa leadership and the CSL. However, it seemed that Goltz and company wanted to push the racial envelope, since several individuals believed it was time for blacks to play in the Cotton States League. The Bathers needed good pitchers, so two African-Americans, Jim and Leander Tugerson signed contracts with the Bathers in the spring of 1953. Jim, 30, was a 6' 4" 194-pound right-handed thrower. Leander, two years younger, also possessed an adequate gift on the mound, but not as talented as his brother.

The Tugerson brothers had pitched for the Indianapolis Clowns of the Negro American League in 1951. The team played legitimate baseball, but also barnstormed as a comedy team, sort of like the Harlem Globetrotters in basketball. The team claimed the Negro American League pennant in 1950, 1951, 1952 and 1954. Leander, the big gun for the Clowns in 1951, posted a 15-4 mark including one no-hitter. Jim spent his first season in professional Negro League baseball hanging up 10 skins on the wall against five defeats for the Clowns.

In 1952, Jim returned to the Clowns where he acquired an 8-2 record and ended the summer playing in the Dominican summer league. Leander signed with Colorado Springs, a White Sox affiliate; however, he soon returned to the Clowns. That same year, the Clowns included a young 18-year-old, cross-handed batter from Mobile who later became a great major league hitter. The Tugerson's new teammate, Hank Aaron played shortstop and led the league in batting with a .467 mark. Midway through the season, the Boston Braves bought out Aaron's contract from the Clowns for $10,000 and the skinny shortstop headed for the minor leagues. In 1954, due to an ailing Bobby Thompson, Aaron took Thompson's place in the Braves lineup in left field and by then, the Braves' new home was Milwaukee. Aaron hit a home run in his first major league at bat and he continued to hit home runs for the Braves for 23 years.[4]

The Tugerson brothers served in the Army Air Corps during WW II, where Jim rose to the rank of Warrant Officer. Jennings reported that they were articulate and displayed "sterling character" on and off the field. He also noted that both had "outgoing personalities, especially Jim." The Bathers seemed to be more interested in Jim, but they were delighted to get both pitchers. Suddenly, there was a snag!

The Attorney General of Mississippi, J. P. Coleman had other ideas concerning the signing of the Tugerson brothers.

Their signing met with immediate resistance. On April 1, 1953, Mississippi Attorney General J. P. Coleman announced that integrated clubs did not have the right to appear on baseball diamonds in this state. Coleman acknowledged that there was no specific statute to that effect, but based his edict upon the emphasis placed on segregation in the Mississippi constitution.[5]

The front-page headlines of *The Sentinel-Record* on April 7, stated "Bathers Ousted From CSL Over Negro Player Issue." Hot Springs was now a club without a league. Al Haraway, president of the CSL, released this communiqué to *The Sentinel-Record.*

In a lengthy executive session at Greenville, Miss. Monday, the Class C league terminated the Hot Springs franchise 'since it is a matter of survival of the League.'
President Al Haraway of Helena issued this prepared statement:
　　At a meeting of the directors of the Cotton States League held in Greenville, Miss. April 6, the membership of the Hot Springs club was terminated under article 5, paragraph 13 of the League Constitution which states in part 'any cause which prevents the League from

functioning properly with such clubs holding membership.' And paragraph 14, which says in part 'by a 2-3 vote of all the clubs that for business reasons the membership of any club is no longer desired.'

Since the Hot Springs club has assumed a position from which it refuses to recede, which will disrupt the Cotton States League and cause its dissolution, which position having been assumed without the courtesy of a League discussion and since it is a matter of survival of the league, or transfer of the Hot Springs franchise, this action was taken.[6]

In a related article on the same page, the headlines stated, "O'Connor Decries Action; Citizens Offer Protests." Officials of the Spa club immediately sent a letter of protest to George M. Trautman, president of the National Association of Minor Leagues. "The protest, it was reported, will be based on the charges that the action was illegal under the constitution and by-laws of the league."

Leslie O'Connor, brought in to assist the Bathers in their squabble with the league, proved a legitimate aide. He was an attorney, as well as former White Sox general manager and longtime secretary to the late Kenesaw Mountain Landis. As the Bathers representative at the meeting, he had much to say concerning the situation. He stated that it was the "most grievous error ever committed in baseball." *The Sentinel-Record* reported information concerning the league meeting.

Hot Springs citizens last night individually and collectively protested the action of the Cotton States League in ousting the Bathers because of their insistence on using two Negro players.

Leslie O'Connor, former assistant to the late Baseball Commissioner K. M. Landis and author of many of the game's key rules during the past three decades, termed the action taken by the league at Greenville, Miss. 'the most grievous error ever committed in baseball.'

O'Connor, a Hot Springs property owner but a resident of Chicago, accompanied the Bather delegation but was not allowed to speak at the executive session. An attorney, he is legal counsel for the Pacific Coast League and a member of the powerful major-minor league baseball council.

The Junior Chamber of Commerce, builders of Jaycee baseball park, now valued at $100,000, and one of the prime forces in keeping professional baseball in Hot Springs, wired its protest last night to League President Al Haraway of Helena.[7]

After returning to Hot Springs from the Greenville meeting, O'Connor expounded upon the meeting and expressed his opinions to the Hot Springs press.

I deeply regret the precipitate action of the Cotton States League in purportedly terminating the membership of the Hot Springs club.

I had hoped to be privileged to submit to the league members for their consideration, before acting upon this matter, observations as to the many factors involved, as I was apprehensive that ill-considered action might be taken which would be extremely detrimental to the general welfare of baseball throughout the nation, and was hopeful that a solution satisfactory to all concerned could be attained if everything involved had proper consideration.

The action of the league is wholly unsupported by anything in the law of the land.[8]

Protests poured in from across the nation as newspapers ran the story of the Bathers dismissal from the Cotton States League. In addition to the two Hot Springs newspapers, *The Sentinel-Record* and *New Era*, a few of the newspapers that printed the story concerning the Tugerson's removal included *The New York Times*, *The Dallas Morning News*, the *Houston Chronicle*, *The Times-Picayune* (New Orleans) and *Jet*, the Weekly Negro News Magazine. Other newspapers that reported the events were *The Commercial Appeal* (Memphis), the *Fargo Forum*, (North Dakota), the *Daily Argus-Leader* (Sioux Falls, South Dakota), the *St. Petersburg Times* (Florida), the

Arizona Republic (Phoenix), the *Atlanta Journal,* now *The Atlanta Journal-Constitution* (Georgia) and the *Arkansas Gazette,* now the *Arkansas Democrat-Gazette* (Little Rock). In addition, many national sports publications, including *The Sporting News*, featured articles concerning the Cotton States League incident.[9]

An editorial by the *Delta Democrat-Times* of Greenville, Mississippi, stated the case to keep the players on the Hot Springs team.

As far as we can determine, no Hot Springs players object to having Negroes on the team. We haven't heard any great opposition from Hot Springs fans or from any other Arkansas city. The biggest objector is Natchez. There has been some outspoken opposition also in Greenville. Those, we believe are the facts.[10]

Even the Methodist women joined the cause. On Monday, April 6, the Women's Society of Christian Service of the Little Rock Methodist Conference assembled at the Grand Avenue Methodist Church in Hot Springs. The 250 women unanimously voted for a resolution introduced by the immediate past-president of the organization, Mrs. E. D. Galloway of Hope. The resolution stated that the Christian organization praised the Bathers ownership for employing the two "Negro pitchers." They "termed the Bathers action in the Christian spirit and said that the group believed the contracts were awarded on the merits of the players and not because of their race."[11]

In order to keep the two pitchers, the team was willing to play the Tugersons only at home and other cities that would allow them to play. Representatives of the Bathers said that they never intended playing the two men in Mississippi. The Bathers issued a joint statement concerning Haraway's philosophy. "We can't see where President Haraway, because of his personal feelings, can ramrod us out of the league on a segregation question." The Bathers officials also stated that they believed that many of the news reporters "seemed to be in agreement with our cause." [12]

Vernon "Moose" Shetler, manager of the Bathers, related the tone of the team and that was, "I'll see the boys at the park at 11 a.m. today." The team continued to practice for opening day. He noted that the Bathers planned to play their opening game at Pine Bluff on April 21, just as scheduled.[13]

"Trautman Halts CSL Ouster of Hot Springs Pending an Appeal by League President" was the headlines in *The Sentinel-Record* of April 11.

The Hot Springs Bathers of the Cotton States League won a temporary victory today when the minor leagues association stopped the team's ouster from the league. The president of the National Association of Professional Baseball Leagues, George Trautman said the action was halted pending a decision on an appeal.

The Bathers were dropped from the Class C loop Monday for hiring two Negro ball players.

On Tuesday, the (Bathers) board of directors appealed to the national association and the national commissioner.[14]

On April 12, *The Sentinel-Record,* printed Haraway's letter and the response of the Hot Springs Junior Chamber of Commerce.

Haraway's letter and response by the Jaycees follows.

Dr. H. King Wade, Jr.
Mr. Ray S. Smith, Jr.
Hot Springs, Arkansas

Dear King and Ray:

Have your telegram of the sixth protesting the termination of the Hot Springs franchise.

No one regrets more than I to see Hot Springs get out of the League, and I am deeply appreciative personally of the splendid efforts you and your committee put forth to continue baseball in Hot Springs when Herbert Anderton gave up the ghost.

My connection with the Cotton States League as a club and league executive covers a period of almost twenty years, during which time there has been a most stimulating spirit of cooperation and always a full discussion of the plans and problems of each of its members as related to the welfare of the league as a whole, and our league meetings have been marked by a complete absence of discord and bickering as is prevalent in many leagues, both large and small. This was completely disregarded by the officials of the Hot Springs Club in the present case, which fact caused equally as much resentment among the league directors as the question of an attempt to break the color line in a Deep South league.

After a meeting in Greenville on January 25th, H. M. Britt and Gabe Crawford approached me on the matter of signing colored ball players for Hot Springs. Feeling that I had a better understanding of the sentiments of the club owners, perhaps than they did, I advised against it and requested that they do not attempt it as this time, knowing the hornet's nest it would stir up; and I tried my very best to convince them of this fact apparently without success. The records in this office show that on February 4 and February 12, the Tugerson brothers were signed to 1953 contracts, in studied defiance of a warning that the people in our league were not yet ready to accept a breakdown in racial barriers. Now, it comes out at the meeting yesterday that these players were signed to a contract late in 1952 or early in 1953, without having discussed such a revolutionary and explosive move with anyone in the league.

Common courtesy would dictate that the other league members have an opportunity to express themselves, and simple ethics that the Hot Springs officials be governed by the wishes of the majority. Instead, they wait until spring training opens then come out in big headlines that two Negro players had been signed, apparently in an attempt to ram them down the throats of the rest of the league knowing full well the time for action was limited.

Add to all this the unyielding attitude of the Hot Springs officials when efforts were made to work out a solution to the problem, and in face of the fact that four clubs had openly declared their intention to withdraw from the league if the Tugersons were kept on the roster of the Hot Springs Club. Since this would have resulted in a complete dissolution of the league, and Hot Springs was apparently unwilling to recede from its position, and seemed perfectly willing for the league to break up if they couldn't have their way, there was nothing left to do but invoke parts of Paragraphs 13 and 14 of Article V, Section 1, of the league constitution (which, incidentally was written by Mr. Leslie O'Connor) which provides that a club's franchise may be terminated for 'cause which prevents this league from functioning properly and for business reasons which make the membership of any club no longer desirable,' both of which would be the case should such actions cause a break up of the league.

I have undertaken to set fourth above, the thinking of the league directors. I realize that it is difficult for Hot Springs with its cosmopolitan population from everywhere to grasp the thinking of Deep South people, and I, personally, feel that in view of the intense opposition the proposal of the Hot Springs Club should have yielded to the wishes of the overwhelming majority.

I am not authorized to speak for a majority of the league directors, but I feel reasonably sure that if the players in question are removed from the roster and no others signed until approval has been given by at least five directors, it will be possible to have Monday's action rescinded. I will be glad to use any influence I may have to that end, and for a restoration of harmony in the league. After the positive declaration of yesterday, I feel it will be useless to suggest any less.

I have a telegram from the Tucson, Arizona, club of the Arizona-Texas League expressing an interest in the Tugersons. If the Club cares to, they can communicate with Mr. George F. Merrick, business manager of the Tucson club.

I hope we can get all this business cleared up and forgotten, so that we can get back to the sport we love so well, and pass the social experiments on to other hands who probably are much better qualified than we.

With all good wishes, I am sincerely yours,
Al Haraway

Jaycees Response to Haraway's letter follows.

Thank you for your letter of April 7. As representatives of the Hot Springs Junior Chamber of Commerce, we have brought your reply before the Board of Directors for consideration and have been instructed to write you as follows:

As you are well aware, the Junior Chamber of Commerce of Hot Springs has always had a high regard and the friendliest feeling for you personally and regret deeply the difference of opinion, which has developed. However, we feel that, when fundamental principles are involved, they are above personal opinions.

We feel that the phrase, 'The unyielding attitude of the Hot Springs officials when efforts were made to work out a solution to the problem,' could more aptly be applied to other members of the league. Hot Springs Bathers officials announced publicly that they would use the Negroes only in Hot Springs and in such other cities that might desire them. We would also like to point out that such 'Deep South' states as Texas, Tennessee, Louisiana and Kentucky have played Negroes.

Today we ask that the League place the problem above personal feelings to the extent of some sort of compromise. We feel that one has been offered by Hot Springs officials but that none has been offered by the League. We do not feel that the time for compromise has passed, and we strongly urge the Cotton States League to consider and, if possible, to offer some type of compromise that might be worked out in this manner.

We are still of the opinion that Hot Springs has been a mainstay of the Cotton States League these past years and has actually helped keep the League from becoming defunct. We believe, from its history in this League, the Hot Springs Ball Club is certainly deserving of every consideration that you and the Board could give them.

We also feel that merit should still be recognized regardless of race or creed. There has been no change in our ideas on the moral viewpoint in this situation.

Sincerely your,

Hot Springs Junior Chamber of Commerce

H. King Wade, Jr.

Ray S Smith, Jr.[15]

The "overwhelming majority" of baseball fans throughout the nation expressed a desire for the Tugersons to play for Hot Springs. However, in this case, the minority became the overwhelming majority.

The annual season ticket sales began the week of April 12. Ticket sales committee included Earle Bowling, Herbert Brenner and W. D. Roddenberry. The Bathers were going full-steam ahead. The business community was selling tickets all over the city. The companies included Lewis Jewelers, Goddard Hotel, Art Kraft Camera Shop, Crawford Drug Stores, Citizen's, Spenser's and Sim's Cigar Stores, Ohio Club, Kentucky Club, Southern Grill, Douglas Flower Shop, Yellow Cab Company, National Café, National Baptist Sanitarium, Copa Cabana Club, Wes Curry Taxi Stand and Town-Talk Barbecue. Goltz, soon-to-be co-owner of the Bathers, continued to push for a full house at Jaycee Park on opening night in Hot Springs.

We want to show the Cotton States League we want baseball, and one of the best ways to do this is to have a packed park April 23, Co-owner Lewis Goltz declared. Fans who want to help keep professional baseball in Hot Springs can do so by supporting the Bathers, win or lose.[16]

Hostility continued to flare on both sides. Neither group wanted to back down. Following the meeting, Goltz said that he called Haraway every name he could think of, but "redneck" was his favorite.[17] On April 14, *The Sentinel-Record* reported that another CSL meeting was in the works, but Hot Springs was not going to send a representative. On April 17, the meeting was verified.

A highly secret session of the CSL was held Tuesday (14) and from it came the brief announcement that the Cotton States League would open April 21 with the present eight clubs. Officials of the Bathers told newsmen yesterday that we are still reviewing the whole situation and may have an announcement made Saturday.

It was reliably reported Thursday that the Cotton States League and the Southern Association are the only loops in the South, which are not permitting the use of Negro players this year...

...Nothing on what transpired at Tuesday's meeting has been made public. League directors are under threat of a $1,000 fine if news of the secret session is made public, it was reported.

Meanwhile the Tugersons are going ahead with training. Jim Tugerson is scheduled to pitch against the Millington Naval Air Station tonight.[18]

Gabe Crawford, still president of the Bathers, reported that he received a recent telegram from Major League Baseball Commissioner Ford Frick. The telegram stated, "Copy of your protest received and hereby acknowledged. I will be prepared to make a quick decision if and when the matter comes to me." The Bathers were waiting on communication from George M. Trautman, minor league czar.

The most eloquent, emotional reply to the ouster came from the Tugersons themselves. They issued a joint statement, which read in part, 'Are we fit to work in your homes and fields only? We can talk for you and help elect you when it is time for voting. When you were young was it fair for a Negro maid to raise you? Now we're the forgotten ones. You haven't been fair to us in the South. We don't want to, as Negroes, stay with you or eat with you. All we want to do is play baseball for a living...As long as the club wants us, we will stay here and fight.'[19]

On April 15, Trautman sent a scorching telegram to the CSL officials. He strongly stated that reinstatement to the Cotton States League was the only answer for the Hot Springs Bathers. The telegram stated:

The employment of Negro players has never been, nor is now, prohibited by any provision in the major-minor league agreement. Whether a National Association club chooses to employ a player of any race, color or creed is a decision for the club itself to make.[20]

The reinstatement of the club meant to the CSL officials that they could play in the CSL, if they didn't use the Tugerson brothers. The emotional war of words continued. The telegram wasn't completely true. Major and minor league baseball didn't allow players of color to play in the all-white leagues for many years. It was true that "the employment of Negro players has never been prohibited by any provision." But, as Jackie Robinson found out, there was a custom that blacks did not play in all-white leagues. However, Trautman made his point heard loud and clear.

Who was this Trautman fellow? Selected as the fourth president of the minor leagues in 1947, the experienced Trautman seemed ready for the task. At that time, World War II was over, it was peacetime and people wanted a diversion from their work schedule. Baseball was the answer. The year, 1949, was the "high water mark" of Trautman's administration. Nearly 40 million fans walked through the minor league turnstiles as they backed 448 teams in 59 leagues.

Trautman won varsity letters in football, basketball and baseball at Ohio State University. Following graduation, he became the assistant athletic director at his Alma Mater. He soon became the head basketball coach at Ohio State, but this didn't work out very well because he finished his three-year coaching career with a dismal 29-33 record. In 1933, he became the president of the Triple-A, Columbus Red Birds, a minor league baseball team in Ohio. George continued to climb the administrative baseball ladder, as he became the president of the American Association, one of two Triple-A leagues in the country. Triple-A was the highest minor league classification in professional baseball, one-step away from the major leagues. Named President of the National Association of Professional Baseball Leagues in 1947, Trautman held that position until his death in 1963.

In the meantime, the Bathers continued to practice for their opening game with Pine Bluff. Intersquad games produced excellent results concerning the Tugerson brothers. Both men hit and pitched well during the practice games. On April 17, the Bathers played an exhibition game at home against Millington Naval Air Station from Memphis. Jim Tugerson, 6' 4", 194 pounds, from Florence Villa, Polk County, Florida, started on the mound for the Bathers and Hot Springs sailed over the Navy boys 17-5. Jack Bales, former Bathers catcher said, "We didn't have any problem having the Tugersons playing on the team."[21]

On April 18, Maurice Moore, local sports editor, posed a question, which was, "Where To Go From Here?" He stated that the Bathers are putting up a good fight, but when it all comes down to it, they have four courses of action. The possible actions included "(1) play the Tugersons, (2) sell them, (3) trade them, or (4) option them out." His article continued:

The Bathers possess a historic ruling on this whole issue from President George M. Trautman of the National Association of Professional Baseball Leagues....Whether the Bathers profit or not by this fight, at least they have made a major contribution to the future welfare of a great American sport...This is a consolation measured in sentiment and courage to stand by a principle.[22]

On April 20, before the first regular-season game, the Bathers decided to send the pitchers to Knoxville with an option to recall them. This action put the Spa's mound staff in a dilemma. The team had only "two veterans, a limited service twirler, and three rookies." On opening night, April 21, manager Vern "Moose" Shetler tapped veteran hurler Ed Baski to toss the season opener on the road against Pine Bluff. Following mid-season in 1952, Baski compiled a 4-6 record for the

Bathers, mainly in relief. The opening Bathers lineup included hometown product Jackie Bales, formerly of the Detroit Tigers system, who started at catcher. "Moose" Shetler was at first, veteran Bob Passarella took care of second base, while another veteran, Babe Tuckey handled the hot corner and rookie, 6' 3" Charles Ekas played shortstop. Hard-hitting Hal Martin roamed in the center pasture, while two Arkansas rookies covered Martin's flanks. John Greenway, from Paron, Arkansas, patrolled left field and Rison native John Trucks protected the right side of the outfield.

Jack Bales stated that Hal Martin was a "guess hitter" with tremendous wrist power. He would go to the plate to hit and guess at every pitch. Sometimes he would miss it a mile and other times he would knock the cover off the ball. Jack recalled Martin connected on a ball that flew over the left field fence and he was sure it went at least 500 feet in the air before landing. There was nothing but Roosters Field and wide-open spaces over the left field fence. He said that it was no telling how far that thing rolled after it hit.

Hot Springs lost their first two games of the season at Taylor Field in Pine Bluff. They were ready to get back home for their opening night. However, first it was the opening-day festivities. In the afternoon, there was a "Meet Your Bathers" parade, which began at Fountain Street and continued down through the heart of downtown on Central Avenue. The players, led by manager Vernon "Moose" Shetler, rode in convertibles.

Big happenings were on tap at Jaycee Park for the Bathers home opener with Pine Bluff on April 23. Events included two games for the price of one and the performance of the John Roddy's Stringbusters band. In addition, everyone enjoyed watching a six-horse hitch of Clydesdales from the Wilson Packing Company.

The pregame festivities began at 7:30 p.m. as the civic leaders and dignitaries took the field. They showed the fans how not to play the game of baseball. "Blind Bill" Durant umpired the game and "called 'em like he saw 'em!" Those taking part in the "liniment" game included Jack McJunkin-1B, Van Lyell, Sr.-2B, Jimmy Phillips-SS, Judge Floyd Huff-3B, Clyde McMahan-LF, Milton Nobles- CF and Will Lake-RF.

Former Bathers pitcher "Spike" Hunter toed the rubber for the entertaining game, while his catcher was Dr. H. King Wade, Sr. Designated batters were Chancellor Sam Garratt, Mose Klyman and Sherriff Will Lowe. Other dignitaries included Earl Ricks, Q. Byrum Hurst, Judge Clyde Brown, Warren Angel, Lewis Goltz and Dr. H. H. Blahut. Due to illness, Mayor Floyd Housley did not attend that night.

With a few light showers, an opening night crowd of 1,172 watched the Bathers take the field with Kenny Seifert on the mound for the Spa. The fans didn't have to wait long for action. In the first inning, Pine Bluff tallied a run and Hot Springs repeated Pine Bluff's challenge and added one in the bottom half of the first. At the end of three frames, it was 3-2, Hot Springs. Things were looking good for the Bathers at the end of six innings as the hometown team took a commanding 6-3 lead. The Judges rallied in the seventh inning to make it a new ball game at 6-6. Seifert, the lanky veteran right-hander from St. Louis, continued to pitch well, except a few times when the wild bug bit him and two gopher balls flew over the fence. In the ninth frame, Trucks singled Martin home from second base for the winning run as the Bathers took the opener 7-6. Seifert pitched a neat six-hitter.

Another event was in the works just outside the baseball field. The American Circus Association (ACA) presented the Hennies Show at the Jaycee Recreation Park from May 1-9. The Jaycees sponsored the circus and rides. It was a good moneymaker for the Jaycees as families from the area visited the circus and it may have increased baseball attendance.

On May 8, a single by Passarella in the seventh frame scored two runs as the Bathers toppled the Judges 6-5 at home. Beginning May 12, the rains came. From May 12-16, it washed out six games, including a doubleheader. On May 17, the Bathers finally played baseball as they beat Jackson twice on the road. Hal Martin topped the CSL hitters with an astonishing .438 batting average. On the same day, Lewis Goltz won the Jaycee Award for his civic spirit. It was a tremendous honor presented to a person with an electrifying personality. On May 19, Hot Springs returned to their losing ways as Meridian defeated the Bathers 4-2, as 16 Bathers went down swinging.

Within a month of the option, Jim Tugerson accumulated a 6-2 record for the Knoxville Smokies before the Bathers recalled him on May 18. On May 20, Tugerson, the commuting pitcher, was in the Hot Springs lineup slated to pitch against the Jackson Senators of Mississippi at Jaycee Park. More than 1,800 fans packed the stands and bleachers. In addition, several hundred enthusiasts anxiously waited in line at the ticket windows in hopes of getting a ducat to attend the historic event.

Jack Bales, Hot Springs' catcher, was warming up Tugerson on the sidelines. The Bathers tagged Tugerson and Bales as the Spa batteries that night, but Jack said, "I knew we weren't going to play."[23] The late Bob Passarella, infielder/outfielder for the Bathers, said, "Jim was a good pitcher" because I faced him during intersquad games.[24] At the last minute, Bathers front office gave manager Shetler an option. He could decide to back out and not pitch Tugerson or leave big Jim in the lineup. Shetler nixed the idea of backing out.

The Management told me at 10 a.m. today to pitch Jim Tugerson. At 7:50 p.m. they asked me to get somebody else ready. I refused to do this on the basis that it would not be fair to the fans who came to see Tugerson pitch. What the management wishes to do now is up to them.[25]

Shetler met with Jackson manager Duke Doolittle at home plate and exchanged lineups. Plate umpire Thomas McDermott of Baltimore, Maryland, and base umpire Charles Behrens of Miami, Florida, accepted the lineups of both teams. At that moment, "Umpire McDermott turned toward the grandstand shortly after 8 p.m. and announced that the game had been ordered forfeited by the league president for Hot Springs' use of an ineligible player." The crowd let their feelings known to the public by booing loudly. Jackson won automatically by the score of 9-0. At that point, Jewell Thomas, Bathers general manager, read two telegrams over the public address system. The first telegram was from Haraway stating that the game was a forfeit and the second telegram was a reply from the Bathers' ownership.[26]

A news article appeared in the *Ryukyuan Review*, a United States Army Air Force, Navy and Coast Guard newspaper in Okinawa. The headlines stated, "Hot Controversy Hits Cotton States League – Negro Pitcher Is Barred."[27]

Surely, Jim Tugerson was irritated, aggravated and discouraged; however, he showed tremendous self-control.

He did, however, drop a hint that rocked the baseball world, telling a reporter, 'It's possible that I may sue (Haraway), I'm not bitter, but I think he did the wrong thing in making Hot Springs forfeit that game. I hope I land in the majors some day. I want to be in a league where they will let me play ball.' [28]

The Tugersons were tired of being in the middle of a squabble because they wanted to play baseball. Jim and Leander requested an option to play in another league. Jim, the spokesperson of the two, said that they appreciated the management's efforts and the players were very good to them. Finally, he stated, "We hope that someday we might be able to return." The Bathers granted their option. The Tugersons returned to the Knoxville in the Class D, Mountain States League, but the door was still slightly ajar for them to return to Hot Springs.

It was the second season at Hot Springs for Bob Passarella and he was looking forward to a better season because in 1952, he only hit .231. At times, he and "Moose" Shetler, Bathers manager, disagreed about certain things. They respected one another, but they were "up front" with each other. Bob recalls when he was in a batting slump; "Moose" dropped him to the eighth spot in the lineup. "Passie" understood the strategy, but the manager made him take pitches that he did not usually take. When he took pitches, it would put him behind in the count and Bob said it was difficult to raise his batting average by letting strikes zoom past him. On one occasion, Bob saw the "take" sign, but he was tired of taking, so on the next pitch Bob swung and connected. No, it wasn't a home run, but he hit a hot shot up the middle, but the infielders turned a double play. In the dugout, "Moose" didn't waste any time telling Bob what he thought, but things were soon smoothed over between the two players.

On May 24, Meridian won 9-6, but "fence-buster" Martin got his licks in. There were five homers hit that night and big Hal accounted for two of them. On May 26, the Bathers took care of Meridian 12-9, as Hot Springs registered four homers by power-hitters, Shetler, Tuckey, Martin and Adcock. The Bathers played good ball, but many times, they came up on the short end.

On May 30, in the 6th inning of a Monroe game, Korfonta was out at home. A big discussion between players and umpire broke out. Umpire Neil Kent got his ear full as manager Shetler and right fielder Steve Korfonta disagreed with the ump's call. They continued to argue a little too much, so umpire Kent gave the two players the "thumb" of ejection. The Spa Team lost 3-1, but they pulled off a rare triple play in the 8th inning.

Many people remember the Bathers' batboy nicknamed "Swifty." His real name was Claude Dick and he seemed to be at the park most of the time. Jack Bales stated that the teenager was a good batboy and assisted in keeping the locker room in good shape. "Swifty," who began his batboy duties in 1947, received his name due to his "fleetness in chasing foul balls." In 1953, "Swifty" got a chance of a lifetime. The Bathers needed pitching. "Swifty" was a good pitcher on the Boys Club and semi-pro teams, so the Bathers decided to sign the right-hander to a contract. The records show that he pitched in one game in 1953. After that night, Bales said "Swifty" continued to be an excellent batboy.[29]

The last of May and early June, the Bathers bats and pitching came together. On May 30, Kenny Siefert won his fifth tilt by blanking the Monroe Sports 7-0 on a six hitter. A few days later, The Bathers halted Natchez 10-2 as Ronay hurled a five hitter. The next evening, Shetler poled a four-bagger as the Bathers passed Natchez in the 13th inning, 3-2. The Bathers were rolling. On June 5, Bales homered in the ninth frame to take away a win from Pine Bluff. Even though the

Bathers strung several wins together, they were in fifth place. However, they only needed to get to that fourth spot for a playoff berth. Martin remained in the lead in the CSL batting race with a terrific .438 mark.

During the same season, Hal Martin, Bathers speedy center fielder and batting hero, seemingly was the media darling. On June 7, *The Sentinel-Record* sportswriter penned an article about the CSL star. The title of the article was "From Nightmares To Diamond Dreams." In 1953, Martin was connecting at the plate. Due to his heroic past, it was amazing that he was walking, much less playing baseball at a professional level. In 1943, during WW II, Army Staff Sergeant Hal Martin was in a firefight at the Battle of Kasserine Pass in Tunisia, North Africa. Martin, wounded in the stomach and the left knee by German Field Marshall Rommel's forces, became a prisoner of war in February 1943.

One of the first issues Martin considered was his baseball future. The Germans frequently moved the American prisoners to other camps in order to stay out of range of the approaching Allied Forces. The Germans allowed the American prisoners to participate in recreational activities and, as his health slowly improved, Martin began to play a little softball. "He revealed that the American prisoners were allowed to play the sport five times a week," but he said they were not permitted to play baseball. One of his softball opponents was Mickey Grasso, the light-hitting catcher who, after the war, played major league baseball. In fact, when Martin was playing for the Bathers in 1953, Grasso was catching for the Washington Senators.[30]

Martin said he was located at POW camps in Sicily, Italy, Austria and Germany. "His day of liberation came on April 22, 1945. The Russians had reached the camp first and he was back in American hands a few days later." He was a prisoner of war for two years, two months and two days. He returned to the United States in June and the Army discharged him in August 1945. A Bronze Star and a Purple Heart were among his military honors.[31]

Before the war, Martin broke into professional baseball with a farm team of the Cincinnati Reds in 1939. After WW II, he returned to the minor leagues but soon became discouraged, so he re-enlisted in the Army. After his discharge the second time, he began playing baseball again. He moved around from team to team, mainly on the east coast. In 1953, he signed with the Greenville Bucks in the Cotton States League, but had a dispute with the leadership during spring training. The Bucks released him and Hot Springs picked him up. His goal in 1953 was to win the CSL batting title. The 33-year-old outfielder was married and had a three-year-old daughter at that time. During the off-season, he lived in South Carolina and Virginia. Hot Springs was delighted to have the talented Martin on their side.

Meetings, concerning the possible return of Jim Tugerson, continued at Hot Springs and within the CSL. "Baseball Club Directors To Reorganize Wednesday" was one the sports headlines in *The Sentinel-Record* of June 9, 1953.

Stockholders and board of directors of the Hot Springs Baseball club will hold a reorganization meeting Wednesday at 1 p.m. at the Goddard Hotel.

It is a good possibility that the club officials will discuss whether or not to recall Negro Pitcher Jim Tugerson from Knoxville, Tenn., of the Class D Mountain States League because of an undisputed ruling given Saturday by Minor League Czar George M. Trautman at Columbus, Ohio.

A decision on this issue, which had been boiling in the Cotton States League since April, could come earlier than the meeting.

The board of directors has not formally been reorganized since brothers H. M. and Garrett Britt and Lewis Goltz became co-owners succeeding Druggist A. G. (Gabe) Crawford and Tom Stough. Goltz has been serving in the capacity of acting president; H. M. Britt, vice president; Garrett Britt, treasurer; Chancellor Sam W. Garratt, club chairman; W. D. Roddenberry is club secretary and Jewell Thomas, general manager.[32]

Rain, heavy wind and power outages cancelled the game in Hot Springs with Pine Bluff on June 11. Heavy winds blew a tree across a power line serving the park and the result was total darkness for more than an hour. Following the power restoration to eight light poles, a heavy downpour flooded the baseball park. A few days later, Hot Springs lost its seventh straight contest; however, the next night they broke the jinx and split a twin bill with Greenville. The Bathers were losing ground. Now they were in seventh place. On June 16, the Bathers and Monroe were deadlocked 3-3 when Martin solved the problem with his 21st round-tripper that led to a 6-3 Spa win. It was the first home run at Monroe's Memorial Stadium of the 1953 season.

Martin's two homers helped the Bathers hobble the Jackson Senators 11-7. The former Army sergeant continued to rip down the fences with four-baggers. The Bathers rolled to their fifth consecutive victory on June 23, by plastering the Meridian Millers 10-0.

In late June, the Junior Chamber of Commerce was energetically organizing and promoting other events in the city. The Jaycees crowned Janet Gray, "Miss Hot Springs." The event was always a popular activity for the city. In addition, the Jaycees sponsored the Rogers Rodeo and Circus, a two-day affair, held at the Jaycee Park recreation area. Admission for the event was $1.00 for adults and $.50 for children. Two big events were in the Bathers plans. The management arranged a big "wing-ding" for Hal Martin on Thursday, July 2. Martin was a top-notch player and popular with the fans. Another big coming event was the annual Cotton States League All-Star contest, hosted by the Bathers.

Too much rain washed out the baseball game on July 2, but not until Hal Martin received a personal shower as over 1,100 fans showed up for "Hal Martin Night." It was the largest crowd in weeks. The "Home Run Happy" Martin led the CSL at mid-season with 28 homers, only 12 behind the all-time season record. Not only was he cranking the ball out of the park, he was slapping it all over the park, as he led the Cotton States League in hitting with over a .370 average.

The Martin family, Hal, Mrs. Martin and four-year-old daughter Patti, were grateful for the outpouring of support and the presents given to them by the fans. The family received over 50 gifts, but Hal's favorite gift was a set of golf clubs, "that he always wanted." Hal received a watch, house wares, at least six free meals to local restaurants and free local movie passes. Estimated value for the gifts was around $500.00. "And the Martins were even promised their Thanksgiving turkey for November. It will be sent to them wherever they are."

The "Hal Martin Night" game progressed all the way to the second inning, but that was all the umpires could take, so they called it off. The umpires checked the field twice before cancelling the tilt, but it was a perfect time for Hot Springs to stop the contest. Natchez was ahead 1-0 and the bases were full of Indians.

Sportswriter Maurice Moore wrote about "No Moon Shine" on Sunday, July 5, in *The Sentinel-Record*.

Manager Moose Shetler has been in baseball a long time, and thought he had heard every-thing, but recently-released Hot Springs hurler, Herb Fleischner, stopped him cold with this remark: 'Skip, I pitch best when the moon is full.' Fleischner's 'moon' eclipsed last week.[33]

On Tuesday, July 14, around 2,000 fans packed Jaycee Park to observe the sixth annual CSL All-Star clash. Four teams from Mississippi challenged the Arkansas-Louisiana squad. Meridian Millers, Jackson Senators, Greenville Bucks and the Natchez Indians formed the All-Star squad from the east side of the Mississippi River. On the west side of the river, the Arkansas-Louisiana All-Stars representatives were the El Dorado Oilers, the Pine Bluff Judges, the Hot Springs Bathers and the Monroe (LA) Sports.

The 1953 All-Star team included three Bathers Jack Bales – catcher, Hal Martin - center field and Bob Adcock - right field. In a special pregame ceremony at home plate, president Al Haraway presented each player with an engraved cigarette lighter. The Arkansas-Louisiana All-Stars tallied twice in the second inning, but Mississippi scored a lone run in the fourth stanza and one more in the fifth for a 2-2 tie. In the bottom of the seventh, Hal Martin singled in a run as the East squad went up 3-2. In the top of the ninth inning, third baseman Ray Posipanski of Greenville, clouted a solo home run to put the contest into a 3-3 dead heat. Still in the ninth inning, with a man on third and one out, Roy Jayne, Mississippi's third pitcher, slapped a sacrifice fly to center, driving in the runner from third.

The west team managed to get two men on base during the bottom half of final frame, but left them stranded as Mississippi won the sixth annual All-Star contest by a 4-3 margin. Chosen the game's MVP was Greenville's third-sacker Ray Posipanka. Hal Martin led all hitters with a 3-4 outing, including an RBI. Due to a thumb injury to Pine Bluff's catcher Chuck Thomas, Jack Bales caught the entire game and scored a run. Thomas, used as a pinch hitter in the ninth inning, singled, but a force out at second ended the threat.

The winning hurler was Roy Jayne of Natchez, while Hugh Blanten, from Monroe, suffered the loss. Greenville pitcher, Tom Pollet gave up only one hit during his three-inning twirling duties. "Right fielder Gene Pompelia of Meridian turned in one of the most spectacular catches of the game when he raced full speed near the scoreboard in right center field to haul in what seemed to be a sure-hit by Pel Austin of El Dorado." Umpires for the game were Behrens, Cargill, Kent and Duncan. Time of the contest was two hours flat and at the All-Star break, Hot Springs was in sixth place in the standings.

An editorial under "Opinion" in *The Baltimore Afro-American* stated that the editor believed that Tugerson should make the league pay.

The decision of Jim Tugerson to fight back is as cheerful a bit of news as we've heard this week.

Tugerson, with his twin brother, Leander, you may remember, had signed contracts to pitch this year for the Hot Springs (Ark.) Bathers…

…Before Tugerson could pitch the first ball, Cotton States League President Al Haraway ordered the game forfeited to Jackson (MS).

Because the team insisted on keeping the two pitchers, the Hot Springs Bathers were ousted from the league. Minor League President George Trautman ordered it reinstated.

But the Tugersons were still not permitted to pitch. So Jim hired a lawyer and has filed a $50,000 suit in the U. S. District Court at Hot Springs.

Moreover, he charges that he was barred from playing with the Bathers because of his race, thus denying him his rights as a citizen...

...Jim Tugerson's suit is therefore timely. If President Al Haraway and the Cotton States League insist on keeping this desert of discrimination amid the green outfields of America's greatest pastime, they should be made to pay for the privilege.[34]

Once a year, the Jaycees picked one game of their choice and "Jaycee Night" of 1953, occurred on July 27. The purpose for the special night was for the Jaycees to use the revenue generated from admissions and concessions to help develop Jaycee Recreational Park. In addition, the Jaycees donated a bicycle to one lucky youngster. The Bathers won the game 5-3 over El Dorado as they blasted four round-trippers.

Elated Knoxville Smokies' baseball fans welcomed back Jim Tugerson. The return of Tugerson boosted gate receipts, and as someone said, "He has meant their salvation." Earlier in the season, the Smokies forfeited a game because they had no baseballs. Circumstances change as Tugerson's hurling record for the Smokies was a hefty 21-7 mark, the best in Organized Baseball. The fans wondered what his record would have been if he hadn't taken those trips to Arkansas. [35]

"Tugerson Returning to Spa; Bather Officials Won't Say If He Will Play," was the headline in the local paper. Well, here we go again! Hot Springs was making a last-ditch effort to recall Jim Tugerson. The article stated that the Associated Press had reported that Tugerson had filed a $50,000 civil rights suit against the Cotton States League and various individuals. The article said that he was going to the Spa City on the advice of his attorney.

Tugerson, who was center of a controversy which resulted in the Cotton States League taking disciplinary action against the Hot Springs club on two different occasions charged in the suit filed by Attorney Jim Wood Chesnutt Monday that CSL officials conspired to keep him from playing because he was a Negro.[36]

The CSL officials were at a "social" in the Willow Room at the Phillips Drive-In on Park Avenue when they received "papers" concerning the civil rights suit.

Officials of the CSL have said privately that if the Negro played, the league schedule would be terminated within a 'very short time.'

Henry Britt, attorney for the Hot Springs Baseball Club and son of the owner, H. M. Britt, said last night on being told Tugerson was coming back to the city, ' I won't believe it until I see it.'

Tugerson reportedly has been on option to Knoxville on a 24-hour recall basis. This was the case when he was recalled on May 20, but there is some mystery as to his status now[37]

The main sports headline in *The Sentinel-Record* on July 17, stated, "Tugerson Returns to Knoxville Today; Bathers Give Up Efforts to Play Him," Mr. Haraway appealed Trautman's "ruling setting aside the forfeiture of a Hot Springs game against the Jackson Senators on May 20." Trautman filed the appeal "last week" and he said, "He is awaiting a three-man committee ruling." The rhetoric continued, but Tugerson never pitched for Hot Springs. He eventually dropped the suit since the parties reached a compromise.[38]

The Bathers last week sold pitcher Jim Tugerson, the controversial figure in this debate, to the Dallas Eagles of the Texas league.

As a result, Tugerson announced he was dropping his $50,000 suit against the Cotton States league. He had charged the league with denying him an opportunity to work because of his race, thereby violating his civil rights.

Tugerson wired his withdrawal to his attorney, James W. Chesnutt, asking him to seek dismissal of the court action. He wrote:

'I am withdrawing my suit. I made the statement before that I wanted to play high-grade baseball-AA or better. Now that I have the opportunity, I am dismissing the suit with no hard feeling towards anyone."[39]

However, Jim Tugerson was on his way to becoming the best minor league pitcher in the country in 1953. Even as the hullabaloo continued in the CSL, Jim played in 46 games for Knoxville, started 37 games and recorded a league high of 29 wins against 11 setbacks with an ERA of 3.71. He led the Smokies to a second place finish in the 1953 regular season, but Knoxville won the playoffs. Ken Buckles, a former Knoxville teammate of Jim and Leander, stated that Leander developed a sore arm in mid-season and returned to his home in Florida.[40]

Jack Bales and Bob Passarella stated that they vividly remembered a certain batting practice in 1953. The team was taking pregame batting practice at Jaycee Park. Suddenly, the players noticed the wind picked up and the sky darkened. Bales looked in the distance above the left field fence and saw the Hot Springs Tower, located on Hot Springs Mountain a few miles away, disappear in the clouds. At first, light wind and rain followed the darkness. Passarella, from Scranton, Pennsylvania, had never seen a tornado or high winds, but he saw most of the "Rebels" (as he called the players from the south) running up the hill to seek shelter in the new Hot Springs Boys Club building. Since the southern players knew more about tornadoes than he did, he quickly scampered up the hill, hot on the heels of his "Rebel" teammates and players from the visiting Pine Bluff Judges. The solidly built Boys Club building was a safe haven.

On the other hand, homegrown, Bales took another route to safety. Jack said his father was at the park watching batting practice. Jack's father noticed the windy weather heading their way and he quickly exclaimed to his son, "Let's go!" Jack said his father outran him to the railroad tracks located behind the bleachers and up the hill. The duo climbed over the tracks and down the gulley on the other side. The tracks were on top of the embankment and the two men crouched low on the other side of the tracks away from the on-coming wind. It was a perfect shield from the winds as they sought safety. Jack said they withstood the high winds, but father and son were drenched.

When the weather blew in, Jack said that the Bather star outfielder Bob Adcock was in the dressing room under the stands sound asleep. Bob slept through the whole ordeal! The dressing room was made of wood, but amazingly, it wasn't damaged. Following the high winds and rain, everyone seemed surprised that the wooden part of the stands and dressing room remained intact. As the players returned to the field, they noticed that the high winds took a toll on the field. The weather blew down a few of the outfield lights, wiring and part of the large wooden right field fence. They cancelled the game, but within a few days, work crews repaired the damaged structures.

On Sunday afternoon, August 3, Dolph Regelsky, Meridian's flashy shortstop tied an all-time record as he blasted four consecutive homers. At six-feet-four inches tall, the Meridian Millers shortstop set several records that day at Buckwalter Stadium. Regelsky started out with a single and then the powder keg blew. He led off the third, fourth and sixth innings with homers. In the seventh stanza, the drive came with two men on. The homers were Dolph's 12th, 13th, 14th and 15th round trippers of the season. Suddenly, his RBI season's total was 65. Finally, somebody wised up. The best play all day for the Bathers occurred on Regelsky's last at bat. He took a free hike down to first base! Three Cotton States League one-game records were set that day by Regelsky. He smacked the most home runs (4), hit the most-consecutive home runs (4) and collected 17 total bases. The result resembled a football score as Meridian took the game 21-6. However, as one 1940s radio announcer stated …"There's good news tonight." The good news was that the Bathers scored six runs on 12 hits as Martin slapped two out of the park and Bales popped a four-bagger. In addition, Martin went 3-5 at the plate.

In early August, the Bathers grabbed eight victories in nine games, but the Spa team was still in the sixth place. On August 16, Martin continued to unleash his potent powers as he tied the Cotton States Loop home-run record by knocking his 40th with a game-winning, grand slam to thump the Greenville Bucks 7-5. He tied El Dorado's Ralph Weingarner's 1930 record. It was a strange twist to a great night. Hal wasn't in uniform when the game started "for reasons he wouldn't care to discuss." He meandered around the stands chatting with the fans and "sat a spell" in the press box. He told the media, "Don't be surprised if you see me in there before the game is over." Hal called it correctly. Martin entered the game in the seventh inning and one inning later, hit a grand slam homer, tied the record and won the game. In addition, Martin had a chance to set the CSL batting mark.

On August 20, Manuel Fernandez singled in a run in the 13th inning on the road, as Hot Springs defeated Greenville 8-7. Hammerin' Jack Bales sent the game into extra innings in the ninth frame by banging out a 340-foot home run that evened the score 6-6. Both teams scored in the 10th, but the game was scoreless in the 11th and 12th stanzas. In the last of the 13th, Fernandez came to the Bathers rescue as he singled home a run.

Martin set the CSL's single season home run record on August 22, by clouting his 41st round tripper, a solo shot, as the Bathers thrashed the Judges 11-5 at Jaycee Park. The 33-year-old center fielder from Cincinnati sent Pine Bluff's southpaw hurler, Frank Callahan's first-inning pitch, flying to deep center field, 390 feet from home plate. His excited teammates carried the slugger off the field. The explosion electrified the 2,000 home fans that jammed the ball yard. Shortstop Bob Passarella added to the excitement in the second inning as he plastered a grand slammer to help lift the Bathers into a tie with Jackson for fourth place. Martin and "Passie" weren't finished as Martin added two hits and Passarella punched a single to add to his hit collection.

At the last regular season game, a combined "Bathers-Bales Appreciation Night" occurred. Jack was the only homegrown product on the Bathers team. The Bathers divided a gift of $294.40 from the fans. Included in the sum, was the $30.00 that Charlie Williamson donated for the 41st home-run ball hit by Hal Martin. In addition, the fans gave a tie to each team member of the visiting Pine Bluff Judges.

Players' salaries were low; therefore, the players appreciated any added funds. Bales said that they received $3.00-$3.50 per day for meal money when they went on the road. The management would pay them in cash at the beginning of each road trip and expected the players to spend their per diem wisely. Some players spent their money too fast and didn't have any left at the end of the road trips. Others tried to borrow from the players who still had a few bucks. Some loaned it, some didn't. Bales said that "Dino" of Dino's Men's Store gave him a suit. Charlie Williamson, Mrs. Edward Harnik, Dorsey Roddenberry, Mrs. Harold Lockwood and Dick Dickson supervised the arrangements for the special night.

Bales, born and reared in Hot Springs, began playing baseball, basketball and football at a young age. In high school, he was an excellent basketball and football player for the Trojans. Since the high school didn't have a baseball team, all the baseball players jumped on the American Legion team. Following high school graduation in 1948, he signed a pro contract with the Montgomery Rebels of the Class B, Southeastern League. In July, Jack signed another contract with Polly, his high school sweetheart. They were married on July 8, 1948.

The Bathers ended the season in a tie for the fourth playoff spot with Jackson. Hot Springs needed to beat Jackson to get into that fourth position to assure a playoff berth. On August 27, at Jaycee Park, 2,600 fans turned out to witness the important one-game playoff struggle. However, Jackson beat the Bathers 6-2, thereby eliminating the Spa team from the playoffs.

It was official! The league sportswriters selected Hal Martin, center fielder of the Hot Springs Bathers, as the Cotton States League Most Valuable Player. The outfielder accepted the award from "Miss Hot Springs," Janet Gray, in ceremonies preceding the Hot Springs-Jackson playoff game.

"Miss Arkansas," Miss Joyce Reed, also of Hot Springs, assisted in the ceremonies. Martin was the third Bather to win the significant award. Herb Adams won the prize in 1948, while Alex Cosmidis shared the trophy with Jack Ramm of Pine Bluff in 1950.

Martin established a new CSL home-run record of 41; however, he was the top dog in several other 1953 categories. He was first in triples-13; most hits-169; most total bases-350 and highest slugging average of .713, far surpassing the runner-up by .101 percentage points. Friend News Service printed the results in *The Sporting News* and they listed Martin tops in the RBI department with 111. Steve Korfonta, Martin's teammate, put on a late surge to surpass the center fielder in hitting as Korfonta wound up in second place in the CSL hitting race with a .346 average. Martin, the batting frontrunner for most of the season, ended up in third position with a .344 mark. Hugh Glaze of Meridian slipped in at the last minute to win the batting crown with a .355 grade. Manager Vern Shelter was the only other Bather to hit above .300, as the manager hit for a .308 average. Following the Bathers' season, Martin and Korfonta moved to Texas to play the last few games with the Beaumont Exporters in the Double-A, Texas League.[41]

The Bathers pitchers finished the season with the following numbers: Ken Siefert (15-11), Alex Ronay (12-12), Clyde Baldwin (13-5), Robert Gibbons (10-5), Manny Fernandez (9-4), Nelson Campver (9-11), Tom Ward (3-3), Everett Sullivan (2-4), Ed Baski (1-3), Nick Demus (1-0) and John Kuchta (1-0). Other pitchers included Robert Fortmann, Dee Jarvis, Gene Jensen, Tom Moore, Ben Odem and Wayne Parks.

An ironic twist occurred following the season. Jim Tugerson began to barnstorm with the Negro All-Stars and on September 25, Tugerson pitched against the Indianapolis Clowns in front of 1,200 enthusiastic fans at Jaycee Park! Yes, at Jaycee Park! The big man from Florida pitched for the Negro All-Stars and beat his former team, the Indianapolis Clowns, at his former team's field, Jaycee Park, 14-1. Tugerson helped his cause by blasting a home run.

Jim continued to pitch in the minor leagues, including Dallas, for six more years. He retired at the end of the 1959 season and moved back to his home in Florida. Leander developed a sore arm during midseason of 1953 and retired from baseball. Both brothers died in their native Florida. Leander, at 37 years of age, passed away in 1965, while Jim died in 1983 at 60 years old.

Bob Passarella played for the Bathers in 1952 and 1953. The six foot, 180-pound infielder/outfielder, said that the 1953 team was a much better team than the 1952 team. Passarella stated that he thought outfielder Bob Adcock was the best player on the 1953 team. "Bales and Martin were good, but Adcock seemed to be the best all-around player," said Passarella. The Bathers were only about one good pitcher away from the playoffs and maybe the championship, Passarella noted. He thought that they might have won the championship if Jim Tugerson had a chance to play with the Bathers. Passarella played three years in Class-D ball before advancing to Hot Springs in 1952.[42]

During football season, on Thursday night, October 22, they were still playing baseball at Jaycee Park. Jackie Robinson of the Brooklyn Dodgers brought his barnstorming troupe to the Springs. Robinson's team consisted of major league All-Stars that included three well-known stars, big Luke Easter, first baseman for the Cleveland Indians, Gil Hodges of the Dodgers and Robinson. The Negro League All-Stars, Robinson's opponents, hooked up in an exhibition contest in which the Negro League All-Stars took it to the major leaguers 14-9. In the all-offensive melee, the Negro League All-Stars rolled up 20 hits to 12 safeties for the Robinson All-Stars. Sammy Williams of the "Robinsons" and Ted Richardson, of the Negro Stars went all the way on the hill for their respective teams.

Hodges, first sacker for Brooklyn, was one of four players that hit round trippers that night, but in a losing effort for his team. An incident occurred that probably happened only once in the history of Jaycee Park. It involved Gil Hodges who was playing the outfield that evening. Third basemen of the Negro Stars, Fate Sims blasted a home run over the right field fence. On the other hand, was it a homer?

It was on this round tripper that Hodges appeared to have made one of the most brilliant fielding plays ever seen at Jaycee Park.

But the jolly 'Mr. Comeback' of Major League baseball this past season was just having his fun.

As Sims' wallop sailed into right, Hodges leaped up at the fence and appeared to have speared the sphere.

But eagle-eye Umpire Tom (Dutch) Moore had watched Hodges take a ball from his pocket and put it in the glove as Sims' hit took flight.

Hodges came off the field smiling and received applause for, at least, pulling the wool over the spectators' eyes.[43]

The next night the two All-Star teams journeyed 60 miles north to Traveler Field, later called Ray Winder Field, in Little Rock. It was the home, at that time, of the Little Rock Travelers of the Southern Association. The Robinsonites got a win as they eased past the Negro Stars 7-6 in the Capital City. "Luscious Luke" Easter was the hitting star as he uncorked two tape measure home runs. Robinson got a double and a single in Hot Springs and he duplicated the feat at Traveler Field.

Chapter 15

Williamson to the Rescue
1954

"Uvoyd Reynolds, 18, son of Mr. and Mrs. Willie Reynolds of Hot Springs, last night broke the color line in the Cotton States League." – The Sentinel-Record

Paul "Daffy" Dean, former St. Louis Cardinals pitcher and brother of "Dizzy" Dean, purchased the 1954 Bathers from Lewis Goltz, H. M. and Garrett Britt in November 1953. He planned to move his family from Dallas to Hot Springs within a month.

Dean purchased 200 shares of stock owned by the Britts. An additional 37½ minority shares are the property of the Junior Chamber of Commerce and varies individuals.[1]

At first, Dean was not sure if he wanted to be both the general manager and skipper of the Bathers. However, later, he decided to head up the positions. The non-playing skipper said, "I want to see that my boys are taught the best."

Since the Bathers had a working agreement with the Columbus, (GA) Red Birds of the Class A, Sally League, the majority of the players would funnel through the St. Louis Cardinals farm system. The Cardinals had 22 farm teams and the Bathers entered into a "limited agreement" with them. Dean said he was "greatly encouraged" due to the recent increase in advertising and box seats sales. Previously, he had been discouraged due to the lagging sales and considered moving the franchise to Texarkana.

All the Cardinals farm hands gathered at Albany, Georgia, about the middle of March and Dean picked out eight players to be the nucleus of the Bathers club. Nine former Bathers, from the 1953 squad, received early 1954 contracts and Dean received only one signed contract by the middle of March. Claude Dick, who pitched sparingly during the 1953 season, returned his signed contract to Dean. However, he remained the club's batboy. Among the eight other players who were sent contracts were Jackie Bales, catcher; Babe Tuckey, third base; Al Ronay, Nellie Campver, Manuel Fernandez, pitchers; Bob Passarella, shortstop/second base and Nick Demus, catcher.

The league consisted of six teams, two less than the 1953 version. In addition to Dean, skippers of each team were eager to start the season. Frank Lucchesi returned to lead the Pine Bluff Judges program. Bill Adair and Tommy Davis returned as mangers of the El Dorado Oilers and the Meridian Millers, respectively. Willis Hudlin, former major league pitcher, was the field boss and general manager of the Greenville Bucks, while Ed Head, former Brooklyn Dodgers pitcher, was the pilot of the Monroe Sports. The Baltimore Orioles owned the Judges and the Detroit Tigers owned the Greenville Bucks.

Dean instructed Steve Sitek, former minor leaguer who was living in Hot Springs, to travel to Deland, Florida and Albany, Georgia, to sign a few players for the Bathers. The owner-manager stated that he had a few advertising concerns to work out. Mrs. Dean assisted her husband in the business office. The Bathers sold a coupon book of 20 grandstand tickets for $14.00.

Judge Emmet Harty, president of the Cotton States League announced the returning league arbiters were Charles Behrens of Miami, Florida; James Duncan of Brinkley, Arkansas and Charles W. Smith of Sandy Springs, Georgia. The three new umpires were Joseph F. Hickey of Bergenfield, New Jersey; Walter E. Lipp of Fort Wayne, Indiana and Pat Vastano of Brooklyn, New York. The two substitutes were John Metro of El Dorado, Arkansas and Tom Hobart of Greenville, Mississippi. The mediators planned to report to Greenville on April 16, to receive their 120-game schedules.

Jackie Bales, catcher from the 1953 Bathers club, inked his 1954 Bathers contract in early April. The Bathers finished in a tie with Jackson in 1953, but lost the one-game playoff, shutting the door on their playoff hopes. Bales batted a strong .279 in 1953. He began his pro career as an 18-year-old, with the Montgomery (AL) Rebels in the Class B, Southeastern League. After moving around in the B, C, D leagues, Bales wound up in the Cotton States League, playing for Greenville and Hot Springs in 1952.

Paul Dean wrote Bob Passarella a letter in late 1953, and stated that he wanted "Passie" to play for the Bathers during the 1954 season for $250 a month. Dean noted that if the financial situation worked out with the team, he might be able to raise his pay as the season progressed. A second letter, printed below, stated that Dean still wanted the infielder to play for the 1954 Bathers.

PAUL DEAN	*DOROTHY DEAN*
President	*Sec.-Treas.*

Hot Springs Bathers
Baseball Club
Telephone 5358 - P. O. Box 1128
Hot Springs National Park, Arkansas
March 18, 1954

Dear Bob,

We received your letter and contract. I will give you $250.00 per month. If you are interested in this, you can sign your contract when you come to Spring Training.

Sorry I couldn't go any higher, but it is rough making ends meet in Minor League Baseball. I am sure if you come here and have a good year the Cardinals will see that you advance to higher ball. I am sure you will enjoy being with our club.

Sincerely,
Paul Dean[2]

However, Passarella declined Dean's offer and remained in Scranton to assist caring for his ailing father. Bob found work in a factory and played semi-pro baseball until he was 40-years-old. In addition, he volunteered his time as baseball coach at a parochial school for six years because he enjoyed teaching youngsters the game of baseball.

Up to 1954, there was no participation of black players in the Cotton States League; however, the CSL watched racial events unfold in the South Atlantic and Southern Association Leagues. An article appeared in *The Sentinel-Record* entitled, "Cradle of Confederacy Accepts Non-Segregated Baseball Teams."

The really big news, however, will be made in Montgomery Tuesday when the South Atlantic League Rebels, first white pro team in Alabama history to sign Negro players, gets its season underway.

Montgomery, 'Cradle of the Confederacy,' is putting a large share of its pennant hopes this year on the burly shoulders of 220-pound big John Davis, who set a new home run record in the Florida International League last year with 35 round trippers.

Davis, though only one of the three Negroes originally signed by the Rebels, is the first.

And Rebel manager Marvin (Sparky) Olson says that with Davis on the scene, the Montgomery outfit has a 'great' chance to end up in the top slot in the class A Sally League.

Big John, 33, is a native New Yorker who now calls Florida home.[3]

Davis had over nine years of professional experience in the Negro leagues, the winter leagues and the Pacific Coast Loop. Manager Olson stated that the team relations are 'tops' and the players were getting along "wonderfully." Increased league box-office sales were highly successful. "Negro attendance at Rebel home games two years ago was 3,000. Last year, after other Sally teams signed Negroes, it climbed to 13,000."[4]

By mid-April, the Bathers were working out daily at Jaycee Park. Dean was scrambling around attempting to upgrade his team, selling advertisement, writing contracts and countless other duties. The league allowed each team a 16-player limit and only seven could be veterans. The rest of the players were limited service players or rookies. "Limited Service" players included men who were former military personnel.[5]

The Bathers popped the cork on the 1954 campaign by cutting off a rally 6-5 to seize the opener at Pine Bluff. The Judges could only muster a one-run rally in the ninth inning as an estimated crowd of 1,800 viewed the opening game of the season at Taylor Field. Three-year Bathers' veteran, Jackie Bales, belted a home run over the right field fence in the fourth inning to help the Spa cause. Rain cancelled the second game with the Judges as the teams moved to Hot Springs for the Spa opener.[6]

A parade and pregame festivities kicked off the 1954 Bathers home baseball season. The parade began at 4:15 p.m. at the junction of Whittington, Park and Central Avenues. Five bands marched in the parade including the Hot Springs High School Trojans, Langston High School Bulldogs, Lakeside High School Rams, Hot Springs Junior High Spartans and the combined bands of the elementary schools of Hot Springs. Riding in the parade were owner-manager Paul Dean, members of the Hot Springs Bathers, Janet Gray-"Miss Hot Springs 1953," Mayor Floyd Housley, George Earnshaw-former Philadelphia Athletics pitcher and a member of the Spa Bathers board of directors, W. L. Clark-president of the Chamber of Commerce and other dignitaries.

Opening night ducats sold for a buck, but lower prices would kick-in following the first game. Due to a power outage, much of the planned opening pregame festivities went by the wayside, but the main, field lights were bright and beautiful. The lack of grandstand lights didn't seem to disturb the crowd as an estimated 2,200 fans jammed Jaycee Park. Among the VIPs on hand were George Earnshaw, Mayor Housley and "Angel," an internationally known professional wrestler. The game got underway at 8:05 p.m.

Pine Bluff jumped on the hometown pitchers for a 14-hit attack, while Hot Springs managed only half that number. The Judges pitching didn't seem to bother Jackie Bales who cranked out two home runs and scored three runs. At game time, the fans or players didn't realize that they would witness a marathon; in fact, it was the longest game in the history of Jaycee Park. At 12:05 a.m., after four hours of baseball, the visitors completed a three-run rally in the ninth inning spoiling opening night as the Pine Bluff Judges outlasted the Bathers 12-11.

Bales got a break on May 3, but not a break he wanted. The standout catcher was guarding home plate when the Oiler catcher, Luther Tucker slid into him breaking Bales' ankle. Bales said the he blames himself for the break because he wedged his foot against the plate. Bales was out for six weeks, but the young catcher said he still wanted to make 1954 his best season. In the two previous games, Bales connected for three home runs in five trips to the plate.[7]

On May 5, the Bathers journeyed over to Mississippi to play the Greenville Bucks. Perhaps they probably should have stayed at home because the Bucks smothered the Hot Tub Boys 12-4, as the Bathers committed 10 errors. On the heels of the loss, Dean sent a letter to August A. (Gussie) Busch, owner of the St. Louis Cardinals, appealing for more good players. St. Louis had twenty-two teams in their farm system and it seemed that there weren't enough talented players to go around.

Several major league front office personnel discussed having three major leagues, but most everyone believed that would water-down big league talent even more. At the end of the 1953 season, the Yankees won the American League pennant, beating Brooklyn four games to two in the World Series. The Cardinals ended up in a tie with the Phillies for third spot in the senior loop. However, the Cardinals continued to send players to help the Bathers.

George Earnshaw, retired major league pitcher and Navy Commander, was a "gentleman farmer" living on Lake Hamilton in Hot Springs. However, busy George always had time to relate a baseball story or three. Maurice Moore reported a story in *The Sentinel-Record* about an incident that occurred in Hot Springs in the 1930s involving the Dean brothers and Earnshaw.

Earnshaw chuckles every time he recalls the first time he met the Dean brothers-Dizzy and Paul. Believe it or not, it happened right here in our town way back yonder in the early 1930s. Dizzy was a rising star and Earnshaw just finished appearing in the World Series. The meeting took place in a hotel café. Earnshaw was dining with a friend. Diz and Paul were at another table. Earnshaw recognized the elder Dean and thought he would have some fun. He walked over and asked: 'Aren't you the great Dizzy Dean?' 'Could I please have your autograph?' George remembered asking. Diz agreed but had to supply his own paper and pen. 'Usually, us Major Leaguers don't give this kind of accommodation,' Diz said.

Then Earnshaw asked Dean if he had an old bat, ball or glove to autograph. Diz popped loose, 'Now us Major Leaguers don't carry such things around. Say young fellow, you look like you might could play ball. Ever try?'

Earnshaw told him he had a 'tryout' with the Baltimore Orioles and was released-that is released to the Philadelphia A's.

'Say, who are you anyway?' Diz exploded. So Mr. Earnshaw and Mr. Dean, two great pitchers, became acquainted. Seasons afterward, players still ribbed Dizzy (about Earnshaw), asking him if he had a bat or glove to autograph. It's all in fun, and makes baseball tick.' [8]

On May 16, at Monroe, the Bathers crushed the Sports 14-4. The Spamen collected 15 hits off four Monroe hurlers. Kenny Seifert issued 14 hits for the Bathers, but went all the way for the win, as he chalked up his first victory of the season. Shortstop Frank Cooper paced the winners with a four-hit attack, including a double. In their last two games, the Bathers scored 28 runs, but were still in fifth place in the loop standings.[9]

On May 23, Greenville led the league as Hot Springs and Meridian were in third spot, only two games behind. A week later, Cooper and Korfonta were among the top five hitters in the CSL.

Frank Cooper hitting a nifty .357 was in third position and ranked fifth was Steve Korfonta averaging .350. The Bathers placed third in team batting with a .249 mark, while Meridian led with a .283 average. In team fielding, Hot Springs ranked last. Not much was happening on the pitching front for the Bathers.

The Cotton States League attendance was the lowest of the post-war era. Many minor league small markets were having difficulty keeping their financial heads above water and Hot Springs was no different. Owner Dean began to think about moving the franchise or even folding the team. Why were fans not showing up for the games? Maurice Moore gathered information concerning attendance figures in the CSL. Early season average attendance numbers included Greenville-850, Meridian-700, Hot Springs-700-900, El Dorado-500-900, Monroe-400-600 and Pine Bluff-400. Moore gives some reasons for the decline of the fan base.

Television is blanketing this baseball area for the first time, and the clubs, like theaters and other sports events, are feeling the impact. The big question is, 'Can baseball survive?' Television, like radio and the movies, is progress, and there is no reason to try to fight it. The best thing minor sports, (including) baseball, small college and high school football and basketball, can do is to join in. The time will come when the novelty wears off, and fans will trek back to the sports arenas and because of television, they may be stronger than ever before, if they can hang on.[10]

In addition, Moore believed that more importantly the problem was the "tightness of the money." The Bathers tried promotions in order to entice the fans to show up for the games, but that didn't work. The economy was tough. The United States Bureau of Labor Statistics stated that the average annual salary in the United States in 1954 was a little less than $3,000.00, while the minimum wage was $.75 an hour. About 50% of American families owned television sets and the number was rising.

To help save the league, Paul Dean suggested stopgap solutions. He proposed to the league president that each team reduce player limit from 16 to 15 and cut the number of veterans on each club from seven to five. He said if the league would follow his suggestions, each club could save from $400-$700 a month. With the cuts, he thought teams could survive with an attendance of 500-800 fans per game. He also stated that there were "too many class men," meaning that the veterans, players who played for several years, were making higher salaries than the first or second-year-players. The league would not penalize a player who returned from the military.[11]

The Pine Bluff Judges were close to resigning from the league due to small attendance. The weather appeared to be the culprit for the lack of attendance in the Arkansas city. "A member of the board said the Judges had received enough financial help to operate for another two weeks." However, he revealed that three cities were interested in taking Pine Bluff's place if they went under. Vicksburg, Mississippi, expressed an interest in rejoining the league, as did Fort Smith, Arkansas and Texarkana, Arkansas/Texas. Judge Emmet Harty, league president, said that the leading candidate was Vicksburg.[12]

"Dean has told members of the board that attendance has fallen far below expectations and that he did not want to sacrifice his money in a 'losing proposition.'" Hot Springs started out with a large opening night attendance of 2,296. The club lost several games in the first few weeks, but "recovered" and won 14 of 19 games; however, no crowd had been larger than 900 since opening night. If Dean decided to fold, the Bathers' former owners, H. M. Britt and Garrett Britt had a seven-day option period to return as owners.[13]

On June 5, the Bathers were in fourth place, six games behind circuit-leading El Dorado. Harty announced that the league planned to vote on Dean's proposal of cutting veteran strength from 7-5 per team and the player limit reduced from 15 to 16 per team.[14]

Dean thought that some "money players" or "hangers-on" were a detriment to the league. Maurice Moore wrote that some of these "money or class players" go through the motions of playing games and receive a paycheck. Dean said he was in professional baseball to make a living and he was having a difficult time succeeding. He knew the "money players" are taking a big slice out of the club's pie. However, the players who just completed their military service were called "national defense players" and didn't count as "a class player."

Dean had enough! Daffy decided to throw in the towel because he was simply losing money. A few days later Charlie Williamson, local used car dealer, bought the Bathers franchise from Dean. The former owner expressed regret that the team didn't receive sufficient support, but he wished the new owner the best. For the time being, the Deans planned to remain in Hot Springs for Paul Jr. to finish out the school year.

On June 9, Williamson officially took over as the new owner and one of his first acts was to make Jackie Bales the manager. Due to an ankle injury, Bales was out of action for several weeks. The time was near for him to resume his catching duties. The new manager had an interesting career. Jackie played every position on the field except shortstop and center field since he was seven years old. The Hot Springs resident signed a 1948 contract with the Detroit Tigers who sent him to Montgomery, Alabama via Little Rock. He moved around a lot as young players do. The next year, he played for Durham, North Carolina and Thomasville, Georgia. He hit .277 for Rome, New York and he said he never knew what position he would be playing. In 1951, he was with Davenport, Iowa, in the Class B, Three-I League where he hit .284. In 1952, he traveled to the Cotton States League and started the season with Greenville, Mississippi. In mid-season, Greenville sold him to Hot Springs. As a Bather, he hit .279 including 12 home runs and the writers selected him to the annual league All-Star roster at catcher.[15]

The new owner also re-hired concessioners and attendants who had been serving the fans at Jaycee Park for years. Concerning the purchase of the club, Williams stated,

I felt like I was obligated to take over the Hot Springs franchise. I helped sell much of the fence and program advertising and consider it a duty to see that the club completes the season.[16]

President Harty related that since school was out and warmer weather, he believed that Hot Springs would fair better at the gate because more students and families would attend games. When the league released attendance figures, numbers weren't great for the Bathers, but they were still ahead of the league-leading El Dorado Oilers. The breakdown of each club's total attendance was as follows: (1) Greenville-17,081 (2) Meridian-10,889 (3) Monroe-9,843 (4) Hot Springs-9,399 (5) El Dorado-8,300 and (6) Pine Bluff-4,078.

It was not a good welcoming ceremony for the new owner, because the Bathers lost their ninth straight game, this time to El Dorado. The Bathers broke the nine-game losing streak the next day by thumping the Oilers 11-0, in the first end of a double-header, but they lost the nightcap 10-2. In other news, the league voted to retain the "7-Vet" rule. Previously, the vote was 5-1 in favor of reducing the number of veterans (players with more than two years of professional baseball experience) to five per team. However, after further discussions with team owners and managers, "in order to keep peace in the family," the league decided to retain the 7-vet rule and the 16-player limit per team. "[17]

By June 13, Hot Springs slipped to last place in the standings, thirteen games behind first place El Dorado. Bathers' problems continued. The Spa team lost 12-7 to Monroe on June 18, at Jaycee Park as the Sports blasted three home runs during their 14-hit attack. Korfonta and Adcock collected two hits each in a losing effort as a slight crowd of only 300 showed up for the contest. Korfonta, listed in the sixth position in the CSL batting race, was the hitting star in the Bathers lineup.

Here we go again! It took Williamson a little over two weeks to determine he wanted out. He just could not see an upside to owning the Bathers. He tried, but ran into the same problems that Dean experienced...lack of fans in the stands. Williamson telephoned Emmet Harty and told him of his decision. "Williamson suggested that in view of the financial woes suffered by virtually all members of the league, arrangements are made to terminate the season after the All-Star game,

July 12." The used-car dealer offered the team, free and clear, to any Hot Springs citizen, group or civic club that would insure the stability of the organization until the end of the season.

In the meantime, Texarkana contacted the league president and told him that they were interested in taking over the Hot Springs franchise. In 1953, Texarkana played in the Class B, Big State League, but they did not field a professional team in 1954. The Sports Editor of the *Texarkana Gazette* told *The Sentinel-Record* that "unusual interest" existed by baseball leaders in the Twin Cities area, concerning the possible takeover of the Bathers. They were looking at the transaction to occur following the All-Star game on July 12.

On June 13, Charlie Williamson named 36-year-old Louis "Red" Lucas to be the new Bathers pilot. The player-manager was a third baseman who came from Jackson, Tennessee, where he was the player-skipper. The hard-luck manager, who hailed from New Jersey, departed Jackson because the team went out of business. The Generals, of the Class D, Kitty (Kentucky-Illinois-Tennessee) League, lost 26 straight before winning one. After that, simply put, the team folded. On June 24, the new manager-third baseman Lucas, poled two homers for the Bathers in a 14-3 thumping of the Meridian Millers at Jaycee Park. By this time, he had rung-up six homers for his new team and he had been in a Bathers uniform less than two weeks.

Williamson said he would try to continue Bathers operations until the end of the season if he could raise $4,000. If the Bathers could average 800 fans per night for the last 34 home games, Charlie believed he could make it. Attendance recently had been hovering around 300-600 fans per game. He said that he was losing $100-$150 a day. [18]

At 8:50 p.m. on the night of June 21, Texarkana received a call from Hot Springs. This could be it! The Bathers may go down the tube and Texarkana would take over the organization. Baseball fans in the Twin Cities were excited…until they heard the news. Hot Springs collected over $5,000 to continue operations through the end of the season. Hot Springs was elated and Texarkana was disappointed. Moore said, "June 21 was a red-letter day." Baseball fans pulled together to rescue a sinking ship. "Hail to the Fans," was the title of his sports column.

It's hard to tell how many participated in this splendid effort, but the response was heart-warming to city leaders who have butted their heads against a stone wall for other causes probably just as important or more so than baseball.[19]

It was an exciting article, but the Bathers continued to lose; in fact, they lost big on June 28, when the Oilers rapped out 27 hits, humbling the Bathers 25-4. By July 1, Hot Springs was searching for winners and they found one. The team sought someone to hold the title of "Miss Bather." The club was "staging a whirlwind beauty contest to select a girl to represent the resort at the "Miss Cotton States League" contest July 12, at El Dorado." The winner would represent the league at the annual minor league convention in Houston. Local competition planned to take place at the Hot Springs-Greenville doubleheader intermission on Thursday, July 8. The competition, solely a beauty contest, included several young women parading in swimsuits in front of three out-of-town judges. Charlie Williamson appointed businessman, Lewis Goltz as committee chairman. The event had proven popular in other baseball leagues across the United States.[20]

George Silvey, supervisor of the Cardinals C and D class teams, visited the Bathers to see what he could do to boost the talent level. Due to the large number of farm teams in the Cardinals system, many of those teams had a difficult time, much like the Bathers. There weren't sufficient numbers of skilled players to go around. He said that the Cardinals explored the idea of reducing the number of farm clubs next year. One of the sticking points was that major league teams didn't want to send their youngsters against "old-head money" performers. The Bathers had a 30% change in personnel since spring training. Mr. Silvey departed the Springs, leaving the Bathers front office with little optimism. He said, "I'll see what I can do."[21]

Despite the Bathers poor record, on July 4, there were five Hot Springs boys hitting over .300. Lou Lucas, Steve Korfonta, Frank Cooper, Jackie Bales and Tom Burks were all above .300 in the batting statistics. The Bathers dominated the cellar in fielding and next to last in club batting. Pitching wasn't much better as John Hreljac with a 5-5 record, was the ace.

By early July, Williamson relieved Lucas as manager and selected Jackie Bales, Bathers catcher, to take over the managerial reins of the Bathers. Lou "Have Bags Will Travel" Lucas came to Hot Springs from the Jackson Generals/Central City Rebels where they folded earlier in the season. Leaving Hot Springs, the Greenville Tigers signed him to a short-term contract.

On July 12, Miss Sue Nooner, 21-year-old daughter of Mr. and Mrs. E. C. Nooner, won the "Miss Bathers" contest and represented Hot Springs at the league's All-Star game in El Dorado. Selected among six candidates during the intermission of the Bathers doubleheader on July 8, Nooner was a student at the University of Arkansas. Runner-up was Joan Sitek, 18-year-old daughter of Mr. and Mrs. Steve Sitek. Other contestants were Nola Terry, 17-year-old daughter of Mr. and Mrs. Roy Terry; Betty Pullen, 18-year-old daughter of Mr. and Mrs. Cue Pullen; Rita Meeks, 20-year-old daughter of Mr. and Mrs. John Meeks and Helen Burks, 18-year-old daughter of Tom Burks. Around 650 fans watched the crowning.

There were more league grumblings at Meridian. The Millers were having the same problem as Hot Springs, lack of fan attendance. Meridian's general manager C. B. Rawlings said the future looked bleak to continue supporting a team in the Cotton States Loop. He planned to resign and cease club operations

The selection of "Miss Cotton States League" of 1954 occurred in pregame festivities at the league's All-Star game in El Dorado. It was the first season that the league selected a queen. Moreover, the winner was Miss Sue Nooner, pretty college student from Hot Springs. Miss Nooner, entering her first beauty pageant, won over contestants representing Meridian, Pine Bluff and El Dorado. The winner received an all-expense paid trip to Houston in December where she competed for the title of "Miss Baseball."

The CSL All-Stars went down to defeat 9-6 at the hands of the first place El Dorado Oilers at Griffith Park in the Oil City. Over 2,500 fans witnessed the "home" team rally for four runs in the seventh inning to overtake the All-Stars. The All-Stars out hit the Oilers 13-9, as both teams erred only once in the field.

That negative word "fold," reared its head again. The owners and managers were not only talking about one team closing its doors, they deliberated about terminating the league! The culprit was the lack of attendance, which really meant fund deficiency. The league kept a close eye on attendance figures. League officials reported the current average attendance as follows: Greenville-908; El Dorado-584; Meridian-614; Monroe-554, Pine Bluff-466 and no report from Hot Springs.

The sportswriters of each CSL city agreed to cease pleading with the people for support. One writer said, "It's up to "King Public." On the other side of the coin, fans were tired of reading about the problem and the writers were weary of writing about the difficulties. If they play, they play; if they don't, the league will fold. Maurice Moore commented, "Everyone would like to end the season early, but no team wants to be the first to throw in the towel." [22/23]

It wasn't getting any better for the Spa team. The Bathers remained in last place 28.5 games behind El Dorado. Suddenly, the Judges decided to withdraw from the league, but Sam Cook, president of the Pine Bluff team, stated that a team must give at least five days notice to the league office and to their parent team, the Baltimore Orioles, before withdrawing. Under league rules, a one-day notice was not sufficient lead-time. The members of the Pine Bluff organization soon changed their minds and remained in the league. [24]

Owner Charlie Williamson thought the timing was ripe to sign a black player to the Bather's roster. Fresh in the memory of everyone was the attempted signing of the Tugerson brothers the year before. However, this was a new year and a new league president. Therefore, the owner decided to sign the first black to play for the Bathers. After the 1953 season, this was an enormous challenge. Hot Springs seemed to be the team determined to break the color line in the CSL. Team officials hoped that the league was ready for the "cosmopolitan city" to sign a black player.

Williamson notified League President, Judge Emmet Harty of Greenville, Monday that he intended to hire Negro players in an effort to bolster his last place club and try to increase badly sagging attendance.

However, he told the Associated Press that he had contacted the president of the league and five other clubs and none had anything to say either.

He said that the directors indicated they probably would take no action until Hot Springs made the first move. [25]

Williamson revealed his intentions to officials of each team and they told him "to go ahead with his plans." The owner planned to sign "Negro first baseman Ezel Howard of Wichita, Kansas" on July 20. However, there was a snag. This time, the hitch came from the player and not the league. Howard was a star player for the Boeing Aircraft Company, a semi-pro team. The company would not release Howard from his contract, so Williamson went in another director.

Williamson was open to contact any good black player or players. Local Negro sports leaders recommended to Williamson, an 18-year-old individual just out of the all-black Langston High School in Hot Springs. Uvoyd Reynolds, former three-sport letterman, played quarterback for the 1953 Negro state football champion Bulldogs. He was a teammate of Charles Butler and Bobby Mitchell. Butler and Mitchell both played their college football at the University of Illinois. The speedy Mitchell later played in the NFL with the Cleveland Browns and the Washington Redskins. He is a member of the NFL Hall of Fame. Reynolds had a chance at several college football scholarships, but turned them down to play professional baseball, the game he loved. Reynolds was playing semi-pro baseball at Mt. Pine, a community just outside Hot Springs.

Williamson decided to sign Reynolds. This was history! Hometown teenager, Uvoyd Reynolds broke the color barrier in the Cotton States League in 1954. The Bathers put the young player in right field, although Uvyod said his best position was second base, but he was delighted to play any position. He was now a professional baseball player playing in his own hometown and in front of some of the fans who watched him play high school football. He stood 5' 11" tall and weighed 182 pounds. Before his first game, Reynolds told *The Sentinel-Record*, "It's always been my dream to play professional baseball and I consider it a high honor to be the first of my race in the Cotton States League. It's a big opportunity for me."[26]

The Meridian Millers were in town and on Tuesday, July 20, at Jaycee Park, Reynolds started in right field to begin a new era of baseball in Hot Springs and the Cotton States League. More than 750 fans, over 125 blacks, watched the Hot Springs product walk to the plate in a pressure-packed setting. It was his historic first at bat and his first pro game. In addition, he was the first black player ever to play on an all-white Hot Springs team and in an all-white league. To put a little more pressure on the young Bather, his opponent was a Mississippi team. To add more fuel to the fire, the bases were loaded! Uvoyd was patient and waited for the right one to hit, but he didn't have to hit the ball because the pitcher threw four balls! He took a free pass to first. That was his first walk and his first RBI. The second time Reynolds came to the plate, guess what happened? The bases were loaded! Amazingly, the "ultra-patient-at-the-plate" Reynolds took another stroll down to first base and added another RBI. It went in the record book that Reynolds acquired two RBIs without a hit.

Hot Springs was leading 7-5 going into the seventh inning, but Meridian exploded for seven runs in the last three innings to whip the Bathers 12-7. Even though the Bathers lost, they won! The city of Hot Springs, the Cotton States League, the Bathers and Reynolds won. Uvoyd went 0-3 with two walks and two RBIs, but that night will always remain special to Uvoyd Reynolds, to the Bathers and their fans. There were no repercussions from any players or fans that night.

The next night, July 21, Joe Scott, debuted at first base for the Bathers against the same Meridian Milliers. The 27-year-old African-American, a part-time performer for the Memphis Red Sox, was small for a first baseman, standing 5'8" tall, weighing 165 pounds. He also could play the outfield. He went 1-4 at the plate, walked twice and scored twice. In the field, he made nine putouts at first. Reynolds played defense only in the ninth inning with no plate appearance. Meridian thrashed the Bathers 19-12.

Records stated that Scott only played two games with the Bathers. The reason for the quick release was that the Bathers would have to pay Scott's parent team, the Memphis Red Sox, $500.00

to keep Scott in a Bathers uniform. In order to pay the rest of the Bathers, Williamson had no other choice than to discharge Scott. However, Williamson was considering signing other black players. The owner decided to take Reynolds on the road to El Dorado, since he hadn't heard any negative reaction to taking the young men on road trips.

'The other cities haven't said anything one way or another, but I will play them out of town if so requested,' he declared.

'I wouldn't anticipate any trouble but I don't want to take any chances,' Williamson said. [27]

Reynolds and the Bathers headed to play at the Oil City. Headlines on July 24, in the local paper stated, "Spa Tops Oilers 5-3 In 11 Innings; Reynolds Plays." The first sentence of the sports article from El Dorado related, "Reynolds was the first Negro to play with a white team in Organized Baseball here…" and "here" meant El Dorado. Reynolds recalled when he played at El Dorado, as he walked to the plate, an elderly white man in the stands said, "Hey, N— —, where ya think you're going?" However, Reynolds said that was about the only time he heard any negative remarks. Remember, this was six years <u>after</u> Jackie Robinson broke the color barrier in the major leagues. Other than that one incident, the crowd of 736 showed no opposition to Reynolds or the Bathers. Reynolds, who played left field, went 1-4 at the plate.[28]

The Bathers produced another positive that night. Last place Hot Springs pulled off a triple play against El Dorado, the first place team. The scorekeeper recorded as follows: "Shortstop Joe Miller hauled in a line drive for one out, stepped on second to catch the runner off for No. 2, and then, hurled to Vance Byrd at first for the third out." [29]

Negative headlines occurred again in the local paper! Sports headlines stated, "Bathers To Cease Operations; CSL To Hold Emergency Meet." After all the Bathers went through to get to this point in the campaign, Williamson wanted out! The owner was losing too much money! The last game only drew 286 fans. It's difficult to run a ball club with few fans in attendance. If all of the $5,000 pledged money came in, he could make the team last until the end of the season. However, $1,500 remained outstanding. After conferring with several "in the know," including George M. Trautman, president of minor league baseball, big Charlie decided to pull the plug.[30]

However, a big surprise occurred as the fans read the headlines of July 25. *The Sentinel-Record* wrote, "Fans Kick In $1,500 To Keep Bathers In Operation." Actually, the "fans" were Williamson, Mr. and Mrs. H. M. Britt and Garrett Britt. Charlie said that the money would pay the players' payroll through August 15, noting that to cover expenses for the last 14 home games; he needed 300-500 fans paid attendance per night.[31]

Near the end of July, even though the Bathers were going through difficult times, a couple of players were swinging the lumber for effect. Outfielder Steve Korfonta ranked sixth in the CSL batting race with a .332 mark was the team leader, while center fielder Frank Cooper was next with .319. Greenville catcher, Frank Shell was the loop leader with a mark of .377. Last place Hot Springs lagged 30.5 games behind league leading El Dorado and 15 games behind Pine Bluff, the fifth place team.

Williamson hired another African-American, John Parker, who played first base and stayed with the Bathers for 32 games. Parker was in the lineup when the Bathers traveled to Meridian on July 27. The first baseman went 0-4, but had 12 putouts at first. Meridian's Jimmy Dupuy, former Bather, shackled his former teammates on two hits, as the Millers bombarded the Bathers 21-0.

However, Williamson continued attempting to improve the record and gate receipts. Williamson was en route to Hot Springs when another black player arrived at the Springs via New Mexico.

Owner Charlie Williamson last night announced the acquisition of Negro Pitcher William Ray Mitchell from Artesia, New Mexico of the West Texas-New Mexico League. His contract was obtained through the Dallas Eagles of the Texas League. [32]

Mitchell was a 23-year-old "limited service" player who had a 7-2 record with his current New Mexico team. With the same club last year, he ended up with an 11-10 mound record. Earlier in the 1954 season at Artesia, he was a teammate of Jim Tugerson.

Meridian announced the first African-American, representing a Mississippi team in the Cotton States League, played on Monday, July 26. The newspaper related there was an "appreciable jump in attendance" from the first night he played. Now, Pine Bluff was looking at the possibility of signing a black player. "So far there have been no objections from white fans that turn out nightly to watch the games," in Pine Bluff.

At Pine Bluff, for instance, where attendance has been limited to skeleton crowds all season, spectators nearly doubled in number when the Hot Springs Bathers came to town with their classy-fielding Negro first baseman.

Thursday night's crowd numbered 791 and 385 of those customers were Negroes. Friday night's crowd drew even more Negroes, when the word got around that John Parker handled first base like a charm. The attendance was 935 and 538 of those were Negroes. [33]

Manager Jackie Bales drove in six runs, including two fence busters, as the Spa hung an 8-2 loss on Pine Bluff at Jaycee Park, July 31. After rehabbing his ankle, Bales began his quest to put the bat on the ball as he connected on three hits on four trips to the plate. A scant crowd of 379 faithful fans observed the Spa Boys, as they scored eight runs on 13 hits to Pine Bluff's two runs on five scattered hits. Rookie right-hander, James Hicks shared the spotlight with Bales as he threw a five hitter and pitched the complete game. Hicks, a former University of Oklahoma product from Lawton, Oklahoma, won his fourth game in a month as a Bather.

Applause was in order for Charlie Williamson, the man who instigated signing black players in the Cotton States League. He was the "Branch Rickey" of the Cotton Circuit. Many problems embraced the league the year before as Hot Springs stood alone attempting to sign the Tugerson brothers. The league slammed the door shut on the Spa and kicked them out of the league. However, reinstatement of the team laid the groundwork for history to occur in 1954. Hot Springs wanted black players to be a part of the team, so more people would wind up in the seats, thereby improving the financial problem. In addition, it allowed many black players to play professional baseball in what was an all-white league. The major leagues accepted integration by hiring such players as Robinson, Doby, Irvin, Paige, Banks, Mays, Campanella, Newcombe, Black, Thompson and Jethroe. Therefore, it seemed that it was past time for the CSL to follow suit.

In Pine Bluff, the crowd shot up considerably when Hot Springs came to play at Taylor Field, the Judges home stadium.

At Meridian, attendance jumped to more than 2,100 in two nights...more than had attended a half dozen previous games. The Millers even broke precedent and hired a Negro player of their own. But at home the Hot Springs crowds swelled up for a couple of nights, then bounced back to usual. Even though the shaky condition of the club has kept the league in a dither for the past several weeks, introduction of Negro players at this time into the league by Williamson had undoubtedly helped preserve it.

Charlie will be remembered for that, sure. But, back to Pine Bluff. He was introduced to the crowd, and received a rousing ovation, led by the Negro fans. Several of them told him, "We won't come back until you'all are here," and they complimented him highly. So let that be Hot Springs and Charlie's main contribution this season.[34]

Even though the loyal Spa fans were small in number, Charlie appreciated them. He wrote a letter to Maurice Moore and asked him to print it. In essence, he wanted to thank the fans for hanging in with the Bathers, even though they were very deep in the cellar. He said he did not pay himself "one dime" to run the team. In fact, he said, "I have furnished cars off my lot to take the boys on their road trips and have paid the gasoline bills out of my own pocket." Three major events of which Williamson was proud included (1) signing the first black player to play for Hot Springs and in the CSL; (2) the Bathers executing the only triple play of the season and (3) Miss Sue Nooner's selection as Miss Cotton States League. A few lines of Charlie's letter appear below.

Monday night has been designated as 'Baseball Appreciation' night. I don't want any credit other than the appreciation of the fans. If you appreciated what I have done for Hot Springs, then come to the games and bring someone with you. I shall always remember you loyal fans because it has been a pleasure to do what I have done.' [35]

On August 2, the Bathers were 36 games out of first place. Ten bulldozers, working around the clock until the end of the season, couldn't excavate the Spa team out of the doldrums. El Dorado led the league, while Greenville was five games behind. Third place Meridian was eleven games out, while Pine Bluff and Monroe were 23 and 24 behind, respectively.

Over 760 fans, witnessed the Bathers' newly acquired black pitcher, Bill "Double Thumbs" Mitchell. He scattered nine hits, against the league-leading El Dorado Oilers to win his first CSL triumph 12-8. Mitchell pitched a good game on August 2, his first game in the CSL, but it was an atrocious night for Bathers fielding, at least in the early going, as they committed six errors. Soon, they settled down and the bats took over. The Bathers collected 16 hits during the encounter. Mitchell, well received by the Hot Springs crowd, remained focused on the batters as the crowd displayed excitement throughout the tilt. Healthy player-manager Jackie Bales had a blast...over the right field fence that drove in three runs. It was his fourth explosion in three days. Jackie Bales was an unusual combination of a right-handed thrower and a portside striker. Outfielders Korfonta and Cooper had an awesome night at the plate. The leading Spa batters went 4-4 at the dish and each had a pair of doubles. In addition, Miller had a good night at the plate contributing a single, a double with two RBIs and scored twice. People were discussing Mitchell's "double thumb." Bales said that he actually had a split thumb on his pitching hand. It looked odd, but it didn't bother the pitcher.

In early August, Pine Bluff decided to sign a black player. The Judges became the third team in the Cotton States League to sign at least one black player. President of the Pine Bluff Judges, Sam Cook signed a 22-year-old outfielder, Silvester Rogers of El Dorado, Arkansas. The speedy player, timed at 9.5 in the 100-yard dash, played with Negro baseball teams for seven years. During those years, Rogers hit above .300 every year except one. His stay was brief, but he did break the color barrier for Pine Bluff baseball.

On Friday night, August 6, an estimated crowd of 3,000 saw the Bathers lose 4-3 to the Greenville Bucks at Jaycee Park. Why did a huge number of fans show up for this regular-season game? Before the game, local political candidates spoke briefly from 7:00-8:00 p.m. Perhaps some did come out for the purpose to listen to political speeches, but the main reason for the large crowd was that the admission was free! The game, purchased by Judge C. Floyd Huff, starred homegrown right fielder, Tom Burks who went 3-4 including a triple. Tom was a 1950 graduate of Hot Springs High School and a good friend of Jackie Bales. Manager Bales said that he and Burks used to go fishing at Burks' family place on Lake Hamilton. Bales stated that the slender Burks "really enjoyed playing the game." [36/37]

Uvoyd said he stayed with the Bathers for about six or eight weeks and batted around .200. He received about $250 a month and was happy to get money for playing baseball, the game he loved. Near the end of his stay with the Bathers, Charlie Williamson discussed his future with the first black player to play for the Bathers. Williamson told the young player that he gave him every chance to make the team, but he was not pulling his weight, so Williamson let him go. "Mr. Williamson was right; I really wasn't pulling my weight," Uvoyd remarked. Uvoyd appreciated what Williamson did for him, but Reynolds said, "I was not helping the team." Uvoyd tried to catch on with the Indianapolis Clowns and another black baseball team, but didn't make it. He moved to California, got a job, started a family and remained there until 1983. He then moved to Oklahoma. After retirement, he moved to Milwaukee where he lives today.[38]

By the middle of August, the Bathers hadn't won a game since August 2 and that seemed to be the key reason there were less than 100 fans at Jaycee Park on August 15. To be exact, the paid admission was 91. However, Korfonta and Cooper continued to bat well. The duo remained in the top 10 in the loop's batting race. Steve Korfonta was in the ninth position with a .323 average, while Frank Cooper was close behind in the tenth spot posting an average of .317. Hot Springs was last in league standings, last in fielding and next to last in batting.[39]

The Bathers pulled one of the lowest crowds, again, the next night, when Monroe visited Jaycee Park. Hot Springs lost their 15th straight tilt, this time to Monroe, 8-1. Only 157 very loyal fans witnessed the Bathers lose one more time. However, the assembly was larger than the 91 that showed up a few days earlier. On the same night, Dorsey Roddenberry, local commercial photographer, laid aside his camera for a few hours because the league officials called him to assist umpire Bob Vastano at Jaycee Park. Dorsey was a full-time ump in 1947. Since that time, the league used the local shutterbug in emergencies and the Monroe series was one of those times. Roddenberry replaced Jim Duncan who entered a Little Rock hospital for treatment.

Charlie Williamson decided to admit fans free to the first game of the Meridian three-game series on the night of August 18. "There will be money buckets at the gate and fans can give what they want." Charlie was doing his best. At the "free game", the Bathers snapped a 15-game losing streak as more than 850 fans observed the Meridian loss to the Bathers 15-7. The "high flying" Bathers, at least this night, heaped on 14 runs in the first three frames to coast to the win. Manager Bales set the tone for the night when the lefty blistered the Meridian hurler's offering over the right field fence for a grand slam trotter. Williamson, delighted in the turn out, planned to repeat the idea the following night. "Free-will offerings reportedly totaled more than what would have been taken in through the gates considering the low attendance of recent games."[40]

The Bathers won the second game of the "free game" series and attempted a series sweep against the third place Millers on August 19. Big Charlie stayed with his "free-game" scheme. Williamson was elated because more than 800 fans took advantage of the third freebie game. Any way you look at it, over 2,500 fans attended the last three "free-donations accepted" games. The third game was tight, knotted at three, until the seventh inning. The bases were, "FOB," full of Bathers, as "Mr. Spark" himself, Jackie Bales stepped into the batters' box. Johnny Dupuy, former Bathers pitcher, toed the slab for Meridian. Bales, hit by a pitch in the fourth inning and issued a free pass in the sixth, didn't wait for the second pitch this time. He decided to swing harder and unloaded a grand-slam home run over the right field fence! Hot Springs called for relief support in the eighth frame. They added an insurance run in the bottom of the eighth to take an 8-6 triumph to sweep the series.

With a few games left, *The Sentinel-Record* revealed the league's home run statistics. Hot Springs and Pine Bluff's pitchers gave up the most home runs in the league. The Bathers surrendered 112 round trippers, while the Judges were seven behind with 105. The Twin Cities Sports (Monroe and West Monroe, LA) yielded the least at 58. The biggest splurge of "over the fence orbs" occurred on June 22, when Hot Springs and Pine Bluff collided at Taylor Field. The Bathers parked five outside the fence, while the Judges blasted four homers. The nine home runs accounted for most of the 23 runs scored by both teams.[41]

Maurice Moore, *The Sentinel-Record* sportswriter, praised Judge Emmet Harty, league president. The Judge did everything in his power to keep the league afloat. When sportswriters, fans and others stated that the league should fold early, Harty decided to take the opposite view. He wanted to keep the league floating. There were many difficult decisions by Harty, but somehow the league made it through. "We can't think offhand of anyone who would have wanted to have been in a similar predicament," declared Moore. Excerpts from Judge Harty's letter appear below.

This has been possibly the most difficult season in our history, but somehow we have managed to stagger through. The owners have taken a terrific licking but have honorably performed their contractual obligations to their advertisers and patrons…

…Strange as it may seem, the owners are already discussing a more stable organization for next year with clubs financially responsible to guarantee a completion of the schedule without this constant talk of folding, which was most harmful, not only to the attendance but to the efforts of owners to collect for advertising. For the first time since Korea, I have had an inquiry from a major organization as to the possibility of a working agreement in this league for next year. So, it would seem, we are not dead yet.[42]

Moore stated that he thought that the league should have folded earlier but the clubs made it to the finish line. Many financial grenades hit the league, but somehow the league dodged and ducked the fatal shrapnel. Moore related his thoughts concerning the league.

Hot Springs has done a little bit of everything this season, except win its share of games. The Bathers have had two different owners, a 'save baseball' drive, three different mangers, over 60 players, an attendance as low as 91, and as high as 3,000, a nine-game winning streak, a 15-game losing streak and free games. Oh yes, let's not forget free programs too. Owner Charlie Williamson has given away about everything except concessions in an effort to draw crowds.[43]

The Bathers' last game of the season on August 26 pitted the two worse teams in the league, the Bathers and the Judges. It was one of those "who cares" games at Jaycee Park. The newspaper writer called it "dizzy" and "topsy-turvy." Moore said that the antics rivaled the famed Bud Abbott and Lou Costello's skit called, "Who's on First?" All the players played in a game where positions meant little. It was sort of like a physical education class. It was a zany game, but the players seemed to enjoy the relaxed atmosphere. Both teams popped the ball around for 11 hits each, but surprisingly, it was a low scoring game. The Bathers won 5-4. "At least Hot Springs ended the campaign as it started – beating Pine Bluff. "Following the game, John Parker, Bathers' first baseman, planned to travel to Memphis and join the Indianapolis Clowns of the Negro American League. Later in the year, he would hook up with the Jackie Robinson All-Stars. [44]

Near the end of the season, Greenville caught fire and made a mad dash to the finish line attempting to overtake league-leading El Dorado. On the last day of the season, a combination of an El Dorado 2-1 loss to Monroe and a 10-inning, 3-1 Greenville triumph over Meridian nailed down the league championship for the raging Bucks. The Oilers, league leaders, most of the season, bowed to the Bucks in the final standings by ½ game. Third place Meridian and fourth spot Monroe rounded out the playoff positions. Pine Bluff and cellar-dweller Hot Springs didn't figure in the post-season play. [45]

Frank Walenga, El Dorado's first baseman, clinched the CSL batting honors with a blistering .394 average. In addition, his 173 total hits topped the circuit. The three big-batting guns for Hot Springs were outfielder Steve Korfonta, infielder-outfielder Frank Cooper and shortstop Bud Miller. Korfonta ended up in the top ten listing as he smacked the ball around for a lofty .321. Cooper ended with a strong .311 batting average and steady Jim "Bud" Miller, shortstop, who started with Hot Springs around early May, finished with a healthy .283 mark.

In the 1954 championship series, Willis Hudlin, former major league pitcher, coached the Bucks, while Bill Adair, long-time minor league player-manager, piloted the El Dorado Oilers. The Oilers downed the Greenville Bucks, four games to two, to win the CSL post-season championship.

Chapter 16

The Last Hurrah
1955

"If you pick up The Sporting News any week, you'll see the same story of financial plights and clubs folding." - Maurice Moore

A ticket campaign called "Operation Baseball" kicked off the 1955 season on March 14. Milan Creighton, chairman of the Chamber of Commerce's general sports committee, announced plans to "cover the city" with advertisement. Creighton a former Razorback football player, NFL player-coach for the Chicago Cardinals and former head coach for the local Hot Springs Trojans high school football team, was familiar with the sports arena. The game plan was to sell 400 books of Bathers' season tickets for $25.00 per book. Each book contained 59 tickets, one grandstand ticket for each home game, excluding opening night.

Local car dealer, Charlie Williamson, 1955 Bathers owner, said he needed $27,000 in the bank by the Bathers first game of the season on April 26. Mr. Williamson operated at a loss during the previous season; however, he secured a limited working agreement with the Kansas City Athletics for the 1955 season. So, Charlie Williamson, number one Bathers' fan, again, planned lead the Bathers charge. Joe Lutz, former Triple-A player, took over the helm as Bathers manager. During the winter months, Lutz taught school in West Burlington, Iowa. Spring training for the Bathers began at the Athletics central training facility on March 23, at Savannah, Georgia. The pact with the Athletics "guarantees five players and a manager, but the A's are expected to assign more as soon as their spring training program jells."[1]

However, a few days following the opening day of the ticket campaign, a gloomy sports article appeared in *The Sentinel-Record*. The headlines said it all, "Outlook For Baseball, Dark As Season Ticket Campaign Opens Here." Here we go again. Maurice Moore stated there were several unanswered questions concerning the Bathers financial condition. Perhaps the Bathers needed a "sugar daddy." When the White Sox owned the club, there seemed to be less strain on the club's pocket book. Financial setbacks distracted the Bathers since 1950, when private ownership, with little or no assistance from the major league clubs, took over the reins. Fans and ownership hoisted the club out of the doldrums several times. The owner and fans were jittery about investing in the club because they weren't sure they wanted a horse in this race.

Williamson was too skeptical about owning the club, so he saw a chance to sell the club. Within a few days, Williamson sold the Bathers to George "Mickey" O'Neil, a 38-year veteran of baseball. O'Neil, a native of St. Louis, spent nine years as catcher in the majors and several years in the minors. The new, experienced owner-president's minor league profile included performing as player, manager, business manager and owner. "The diamond-wise" O'Neil moved from Missouri to Hot Springs to become a hands-on owner.

Milan Creighton, chairman of the sports committee, called a meeting of the new 14-member Board of Directors of the Bathers Baseball Club and met with the new owner. The board included Creighton, Sam Garratt, J. C. McWha, Williamson, Bill Armstrong, Tommy Reed, Angelo Pappas, C. J. "Gus" Dickson, Prince Cook, Lewis Goltz, Dr. F. S. Tarleton, W. D. Roddenberry, Garrett H. Britt and Marshall Carlisle.

O'Neil received "blessings" from the Kansas City A's, as well as the president of the Cotton States League. Judge Emmet Harty and O'Neil were longtime acquaintances. O'Neil received a telegram from Harty stating, "Directors of the CSL unanimously approved transfer of the Hot

Springs franchise. I congratulate Hot Springs and am delighted to have you in the league." Harty also sent a telegram to outgoing owner, Charlie Williamson that stated, "You have rendered great service to your community in particular and baseball in general and I regret your passing from the scene. Personally, I shall always be grateful for the cooperation extended to me at all times."

The Bathers opened spring training in Savannah, Georgia, on March 27, where six farm affiliates of the Kansas City A's practiced at the same location. The ownership was pleased that Hot Springs had a limited working agreement with the A's. This year was the first time in the post-war era that the Bathers traveled away from the Spa for spring training. One major rule had changed since the 1954 season. The CSL limited each team to only four experienced or veteran players. Therefore, teams could have 12 rookies and "limited-service players" plus 4 former professional players on the 16-man roster. A "limited-service player" was a player who was in professional baseball at the time he entered the military. Upon his return from the military, he could continue playing professional baseball, provided he made the team. The league did not rule this type player a "veteran player." The idea was to attempt to get more rookies and limited service players a chance to make the grade into professional baseball.

On April 1, the Jaycees formally leased the baseball park to Mickey O'Neil, the new owner of the Bathers. Since the Junior Chamber of Commerce helped revive professional baseball by constructing Jaycee Park in 1947, the stipulations remained the same.

The lease, signed by Jaycee president Bill Harper, Tommy Ellsworth, chairman of the park board, and Renaford Caldwell, secretary of the organization, gives O'Neil lease of the park for one year with a five-year option.

In return, the Jaycees receive 20 per cent from the sale of all fence signs, and 1 game from which they derive all proceeds.[2]

On April 14, a local sports enthusiast, Paul Longinotti, 39, succumbed to an apparent heart attack at his home on Clinton Street. During his high school days at Hot Springs, he was All-Southern quarterback and made the All-State team twice. He quarterbacked the powerful 1934 Trojans to the state high school football title. A knee injury curtailed his college career. Longinotti was one of the organizers of the grade school football program in the city. Coaching at St. Johns and Ramble schools, he tutored Ramble to the "Little Hot Water Bowl" grade school city football championship in 1949. Longinotti was a member of St. John's Catholic Church, the Catholic Men's Club, Elk's Lodge #380 and the American Legion.

The six-team CSL preparing to crank up the season included three Arkansas teams from Hot Springs, Pine Bluff and El Dorado. Greenville and Vicksburg represented Mississippi and the Louisiana representative, Monroe rounded out the league. On Monday, April 25, one day before opening night with Pine Bluff, the Bathers held two workouts at Jaycee Park. The morning workout began at 10:00 and the afternoon practice began at 7:00 and finished at 8:30. Manager Lutz wanted the players to become comfortable with the lighting. Following the night practice, the Bathers journeyed to radio station KWFC to broadcast a 30-minute program called "Meet the Bathers." On Tuesday afternoon, several hours before game time, the Bathers paraded down Central Avenue.

Brief pregame ceremonies at Jaycee Park marked the opening night of the 1955 baseball season for the Hot Springs Bathers. Mayor Floyd Housley, Circuit Judge C. Floyd Huff, Jr., Sheriff Leonard Ellis and Municipal Judge M. C. Lewis, Jr. took part in a pseudo baseball game before the real game started. Jewell Thomas headed up the concessions. Thomas had been involved in Bathers baseball since 1951, when he was assistant concessions manager. In 1953, he was general manager of the Bathers and volunteered to assist with the concessions in 1954. In addition, Mr. Thomas was active in youth sports in the Hot Springs area for many years.

The Bathers jolted the Judges 12-6 as 2,240 fans witnessed the initial 1955 contest in Hot Town. The Spa Boys out hit Pine Bluff by a 14 to 8 margin as Bathers third baseman Howard Warrell led all batters with three safeties, including a round tripper. Outfielder Bill Brashear, the bespectacled leadoff hitter and "speed merchant" went 2-4 at the plate, including a three-run homer, five RBIs and scored twice. The Spamen scored a combined seven tallies in the seventh and eighth innings to help their cause as they used four tossers to connect with the win. Starter Rodney Tangeman, a rookie from Iowa, showed good arm speed until the fifth frame when he was touched with four runs. With two outs in the fifth, lefty Don "Spook" Miller took over on the mound followed shortly by Jim Williams. Lefty "Fireman" Joe Graham doused the flames in the eighth and ninth frames to allow the Williams win.

The next night, the Bathers zipped past Pine Bluff 9-3. What a difference a day makes. The first game of the season took 3 hours and 13 minutes to complete, but the second game with the Judges was an hour shorter. Over 2,200 fans showed up at opening night, but the second night attendance was only 509.

The CSL again had a problem of allowing blacks to play. *The Sentinel-Record* reported on May 5, that Pine Bluff had three black players on their roster. However, implications came from others in the league that Pine Bluff was not to play the black players.

Officials of the league met at Greenville, Miss., today but refused to say what they had talked about. Later Virgil Wooley, business manager of the Judges, said he was told not to play the Negroes.

Wooley said he appealed to George Trautman, boss of Minor League baseball, but Trautman said he would not interfere with the league ruling. The Negroes were held out of tonight's game with Greenville.[3]

The black players from the Negro American League were Charles Peppers – outfielder and Russell Moseley - shortstop from Memphis. Pitcher Charles Chapman played with the Detroit Stars.

Due to lack of attendance, Pine Bluff considered pulling out of the league. Judge Harty, president of the league, didn't say anything about the meeting, but he noted that if Pine Bluff pulled out of the league, he knew of several cities that would be interested in taking over their spot.

The Indianapolis Clowns battled the New York Black Yankees in an exhibition game at Jaycees Park on May 6. It was the first of several summer games involving black baseball teams in Hot Springs. The Clowns had been a great draw for 25 years and the Black Yankees were one of the top contenders for the American Negro League pennant. Several players from the Black Yankees were playing in the major or minor leagues. In the exhibition game, the Black Yankees doubled up the Clowns 8-4.

On May 7, *The Sentinel-Record* reported that the three black players, who were supposed to play for Pine Bluff, sat in the stands at Pine Bluff, "sidelined by a league rule against Negroes." Virgil Wooley, Pine Bluff's business manager, stated that the umpires were "instructed to call a forfeit on Pine Bluff in any game in which the Negroes played." Wooley appealed to George M. Trautman who was president of the National Association of Minor Baseball Leagues. Trautman said that his office would not approve any rule that prohibited any player from playing baseball. However, he said that the CSL officials had not confirmed the report.[4]

"Wooley had quoted Trautman earlier as saying, 'If you people can't operate without Negroes, why don't you quit?'" However, Trautman stated that he didn't make those remarks. Trautman did say there is no place in baseball for prohibitive legislation and it'll never be approved here. There are no lines on color or creed and there won't be."

The next day, a report stated that Pine Bluff dropped the three black players from their roster. One of the officials in the Pine Bluff front office blamed a league ruling for dismissing the players.

At Greenville, Miss., today, however CSL President Judge Emmet Harty said he knew of no league ruling against using Negroes. He also denied statements of Pine Bluff officials that they had been advised their games would be forfeited if the Negroes played. [5]

Maurice Moore reported in *The Sentinel-Record,* on May 8, that he seemed to be tired of hearing about all the racial matters. He wanted the league to allow blacks to play and get on with baseball.

It's too bad that this dispute can't be resolved, and if American principles are best served, there can be but one answer. The Cotton States league and Southern Association are the last bulwarks against Negro players and sooner or later the courts will probably have to give the answer. But, you can look at the situation in two veins and different lights. Negro players would probably bring out a substantial number of colored fans wherever they performed. They did last year, but it seems to us that principles should be deeper than just 'exploiting' them for what additional crowds they might bring...A definite stand is needed to bolster the confidence of the fans both white and colored.[6]

In the same day's paper, Moore reported about a previous incident involving manager Lutz and L. E. Biles, owner of a music store in the city. Moore noted that he thought it was a small world. Lutz, a Marine during WW II, saw action at Guadalcanal and ended up with the 22nd Marines on Okinawa. While Lutz was in the Marine program at Millsaps College in Jackson, Mississippi, his commanding officer (CO) was L. E. Biles. Biles organized and directed the Hot Springs High School band for several years. In 1942, Biles enlisted in the Marine Corps. Following the war, he returned to Hot Springs and opened a music store. Lutz found out that his former CO owned the music store, so the Bather manager skedaddled down to Biles Music Store. The first thing out of the mouth of Lutz was "Capt. Biles!" That was his rank when Lutz knew him. However, at that time, Biles had risen to the rank of Major. Thus, an old friendship was rekindled.[7]

On Sunday, May 8, Hot Springs was the hottest team in the young CSL season. The Bathers (10-6) were up by half a game in first place over El Dorado. The Spa team was second in club batting with .265, behind Monroe's .295 team average. In club fielding, Hot Springs was in first place with a .949 clip, .001 point better than El Dorado. Five Bathers were hitting over .300 as Rudy Mayling was in second place in the league with a rousing .391. "Gabby" Hays had a .333, Brashear posted a .324 figure, Howard Warrell was batting .314 and Larry Good stood at .306. No Hot Springs pitcher had more than one win; however, Ed White was undefeated at 1-0.

Also on Sunday, May 8, it was "Ladies' Day" at Jaycee Park and the Bathers presented corsages to the oldest and youngest mothers in attendance. Mrs. Annie Atwood, 77, received the corsage for the oldest mother. She had three children, five grandchildren and four great-grandchildren. Jane Chesser, 19-year-old mother of one child, "won" the youngest mother award.

Lutz blasted a pair of homers, while Warrell added a solo round-tripper as Don Miller limited the Judges to five hits. The Bathers posted a 9-0 win over Pine Bluff on Monday, May 16. Only 407 customers saw the Bathers play one of the best games of the season as Miller went all the way for the Spa Boys. After hit by a pitch on Saturday night, shortstop Kirby Dickens was back in the line up. The sure-handed infielder went 1-4 at the plate.

About a week later, Rookie Rod Tangeman tossed a six-hit shutout as the Bathers blasted the Bucks, 10-0. Right fielder Mayling, first baseman Al DelleValle and John Janocha the Spa's backstop, posted two hits each. Included in Janocha's totals was a four-bagger. The Bathers were alone in second place in the tight CSL race.

Mrs. Lovell Mantle of Commerce, Oklahoma, posed for a picture with three of her sons Larry (14), twins Roy and Ray at Jaycee Park on Saturday May 28. Roy and Ray played outfield for the Monroe Sports. Larry played infield for the Commerce junior high team. Her other son, Mickey, was a star outfielder with the New York Yankees. Mrs. Mantle and Larry were guests at the Goddard Hotel. Within a few days, she and Larry planned to watch Mickey take his cuts against the Browns in St. Louis.

By the end of May, Rudy Mayling, outfielder for Hot Springs, climbed to the top of the batting heap in the CSL with a .360 record. Five teams were bouncing around from first to fifth place in the sticky league standings; however, Hot Springs hovered around third place.

It seemed the end of the road for Pine Bluff! The management of the Judges decided to bail out of the league due to the lack of capital. League president Judge Harty stated that the Junior Chamber of Commerce of Pine Bluff considered taking over the franchise by raising $12,000 within 15 days. However, until that time, the Judges were under the operation of the Cotton States League. If the Jaycees could not maintain ownership, Meridian, Mississippi, was waiting in the wings to take control of the Arkansas team.

Meanwhile, baseball continued in the CSL. On June 2, the Bathers rapped five homers as they downed the Judges 16-11 at Pine Bluff. Hot Springs clouted 18 hits to the Judges 14. Lutz collected three hits, including a homer. Other Bathers hitting homers were Al DellaValle, shortstop Ken Kortum, third baseman Howard "Boots" Warrell and outfielder Bill Brashear. Joining Lutz with a three-hit attack were "Whitey" Bragg and Brashear.

Since many players traveled through the Bathers dugout in 1955, the team released a revised team roster. The new roster included pitchers (right-handers) John White, Ed White, Fred Martin, Rodney Tangeman, Carl Montangna and William Shannon, (lefthanders) Don Miller and Bill Kirk. Infielders were Joe Lutz, first base/manager; Al DellaValle, first base/second base; Larry Good, second base; Howard Warrell, third base and Ken Kortum, shortstop. Outfielders included Rudy Mayling, right fielder; Gordon Bragg, center fielder; Bill Brashear, left fielder; catchers: John Janocha and Stephen Durst.

In early June, the Bathers launched "Baseball Day," a continuing campaign to raise attendance. Average attendance lingered around 500 per game, but even at that, the team stayed in first division most of the season. The Downtown Lions Club planned a picnic and afterwards the group attended a Bathers game. The Elks followed suit. The Bathers needed people in the stands. Another idea conceived by a committee of Bathers supporters was to advertise in surrounding areas such as Mt. Ida, Glenwood, Malvern and Benton. "All we need is fans," declared Mickey O'Neil, club owner. "Everything else is okay. The turnstiles need to click more," O'Neil related.[8]

The Bathers spotted Greenville six runs as the hometown boys came from behind to squeeze past the Bucks in 10 frames, 12-10. The nine-error, 33-hit game lasted nearly three hours.

After sweating through the top of the 10th, which saw the Bucks get one player as far as second, the Bathers came to the 'time of decision.'

Mayling, first up, beat out an infield roller for a single. (Manager Joe) Lutz looked as if he might try to sacrifice so Mayling could get in scoring position.

But with two strikes against him, the loop's top homer hitter sent a pitch sailing over the right field fence, and that was the wind-up after two hours and 55 minutes of grueling competitive play.[9]

A few days later, O'Neil informed *The Sentinel-Record* the Bathers may fold due to the open spaces in the grandstand. The city heard this statement repeatedly through the years. However, the South Hot Springs Lions Club jumped on the baseball bandwagon and sponsored a "Bathers Night."

It was football weather out at Jaycee Park on June 10; however, about 600 fans braved the 50-degree weather to watch Lutz slam three home runs as the Spa Boys divided a twin bill with the Billies of Vicksburg. The Bathers took the first game 7-4, but lost the nightcap in a come-from-behind victory by the Billies 8-7. The long ball was the star of the night as Lutz plastered one over the fence in the first game and two more orbs found their way on the outside of the fence during the second contest. Bathers' catcher John Janocha and third baseman "Boots" Warrell contributed one homer each during the evening. The Billies added three more round trippers to their side of the ledger, which totaled eight home runs between the two teams during the doubleheader.

The ticket campaign got off to a flying start as city officials supported the ticket thrust via radio and the newspapers. Owner Mickey O'Neil reiterated that he was not moving the team and planned to make the city his home. However, down the road about 60 miles east of Hot Springs, the Pine Bluff Judges were also having a numbers crunch. The Junior Chamber of Commerce still tossed around the idea of raising $12,000 to continue their baseball program. The future looked bleak for the Judges. [10]

Hot Springs battered Monroe 16-2, on June 15, to move into a tie for second place with El Dorado and only two games behind league-leading Monroe. On "Children's Night," a crowd of 500 watched the Bathers jog around the bases all night. The Spa scored seven runs in the fourth inning and another five more in the seventh stanza to ice the contest. Two nights later, the Bathers swept two games from Greenville 4-0 and 8-4 to move into first place by a ½ game over El Dorado and Monroe. The double triumphs extended the Bathers win streak to five straight and eight out of their last 10 games. Pitcher Bill Kirk went all the way for his first shutout of the season as he registered his third straight triumph.

Jaycee Park was a busy place on June 22. Sponsored by the Hot Springs Elks Lodge No. 380, admission was free to children under 12. In addition, a pregame contest took place between the mighty Elks Athletic Committee and the talented Elks Entertainment Committee. Manager of the Athletic Committee, Alton Baldwin, former Green Bay Packer player and Ish Thomas, Baldwin's counterpart for the Entertainment Committee, assumed their duties at 7:00 p.m. Exalted Ruler J. R. Smith summoned all Elks to the game. Even a band serenaded the crowd during the pregame activities.

Manager Lutz returned to the Bathers after a 10-day layoff due to a shoulder injury and a five-day suspension from the league for vociferously disagreeing with the home plate arbiter. The previously heated discussion between Lutz and the umpire was hot enough that the ump gave one of the best power hitters in the league the old heave-ho. At this point, the Bathers were two games out of first place behind El Dorado and Monroe who were even with a record of 31-21 each.

The Bathers finished the first half with vengeance and their prey was the Meridian Millers. After a game total of 42 hits and 29 runs, Hot Springs chalked up a 20-9 victory on June 24. There were only 550 fans at Jaycee Park to witness the merry-go-round contest that lasted two hours, forty-five minutes. Newly acquired second sacker, Ken Hartman, who had been with the club for less than two weeks, gathered four singles and a double during his six trips to the plate. He scored four runs to boot.

Judge Harty announced that the league directors decided for a split season. The first half of the season ended Friday, June 24, while the second session began on Saturday, June 25. The first half standings, in order, included Monroe, El Dorado, Hot Springs, Greenville, Meridian and Vicksburg. The Bathers stood 3 ½ games out of first place.[11]

The split-season format was new to the CSL and it seemed nobody knew too much about the plan. They did realize that the second division teams had new life, so that was a plus for them. In addition, several of the teams in the CSL continued to financially struggle.

If you pick up The Sporting News any week, you'll see the same story of financial plights, and clubs folding. Somebody has to come up with a solution or Minor League baseball will be reduced to little more than skeleton-size. In these days of high prices, it's hard to keep costs down. For instance, the light bill for eight games at Jaycee Park, Owner Mickey O'Neil revealed, amounted to more than $320. It's tough to make ends meet.[12]

The paper reported an incident concerning "Satchel" Paige. He continued to have speed even into his late 40s or whatever age he was in 1955. The "ageless wonder" pitched for the Kansas City Monarchs in 1955, but he monetarily assisted the Indiana police. He plead guilty to a speeding violation in Auburn, Indiana, and paid his $5.00 (plus cost) ticket. His driver's license listed him as 49 years old. "But he told Justice of the Peace: 'Don't you believe that.' He didn't and we don't."[13]

Hot Springs ended the intermission in fourth position in club batting and first spot in club fielding, although newly acquired outfielder, Bill Anderson hit .395 in 10 games. Gordon Bragg, Hot Springs outfielder turned in the week's best average with a 15 for 36-pace at the plate. Al

DellaValle and Lutz were hitting .333 and .330 respectively. Newcomers Bill Kirk and Tom Grant each had hurling records of 3-0.

Early in the second half, the Bathers slid to last place with a 1-4 record, while Vicksburg was undefeated with a 3-0 mark. During the first few days of the new season, Joe Lutz's Kansas City A's farmhands sprinkled enough hits and runs to beat the Greenville Bucks 5-3 at Jaycee Park. A crowd of 625 watched Richard Jack, Hot Springs' newest pitcher throw for 7 1/3 innings to cop his initial victory. Standing at 6' 9", Jack, from Toronto, Canada, was the tallest player in professional baseball.

On July 4, Willis Hudlin, manager of the Greenville Bucks notified Judge Harty, president of the CSL, that finishing the season for Greenville, looked dark. He said the team was losing too much money. A few days later, the league stated that the Bucks got a new lease on life. "The Class C league voted to send the deficit-plagued Greenville Bucks on a 4-day road trip at league expense. After that, a Greenville citizens' group will take over the team."[14]

On July 10, following the game with Monroe, the Bathers, wives and guests journeyed to the home of Mr. and Mrs. A. D. Watkins on Lake Catherine for a barbecue chicken dinner with all the trimmings. Hosts for the event were Charlie Williamson and the Watkins family. Other cuisine contributors included Borden's Milk Company, Coca-Cola, M. L. Stueart Grocery, Ark Bakery and Wally Matthews.

The Sentinel-Record reported on July 9, Arch Ward, sports editor of the *Chicago Tribune* for 25 years, passed away of a heart attack in Chicago. The veteran sports authority originated the All-Star baseball (1933) and All-Star football games (1934). Chicago's Comiskey Park hosted the first Major League Baseball All-Star Game in 1933, in which the American League eased past the National League 4-2. "The Arkansas Hummingbird," Lon Warneke, Cubs hurler, pitched well as he tossed six innings and allowed only one run in the first All-Star contest. At the plate, Warneke tagged the first All-Star triple.

On July 11, the Cotton States League All-Star Game pitted the first place El Dorado Oilers against the All-Stars of the remaining five teams in the loop. Center fielder Gordon "Whitey" Bragg (.325), shortstop Ken Kortum (.283) and outfielder Rudy Mayling (.311) represented Hot Springs in the mid-season classic at El Dorado's Jim Griffith Field. Neither team scored until the eighth inning when Marshall Gilbert, first baseman of Monroe, blasted Rene Masip's fastballs over the right field fence. In the same inning, Rudy Mayling of Hot Springs doubled off the left field fence to drive in Bernie Tomicki of Meridian for the second run of the night. The All-Stars took the Oilers 2-0 as the three All-Star pitchers Drummond (Monroe), Wiltse (Greenville) and Shipman (Monroe) tossed the first no hitter in CSL All-Star history. Gilbert was the only player to acquire two hits in the game.

Prior to the All-Star game, Harty was fuming when he talked to the Sportswriters Association. He believed that all the CSL teams would complete the season in 1955, but he was not sure about the 1956 season. Due to financial problems, Pine Bluff transferred their franchise to Meridian, Mississippi. He thought that the major league teams should provide more financial support to the minor league teams in order for the minors to survive. Subsequently, he told them what he thought.

'Some of the clubs in our league have contributed as much as $75,000 over the past five years to develop young talent for the Major Leagues,' said Harty. 'The big leagues cannot expect us to keep on carrying the burden while they reap all the profits.'

Harty criticized the radio and television live coverage of Major League games in towns, which have Minor League clubs as the major factor in the steady decline of attendance at Cotton States League games.

'The people are saturated with baseball,' he said. 'They talk of nothing but the Major League races. The big league club owners could stop this by prohibiting the broadcasting and telecasting of games in a Minor League club's area, but they won't do it because they are too selfish.'

Harty also apologized to the sports editors for a recent quote attributed to him in which he accused 'the dumb sports writers of trying to break up the league.' Harty said he made the remark because of irritation over the repeated speculations that the Cotton States League would fold.[15]

At the All-Star break, El Dorado was in first place by three games (12-5), followed by Vicksburg, Monroe, Hot Springs, Meridian and Greenville. It was early in the second half so anything could happen in the tight CSL race.

Hot Springs was hurting. Manager Lutz had a "pesky shoulder-neck injury" and played only sparingly. Center fielder Gordon "Whitey" Bragg was not in the All-Star lineup because he found a better paying non-baseball position in Blackwell, Oklahoma. He was hitting around .300 when he departed, but he roamed around the minors for about eight years and finally threw in the towel. So, Lutz is scrambling to find decent talent to continue the season.

The longest game ever played at Jaycee Park occurred on Sunday, July 17, 1955. It was fortunate that the game started at 2:47 p.m. because it concluded four hours and forty-five minutes later. The Bathers and the Vicksburg Billies struggled for a record 17 innings as Hot Springs edged the Billies, 3-2. With two out in the bottom of the 17th frame, outfielder Bill Anderson slashed a double into left field. The next batter, Kenny Hartman, second baseman, slapped a single past Carr at third and the fleet-footed Anderson scored to break up the marathon. Both sides turned in excellent defensive maneuvers as only two Hot Springs errors and no Billies errors showed up on the scorecard. Both teams scored one run each in the ninth frame to prolong the contest.

Money woes continued to strike the Bathers. The club was two weeks behind in salaries, but with a little push from the public, the Bathers would probably be back in business. They postponed a trip to El Dorado due to lack of money, but if the resources came in, they planned to play a doubleheader to make up the game. The total amount owed to the players in back wages was around $3,200 and the Kansas City Athletics, the parent club of the Bathers, would pay $1,500 of that amount if the fans could raise the rest. O'Neil announced that pledge money of $1,275 arrived and was ready for the bank deposit that morning. Henry Peters, farm director of the Kansas City club, stated that his main objectives were to pay the players and if the team folded, assign the players to other affiliates.

O'Neil thanked the 500-600 loyal fans who help pay the bills, but blamed the financial dilemma on poor attendance, bad weather, poor preseason sales and the "general economic conditions of the city because of the closing of the Army-Navy Hospital." Within 24 hours, the fans came through with $1,700 to pay the back salaries of the players. The Bathers accumulated enough cash to travel south to El Dorado to play the doubleheader. At that point, the Bathers hung around fourth place in the CSL on July 22.

Lanky 6' 9" Richard Jack helped snap a four-game losing streak as he pitched the complete game for the Bathers. "Big Richard" scattered 10 hits to win over the Meridian Millers 8-4 on July 25. It was Jack's second win in a Bathers uniform since joining the crew three weeks previously. The Bathers blanked Vicksburg 4-0 on the last day of July, but they were still in fourth place, nine games behind league leader El Dorado.

Manager Joe Lutz resigned as owner Mickey O'Neil, former major league catcher, took over the club as field general. Lutz came on board as a playing manager, but was unable to play due to his sore neck and shoulder injury. When Kansas City got wind of the forced resignation of Lutz, they were hot because they thought Lutz was doing a good job under the circumstances. The Athletics threatened to pull out the whole club since 14 of the players belonged to them. O'Neil contacted Trautman at the national offices and president Harty at Greenville, Mississippi. Trautman stood behind O'Neil and stated, "Kansas City had no jurisdiction" in the matter. O'Neil planned to save the manager's salary since he will manage at a reduced salary or pro bono. "The difficulties with the Athletics could possibly resolve themselves if the record is good the remainder of the way."[16]

The five-hitter tossed by Jack Kenney helped the Bathers defeat the Monroe Sports and the Mantle twins, 6-3, on August 11, in Monroe. Outfielders Rudy Mayling and Bill Brashear were "the sparkplugs" at the plate and on the bases. Brashear popped a two-run homer in the second inning. Mayling was a triple threat as he stole three bases and stepped on home plate three times. Roy Mantle doubled, but Ray fanned in the ninth inning as he batted for Monroe's pitcher Madden. On August 11, Hot Springs was in fifth place, 7.5 games behind league leading, Monroe, a New York Yankees affiliate.[17]

The Shaughnessy playoffs were looming in the wings and it looked as though the Bathers may end up in fourth place, high enough for a playoff berth. However, O'Neil had "a piece-meal" club since injuries and school interests have robbed him of some of his key players. Following the game on August 21, with El Dorado, the club was in fourth place, 13.5 games behind Monroe.

The El Dorado game was "zany" as the Oilers outslugged the Bathers 14-7. It was a wild and wooly night as substitute umpire Paul Dean filled in as an arbiter, since the league was short of umps. Dean, whose strident attitude toward umpires during his playing days was well known, didn't dress like an umpire. He wore light colored pants and a sport shirt and the only thing that made him resemble an umpire was a baseball cap. He fared well as he umpired the bases, but the fans didn't treat Dean's counterpart, plate umpire, Serge Schuster as kindly. Schuster ejected two Bathers for arguing. O'Neil became a "master manipulator of sorts to keep nine players on the field." He came close to donning a glove because few Bathers remained on the bench. The manager used seven pitchers in the game – only two did the hurling on the mound. The other pitchers filled gaps on the roster in order to play the game.

First off, Shortstop Kenny Kortum was slammed hard in the face by a grounder that took a bad hop, and he was taken to Ouachita Hospital, and kept overnight for observation. He was not believed seriously hurt.

So, O'Neil pulled Bill Brashear out of center and inserted left-handed moundsman, Loren Oliver. White (catcher) was ejected in the fifth inning for arguing and Al DellaValle was pulled from third and put behind the plate. Ron Slawski, who started in rightfield moved to third, and Bill Kirk, also a southpaw mounds man, went to right.

In the seventh, Martin (1B) and Schuster started rhubarbing and Martin got the heave-ho. So, Kirk went to first, and another southpaw moundsman, Bob Nonenmocher, took over the outfield spot.

Somehow, the Bathers managed to finish the game without any more switches. O'Neil still had two more twirlers, Jack Kenny and Rod Tangeman, on the standby.[18]

Bathers' twirler Jack Kenny whiffed 15 Sports as he pitched Hot Springs to a 4-1 victory over Monroe. It took the Louisiana team nine innings to cross the plate one time, as Kenny, the 6' 5" moundsman, gave up nine hits. Monroe's pitcher, Mickey Madden, gave up only seven hits on August 22, but he was the batting star, collecting three hits for four times at bat. Roy Mantle hit safely twice and twin Ray singled once.

It was "Charlie Williamson Night" at Jaycee Park on August 23, as the Monroe Sports and the Bathers clashed in the final two games of the 1955 season at Jaycee Park. The first of two seven-inning games began at 6:30 p.m. O'Neil honored Williamson, a local car dealer and former Bathers owner, because of his efforts to keep professional baseball in Hot Springs. Williamson furnished all of the club's road-trip transportation during the 1954 and 1955 seasons.

The Bathers went on the road for their last two games of the season against the Meridian Millers losing both contests 4-3 and 9-6. Even though the Bathers lost the last two games, their overall record in the CSL put them in the playoffs at the number four position. It was unfortunate for Hot Springs that they lost three key players in a two-week span, but one returned to the makeshift lineup. Shortstop Kenny Kortum received a bad hop in the jaw at shortstop a few days previously, but was ready to go by playoff time. Catcher John Janocha suffered a broken finger and was out of action for the playoffs. It was time for college students to return to their respective campuses, so the 25-year-old Rudy Mayling, returned to his campus of higher learning. The Bathers outfielder left the club hitting a strong .281 batting average with 13 homers.

Shortstop Ken Kortum was the only Hot Springs player selected to the "end of the year" CSL All-Star team. The CSL 1955 All-Star Team included first base – Marshall Gilbert, Monroe; second base – Bob Maness, Monroe; third base - Jim Davenport, El Dorado; shortstop – Jose' Pagan, El Dorado and Ken Kortum, Hot Springs (tie). The left fielder was George Blash, Meridian; center field - Banks McDowell, Greenville and right fielder - Roy Mantle, Monroe.

Selected, as All-Star catcher was Wally Widholm, Vicksburg, while the utility player was Doug Kassay; Meridian The pitchers included Bill Drummond, Ed Dick and Bob Shipman of Monroe; Dick Malbauer, El Dorado and Joe Blasko, El Dorado. The manager's ballot was a tie between Ed Head, Monroe and Francis (Salty) Parker of El Dorado.

Final CSL figures reported that Jim Davenport, third baseman for the El Dorado Oilers captured the CSL batting title with a .363 average. Al DellaValle was the highest Bather on the batting list with a .294 average and finished in the CSL's number-nine slot. Hot Springs finished fourth in team batting and team fielding, but the Bathers were rather quiet on the pitching front. A few of the top tossers for the Bathers were Tangeman 12-8, Grant 5-2, Martin 5-5, Kenny 6-5, Kirk 7-7 and John White 4-4.

The Bathers finished the second half in fifth place 15.5 games behind first place Monroe, but the overall record from the first half sneaked the hometown boys into fourth place to cop the last playoff berth.

1st Round Playoffs

(Best of 7)

Game 1 - Saturday, August 27, 1955 at Monroe, Louisiana

Monroe – 7 Hot Springs – 2

The playoff openers pitted (1) Monroe vs. (4) Hot Springs and (2) El Dorado vs. (3) Meridian. Monroe defeated Hot Springs in the first game of the CSL playoffs 7-2 as the limping Bathers managed only four hits. Ray Mantle was one of the leaders for Monroe socking a double and a triple and added two RBIs. Bathers' Rod Tangeman limited the first-place Sports to only eight hits, but it was too much to overcome for the Bathers. Over 1,400 witnessed the event in Monroe.[19]

Game 2 – Sunday, August 28, 1955 at Monroe, Louisiana
Monroe 17 HS – 0

Monroe trounced the Bathers 17-0 in the second game of the playoffs at Monroe. Ray Mantle and Rod Kanehl ignited the Sports for four hits each, as Kanehl went on a rampage driving in six runs. Monroe's southpaw Ed Dick allowed the Bathers only six hits, while fanning seven in the runaway. Over 1,100 fans came out to witness the Sports demolish the Bathers, 17-0. Lipp and Duncan were the umpires.[20]

Game 3 – Tuesday, August 30, 1955 at Hot Springs, Arkansas
Monroe – 11 Hot Springs - 7

It rains very little in August in Hot Springs, but it did on Monday night, August 29. The clubs clashed again on Tuesday, August 30. Hot Springs lost another player as Al DellaValle, third baseman, returned to New York. Usually 12 hits are enough to win a game, but not this one. Monroe outhit the Bathers 15-12 and ended up scoring five runs in the ninth frame beating the Bathers 11-7, as the Sports went up 3-0 in playoff wins. The highlight for the Bathers was Bill Brashear, Bathers center fielder, who collected three hits for his four trips to the plate. Attendance at Jaycee Park was a dismal 341.[21]

Game 4 – Wednesday, August 31, 1955 at Hot Springs, Arkansas
Monroe – 9 Hot Springs - 4

The Sports slammed the lid on the Bathers hopes at Jaycee Park as they ran past the Spa Boys 9-4 to sweep the best of seven-game series. The 200 faithful fans at Jaycee Park were the last to see professional baseball in Hot Springs. Bill Brashear, center fielder, one of only two original 1955 Bathers, started and ended the season with a homer. Fred Martin, a pitcher who played first base was the hitting sparkplug for the Bathers, collected three hits for five trips to the plate. Most of the Bathers scattered to the four winds the following day, but Monroe returned to the Twin Cities to await the winner of the Oilers – Millers series. El Dorado took care of the Millers, but in the championship series, Monroe slid past El Dorado four games to three to win the 1955 CSL championship.[22]

The 1955 Bathers may have been one of the most underrated teams in the history of the organization. They withstood constant financial problems. In fact, at one point, the players played without receiving paychecks, but eventually they were paid. They survived two managers as well as two owners. The Bathers attempted to play black players, but the league muffled that idea. Near the end of the season, they lost several players due to school or work circumstances. The team scratched and clawed their way into fourth spot, just high enough to squeak into the playoff picture. It seemed that their talent was mediocre, but they played as well as they could, under the circumstances. Only two of the 1955 Bathers, besides the two managers, saw action in the majors. Bill Kirk saw limited action in the major league, but pitcher George Brunet collected about 15 years with several teams in the majors.

The long-running Class C, Cotton States League folded following the 1955 season. There were too many financial roller-coaster years for the league. All teams and leagues must have money to survive, but not enough moo-lah existed in the Cotton States League. However, special memories remain with the people who recall those unique times with the Hot Springs Bathers.

"I have fought the good fight, I have finished the race, I have kept the faith. Now there is in store for me the crown of righteousness, which the Lord, the righteous Judge, will award to me on that day—and not only to me, but also to all who have longed for his appearing." II Timothy 4:7-8 (NIV)

Chapter 17

Bathers Memories

"How about that?" – Mel Allen (Famed Yankee announcer)

Interviews are from former Bathers and friends of Don Duren

Mamie Ruth Abernathy

Mamie Ruth was associated with the Bathers by working in the Bathers front office during the late 1930s and early 1940s. She recalls typing several letters from Bathers president Lloyd Adams to Judge Kenesaw Mountain Landis, Commissioner of Baseball. Hot Springs got in hot water by covering up players. Hot Springs was one of the many minor league teams that lost players due to the "cover up." She also recalls George Raft, movie star, visiting a Bathers game.

Herb Adams – former Bathers center fielder – 1948

The 1948 Bathers were returning on the team bus from a game in Greenwood, Mississippi. It was about midnight, when suddenly the bus driver and several of the players noticed a body on the side of the road. Startled, the driver stopped and the players rushed off the bus to render care to the person. Suddenly, the man on the side of the road jumped up and ran into the nearby dark woods. The players noticed four or five men followed the man into the darkness for the getaway. Herb surmised that the men were waiting for a car to come by so they could "waylay" the unsuspecting motorist. Those guys didn't expect a bus to stop, especially one that was loaded with professional athletes. The team returned to the bus for the ride back to Hot Springs.

Herb said that in 1948, Rogers Hornsby was his batting instructor. Adams said, "Hornsby could hit better than anyone at 60-years-old." Herb remarked that Hornsby enjoyed betting on the horses. Jack Bales also said that Hornsby enjoyed checking out the horses at Oaklawn.

Orval Allbritton

Orval noted that there was no lighting at Ban Johnson Field, except during game nights. However, the Arkansas Power and Light Company ran special lightning for games. Roy Bosson, sports editor for *The Sentinel-Record/New Era* was the scorekeeper. He used a 40 or 60-watt bulb in his lamp so he could see to keep score. Bosson sat in the grandstands directly in line with the pitchers. The pitchers complained that the light bothered them. Bosson added a lampshade over the bulb and the pitchers were satisfied.

Orval was a member of the Bathers Knothole Gang in 1938. Jack McJunkin organized and paid for the "gang," so kids could get in free to the games. He enjoyed kids having fun, so he did what he could for them.

Mayor Leo McLaughlin of Hot Springs gave the concessions at Rix Stadium (high school football field) and Whittington Park to Jack McJunkin, a city firefighter. Bud Canada's family didn't have much money, so Jack McJunkin helped Bud in several ways. Bud worked at the concession stand at Whittington Park. Bud was a star athlete in football and track at high school and continued his sports career at the University of Arkansas. McJunkin assisted financially to Bud while he was at the university. He was a Korean War veteran and later became a state senator for many years. Canada passed away in Hot Springs in 2009.

Many business owners helped support the Bathers. Dave Lockwood, owner of Lockwood's Men's Store, donated clothing to the Bathers who hit home runs. A barbershop gave discounts or free haircuts to the players. Fincher's restaurant gave the players free or reduced rate on meals. Some property owners reduced the monthly rent for players. Mayor McLaughlin would support the team by asking others to support the Bathers.

For several weeks during the 1940 or 1941 baseball season, Orval noticed two Bathers baseballs that were stuck in the gutter at the top of the grandstands at Ban Johnson Field. He wanted the baseballs, but waited until after the season. On a quiet September Saturday morning, he traveled to the park, climbed a tree next to the grandstand and eased over on the metal roof atop the 30'-40' high grandstand. He crawled over to the gutter, reached into the gutter and retrieved his treasures, which were two weather beaten, used, Cotton States League baseballs. He crawled down and the happy young boy enjoyed the two baseballs for about two years.

Orval recalls, in 1947, the workers were on a fast track to complete building Jaycee Park in order that the facility would be ready for the beginning of the 1947 home opener.

Jack Bales (wife Polly) – former Bathers manager-catcher from 1952-1955

Jack and Polly Bales were married on July 8, 1948. They didn't have much money to spend on a honeymoon, so the newlyweds stayed a few days at "Spike" Hunter's Motel in Hot Springs. Jack and Hunter knew each other and when Jack went to pay his bill, "Spike" told Jack, "You don't owe me anything. That's my wedding present to you and Polly."

After a game, catcher Jack went home and told Polly that he had had a good day today. Jack said, "I only got hit four or five times today by foul balls." In a game at Jaycee Park, a batter swung and tipped the ball. Suddenly, Jack couldn't see the pitcher. The ball stuck between the bars in his catcher's mask.

A batter fouled off a ball and hit Jack on his right bicep. He said it "frogged up" so big he looked like Popeye (a cartoon character of that era). Several batters later, another foul ball hit him on the left bicep and he jumped up, throwing his glove up in the air. It hurt. He told the batter, "You guys are making me look like Charles Atlas." The batter just laughed like crazy.

Jack was playing baseball in Canada and a teammate, Nick Balikes from Florida, came by Jack's apartment and said, "Let's go to breakfast." It was about 7:30 a.m. and they had played the night before. Jack didn't want to get up, but he did. Jack put on his clothes, donned a windbreaker and walked out into the fresh, early morning Canadian air. It was springtime. Jack stopped, turned around and told Nick, "It's too cold to get out here!" Jack went back in the warm, cozy apartment and went back to sleep. He woke up when it warmed up.

Bales claim to fame – He caught Jim Bunning at Davenport, Iowa and Paul Foytack at Thomasville, Georgia. Selected to the Baseball Hall of Fame, Bunning was a United States Senator for several years.

In 1950, Bales' manager in Rome, NY was Eli Gall. Jack was playing about every position on the team. In the dugout before the game, Bales tossed three different gloves into the lap of manager Gall and said, "Pick one!" The gloves included a catcher's mitt, fielder's glove and a first baseman's glove. Jack said, "Where do you want me to play today?" Gall said, "Catch."

Bales said that Hal Martin, as a batter, had tremendous wrists. Jack said that Martin was a "guesser" at the plate. He tried to out-guess the pitcher as to what he was going to throw at him. His strong, quick wrists made up for some of the wrong guesses. He said he saw Martin hit a home run over the left field fence and it landed across the road in the Boys Club field, called Roosters Field. He said that thing probably landed 500 feet from home plate. It was the longest ball he ever saw hit out of Jaycee Park.

Jack didn't drink (and still doesn't), but one evening the players had a party at the home of one of the Bathers. Jack stopped by to see how things were going. Hal Martin had a little too much to drink and he threw-up in the bathroom.

When he did that, he lost his false teeth down the toilet and had to order new ones through the Veterans Administration (VA). Jack said that Martin looked like an old man for several days until the new dentures arrived.

One night at the park, due to a rain shower, the grounds were muddy. He slipped on his "mudder cleats." They were special shoes for playing in wet weather. The Bathers' stadium announcer, Bill Bailey, who also worked at a local radio station, looked at Bales' shoes and said, "What do you have on?"

Jack told him that he was wearing mudders. Bailey told him that they looked terrible. He said, "Jack, if you hit a home run tonight, I'll buy you a pair of shoes." Jack did hit a screaming line drive over the right field fence and when he rounded third base, Jack pointed up to the press box just to let Bailey know that he expects new shoes shortly. Bailey announced to the crowd, "I told Jack Bales that if he hit a home run tonight, I'd buy him a pair of new shoes, but I don't have any money. So, I'm going to pass the hat." Jack said he received about $30-$40 for new shoes.

In a game against El Dorado, popular Pel Austin played left field for the Oilers. Jack, a left-handed hitter, usually hit line drives to right field. However, this time he sliced the ball into left field and it curved away from Austin for a base hit. After rounding first base, Jack was laughing. Pel told him later, "You made me look silly." Pel had never seen a ball curve that much and he was unable to get a glove on it. Pell said the ball came off the bat, "screwy." Jack told Pel that he didn't mean to laugh and make him look like that. Jack said, "But Pel, you did look like a drunk guy going for the ball."

Jack Beavers

"Goobers, goobers, get your goobers…a home run in ever sack," said the peanut salesperson at Jaycee Park back in the 50s. Jack's dad, also named Jack, laughed every time he heard the "peanut woman" chant about the goobers. Jack remembers a Bather that chewed gum and when he came to bat, he stuck it to his cap before he batted. Jack said that Babe Tuckey, Bathers third baseman, went to work at the General Motors plant in Hot Springs following his baseball career with the Bathers. Jack Bales helped get him the job.

Dewey Culliver

Dewey remembered the night, in 1953, when the Bathers attempted to integrate the Cotton States League. Jack Bales warmed up Jim Tugerson, a black player, on the sidelines. When the managers approached home plate with the starting lineups, the umpires told the teams that the game was a forfeit in favor of Jackson, Mississippi because Hot Springs had Tugerson slated to pitch.

In the middle 50s, Dewey was the batboy for Rogers Hornsby's baseball school held at Jaycee Park. Dewey received fifty cents a day and all the broken bats he wanted.

He recalled a major league barnstorming team playing at Jaycee Park. Big Luke Easter, the Cleveland first baseman, hit a home run that cleared the lights in right field. Dewey said it was the longest home run he had ever seen hit.

Dewey sneaked over the fence a few times, just like a lot of kids during that time. He recalled Joe Campbell, the policeman, who was in charge of collecting foul balls from the kids. Campbell was a friend to all the kids in Hot Springs.

Culliver used to razz "Babe" Tuckey when "Babe" played for opposing teams in the league. Babe hit one out once and when he returned to the dugout, he hollered to Dewey in the bleachers, "That one was for you, Dewey."

He recalls Pel Austin used to walk over to the Boys Club field, near Jaycee Park and hit grounders to the kids.

"Spike" Hunter gave Dewey an autographed Roy Campenella baseball.

Dr. Guinn Daniel

In 1938, Guinn was the Bathers' batboy when he was around 15 years old. They played in the Cotton States League and all home games were played at Whittington Park (Ban Johnson Field). It was the first year, after a thirty-year layoff, that the Bathers had a professional baseball team. Once, Guinn actually got to travel on an eastern swing with the team. They rode Wolf Bus Line over to Helena, Arkansas and several Mississippi cities that were members of the Cotton States League. He roomed with Robbie Robinson, third baseman, one of the younger players on the team. They stayed in hotels and ate in the coffee shops free. Guinn was living the good life.

Guinn lived in South Hot Springs and he said that while he was batboy he had more friends than anybody in his neighborhood. He gave his friends discarded gloves, broken bats, old baseballs and other rejected equipment. On "George Raft night," at Whittington Park, he obtained Raft's autograph on a baseball. Raft was a movie star during the 30s-50s. There was a big crowd around Raft, but soon, due to rain, Raft left and the game was a washout. Guinn's favorite Bathers were Walt Schafer (P-OF), Joe Barnett (SS) and Art "Robby" Robinson (3B).

Dr. Daniel graduated from Baylor Dental School in Dallas in the 1950s. Shortly after he began practice in Hot Springs, he received a phone call one evening from Dr. D. J. Van Patter, the local oral surgeon. He informed Dr. Daniel that Earl "Oil" Smith was in the hospital with displaced jaw fractures and Dr. Van needed Dr. Daniel's help "in putting Earl back together." Dr. Van said. "Earl had been in a bar-room fight and some guy had really worked Earl over with a metal pipe." Dr. Daniel got to the hospital as fast as he could go. He went directly to the operating room where Dr. Van introduced Guinn to Earl, "which elicited a grunt." Dr. Van told Earl that he was going to receive general anesthesia so they could begin to work on him. Earl began to shake his head, "No." To correct the damage done to his mouth and face, the doctors told him that it was going to be a long and painful procedure. Earl continued to relate to the doctors that he didn't want any anesthesia. The doctors, under the circumstances, never saw anyone refuse anesthesia before surgery. Dr. Daniel's letter continues below:

Finally, Dr. Van Patter said, 'Okay, Earl, we'll start, but if you find you want sedation, raise your hand and we'll sedate you.'

Over an hour later, we had Earl back together and stabilized and Earl had not once made a sound of any kind.

Dr. Van told Earl that we needed to admit him to the hospital overnight to take care of any complications that might arise. Again, Earl began shaking his head-no.

Knowing that he wasn't about to change his mind, we gave him instructions on post-op care. He rolled off the bed, mumbled, 'Thank you,' and left.

Today, hospital procedure requires that patients, upon dismissal, are placed in a wheelchair & rolled outside the hospital.

To this day, there is no doubt in my mind, that Earl Smith is the toughest man I've ever met. However, Earl had a start on self-sedation with that fermented stuff that comes in bottles.

Paul Dean, Jr.

The Bather that Paul (PJ) remembers most is Jack Bales.

Mike Dugan

Mike was too young to remember the Bathers, but he did attend games. He said his grandfather and great uncle took him to the games in a stroller. However, it was a clandestine act. The two men hid refreshments in Mike's stroller. "Nuf said!"

Ron Garner

When Ron didn't have the price of admission, he would sneak into Jaycee Park by climbing the fence behind the bleachers. He said that one guy was the "lookout" for the cops. Ron said that the cops probably knew they were sneaking in.

In 1955, Garner worked his way close enough to the visitor's dugout (Monroe) to see Roy and Ray Mantle, Mickey's twin brothers. In 1950, Ron watched Ryne Duren pitch for Pine Bluff against the Bathers. Ryne, with his coke-bottle style lens, kept the Bathers loose in the batter's box. The pitcher had amazing speed on his fastball, but his control was sometimes lacking.

Few youngsters had the opportunity to talk with Paul "Daffy" Dean. Once, Ron sat in the grandstands behind home plate and listened to Dean talk baseball.

Ron recalls watching games as he sat on the "big hill" overlooking Jaycee Park. He may not have had money or wanted to save his coins. If kids grabbed a foul ball and took it to the ticket window, they would admit you free to the game.

Price Gillenwater

He used to sell soft drinks at Jaycees Park and his take was one penny per drink.

M. D. Graham – Bathers Batboy - 1953

M. D. and Billy Bales (Jack's younger brother) were batboys in 1953. M. D. said that Danny Caccavo, Bathers pitcher, gave him his old glove and he kept it for years. His favorite players were Caccavo, Alex Cosmidis and Hal Martin. Many of the players chewed Beech Nut Chewing Tobacco. Since M. D. wanted to be like the players, he stuck a wad of the tobacco in his mouth… yes, that's right, he got very sick. He never chewed again. M. D. mowed Owney Madden's lawn on Grand Avenue. At one time, Madden owned the "Cotton Club" in New York.

Sara Baswell Harris (Mrs. Don Harris)

Sara attended a Bathers game when she was in the seventh grade. Her family sat in the bleachers, which were on the first base side. The game was running late, so she laid her head on her mother's lap and fell asleep. The family scrambled from an on-coming overthrown ball at first base. The ball hit her face and broke her nose. She had breathing problems for many years.

Dick Holden

As a 14-year-old, Dick was the assistant Bathers concessionaire for a few weeks when Rex McMahan was the manager of the concessions at Jaycee Park. Rex would order all the food, drinks and refreshments for the Bathers games. When Rex resigned to go to work at the GM plant, Dick took over the head job. When Dick was the assistant, he made $2.00 a night, but when he became "the man" his salary shot up to $5.00 a night for all home games. Dick said that was good money for a 15 year old in the 1950s. He also noted that it was much responsibility. However, he related that he learned much about the business world working at the park. He worked there for two summers.

He also recalls Hal Martin. Martin was a tremendous hitter and when the announcer called Martin's name on the loudspeaker, Dick would stop what he was doing and look through a hole in the wall to watch one of his favorite players swing the lumber. Dick said he could almost sense when Martin was going to hit a homer.

Dick remembers Adrian Burk who played first base for the visiting Monroe Sports in 1953. Following a night game at Jaycee Park, Burk was on the team bus ready to leave the park and he asked Dick to bring him a Coca-Cola. Dick fetched the drink and Burk handed him a ten-dollar bill. Holden didn't have change and told Burk to hold up the bus while he ran to get change. Burk told Dick, "That's okay, just keep the ten."

In 1953, Burk, former quarterback for Baylor University, was the quarterback for the Philadelphia Eagles. When he played with Monroe, he was playing baseball in the off-season to keep in shape for football. Burk passed away in Texas in 2003.

Dick recalls the announcer at Jaycee Park roaring out the winner of the lucky number listed in the Bathers baseball program. The winner received a modest prize each night. The announcer excitedly said, "The winner is, Jackie, the blind man's son." The sympathetic fans simultaneously said, "Ah!" Applause followed. There was a man known in Hot Springs as "Blind Bill" Durant and everyone assumed the son of Durant won the prize. Then, the announcer informed the crowd that, "The winner is Jackie Corder, son of the owner of the Hot Springs Venetian Blind and Awning Company."

Dutch Howard

During the summer of 1948, Dutch attended a night game at Jaycee Park and the operator of the manual scoreboard in the outfield was a "no-show." Mrs. Ensminger, secretary for the Bathers, asked Dutch if he would like to substitute for the scoreboard operator. Dutch took the job and the scoreboard operator for about a month. Dutch was in high school and the extra $2.00 a night came in handy.

Earl Hudson

At a Bathers' batting practice, Earl noticed that someone painted an orange. Of course, it was white and the artist drew stitches to look like a baseball. The pitcher threw it to an unsuspecting batter. The batter swing and orange juice went all over the batter. Earl believed that once during a game, a batter tried to use a fungo bat at the plate. Earl isn't sure if the umpire caught the illegal play in time.

Don Kilgore

As a youngster, Don lived near Jaycee Park, so he attended many games and practices. He ventured over to the Bathers' practices and grabbed baseballs that the players hit over the fence. The Bathers gave him several broken bats and Don would tape them up and use them during sand lot games. Don also recalls that several of the Bathers lived in a boarding house across the street from what is currently the YWCA on Quapaw.

Jack McMahan

As a kid, Jack sold programs at Jaycee Park. In high school, Jack was a tremendous American Legion pitcher. Once he threw batting practice for the Bathers. McMahan pitched against Jack Bales during batting practice and Bales hit a pitch out of the park.

The Bathers considered allowing Jack to continue to pitch batting practice regularly while he was in high school. The front office decided against it due to the liability issues. Upon high school graduation, the Bathers offered him $400 a month to pitch for them, but he turned it down because the Yankees organization talked him into playing in their organization. He saw visions of pinstripes dancing in his head, so he decided to sign with the Yankees organization. He said the Cardinals were going to offer him a $20,000 bonus to sign with them, but nobody contacted him before he signed with the Yankees farm system.

In the Three-I League, Jack pitched against Dan Phalen, a popular Bathers player.

Rex McMahan

During the early 50s, Rex sold programs, cushions and later became the manager of the concessions for the Bathers at Jaycee Park. He umpired in the Cotton States League and the Southern Association. He, Jim Elder and Dorsey Roddenberry umpired many black baseball teams that played at Jaycee Park. He said he saw some real good players back then. He recalled two Hot Springs policemen, "Pee Wee" Roberts and "Papa Meathouse," who worked most of the games that involved the black teams. He said the stands were full of fans when the black teams played at Hot Springs.

He umpired the Bathers a few times and he recalled Jack Bales was upset at one of his calls. Bales kept scooting back toward the umpire McMahan. The two knew each other, so Bales thought he could get away with a little more than usual. Rex put his knee in the back of Bales and told Bales, "That's far enough, Jack."

Tom Nichols

Tom is currently employed at KVRE – 92.9 in Hot Springs Village. He lived near Jaycee Park when he was a youngster and he recalls climbing over the fence to watch the games.

Wayne Rice

Wayne recalls riding his bicycle from Park Avenue out to Jaycee Park, leaving it outside the park and it would be there following the game. He also remembers that if you caught a foul ball, he could return it to the ticket window and get in to the game free.

Dr. Pete Smith

In the early 50s, Pete would bag and sell peanuts for a nickel at Jaycee Park. He made a whopping penny off each bag he sold. His grandfather, A. R. Smith, owner of Smith Printers, had a box seat and Pete sat there with him many times. From time to time, his grandfather gave "suggestions" to the Bathers managers since the box seats were located next to the dugout. For a youngster to be that close to the Bathers dugout was a tremendous experience.

Pete was a member of the Bathers Knothole Gang. Also, if he brought back a foul ball that was hit outside the park, the Bathers would give him 10 cents. Sometimes that was tough duty, because other kids had the same idea.

John David Stone

In 1953, John remembers going to a Bathers/Greenville game with his mother and two sisters, Peggy and Kathy, at Jaycee Park. My mother had never been to a baseball game. During the game, the announcer called out several lucky ticket numbers, but each time our family barely missed winning. After eight innings, they decided to head home. As they walked up the hill to the parking lot, they heard the announcer call his Mother's lucky number. One problem, "Mother had thrown away her ticket." Remembering where she tossed the lucky ticket, they hurried back inside the park and found the castoff ticket waiting for them on the ground. The family excitedly hurried back to the box office to claim Mrs. Stone's special prize, a bottle of champagne. The announcer proclaimed the name of the lucky number winner to everyone.

Well, there was another little problem. David's mother was an active member of Second Baptist Church. The church was the largest congregation in the city. John said, "She never had an alcoholic drink in her life." Around 600 fans attended the game that night and John David said, "Probably 200 of them were members of Second Baptist." Later, the Stone family presented the champagne as a wedding gift to a family member. No telling how much teasing she received from church members.

Ed White is John David's uncle. The Chicago White Sox signed Ed to a minor league contract in the early 1950s. In 1954 and 1955, Ed pitched for the Bathers. In his first game for the Bathers in 1954, 23-year-old White was "pumped." He told his nephew John David, that he was going to have a good day against the El Dorado Oilers, the next day, at Jaycee Park. The next day, John David was playing a baseball game at Rooster's Field, a Boys Club baseball field, located next to Jaycee Park. At the same time, White and the Bathers were involved in their game at Jaycee Park. John David could hear the crowd noise and the sound of batted balls rattling against the wooden left field fence. He said that three balls didn't rattle, because they flew over the fence and landing on Rooster's Field where John David was playing.

The day after both games, John David asked Ed how it went. Dejectedly, Ed replied, "They really rocked me!" John David said that he hadn't seen Ed that humble in his life. John David said that they finished their Boys Club game with the three balls that soared over the fence from Jaycee Park.

Mrs. Tom Ward – widow of former Bathers pitcher - 1953

In 1948, Tom graduated from Jackson High School in Alabama and immediately joined the United States Air Force. While serving a four-year hitch in the military he played baseball at several air bases. In 1952, upon his discharge he married Dorothy. Tom went to spring training with the Tulsa Oilers in 1953, a Cincinnati Reds farm team. He signed with Duluth, Minnesota, but due to the cold weather, which he didn't like, moved to the south. Tom pitched for the Bathers for the remainder of the 1953 season at a monthly salary of $300.00.

Mrs. Ward recalls that they didn't have much money to spare, so when Tom hit a home run, he received a free chicken dinner. She said it was a great meal because they were hungry. Soon, Tom and Dorothy were parents. Dorothy recalls that when Tom left on a Bathers road trip, she had one quarter. She saved the quarter until Tom returned home. She saved it just in case the baby needed something while Tom was gone. At the end of the 1953 season, the Bathers received gifts from the fans and front office. She said it was like Christmas in August.

On March 1, 1954, he received a letter from manager Ken Blackman of the Duluth Dukes Baseball Club. The manager wanted Tom to call him collect if he was interested in playing for the Dukes. On March 19, 1954, Bill McKechnie, Jr., farm system director of the Cincinnati Reds, wrote Tom the following letter from the Cincinnati minor league training base in Douglas, GA.

'I hope you can see your way clear to being with us. I doubt strongly that Duluth can raise their offer ($300.00) and we cannot give you a higher contract until you show you can play higher ball. Let me hear from you. Best wishes, Yours, Wm. B. McKechnie, Jr.'

Tom decided to retire from baseball and go into private business. He passed away on January 8, 2008.

Ed White -former Bathers pitcher - 1954-1955

He said it was a lot of fun playing with the Bathers. During his first time on the mound for the Bathers, the bases were loaded and he struck out the sides. His former Brooklyn farm team wanted him to be a relief pitcher but he wanted to be a starter. He said he should have listened to them.

Tony Zini (and A.J.) - former Bather's catcher – 1947-1948

Jim Elder was umpiring at HS and Tony was catching. Jim just returned from a long trip and he told Zini that he was so tired that he was going to lean on him during the game. "Don't give me a rough time today because I'm tired," said Elder. Zini said that he called a good game.

Harry Chozen, Greenville manager, knew that Zini was in a batting slump. Chozen told Zini that his bat was too heavy. Chozen said, "Here use mine." Zini said the bat was one of the lightest bat's he'd ever used. That night Zini hit two homers and Chozen said after the game, "Maybe I should have given you the bat <u>after</u> the game."

Zini recalled that in 1948, a leg injury curtailed left fielder Dick Fuller's playing time. Since Fuller was out of action, on road trips he assisted Bill Bailey, the regular Bathers radio announcer in the press box. Fuller knew the Bathers signals and he told the radio audience what the Bathers planned to do <u>before it happened</u>.

Catcher Zini and Ed McGhee, outfielder on the 1948 Bathers, were second cousins. Tony believed that Art Hamilton was the best pitcher on the team when they were Bathers.

Don Duren

Many of us who played American Legion baseball attended several Bathers games in 1954. Paul Dean, Jr., known as "PJ," pitched on our American Legion team. Once during a Bathers game, he sat behind me in the stands. Suddenly, I felt a whack on the top of my head. "PJ" popped me in the head with his long index finger. Man, he really got my attention. He told me that he had done the same thing to other unsuspecting individuals.

In 1951, when I was 12 years old, I was selected "Boys Club Player of the Week" and was the Bathers batboy at one of the games. The best part about it was that I sat in the dugout with the

Bathers. Radio station KTHS interviewed me at the station. Royal Crown Bottling Co. presented me with a six-pack of Royal Crown Cola.

In 1950, following a game, my Dad and I met Ryne Duren, under the stands at Jaycee Park when he pitched for the Pine Bluff Judges. My dad asked him about his family history. He was from Wisconsin, so we didn't know if we were related.

Paul Dean Jr. was a member of our American Legion baseball team in 1954. His father, Paul (Daffy) Dean owned the Bathers during the early part of 1954 season. The senior Dean would drive his car to our practices. After practice, several of us would stand around his black Buick and talk with him for a few minutes. I noticed tobacco juice on the outside of the car door. Though I enjoyed talking with him, I decided the best thing to do was to leave a little space between the car and me. The claim to fame for all of us on that American Legion team was that we played against Brooks Robinson at a Legion tournament in Little Rock at Lamar Porter Field (1954).

"...but those who hope in the Lord will renew their strength. They will soar on wings like eagles; they will run and not grow weary, they will walk and not be faint" (Isaiah 40:31).

Appendix

Cotton States League Standings
1938-1941 and 1947-1955

1938 - CSL Regular Season Standings

CSL President – J. Walter Morris

Team	W	L	Pct.	GB
Greenville Bucks	88	50	.638	—-
Helena Seaporters	80	57	.584	7.5
Monroe White Sox	78	60	.565	10
El Dorado Lions	74	61	.548	12.5
Clarksdale Red Sox	66	71	.482	21.5
Pine Bluff Judges	60	73	.451	25.5
Greenwood Dodgers	55	83	.399	33
Hot Springs Bathers	45	91	.331	42

1938 – CSL Playoff Results

Winner	Loser	W-L Record
Monroe	Helena	3-1
Greenville	El Dorado	3-1
	Championship	
Monroe	Greenville	4-2

1938 – CSL Individual Top Stats

Player	Team	Stat	Total
Mike Powers	El Dorado	BA	.345
Rudy Tone	El Dorado	Runs	139
Kirby Farrell	Greenville	Hits	182
Mike Powers	El Dorado	RBI	111
Jay Kirke, Jr.	Pine Bluff	HR	18
Buford Rhea	Monroe	SB	79
Chuck Hawley	El Dorado	Wins	22
Chuck Hawley	El Dorado	SO	174
Boyd Perry	Monroe	Pct.	.895; 17-2
Boyd Perry	Monroe	ERA	1.71

1939 – CSL Regular Season Standings

CSL President – Judge Emmet Harty

Team	W	L	Pct.	GB
Monroe White Sox	92	46	.667	—-
Clarksdale Red Sox	77	63	.550	16
Greenwood Crackers	71	63	.530	19
Hot Springs Bathers	**71**	**67**	**.514**	**21**
Greenville Buckshots	61	75	.449	30
El Dorado Lions	59	75	.440	31
Pine Bluff Judges	57	76	.429	32.5
Helena Seaporters	58	81	.417	34.5

1939 – CSL Playoff Results

Winner	Loser	W-L Record
Hot Springs	**Monroe**	**3-2**
Greenwood	Clarksdale	3-1
	Championship	
Greenwood	**Hot Springs**	**4-1**

1939 – CSL Top Individual Stats

Player	Team	Stat	Total
Steve Carter	**Hot Springs**	**BA**	**.369**
Andy Gilbert	Clarksdale	Runs	136
John Rowe	Helena	Hits	202
Steve Carter	**Hot Springs**	**RBI**	**132**
John Yelovic	Monroe	Wins	21
Earl Harrist	El Dorado	SO	223
James Hogan	Helena	ERA	3.14
Al Gardella	**Hot Springs**	**HR**	**32**

1940 – CSL Regular Season Standings

CSL President – Judge Emmet Harty

Team	W	L	Pct.	GB
Monroe White Sox	82	45	.646	—-
El Dorado Oilers	78	57	.578	8
Helena Seaporters	71	60	.542	13
Greenville Buckshots	70	69	,504	18
Hot Springs Bathers	**67**	**71**	**.486**	**20.5**
Clarksdale Red Sox	61	75	.449	25.5
Greenwood Choctaws	58	76	.433	27.5
Pine Bluff Judges	49	83	.371	35.5

1940 - CSL Playoff Results

Winner	Loser	W-L Record
Monroe	Greenville	3-1
El Dorado	Helena	3-1
	Championship	
Monroe	El Dorado	4-1

1940 – CSL Top Individual Stats

Player	Team	Stat	Total
Thurman Tucker	Clarksdale	BA	.390
Monte Duncan	**Hot Springs**	**Runs**	**127**
Jack Grantham	Clarksdale	Hits	194
Ed Zydowski	**Hot Springs**	**RBI**	**157**
Ed Zydowski	**Hot Springs**	**HR**	***25**
Monte Duncan	**Hot Springs**	**HR**	***25**
Boyd Perry	Monroe	Wins	21
Carl Wentz	El Dorado	SO	238
Dave Smith	Greenville	ERA	2.96

* Tie

1941 – CSL Regular Season Standings

CSL President – Judge Emmet Harty

Team	W	L	Pct.	GB
Monroe White Sox	83	55	.601	— -
Hot Springs Bathers	**77**	**60**	**.562**	**5.5**
Greenville Buckshots	76	63	.547	7.5
Vicksburg Hill Billies	76	64	.543	8
Helena Seaporters	72	66	.522	11
Texarkana Twins	65	73	.471	18
El Dorado Oilers	54	82	.397	28
Clarksdale/Marshall *	48	88	.353	34

*Clarksdale, MS (33-47) moved to Marshall, TX July 10

1941 – CSL Playoff Results

Winner	Loser	W-L Record
Vicksburg	Monroe	3-2
Hot Springs	**Greenville**	**3-0**
	Championship	
Hot Springs	**Vicksburg**	**4-0**

1941 Individual Top Stats

Player	Team	Stat	Total
Roy Bueschen	Greenville	BA	.370
Colman Powell	**Hot Springs**	**Runs**	**136**
Roy Marion	**Hot Springs**	**Hits**	**207**
Mike Powers	**Hot Springs**	**RBI**	**137**
Harry Kelley	Vicksburg	Wins	22
Bill Reeder	Monroe	SO	189
Charles Pescod	**Hot Springs**	**ERA**	**3.00**
Merv Connors	Texarkana	HR	29

1942-1946 (War Years – No League)

1947 Regular Season Standings

CSL President – James Griffith

Team	W	L	Pct.	GB
Greenwood Dodgers	92	38	.708	—-
Greenville Bucks	84	46	.646	8
El Dorado Oilers	61	69	.469	31
Clarksdale Planters	59	71	.454	33
Hot Springs Bathers	**49**	**81**	**.377**	**43**
Helena Seaporters	45	91	.345	45.5

1947 CSL Playoffs Results

Winner	Loser	W-L Record
Greenwood	Clarksdale	3-1
Greenville	El Dorado	3-2
	Championship	
Greenwood	Greenville	4-3

1947 – CSL Individual Top Stats

Player	Team	Stat	Total
Ernest Davis	El Dorado	BA	.340
Roy Lee	Greenwood	*Runs	102
Paul Mauldin	Clarksdale	*Runs	102
H. G. Talbert	Helena	*Runs	102
Paul Mauldin	Clarksdale	Hits	166
Floyd Fogg	Clarksdale	HR	27
Leslie Edwards	Greenville	#Wins	21
Russ Oppliger	Greenwood	#Wins	21
Bob Schultz	Greenville	SO	274
Billy Briggs	Greenville	ERA	1.93
Floyd Fogg	Clarksdale	RBI	112

* Tie - #Tie

1948 CSL Regular Season Standings

CSL President – James Griffith

Team	W	L	Pct.	GB
Greenwood Dodgers	92	44	.676	—-
Clarksdale Planters	85	53	.616	8
Hot Springs Bathers	**82**	**56**	**.594**	**11**
Natchez Indians	74	64	.536	19
Greenville Bucks	65	73	.471	28
Helena Seaporters	54	82	.397	38
Pine Bluff Cardinals	50	87	.365	42.5
El Dorado Oilers	48	91	.345	45.5

1948 CSL Playoff Results

Winner	Loser	W-L Record
Greenwood	Natchez	3-0
Hot Springs	**Clarksdale**	**3-0**
	Championship	
Hot Springs	**Greenwood**	**4-3**

1948 CSL Individual Top Stats

Player	Team	Stat	Total
Herb Adams	**Hot Springs**	**BA**	**.375**
Herb Adams	**Hot Springs**	**Runs**	**123**
Herb Adams	**Hot Springs**	**Hits**	**223**
Jack Parks	Natchez	RBI	96
Jack Parks	Natchez	HR	22
Bill Upton	Clarksdale	Wins	21
Ed Albrecht	Pine Bluff	SO	195
Labe Dean	Greenwood	ERA	1.34

1948 CSL Most Valuable Player – Herb Adams – Hot Springs

1949 CSL Regular Season Standings

CSL President – Al Haraway

Team	W	L	Pct.	GB
Greenwood Dodgers	84	56	.600	—
El Dorado Oilers	80	59	.576	3.5
Natchez Indians	73	66	.533	10.5
Pine Bluff Cardinals	72	66	.533	11
Greenville Bucks	72	67	.518	11.5
Hot Springs Bathers	**64**	**75**	**.460**	**19.5**
Clarksdale Planters	58	80	.420	25
Helena Seaporters	53	87	.378	31

1949 CSL Playoff Results

Winner	Loser	W-L Results
Natchez	El Dorado	4-3
Pine Bluff	Greenwood	4-2
	Championship	
Natchez	Pine Bluff	4-1

1949 CSL Individual Top Stats

Player	Team	Stat	Total
Harold Seawright	Greenville	BA	.325
Ed Sudol	El Dorado	Runs	106
Harold Seawright	Greenville	Hits	172
Harold Seawright	Greenville	RBI	108
Dan Phalen	**Hot Springs**	**HR**	**22**
Ed Albrecht	Pine Bluff	Wins	29
Ed Albrecht	Pine Bluff	SO	389
Stan Poloczyk	Greenwood	ERA	1.82

1950 CSL Regular Season Standings

CSL President – Al Haraway

Team	W	L	Pct.	GB
Pine Bluff Judges	84	54	.609	—-
Monroe Sports	81	56	.591	2.5
Hot Springs Bathers	**77**	**60**	**.562**	**6.5**
Natchez Indians	78	61	.561	6.5
Greenwood Dodgers	69	69	.500	15
Greenville Bucks	63	75	.457	21
Clarksdale Planters	62	76	.449	22
El Dorado Oilers	38	101	.273	46.5

1950 CSL Playoff Results

Winner	Loser	W-L Results
Hot Springs	**Monroe**	**4-2**
Natchez	Pine Bluff	4-1
	Championship	
Hot Springs	**Natchez**	**4-3**

1950 CSL Individual Top Stats

Player	Team	Stat	Total
Ben Cantrell	Pine Bluff	BA	.363
Harry Schwegman	Pine Bluff	Runs	150
Ben Cantrell	Pine Bluff	Hits	189
Ben Cantrell	Pine Bluff	RBI	144
Dick Adkins	Natchez	HR	25
Ryne Duren	Pine Bluff	SO	233
Ronald Lurk	Monroe	ERA	1.55
Clifford Coggin	Monroe	Wins	21
Clifford Coggin	Monroe	Pct.	.808, 21-5

1951 CSL Regular Season Standings

CSL President – Al Haraway

Team	W	L	Pct.	GB
Monroe Sports	89	51	.636	—-
Greenwood Dodgers	83	57	.593	6
Pine Bluff Judges	82	58	.586	7
Natchez Indians	79	61	.564	10
El Dorado Oilers	77	62	.554	11.5
Hot Springs Bathers	**53**	**86**	**.381**	**35.5**
Clarksdale Planters	53	87	.379	36
Greenville Bucks	43	97	.307	46

1951 CSL Playoff Results

Winner	Loser	W-L Results
Natchez	Monroe	4-3
Pine Bluff	Greenwood	4-3
	Championship	
Natchez	Pine Bluff	4-1

1951 CSL Individual Top Stats

Player	Team	Stat	Total
James Gilbert	Natchez	BA	.352
Fred Boiko	Pine Bluff	Runs	125
Fred Boiko	Pine Bluff	Hits	182
Steve Molinari	Pine Bluff	RBI	106
Peter Konyar	Pine Bluff	HR	27
Billy Muffett	Monroe	*Wins	22
Vachel Perkins	Pine Bluff	*Wins	22
Bud Black	Pine Bluff	SO	171
Billy Muffett	Monroe	ERA	2.25
Billy Muffett	Monroe	*Pct.	.710, 22-9
Vachel Perkins	Pine Bluff	*Pct.	.710, 22-9

* Tie

1952 CSL Regular Season Standings

CSL President – Al Haraway

Team	W	L	Pct.	GB
Meridian Millers	78	48	.619	—
Natchez Indians	73	53	.579	5
Greenwood Dodgers	70	56	.556	8
Monroe Sports	66	60	.524	12
El Dorado Oilers	65	61	.516	13
Pine Bluff Judges	62	64	.492	16
Greenville Bucks	47	79	.373	31
Hot Springs Bathers	**43**	**83**	**.341**	**35**

1952 CSL Playoff Results

Winner	Loser	W-L Results
Meridian	Monroe	4-2
Natchez	Greenwood	4-2
	Championship	
Meridian	Natchez	4-3

1952 CSL Individual Stats

Player	Team	Stat	Total
Don Allen	Natchez	BA	.335
Gene Pompelia	Meridian	Runs	102
John P. Jones	Monroe	Hits	163
John P. Jones	Monroe	RBI	91
Ray Perry	El Dorado	HR	15
Bob Harrison	Meridian	Wins	24
John Forizs	Greenwood	SO	252
Bob Harrison	Meridian	ERA	1.82

1953 CSL Regular Season Standings

CSL President – Al Haraway

Team	W	L	Pct.	GB
Meridian Millers	79	46	.632	—-
El Dorado Oilers	67	59	.532	12.5
Pine Bluff Judges	65	60	.520	14
Jackson Senators	63	61	.508	15.5
Hot Springs Bathers	**63**	**61**	**.508**	**15.5**
Greenville Bucks	63	62	.504	16
Natchez Indians	50	75	.400	29
Monroe Sports	50	76	.397	29.5

1953 CSL Playoff Results

Winners	Losers	W-L Results
*Jackson	**Hot Springs**	1-0
Meridian	Jackson	4-2
El Dorado	Pine Bluff	4-0
	Championship	
Meridian	El Dorado	4-0

*Tie – 1 Game Playoff

1953 CSL Individual Stats

Player	Team	Stat	Total
Hugh Glaze	Meridian	BA	.355
Hal Martin	**Hot Springs**	**Runs**	**127**
Hal Martin	**Hot Springs**	**Hits**	**169**
Hal Martin	**Hot Springs**	**RBI**	**111**
Hal Martin	**Hot Springs**	**HR**	**41**
Bob Harrison	Meridian	Wins	19
Bob Harrison	Meridian	SO	172
Bob Harrison	Meridian	ERA	2.15

1954 CSL Regular Season Standings

CSL President – Judge Emmet Harty

Team	W	L	Pct.	GB
Greenville Bucks	80	39	.672	— -
El Dorado Oilers	79	39	.669	.5
Meridian Millers	62	56	.525	17.5
Monroe Sports	53	67	.442	27.5
Pine Bluff Judges	47	71	.398	32.5
Hot Springs Bathers	**35**	**84**	**.294**	**45**

1954 Playoff Results

Winner	Loser	W-L Results
Greenville	Monroe	4-1
El Dorado	Meridian	4-3
	Championship	
El Dorado	Greenville	4-2

1954 CSL Individual Stats

Player	Team	Stat	Total
Frank Walenga	El Dorado	BA	.382
Banks McDowell	Greenville	Runs	121
Frank Walenga	El Dorado	Hits	174
Frank Walenga	El Dorado	RBI	125
Pel Austin	El Dorado	HR	28
Roy Jayne	Meridian	Wins	20
Bobby J. Brown	El Dorado	Wins	20
Bill Halley	Monroe	SO	176
Jerry Dean	Greenville	ERA	1.80

1955 CSL Regular Season Standings

CSL President – Judge Emmet Harty

Team	W	L	Pct.	GB
Monroe Sports	76	41	.650	—-
El Dorado Oilers	70	50	.583	7.5
Pine Bluff/Meridian#	59	56	.513	16
Hot Springs Bathers	**57**	**62**	**.479**	**20**
Greenville Bucks	49	69	.415	27.5
Vicksburg Hill Billies	43	76	.361	34

 # Pine Bluff Judges team moved to Meridian Millers

1955 CSL Playoff Results

Winner	Loser	W-L Results
Monroe	**Hot Springs**	4-0
El Dorado	Meridian	4-1
	Championship	
Monroe	El Dorado	4-3

1955 CSL Individual Stats

Player	Team	Stat	Total
Jim Davenport	El Dorado	BA	.363
Bob Maness	Monroe	Runs	109
*Jim Davenport	El Dorado	Hits	147
*Bob Maness	Monroe	Hits	147
Marshall Gilbert	Monroe	HR	19
Marshall Gilbert	Monroe	RBI	101
Richard Mailbauer	El Dorado	Wins	17
Richard Mailbauer	El Dorado	SO	197
Edward Dick	Monroe	ERA	1.77

*Tie

Bathers Owners, Managers and Major League Affiliation

Year	Owner	Manager	Affiliation/*working agreement
1938	Group/Lloyd Adams, president	"Spike" Hunter – Hal Grant (temp.), Joe Barnett	Independent/*Detroit Tigers
1939	Group/ Lloyd Adams, president	Conard Fisher	Independent/*Detroit Tigers
1940	Group/Lloyd Adams, president	Cecil Combs	Independent/*Detroit Tigers & Nashville Vols. (Southern Assoc.)
1941	Group/Lloyd Adams, president	Mike Powers	Independent/Nashville Vols (SA)
1947	Blake Harper –In May - sold to Chicago White Sox	Joe Santomauro – Joe Kuhel	Chicago White Sox
1948	Chicago White Sox	Joe Holden – George Sobek	Chicago White Sox
1949	Chicago White Sox	Pete Fox – Glen "Gabby" Stewart	Chicago White Sox
1950	Herb Anderton	John Antonelli	*Chicago White Sox
1951	Herb Anderton - Jr. Chamber of Commerce	Rex Carr	Chicago White Sox
1952	A.G. Crawford, Tom Stough	Bob Benish – Jim Hogan	Independent/ *Texas City Texans Class B
1953	H. M. & Garrett Britt, A.G Crawford & Lewis Goltz	Vern Shetler	Independent
1954	Paul Dean – Charlie Williamson	Paul Dean – Jack Bales (temp) – Lou "Red" Lucas – Jack Bales	*St. Louis Cardinals/ Columbus, GA
1955	Charlie Williamson & Mickey O'Neil	Joe Lutz – Mickey O'Neil	*Kansas City Athletics

Team affiliation & other information before 1938 are N/A except 1898 – Mgr. Beatty, 1906 - Mgr. Jack Love & 1908 - Mgr. Art Riggs. Roster & information of all teams are found at www.baseball-reference.com

Major League Players Who Played for Hot Springs

Year in HS	Player	Pos.	ML Teams	Years in ML
1887	Gus Creely	SS	StL (AA)	1890
	John Godar	OF	Balt (NL)	1892
	Frank Hoffman	P	KCC (AA)	1888
	Emmett Rogers	C	Tol (AA)	1890
1898	George Bristow	OF	Clv (NL)	1899
1908	Jim "Hippo" Vaughn	P	NYY (AL), Wash (AL) & CHC (NL)	1908-1921
1938	Otis Brannan	2B	StL (AL)	1928-1929
	Johnny Sain	P	Bos (N), NYY (A), KCA (A)	1942-1955
	Floyd Speer	P	CHW (A)	1943-1944
1939	Ed Albosta	P	Bkn (NL), Pit (NL)	1941 & 1946
	Al Gardella	1B/OF	NYG (NL)	1945
	Jim Hickey	P	Bos (NL)	1942 & 1944
1940	Charlie Mead	OF	NYG (NL)	1943-1945
	Cecil Combs - Mgr	OF	CWS (A)	1914
1941	Mike Powers - Mgr	OF	CLV (A)	1932-1933
	Dutch McCall	P	CHC (NL)	1948
	Ted Pawelek	C	CHC (NL)	1946
1947	Joe Kuhel - Mgr	1B	Wsh (AL), CWS (A)	1930-1947
	Pete Wojey	P	Bkn (N), Det (A)	1954-1957

1948	Herb Adams	OF	CWS (A)	1948-1950
	Ed McGhee	OF	CWS (A), Phi (A)	1950 & 1953-1955
	Dick Strahs	P	CWS (A)	1954
	Joe Holden – Mgr.	C	Phil (N)	1934-1936
1949	Bill Fischer	P	CWS (A), Det (A), Wsh (A), KCA (A), Min (A)	1956-1964
	Glen "Gabby" Stewart -Mgr.	INF	NYG (N), Phi (N)	1940 & 1943-1944
	Pete Fox – Mgr.	OF	Det (A), Bos (A)	1933-1945
1950	John Antonelli - Mgr	2B/3B	Phi (N), StL (N)	1944-1945
1952	Jim Hogan - Mgr	C	Bos (N), NY (N) & Wash (A)	1925-1937
	Bert Shepard	P	Wsh (A)	1945
1954	Paul "Daffy" Dean – Mgr./Owner	P	StL (N), NYG (N), StL (A)	1934-1941 & 1943
1955	George Brunet	P	LAA (A), Wsh (A), Hou (N), At (N), Balt (A)	1956-1971
	Bill Kirk	P	KCA (A)	1961
	Joe Lutz - Mgr.	1B	StL (A)	1951
	Mickey O'Neil - Mgr.	C	Bos (N), Wash (A) & NYG (N)	1919-1927

History of Baseball Parks in Hot Springs

Baseball Park – (behind Courthouse-?)

Year	League	Class	Team
1887	Southwestern League	N/A	Hot Springs Blues

Location – Ouachita Avenue (Behind Courthouse)

Dimensions – N/A

Capacity – 500 - ?

Whittington Park (1894-1910)

Year	League	Class	Team
1894	Arkansas State League	N/A	Hot Springs Bathers
1897	Arkansas State League	N/A	Hot Springs Bathers
1898	Arkansas State League	N/A	Hot Springs Bathers?
1906	Arkansas-Texas League	D	Hot Springs Vapors
1908	Arkansas State League	D	Hot Springs Vaporites
1909	Arkansas State League	D	Hot Springs Vaporites

Location – Whittington Avenue – Home plate to right field – ran along side of Whittington Avenue

Dimensions – N/A

Stands located near Whittington Avenue

Home Plate Location – Facing NE

Ban Johnson Field (Whittington Park)

Year	League	Class	Team
1938-1941	Cotton States League	C	Hot Springs Bathers

Location – Whittington Avenue

Dimensions (LF-CF-RF) 350 – 360 – 270

1939 – Constructed 15' fence in right field

Capacity: 2,000

Home Plate Orientation – Facing SE

Stands located near mountain side

Jaycee Park

Year	League	Class	Team
1947-1955	Cotton States League	C	Hot Springs Bathers

Location – End of Winona St. (near Belding and Carson Sts.)

Dimensions – (LF-CF-RF) 330-390-320

Capacity – ca. 2,500 in 1949

Home Plate Orientation – NE

End Notes

Chapter 1 – The Early Years – 1886-1909

1. The *Sporting News,* March 17, 1886, p. 2.

2. *Sporting Life*, March 31, 1886, p. 5

3. *The Sporting News*, October 4, 1886, p. 4.

4. Ibid., March 5, 1887, p. 1.

5. Ibid.

6. Ibid., June 4, 1887, p. 7.

7. "Arkansas State League-1894:" http://www.baseball-reference.com/minors/ (accessed February 19, 2009).

8. "Arkansas State League-1897:" http://www.baseball-reference.com/minors/ (accessed February 19, 2009).

9. "Southwestern League-1898:" http://www.baseball-reference.com/minors/ (accessed February 19, 2009).

10. *The Sentinel-Record*, June 15, 1902.

11. "Arkansas-Texas League-1906:" *http://www.baseball-reference.com/minors/ (accessed February 19, 2009).*

12. Leslie, James W., *Pine Bluff and Jefferson County, a pictorial history,* Virginia Beach, Virginia, 1981. E-mail: Jefferson County Genealogical Society, November 2009.

13. *Sporting Life*, April 18, 1908, p.12.

14. *The Citizens Daily Bulletin*, April 24, 1908.

15. Ibid.

16. Ibid., July 15, 1908.

17. *The Sporting News*, September 17, 1908, p. 5.

18. Ibid., October 1, 1908, p. 8.

19. Ibid., December 17, 1908, p. 7.

20. *The Citizens Daily Bulletin*, May 28, 1909.

21. *Sporting Life,* July 17, 1909, p. 24.

22. Ibid.

23. Hoo-Hoo organization: http://www.hoo-hoo.org, (accessed March 17, 2009).

Chapter 2 – Major Leaguers Only – 1910-1937

1. *The Sporting News*, April 3, 1913, p. 1.

2. *Sporting Life*, February 10, 1917, p. 5.

3. *The Sporting News*, March 21, 1956, p. 2.

Chapter 3 – Birth of the Modern Bathers – 1938

1. *The Sentinel-Record,* Fourth Annual, "Mail-It-Away" Edition, February 1938.

2. *New Era*, November 8, 1937.

3. *The Sentinel-Record,* November 11, 1937.

4. Ibid., November 19, 1937.

5. Ibid., November 24, 1937.

6. Ibid.

7. Ibid.

8. *New Era*, December 1, 1937.

9. *The Sentinel-Record*, December 5, 1937.

10. *Ibid.*, December 23, 1937.

11. *Ibid., January 6, 1938.*

12. *Ibid., January 12, 1938.*

13. *Ibid.*

14. *Ibid.*, January 11, 1938.

15. Ibid., January 19, 1938.

16. Ibid., February 14, 1938.

17. Ibid., April 15, 1938.

18. "Ban Johnson:" http://www.baseball-reference.com/bullpen/ban_johnson (accessed June 4, 2009).

19. *The Sporting News*, May 12, 1938, p. 11.

20. *The Sentinel-Record,* April 11, 1938.

21. Ibid., April 18, 1938.

22. Ibid., April 13, 1938.

23. Ibid., April 21, 1938.

24. Ibid., April 20, 1938.

25. Ibid., April 21, 1938.

26. *The Sporting News*, April 28, 1938, p. 10.

27. *The Sentinel-Record, May 5, 1938.*

28. Ibid.

29. *New Era,* May 10, 1938.

30. Ibid.

31. The Sentinel-Record, May 13, 1938.

32. Ibid., May 17, 1938.

33. Ibid., June 10, 1938.

34. Ibid., June 12, 1938.

35. Ibid.

36. Ibid., June 19, 1938.

37. Ibid., June 22, 1938.

38. Ibid., June 26, 1938.

39. Ibid., July 5, 1938.

40. New Era, August 1, 1938.

41. Ibid.

42. Ibid., August 3, 1938.

43. The Sentinel-Record, August 9, 1938.

44. Ibid., August 11, 1938.

45. New Era, August 13, 1938.

46. Ibid., August 27, 1938.

47. Ibid., August 30, 1938.

Chapter 4 – Playoff Bound – 1939

1. *The Sporting News,* January 5, 1939, p.1.

2. Ibid., January 12, 1939, p. 1.

3. Abernathy, Mamie Ruth, Telephone interview, August 15, 2009.

4. *The Sentinel-Record*, April 20, 1939.

5. *The Sporting News*, April 27, 1939, p. 12.

6. *The Sentinel-Record*, April 21, 1939.

7. *The Sporting News*, May 11, 1939, p. 12.

8. Ibid.

9. Ibid.

10. Ibid., May 18, 1939, p. 6.

11. *The Sentinel-Record*, June 9, 1939.

12. Ibid., June 19, 1939.

13. *New Era,* June 22, 1939,

14. *The Sporting News*, September 7, 1939, p. 6.

15. Ibid.

16. Ibid.

17. Ibid.

18. Ibid.

19. Ibid.

20. *The Sentinel-Record*, September 5, 1939.

21. Ibid., September 6, 1939.

22. Ibid., September 7, 1939.

23. Ibid., September 8, 1939.

24. Ibid.

Chapter 5 – Landis Cleans House - 1940

1. *The Sporting News,* February 22, 1940, p. 2.

2. Ibid., January 18, 1940, p. 1

3. Ibid., April 25, 1946, p. 9.

4. Ibid., March 21, 1940, p. 6.

5. Ibid., March 7, 1940, p. 7.

6. *New Era,* April 1, 1940.

7. Ibid., April 1, 1940.

8. Ibid., April 20, *1940.*

9. *The* Sentinel-Record, April 22, 1940.

10. Ibid., May 17, 1940.

11. Ibid., May 18, 1940.

12. Ibid., May 21, 1940.

13. Ibid., May 26, 1940.

14. *The Sporting News*, June 20, 1940, p. 12.

15. *The Sentinel-Record*, July 22, 1940.

16. Ibid., August 13, 1940.

17. *The Sporting News*, September 5, 1940, p. 5.

18. *The Sentinel-Record*, September 1, 1940

19. Ibid.

Chapter 6 – "The Little Yankees" – 1941

1. *The Sentinel-Record,* April 27, 1941.

2. Ibid., April 30, 1941.

3. Ibid., May 13, 1941.

4. "Louis, Joe:" http://www.en.wikipedia.org/wiki/joe_louis (accessed November 3, 2009).

5. *The Sentinel-Record*, June 24, 1941.

6. Ibid., July 11, 1941.

7. Ibid., August 12, 1941.

8. Ibid., September 7, 1941.

9. Ibid., September 8, 1941.

10. Ibid., September 9, 1941.

11. Ibid., September 13, 1941.

12. Ibid., September 14, 1941.

13. Ibid., September 15, 1941.

14. Ibid., September 16, 1941.

15. Ibid., September 17, 1941.

16. Ibid., July 22, 1951.

17. Ibid., September 21, 1941.

18. "Pescod, Charlie:" http://www.baseball-reference.com (accessed November 7, 2009).

19. "Pescod, Charlie:" http://www.baseballinwartime.com/in_memoriam/pescod_charlie.htm (accessed November 7, 2009).

Chapter 7 – The War Years – 1942-1946

1. *The Sporting News,* December 2, 1941, p. 11.

2. Ibid., March 26, 1942, p. 15.

3. Ibid., January 14, 1943, p. 14.

4. Ibid., May 10, 1945, p. 1.

5. Allbritton, Orval, Personal interview, November 15, 2009.

6. *The Sporting News*, December 25, 1946, p. 1.

Chapter 8 – Jaycee Park - A New Home – 1947

1. "Sport: Pennant Parade:" September 11, 1944, (Harper, Blake). http://www.time.com/time/printout/9,8816,775242,00html (accessed October 12, 2009).

2. *The Sentinel-Record.* July 20, 1951.

3. Ibid., January 26, 1947.

4. Ibid., January 13, 1947.

5. Ibid., March 16, 1947.

6. Ibid.

7. Ibid., May 4, 1947.

8. Ibid., April 20, 1947.

9. *New Era.* May 4, 1947.

10. *The Sentinel-Record.* May 5, 1947.

11. Ibid., May 14, 1947.

12. Ibid., May 15, 1947.

13. "1927 World Series:" http://www.angelfire.com/pa/1927worldseries.html (accessed July 15, 2008).

14. "Ormsby, Red:" http://www.thedeadballera.com/Obits/Umpires/Ormsby.Red.Obit.html (accessed July 15, 2008).

15. *The Sentinel-Record.* March 23, 1947.

16. Ibid., May 28, 1947.

17. Ibid.

18. Ibid., June 1, 1947.

19. Ibid., May 31, 1947.

20. Calloway, Joel, Phone interview, November 10, 2010.

21. *The Sentinel-Record,* June 5, 1947.

22. Ibid., July 2, 1947.

23. Ibid.

24. Bales, Jack, Phone interview, October 20, 2009.

25. *The Sentinel-Record.* July 22, 1947.

26. Ibid., August 1, 1947.

27. Ibid., August 3, 1947.

28. Ibid., August 28, 1947.

29. Ibid.

30. Ibid., September 1, 1947.

31. *The Sporting News,* October 1, 1947, p. 32.

32. Ibid., October 22, 1947, p. 6.

Chapter 9 – Herbie and the Red Hot Bathers – 1948

1. *The Sentinel-Record,* May 11, 1948.

2. Ibid., May 14, 1948.

3. Ibid., May 20, 1948.

4. *The Sporting News.,* June 16, 1948, p. 33.

5. Zini, Tony, personal interview, July 15, 2010.

6. *The Sporting News,* June 23, 1948, p. 34.

7. Ibid., January 19, 1963, p. 34.

8. Ibid., June 23, 1948, p. 38.

9. Ibid., July 7, 1948, p. 35.

10. Ibid., p. 34.

11. *The Sentinel-Record,* July 10, 1948.

12. Ibid., July 11, 1948.

13. Ibid., July 21, 1948.

14. Ibid., July 18, 1948.

15. Ibid.

16. Ibid.

17. Reichler, Joseph L., ed., "Sain, Johnny:" *The Baseball Encyclopedia*, (New York: McMillan Publishing Co., Inc. and London: Collier Macmillan Publishers, Fifth Edition, 1982), p. 1979.

18. *The Sentinel-Record*, July 29, 1948.

19. Ibid., August 2, 1948.

20. Ibid., August 3, 1948.

21. Ibid.

22. Ibid., August 6, 1948.

23. Ibid., August 7, 1948.

24. Ibid., August 24, 1948.

25. Ibid.

26. Ibid.

27. Ibid., August 28, 1948.

28. Ibid., September 1, 1948.

29. Ibid.

30. Ibid., September 3, 1948.

31. Ibid., September 4, 1948.

32. Ibid., September 5, 1948.

33. Ibid., September 8, 1948.

34. Ibid., September 9, 1948.

35. Ibid., September 10, 1948.

36. Ibid., September 11, 1948.

37. Ibid., September 12, 1948.

38. Ibid., September 13, 1948.

39. Ibid., September 15, 1948.

40. *Greenwood Commonwealth*, Greenwood, Mississippi, September 15, 1948.

41. *The Sporting News*, September 8, 1948, p. 38.

42. Ibid., November 10, 1948, p. 13.

43. *The Sentinel-Record*, September 9, 1948.

44. Ibid., September 16, 1948.

45. Ibid.

46. Ibid.

47. *The Sporting News*, November 24, 1948, p. 18.

48. Adams, Herb, personal correspondence, August 22, 2009.

Chapter 10 - Eight Men Out – 1949

1. *The Sentinel-Record,* March 3, 1949.

2. Ibid., April 17, 1949.

3. Ibid., April 22, 1949.

4. Ibid.

5. Ibid., May 17, 1949.

6. *"Price, Jackie:"* http://www.baseball-reference.com/bullpen/jackie-price *(accessed August 10, 2009).*

7. *The Sentinel-Record,* August 22, 1949.

8. Ibid., August 25, 1949.

Chapter 11 – Antonelli Leads Bathers – 1950

1. *The Sentinel-Record,* February 19, 1950.

2. Ibid.

3. Ibid., February 25, 1950.

4. Ibid., May 2, 1950.

5. Ibid., May 12, 1950.

6. Ibid., July 13, 1950.

7. *The Sporting News*, August 30, 1950, p. 33.

8. Ibid.

9. *The Sentinel-Record*, August 28, 1950.

10. *The Sporting News*, September 13, 1950, p. 34.

11. *The Sentinel-Record, September 8, 1950.*

12. Ibid., September 9, 1950.

13. Ibid., September 10, 1950.

14. Ibid., September 13, 1950.

15. Ibid., *September 14, 1950*

16. Ibid., September 16, 1950.

17. Ibid., September 17, 1950.

18. Ibid., September 18, 1950.

19. Ibid., September 21, 1950.

20. Ibid., September 22, 1950.

21. Ibid., September 23, 1950.

22. Ibid., September 24, 1950.

23. Ibid., September 25, 1950.

24. *The Sporting News*, October 25, 1950, p. 14.

Chapter 12 – Ownership: Fruit Basket Turnover – 1951

1. *The Sentinel-Record, April 8, 1951.*

2. Ibid., April 15, 1951.

3. Back, John & Eubanks, Dewayne, M.D., phone interview, August 24, 2009.

4. *The Sentinel-Record,* May 1, 1951.

5. Ibid., May 6, 1951.

6. Ibid., May 27, 1951.

7. Ibid., May 26, 1951.

8. Ibid., May 30, 1951.

9. Ibid., May 31, 1951.

10. Ibid., June 10, 1951.

11. Ibid.

12. Ibid., June 24, 1951.

13. Ibid., August 4, 1951.

14. Ibid., August 8, 1951.

15. Ibid., August 27, 1951.

16. Ibid., August 30, 1951.

17. Ibid., September 2, 1951.

Chapter 13 – A War Hero and a Future Owner – 1952

1. "Benish, Bob:" http://www.baseball-reference.com – (accessed August 2009).

2. *The Sentinel-Record*, May 4, 1952.

3. Ibid.

4. Ibid.

5. Passarella, Bob, Phone interview, August 30, 2009.

6. The Sentinel-Record, May 30, 1952.

7. Ibid.

8. Ibid., June 19, 1952.

9. Ibid., June 20, 1952.

10. Ibid., June 29, 1952.

11. Ibid.

12. Ibid., July 4, 1952.

13. Ibid., July 10, 1952.

14. Ibid., July 11, 1952.

15. Ibid., July 14, 1952.

16. Ibid., July 20, 1952.

17. Ibid., July 15, 1952.

18. Ibid., July 23, 1952.

19. Ibid., August 5, 1952.

20. Ibid., August 10, 1952.

21. Passarella, Bob, Phone interview, August 30, 2009.

22. *The Sentinel-Record,* August 7, 1952.

23. Passarella, Bob, Phone interview, August 30, 2009.

24. Bedingfield, Gary, "Baseball in Wartime – Baseball's Greatest Sacrifice:" http://www. baseballinwartime.com/player_biographies/shepard-bert.htm (accessed September 3, 2009).

25. Ibid.

26. "Shepard, Bert:" http://www.baseball-reference.com, *(accessed September 3, 2009)*.

27. *The Sentinel-Record, August 10, 1952.*

28. Ibid.

29. Ibid.

30. Ibid.

31. Goldstein, Richard, "An Inspirational Amputee Dies,*" New York Times,* published June 20, 2008, *http://www.nytimes.com (accessed September 2, 2009)*.

32. Bedingfield, Gary, "Baseball in Wartime – Baseball's Greatest Sacrifice:" http://www.baseball-inwartime.com/player_biographies/shepard_bert.htm (accessed September 3, 2009).

33. *The Sentinel-Record,* August 11, 1952.

34. Ibid., August 17, 1952.

35. Ibid., August 21, 1952.

36. Ibid., August 24, 1952.

37. Ilitch Holdings, Inc. e-mail, July 16, 2009.

Chapter 14 – The Tugerson Brothers – 1953

1. *The Sentinel-Record,* April 12 1953.

2. Bull, Madeline Hudson, phone interview, October 17, 2009.

3. Jennings, Jay. The Black Bathers, *Arkansas Times,* July 1991, p. 52.

4. *The New Georgia Encyclopedia,* "Hank Aaron:" www.georgiaencyclopedia.org. (accessed September 10, 2008).

5. Morris, Peter, "Jim Tugerson:" http://bioproj.sabr.org. (accessed October, 17, 2008).

6. The *Sentinel-Record,* April 7, 1953.

7. Ibid.

8. Ibid.

9. Goltz, Louis, Family Scrapbook, October 20, 2009.

10. *Delta Democrat-Time,* Greenville, MS, April 6, 1953.

11. *The Sentinel-Record,* April 7, 1953.

12. Ibid.

13. Ibid.

14. Ibid., April 11, 1953.

15. Ibid., April 12, 1953.

16. Ibid.

17. Jennings, Jay, "The Black Bathers," *Arkansas Times,* July 1991, p. 53.

18. *The Sentinel-Record*, April 17, 1953.

19. Jennings, Jay, "The Black Bathers," *Arkansas Times,* July 1991, p. 53.

20. *The Sentinel-Record*, April 16, 1953.

21. Bales, Jack, telephone interview, October 21, 2007.

22. *The Sentinel-Record,* April 18, 1953.

23. Bales, Jack, telephone interview, October 21, 2007.

24. Passarella, Bob, telephone interview, December 11, 2007.

25. *The Sentinel-Record*, May 21, 1953.

26. Ibid.

27. Goltz, Louis. Family Scrapbook, October 20, 2009.

28. Morris, Peter, Jim Tugerson: http://bioproj.sabr.org (accessed November 20, 2008.

29. Bales, Jack, telephone interview, November 15, 2009.

30. *The Sentinel-Record,* June 7, 1953.

31. Ibid., June 21, 1953.

32. Ibid., June 9, 1953.

33. Ibid., July 5, 1953.

34. *The Baltimore Afro-American,* July 21, 1953, p. 15.

35. Ibid., July 28, 1953, p. 10.

36. *The Sentinel-Record,* July 15, 1953.

37. Ibid.

38. Ibid., July 17, 1953.

39. *The Baltimore Afro-American*, August 15, 1953, p. 18.

40. Buckles, Ken. "Jim Tugerson:" http://www.nlbpa.com/message_ view.asp?imsg=2945. (accessed September 4, 2007).

41. *The Sporting News*, September 9, 1953.

42. Passarella, Bob, telephone interview, December 4, 2008.

43. *The Sentinel-Record*, October 23, 1953.

Chapter 15 – Williamson to the Rescue – 1954

1. *New Era,* November 30, 1953.

2. Passarella, Bob, letter from Paul Dean, March 18, 1954.

3. *The Sentinel-Record*, April 13, 1954.

4. Ibid.

5. Ibid., April 18, 1954.

6. Ibid., April 28, 1954.

7. Bales, Jack, telephone interview, July 10, 2009.

8. The Sentinel-Record, May 9, 1954.

9. Ibid., May 17, 1954.

10. Ibid., May 30, 1954.

11. Ibid., June 5, 1954.

12. Ibid.

13. Ibid.

14. Ibid., June 6, 1954.

15. Bales, Jack, telephone interview, July 10, 2009.

16. *The Sentinel-Record*, June 10, 1954.

17. Ibid.

18. Ibid., June 21, 1954.

19. Ibid., June 27, 1954.

20. Ibid., July 4, 1954.

21. Ibid.

22. Ibid., July 14, 1954.

23. Ibid., July 18, 1954.

24. Ibid., July 17, 1954.

25. Ibid., July 20, 1954.

26. Ibid., July 21, 1954.

27. Ibid., July 23, 1954.

28. Reynolds, Uvoyd, telephone interview, October 17, 2009.

29. *The Sentinel-Record*, July 24, 1954.

30. *Ibid*.

31. Ibid., July 25, 1954.

32. *Ibid., July 28, 1954.*

33. Ibid., August 1, 1954.

34. Ibid.

35. Ibid.

36. Ibid., August 7, 1954.

37. Bales, Jack, telephone interview, October 20, 2009.

38. Reynolds, Uvoyd, telephone interview, *October 17, 2009.*

39. The Sentinel-Record, August 16, 1954.

40. Ibid., August 18, 1954.

41. Ibid., August 22, 1954.

42. Ibid.

43. Ibid.

44. Ibid., August 27, 1954.

45. Ibid.

Chapter 16 – The Last Hurrah – 1955

1. *The Sentinel-Record*. March 17, 1955.

2. Ibid., April 1, 1955.

3. Ibid., May 5, 1955.

4. Ibid., May 7, 1955

5. Ibid., May 8, 1955.

6. Ibid.

7. Ibid.

8. Ibid., June 5, 1955.

9. Ibid., June 7, 1955.

10. Ibid., June 12, 1955.

11. Ibid., June 25, 1955.

12. Ibid., June 26, 1955.

13. Ibid.

14. Ibid., July 6, 1955.

15. Ibid., July 12, 1955.

16. Ibid., August 7, 1955.

17. Ibid., August 12, 1955.

18. Ibid., August 21, 1955.

19. Ibid., August 28, 1955.

20. Ibid., August 29, 1955.

21. Ibid., August 31, 1955.

22. Ibid., September 1, 1955.

Bibliography

<u>Books</u>

Disciple's Study Bible, New International Version (Nashville, TN: Holman Bible Publishers, 1988).

Duren, Don, *Boiling Out at the Springs: A History of Major League Baseball Spring Training at Hot Springs, Arkansas from 1886-1940s* (Dallas, Texas: Hodge Printing Company, 2006).

Honig, Donald, *The American League: An Illustrated History (New* York: Crown, 1987).
_____, *The National League: An Illustrated History (* New York: Crown, 1987).

Reichler, Joseph L., ed. *The Baseball Encyclopedia,* 5th ed. (New York: McMillian and London: Collier Macmillian, 1982).

Scully, Francis T., M.D. *Hot Springs, Arkansas and Hot Springs National Park: The Story of a City and The Nation's Health Resort* (Little Rock: Pioneer Press, 1966).

E-mail

Blaeuer, Mark, Park Ranger, Hot Springs National Park, AR.

Conn, Tim, Son of Billy Conn, Billy Conn information.

Garland County Historical Society, Hot Springs, AR.

Gillette, Gary, Editor, *The ESPN Baseball Encyclopedia*.

Hardwick, Caleb, Whittington Park information.

Henderson, Tom, *Crain's Detroit Business News*, Mike Ilitch information.

Herlein, Sherrie, Eddie Herlein information.

Ilitch Holdings, Inc., Mike Ilitch information.

National Baseball Hall of Fame, Billy Hornsby information.

Pittsburgh Post-Gazette, information on Conn-Louis Boxing Matc.

Society of American Baseball Research (SABR), General information.

Warrington, Bob, VP, Philadelphia Athletics Historical Society.

Watkins, John, Fayetteville, AR.

Wiles, Tim, Director of Research, National Baseball Hall of Fame.

Zajc, John, Society of American Baseball research (SABR) – Collusion.

Zini, Kelly, Hot Springs Bathers information.

Internet

Arkansas State League, 1894: http://www.baseball-reference.com/minors/ (accessed February 19, 2009).

Arkansas State League, 1897: http://www.baseball-reference.com/minors/ (accessed February 19, 2009).

Arkansas-Texas League, 1906: http://www.baseball-reference.com/minors/ (accessed February 19, 2009).

Bedingfield, Gary, Baseball in Wartime-Baseball's Greatest Sacrifice: Pescod, Charlie. http://www.baseballinwartime.com/in_memoriam/pescod_charlie.htm (accessed April 2009).

Bedingfield, Gary, Baseball in Wartime-Baseball's Greatest Sacrifice:
Shepard, Bert:
http://www.baseballinwartime.com/player_biographies/shepard_bert.htm (accessed September 3, 2009).

"Benish, Bob:" http://www.baseball-reference.com/bullpen/Bob_Benish (accessed August 3, 2009).

Buckles, Ken, "Tugerson, Jim." http://www.nlbpa.com/message_view.asp?imsg=2945. (accessed September 4, 2007).

Goldstein, Richard. "An Inspirational Amputee Dies." Bert Shepard. *New York Times,* June 20, 2008. http://www.nytimes.com (accessed September 2, 2009).

Harper, Blake, *Time,* Sport: Pennant Parade. Monday, Sep. 11, 1944. (http://www.time.com/time/printout/0,8816,775242,00.html – (accessed May 2008).

International Hoo-Hoo Headquarters and Museum: www.Hoo-Hoo.com – (accessed January 2009).

"Johnson, Ban:" http://www.baseball-reference.com/bullpen/ban_johnson (accessed June 4, 2009).

"Louis, Joe:" http://www.en.wikipedia.org/wiki/joe_louis (accessed November 3, 2009.

Morris, Peter, "Jim Tugerson:" http://bioproj.sabr.org (accessed October 17, 2008 & November 20, 2008).

"Ormsby, Emmett:"http://www.angelfire.com/pa/1927/worldseries.html – (accessed July 2009).

"Ormsby, Emmett:" http://www.thedeadballera.com/Obits/Umpires/Ormsby.Red.Obit.html-(accessed July 2009).

"Pescod, Charlie:" http://ww.baseball-reference.com (accessed November 7, 2009).

"Price, Jackie:" http://www.baseball-reference.com/bullpen/jackie-price (accessed August 10, 2009).

"Shepard, Bert:" http://www.baseball-reference.com/player/s/shepabe01.shtml (accessed September 3, 2009.

Southwestern League, 1898: http://www.baseball-reference.com/minors/ (accessed February 19, 2009).

The New Georgia Encyclopedia, "Hank Aaron:" www.georgiaencyclopedia.org. (accessed September 10, 2008).

Libraries

Arkansas History Commission, Wendy Richter, director. Little Rock, AR

Garland County Historical Society, Liz Robbins, director, Hot Springs, AR.

Garland County Library, John Wells, director, Hot Springs, AR.

Magazines

Jennings, Jay, *Arkansas Times*, The Black Bathers, July 1991, p. 52.

Sporting Life, Philadelphia, Pennsylvania.

The Sporting News, St. Louis, Missouri.

Newspapers

Arkansas Gazette, Little Rock, Arkansas.

Delta Democrat-Times, Greenville, MS.

Greenwood Commonwealth, Greenwood, Mississippi.

New Era, Hot Springs, Arkansas.

The Citizens Daily Bulletin, Hot Springs, Arkansas.

The Sentinel Record, Hot Springs, Arkansas.

Personal Interviews

Abernathy, Mamie Ruth, worked in Bathers front office and member of GCHS, Hot Springs, AR.

Allbritton, Orval, Bathers fan and GCHS volunteer, Hot Springs, AR.

Bales, Jack, former Bathers manager and catcher, Hot Springs, AR.

Blaeuer, Mark, Park Ranger, Hot Springs National Park.

Garland County Historical Society Staff, Hot Springs, AR.

Moore, Joanne Ensminger, daughter of Joe and Evelyn Ensminger, Hot Springs, AR

Lax, Debbie, granddaughter of former Bather mgr/pitcher "Spike" Hunter. Hot Springs, AR.

Robbins, Liz, Director, Garland County Historical Society, Hot Springs, AR.

Shugart, Sharon, former Hot Springs National Park staff, currently GCHS volunteer, Hot Springs, AR.

Webb, Adam, Employee, Garland County Library, Hot Springs, AR.

Wells, John, Director, Garland County Library, Hot Springs, AR

Zini, Tony, former Bather's catcher, North Little Rock, AR

*Telephone Interviews

Abernathy, Mamie Ruth - see above.

Adams, Herb, former Bathers centerfielder – League MVP & major leaguer.

Allbritton, Orval, see above.

Back, Johnny-Retired Army, Honored at Bathers game in 1951.

Bales, Jack, see above.

Blaeuer, Mark, see above.

Bull, Madeline Hudson, granddaughter of the late Louis Goltz.

Callaway, Joel, former Bathers pitcher.

Conn, Tim, son of pro boxer, the late Billy Conn.

Elder, Betty, wife of Jim Elder - Jim was CSL umpire and Bathers General Mgr.

Elder, Susan, daughter of Jim & Betty Elder.

Eubanks, Dewayne, M.D., friend of Johnny Back, who was Bathers honoree 1951.

Herlein, Ed, former Bathers infielder.

Lax, Debbie, granddaughter of "Spike" Hunter.

Passarella, Bob, former Bathers infielder/outfielder (died 2010).

Reynolds, Uvoyd, former Bathers outfielder.

Robbins, Liz, Director, Garland County Historical Society.

Ward, Mrs. Tom, wife of former Bathers pitcher Tom Ward.

White, Ed, former Bathers pitcher.

Whitehead, Donny, collector of Cotton States League memorabilia.

Zini, Tony, former Bathers catcher.

*Other individuals listed in "Bathers Memories."

Scrapbook

Goltz, Louis' family. Hot Springs, Arkansas.

Black, Mrs. Tom. Hot Springs, Arkansas.

Index

Harper, Blake - 119, 123, 124, 126, 127, 128, 131, 133, 135, 136, 212, 281, 439

Harridge, Will - 45

Harris, Sara - 409

Harty, Judge Emmet – 67, 83, 91, 93, 98, 106, 119, 125, 252, 359, 361, 365, 375, 379, 380, 383, 386, 389, 390, 391, 392, 393

Haschak, Bill – 129, 130, 142, 153, 156, 157, 158, 172, 221, 222, 223, 225, 226, 230, 231, 232, 233, 234, 235, 236, 238, 239, 240, 241, 245

Hebert, Dr. Gaston - 95

Heinen, Pete – 158, 241

Herlein, Ed – 155, 156, 157

Hickey, Charlie - 440

Hicks, James - 370

Hilbert, Don – 185, 293

Hodges, Gil – 349, 350

Hoeft, Bob – 183, 263, 269, 273

Hoffman, Frank – 22, 440

Hogan, Jim – 296, 297, 298, 301, 303, 439, 441

Holden, Dick - 410

Holden, Joe – 156, 157, 212, 213, 214, 215, 216, 221, 256, 439, 441

Hoo-Hoo International - 29

Hornsby, Billy - 219, 220

Hornsby, Roger - xi, 34, 36, 52, 143, 159, 219 220, 285, 401, 405

Hot Springs Blues – 21, 22, 442

Hot Springs Vaporites – xiii, 28, 442

Hot Springs Vapors – xiii, 23, 442

Hotchkiss, Douglas – 35, 36, 37, 50

House of David - 148

Housley, Mayor Floyd – 247, 257, 277, 281, 285, 292, 333, 355, 381

Howard, Dutch - 410

Howington, Jodie – 101, 110, 111, 112, 115, 116

Hudlin, Willis – 38, 70, 72, 146, 352, 377, 390

Hudson, Earl – x, 411

Hunter, Spike – x, 37, 39, 41, 42, 45, 49, 51, 53, 55, 60, 62, 100, 145, 146, 147, 148, 228, 333, 402, 403, 439

Ilitch, Mike – x, 208, 297, 298, 299, 300, 301, 304, 305, 312, 313, 314

Jack, Richard – 390, 393

Jackson, Bill - 156

Jacobson, Ed - 185, 300, 301, 303, 312, 313

Janocha, John – 385, 386, 387, 395

Jarworski, Joe - 273

Johnson, "Dumb" - 95

Johnson, Ban – 44, 45

Jordin, John – 103, 114

Kallsnick, Maurice - 102

Kamis, Jim – 156, 157, 158, 214, 221, 225, 226, 230, 232, 234, 239

Kilgore, Don – 412

Kirk, Bill - 441

King, Cy – 95

Kjellenberg, Warren - 158

Klyman, Mose – 65, 264, 333

Korfonta, Steve – 336, 348, 357, 358, 361, 363, 369, 372, 374, 377

Kortum, Ken – 386, 391, 394, 395, 396

Kramer, Ed – 89, 91, 110, 112, 114

Kuchurek, George - 156

Kuhel, Joe – 134, 136, 137, 138, 140, 141, 142, 143, 153, 164, 165, 166, 306, 439, 440

Kurowski, Russell - 156

Kuta, Ed – 251, 252

Lakics, Bill - 153

Landis, Judge K. M. – 134, 228, 243, 252, 320, 400

Lawrence, Marjorie - 223

Leatherman, Leland – 136, 254, 281

Ledgerwood, Dora Jane – 257, 277

Lee, Marty – 183, 259, 260, 263, 267, 271, 273

Lenczyk, Wally – 130, 132, 153

Lindsey, Eldon – 99, 111, 115

Lockwood, Dave - 64, 66, 86, 402

Loidl, Dr. – 308, 310, 311

Longinotti, Louie - 95

Longinotti, Paul – 95, 381

Louis, Joe – 54, 55, 104

Lowe, Will - 333

Lucas, Lou "Red" – 362, 363, 364, 439

Lutz, Joe – 378, 381, 384, 385, 386, 387, 388, 390, 392, 393, 439, 441

Lylle, Van – 39, 109, 196, 254, 264, 281, 332, 409

Madden, Owney – 56, 57, 409

Mabry, Tom - 153

Magle, Tony – 246, 247

Marion, Roy – 106, 110, 111, 114, 116, 425

Martin, Hal – 195, 200, 333, 336, 337, 338, 339, 340, 341, 346, 347, 348, 349, 403, 404, 409, 410, 435

Mason, J. C. - 283

Mattis, Joe – 278, 290

Mauldin, Paul – 133, 426

Maley, Bill - 183

Mayling, Rudy – 203, 385, 386, 387, 391, 393, 394, 395

McCall, Dutch - 440

McCalman - 185

McDermott, Thomas - 334

McGhee, Ed – 156, 157, 158, 168, 214, 215, 220, 221, 224, 226, 230, 231, 232, 234, 236, 238, 239, 240, 245, 416, 441

McJunkin, Jack – 37, 40, 84, 95, 109, 110, 196, 332, 401

McLaughlin, Mayor Leo – 48, 63, 72, 86, 87, 99

McMahan, Jack – 193, 412

McMahan, Rex – 409, 412

McRae, Joe – 86, 140, 224

"Meathouse" – 59, 412

Miller, Bud - 377

Mitchell, Bill "Double-Thumbs" – 369, 370, 372
Mitchell, Bobby – 366
Mitchell, Rex – 67, 69
Montgomery, Wallace - 69
Montgomery, Harry - 183, 258, 260, 271, 273
Moore, Maurice - 219, 229, 243, 265, 278, 283, 285, 291, 293, 297, 312, 331, 340, 356, 358, 359, 365, 371, 375, 378, 379, 384
Morris, J. Walter – 36, 38, 44, 64, 419
Moses, C. Hamilton - 227
Mosley, Jim - 283
Mowery, Charlie - 140
Murrah, Wilson – 254, 255, 257. 261
Narbut, Frank – 69
Newbecker, Bob – 156, 157
Newman, Bud – 74, 98, 99, 106, 116
Nichols, Tom - 413
Nicksic, Bonnie - 301
Nooner, Sue – 364, 372
O'Conner, Leslie – 133, 134, 135, 136
O'Neil, Mickey – 379, 380, 386, 387, 389, 393, 394, 395, 439, 441
O'Rourke, Frank - 70
O'Rourke, Joe "Patsy" – 135, 136, 143
Offenhauser, Fred - 136
Ormsby, Emmett "Red" – 133, 135, 136, 137, 143
Owens, Olen "Tuffy " – 185, 294, 311
Parker, John – 369, 370, 377
Parks, Wayne - 185
Passarella, Bob – 195, 200, 294, 295, 296, 297, 300, 303, 304, 305, 306, 307, 311, 312, 313, 332, 333, 334, 335, 344, 346, 349, 352, 353, 354
Pawelek, Ted – 100, 108, 111, 115, 116, 440
Peckham, Jeff – 143, 156, 157, 249, 252, 253

Pescod, Charlie – 105, 106, 108, 109, 110, 111, 113, 114, 116, 117, 118, 425
Peters, Marie "Mom" – 141, 142, 178, 179, 223, 246, 247
Pfirman, Cy – 99, 106
Phalen, Dan - 183, 248, 249, 253, 261, 262, 263, 264, 266, 268, 270, 272, 273, 429
Phillips, Norwood - 224
Powell, Coleman – 99, 110, 116, 117, 425
Powers, Mike – 98, 99, 109, 110, 111, 116, 420, 425, 439, 440
Price, Johnny – 250
Rabka, Erv – 183, 266, 273, 277, 279
Raft, George - 56, 400, 406
Ragsdale, Lee - 70
Rapacki, Ray – 156, 158, 215, 226, 230, 239, 241
Rasmussen, Wally - 185
Rentschler, Jim - 275
Reynolds, Uvoyd – 202, 351, 366, 367
Rhodes, Pete – 102, 107, 109, 110
Rice, Wayne - 413
Ricks, Earl – 132, 196, 213, 227, 333
Riggs, Arthur – 26, 27 28
Rigney, Johnny – 143, 158, 213, 224, 244, 250, 256
Robinson, Jackie – 316, 318, 330, 349, 368, 377
Robinson, Robby – 48, 53, 56, 406
Rockey, Ed – 67, 68, 69, 75, 77, 80, 111
Roddenberry, W. D. – 139, 190, 258, 274, 281, 287, 289, 328, 338, 347, 374, 379, 412
Rogers, Emmett – 21, 440
Ronay, Al – 195, 336, 348, 352
Ruth, Babe – xi, 32, 54, 107
Sain, Johnny – 50, 82, 83, 224, 440
Salvatore, Harry – 156, 157, 158, 222, 230, 234, 235, 248
Santomauro, Joe – 127, 128, 130, 134, 439

Schafer, Ed – 183, 260, 264, 266, 268, 270, 271
Schafer, Walt – 55, 59, 63, 72, 73, 74, 75, 77, 406
Schmeling, Max – 54, 55
Schmidt, Charlie – 156, 157, 158, 169, 214, 221, 223, 226, 230, 231, 233, 234, 235, 238, 239, 240, 250
Schmudlach, Don – 252, 253
Schoenfeld, Nathan – 281, 282
Scott, Joe – 367, 368
Seifert, Ken – 333, 357
Selph, Carey – 127, 226, 227, 228
Shepard, Bert – 188, 305, 306, 307, 308, 309, 310, 311, 312, 313, 441
Shetler, Vernon "Moose" – 185, 195, 293, 323, 331, 332, 334, 335, 336, 340, 439
Sitek, Steve – 352, 364
Skidmore, Ken - 246
Smith, A. R. - 413
Smith, Clyde – 99, 113, 116, 119, 254, 257, 277, 281, 292
Smith, Earl "Oil" – 39, 47, 127, 128, 129, 130, 134, 154, 216, 228, 407
Smith, J. R. – 138, 224, 281, 388
Smith, Jack – 125, 281
Smith, Pete - 413
Sobek, George – 158, 175, 216, 219, 221, 222, 225, 226, 230, 231, 232, 234, 235, 238, 239, 240, 241, 439
Solis, Steve – 183, 246, 247, 250, 257, 269, 270 273
Speer, Floyd – 49, 52, 55, 59, 60, 63, 440
Spencer, Earl - 95
Stegman, Harvey - 291
Stern, Joe – 185, 296
Stewart, Glen "Gabby" – 244, 250, 251, 252, 253, 439, 441
Stiglich, Charlie – 230, 235, 252
Stone, John David – 413, 414

CPSIA information can be obtained at www.ICGtesting.com
Printed in the USA
243429LV00004B/3/P